Swift 3 for Absolute Beginners

Third Edition

Gary Bennett
Brad Lees

Apress®

Swift 3 for Absolute Beginners

Gary Bennett
Scottsdale, Arizona, USA

Brad Lees
Phoenix, Arizona, USA

ISBN-13 (pbk): 978-1-4842-2330-7
ISBN-13 (electronic): 978-1-4842-2331-4
DOI 10.1007/978-1-4842-2331-4

Library of Congress Control Number: 2016962063

Distributed to the book trade worldwide by Springer Science+Business Media New York, 233 Spring Street, 6th Floor, New York, NY 10013. Phone 1-800-SPRINGER, fax (201) 348-4505, e-mail `orders-ny@springer-sbm.com`, or visit `www.springer.com`. Apress Media, LLC is a California LLC and the sole member (owner) is Springer Science + Business Media Finance Inc (SSBM Finance Inc). SSBM Finance Inc is a Delaware corporation.

For information on translations, please e-mail `rights@apress.com`, or visit `www.apress.com`.

Apress and friends of ED books may be purchased in bulk for academic, corporate, or promotional use. eBook versions and licenses are also available for most titles. For more information, reference our Special Bulk Sales–eBook Licensing web page at `www.apress.com/bulk-sales`.

Any source code or other supplementary materials referenced by the author in this text is available to readers at `www.apress.com`. For detailed information about how to locate your book's source code, go to `www.apress.com/source-code/`.

Printed on acid-free paper

Contents at a Glance

Contents

About the Authors

Gary Bennett is president of xcelMe.com. xcelMe teaches iPhone/iPad programming courses online. Gary has taught hundreds of students how to develop iPhone/iPad apps. He has created several very popular apps himself, and his students have some of the best-selling apps on the iTunes App Store. Gary also worked for 25 years in the technology and defense industries. He served 10 years in the U.S. Navy as a nuclear engineer aboard two nuclear submarines. After leaving the Navy, Gary worked for several companies as a software developer, CIO, and president. As CIO, he helped take VistaCare public in 2002. Gary also co-authored *iPhone Cool Projects* for Apress. Gary lives in Scottsdale, Arizona, with his wife Stefanie and their four children.

Brad Lees has more than 12 years' experience in application development and server management. He has specialized in creating and initiating software programs in real-estate development systems and financial institutions. His career has been highlighted by his positions as information systems manager at The Lyle Anderson Company; product development manager for Smarsh; vice president of application development for iNation; and IT manager at The Orcutt/Winslow Partnership, the largest architectural firm in Arizona. A graduate of Arizona State University, Brad and his wife Natalie reside in Phoenix with their five children.

About the Technical Reviewer

Stefan Kaczmarek has over 15 years of software development experience specializing in mobile applications, large-scale software systems, project management, network protocols, encryption algorithms, and audio/video codecs. As chief software architect and co-founder of SKJM, LLC, Stefan developed a number of successful mobile applications including iCam (which has been featured on CNN, *Good Morning America*, *The Today Show*, and the "Dog Lover" iPhone 3GS television commercial) and iSpy Cameras (which held the #1 Paid iPhone App ranking in a number of countries around the world including the UK, Ireland, Italy, Sweden, and South Korea). Stefan resides in Phoenix, Arizona, with his wife Veronica and their two children.

Introduction

Over the last seven years, we've heard the following comments countless times:

- "I've never programmed before, but I have a great idea for an iPhone/iPad/ AppleTV app."
- "Can I really learn to program the iPhone or iPad?"

To the latter we answer, "Yes, but you have to believe you can." Only you are going to tell yourself you can't do it.

For the Newbie

This book assumes you may have never programmed before. The book is also written for someone who may have never programmed before using object-oriented programming (OOP) languages. There are many Swift books out there, but all of these books assume you have programmed before and know OOP and computer logic. We wanted to write a book that takes readers from knowing little or nothing about computer programming and logic to being able to program in Swift. After all, Swift is a native programming language for the iPhone, iPad, and Mac.

Over the last seven years, we have taught thousands of students at xcelMe.com to be iPhone/iPad (iOS) developers. Many of our students have developed some of the most successful iOS apps in their category in the iTunes App Store. We have incorporated what we have learned in our first two courses, "Introduction to Object-Oriented Programming" and "Logic and Swift for iPhone/iPad Developers," into this book.

For the More Experienced

Many developers who programmed years ago or programmed in a non-OOP language need a background in OOP and Logic before they dive Swift. This book is for you. We gently walk you through OOP and how it is used in iOS development to help make you a successful iOS developer.

How This Book Is Organized

You'll notice that we are all about successes in this book. We introduce the OOP and Logic concepts in Playgound and then move those concepts to Xcode and Swift. Many students are visual learners or they learn by doing. We use both techniques. We'll walk you through topics and concepts with visual examples and then take you through step-by-step examples while reinforcing the concepts.

We often repeat topics in different chapters to reinforce what you have learned and apply these skills in new ways. This enables new programmers to reapply development skills and feel a sense of accomplishment as they progress. Don't worry if you feel you haven't mastered a topic. Keep moving forward!

The Formula for Success

Learning to program is an interactive process between your program and you. Just like learning to play an instrument, you have to practice. You must work through the examples and exercises in this book. Understanding the concept doesn't mean you know how to apply it and use it.

You will learn a lot from this book. You will learn a lot from working through the exercises in this book. However, you will really learn when you debug your programs. Spending time walking through your code and trying to find out why it is not working the way you want is an unparalleled learning process. The downside of debugging is a new developer can find it especially frustrating. If you have never wanted to throw your computer out the window, you will. You will question why you are doing this and whether you are smart enough to solve the problem. Programming is very humbling, even for the most experienced developer.

Like a musician, the more you practice the better you get. By practicing, we mean programming! You can do some amazing things as a programmer. The world is your oyster. Seeing your app in the iTunes App Store is one of the most satisfying accomplishments. However, there is a price, and that price is time spent coding and learning.

Having taught many students to become iOS developers, we have put together a formula for what makes students successful. Here is our formula for success:

- Believe you can do it. You'll be the only one who says you can't do this, so don't tell yourself that.
- Work through all the examples and exercises in this book.
- Code, code, and keeping coding. The more you code, the better you'll get.
- Be patient with yourself. If you were fortunate enough to have been a 4.0 student who could memorize material just by reading it, don't expect your memorization skills to translate to easy success in Swift coding. The only way you are going to learn is to spend time coding.
- You learn by reading this book. You really learn by debugging your code.
- Use the free `xcelMe.com` webinars and YouTube videos explained at the end of this introduction.
- Don't give up!

The Development Technology Stack

We will walk you through the process of understanding the development process for your iOS apps and what technology you need. However, briefly looking at all the technology pieces together is helpful. These are the key iOS development technology pieces you will need to know in order to build a successful app and get it on the app store:

- Apple's Developer Website
- App Telemetry
- App Analytices
- iPhone Swift SDK

- Swift
- Object-Oriented Programming and Logic
- Xcode IDE
- Debugging
- Performance Tuning

We know this is a lot of technology. Don't worry—we will go through it and will be comfortable using it.

Required Software, Materials, and Equipment

One of the great things about developing iOS apps is just about everything you need is free to develop your app.

- Xcode
- Swift
- macOS Sierra10.12.1 or higher
- Xcode Integrated Developers Environment
- iOS SDK
- iPhone and iPad Simulator

All you need to get started is a Mac and knowledge of where to download everything, which we will cover.

Operating System and IDE

When developing iOS apps, you have to use Xcode and the macOS. You can download both of these for free from the Mac App Store (see Figure 1.)

Figure 1. *The Mac App Store*

Software Development Kits

You will need to register as a developer. You can do this for free at `http://developer.apple.com/ios` (see Figure 2).

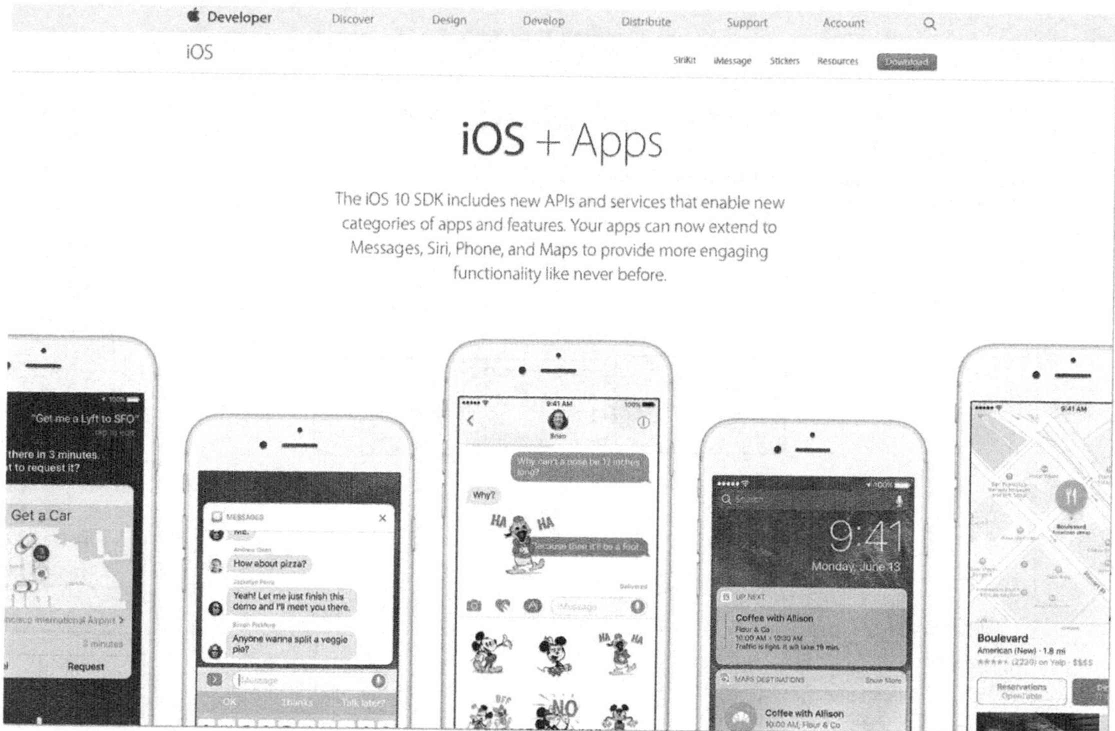

***Figure 2.** Apple's Developer website*

When you are ready to upload your app to the iTunes App Store, you will need to pay $99/year in order to obtain access.

Figure 2 Apple's Developer Website (editor, caption not sure why I can't apply that style)

Dual Monitors [editor not sure why this "Strong" format is doing this]

We recommend developers have a second monitor connected to their computer. It is great to step through your code and watch your output window and iPad simulator at the same time on dual independent monitors.

Apple hardware makes this easy. Just plug your second monitor into the port of any Mac, with the correct adapter of course, and you have two monitors working independently of one another. (See Figure 3.) Note that dual monitors are not required. You will just have to organize your open windows to fit on your screen if you don't have two monitors.

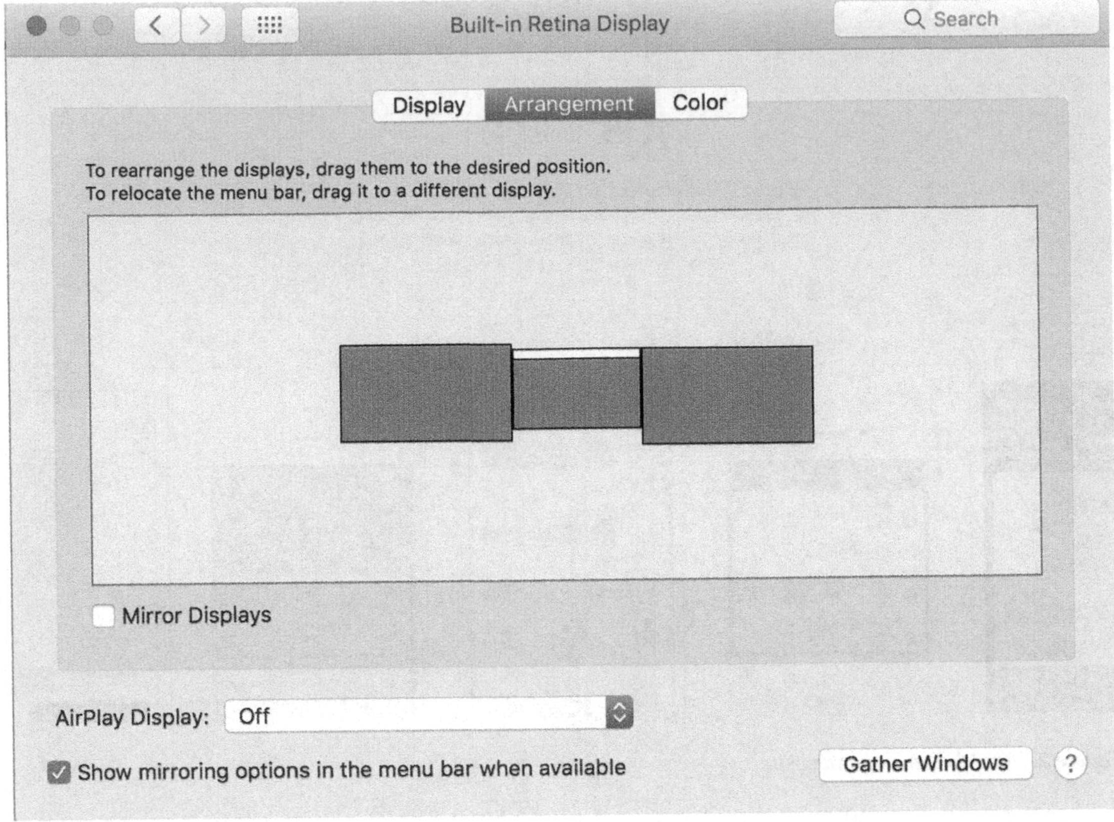

Figure 3. *Configuring a second monitor*

Nearly every week, we have live webinars and discuss a topic from the book or a timely item of interest. These webinars are free, and you can register for them at `www.xcelme.com/latest-videos/`. See Figure 4.

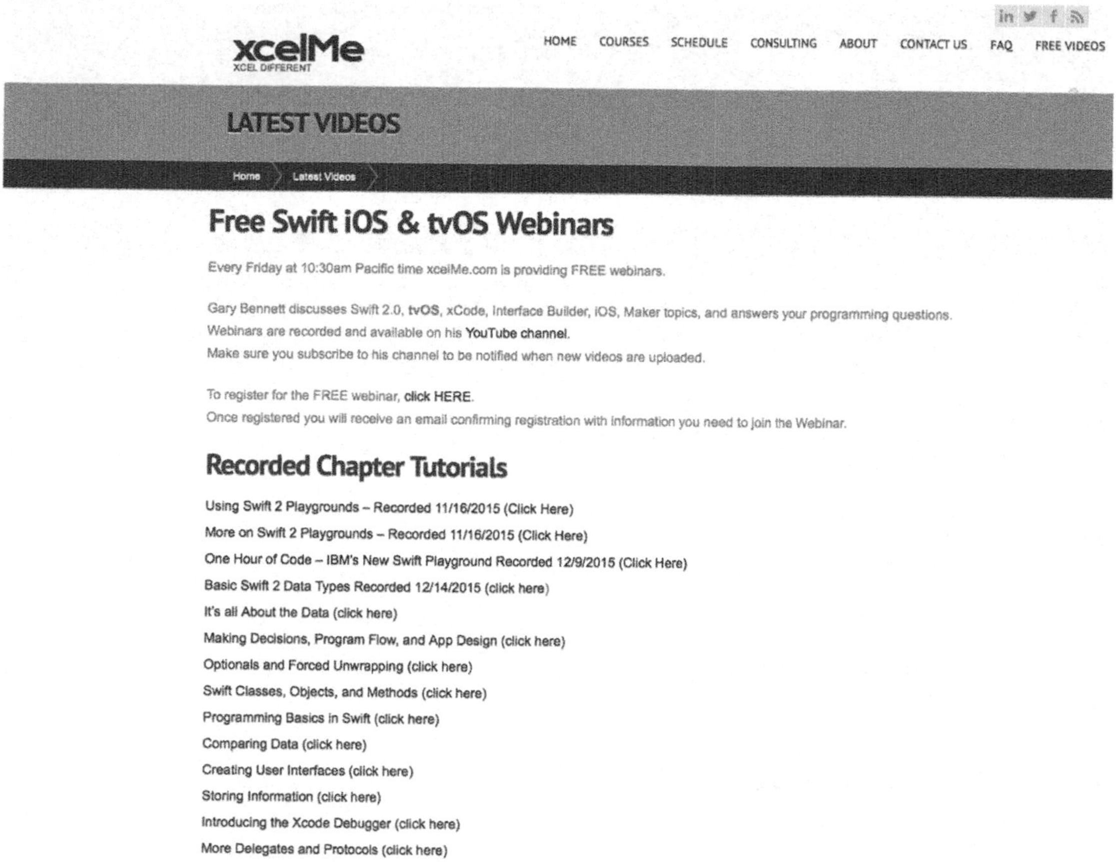

xcelMe
XCEL DIFFERENT

HOME COURSES SCHEDULE CONSULTING ABOUT CONTACT US FAQ FREE VIDEOS

LATEST VIDEOS

Home > Latest Videos

Free Swift iOS & tvOS Webinars

Every Friday at 10:30am Pacific time xcelMe.com is providing FREE webinars.

Gary Bennett discusses Swift 2.0, **tvOS**, xCode, Interface Builder, iOS, Maker topics, and answers your programming questions.
Webinars are recorded and available on his **YouTube channel**.
Make sure you subscribe to his channel to be notified when new videos are uploaded.

To register for the FREE webinar, **click HERE**.
Once registered you will receive an email confirming registration with information you need to join the Webinar.

Recorded Chapter Tutorials

Using Swift 2 Playgrounds – Recorded 11/16/2015 (Click Here)
More on Swift 2 Playgrounds – Recorded 11/16/2015 (Click Here)
One Hour of Code – IBM's New Swift Playground Recorded 12/9/2015 (Click Here)
Basic Swift 2 Data Types Recorded 12/14/2015 (click here)
It's all About the Data (click here)
Making Decisions, Program Flow, and App Design (click here)
Optionals and Forced Unwrapping (click here)
Swift Classes, Objects, and Methods (click here)
Programming Basics in Swift (click here)
Comparing Data (click here)
Creating User Interfaces (click here)
Storing Information (click here)
Introducing the Xcode Debugger (click here)
More Delegates and Protocols (click here)

Figure 4. *Register for free webinars at* `www.xcelme.com/latest-videos/`

At the end of the webinars, we do a Q&A. You can ask a question on the topic discussed or any topic in the book.

Additionally, all the webinars are recorded and available on YouTube. Make sure you subscribe to the YouTube channel so you are notified when new recordings are uploaded.

Free Book Forum

We have developed an online forum for this book at `http://forum.xcelme.com`, where you can ask questions while you are learning Swift and get answers from the authors. You will also find answers to the exercises and additional exercises to help you learn. (See Figure 5.)

FORUM	TOPICS
How To Access Your Course Webinars And How To Use The Forum New students need to download the attached pdf and follow instructions to register for your webinars after you purchase the class. Additionally, there are directions and updates on how to access your course and forum, post questions, navigate the message board, watch training videos, etc. **Moderator:** gary.bennett	3
Book -> Swift 2.0 for Absolute Beginners: iPhone and Mac Programming Made Easy 2nd Edition This forum contains answers readers may have for each chapter as well as any corrections to the book. The forum also contains the Source Code for the book. **Moderator:** gary.bennett	17
Book -> Developing for Apple TV using tvOS and Swift This forum contains answers readers may have for each chapter as well as any corrections to the book. The forum also contains the Source Code for the book. **Moderator:** gary.bennett	10
Book -> Objective-C for Absolute Beginners: (2nd Edition) iPhone and Mac Programming Made Easy This forum contains all the assignments and questions readers may have for each chapter. **Moderator:** gary.bennett	20
Free Live Webinars for iPhone Developers This forum lists the schedule for upcoming live webinars for iPhone developers. Webinars are live and have limited seats. Current and former students get first notifications. Seats for all others is first-come-first serve. The sessions are recorded and will be made available to current and former students on this forum. **Moderator:** gary.bennett	1
Current Student & Alumni Recorded Webinars and More This Forum is for current and former students **Moderator:** gary.bennett	0
Student/Instructor AppStore Applications Applications that xcelme instructors and students have successfully posted on iTunes AppStore. **Moderator:** gary.bennett	39
tvOS using Swift 2.0 for the new Apple TV **Moderator:** gary.bennett	11
Swift 2.0 Course 1 - Intro to OOP and Logic Swift Course 1 - Intro to OOP and Logic **Moderator:** gary.bennett	11
Swift 2.0 Course 2 - Swift for iOS Developers Swift Course 2 - Swift for iOS Developers **Moderator:** gary.bennett	11
Swift 2.0 Course 3 - Cocoa Touch for iOS Developers Swift Course 3 - Cocoa Touch for iOS Developers **Moderator:** gary.bennett	11
Swift 2.0 Course 4 - iPhone and iPad Programming Part 1 Swift Course 4 - iPhone and iPad Programming Part 1	11
Swift 2.0 Course 5 - iPhone and iPad Programming Part 2 Swift Course 5 - iPhone and iPad Programming Part 2 **Moderator:** gary.bennett	11
Swift 2.0 Class 6 - iPad Programming Swift Class 6 - iPad Programming, Apple Watch, HealthKit **Moderator:** gary.bennett	10

***Figure 5.** Reader forum for accessing answer to exercise and posting questions for authors*

CHAPTER 1

Becoming a Great iOS Developer

Now that you're ready to become a software developer and have read the introduction of this book, you need to become familiar with several key concepts. Your computer program will do exactly what you tell it to do—no more and no less. It will follow the programming rules that were defined by the operating system and the Swift programming language. Your program doesn't care if you are having a bad day or how many times you ask it to perform something. Often, what you think you've told your program to do and what it actually does are two different things.

Key to Success If you haven't already, take a few minutes to read the introduction of this book. The introduction shows you where to go to access the free webinars, forums, and YouTube videos that go with each chapter. Also, you'll better understand why this book uses the Swift playground programming environment and how to be successful in developing your iOS apps.

Depending on your background, working with something absolutely black and white may be frustrating. Many times, programming students have lamented, "That's not what I wanted it to do!" As you begin to gain experience and confidence in programming, you'll begin to think like a programmer. You will understand software design and logic, and you will experience having your programs perform exactly as you want, and you will enjoy the satisfaction associated with this.

1.1 Thinking Like a Developer

Software development involves writing a computer program and then having a computer execute that program. A *computer program* is the set of instructions that you want the computer to perform. Before beginning to write a computer program, it is helpful to list the steps that you want your program to perform in the order you want them accomplished. This step-by-step process is called an *algorithm.*

If you want to write a computer program to toast a piece of bread, you would first write an algorithm. The algorithm might look something like this:

1. Take the bread out of the bag.
2. Place a slice of bread in the toaster.
3. Press the "toast" button.
4. Wait for the toast to pop up.
5. Remove the toast from the toaster.

G. Bennett and B. Lees, *Swift 3 for Absolute Beginners*, DOI 10.1007/978-1-4842-2331-4_1

At first glance, this algorithm seems to solve the problem. However, the algorithm leaves out many details and makes many assumptions. Here are some examples:

- What kind of toast does the user want? Does the user want white bread, wheat bread, or some other kind of bread?
- How does the user want the bread toasted? Light or dark?
- What does the user want on the bread after it is toasted: butter, margarine, honey, or strawberry jam?
- Does this algorithm work for all users in their cultures and languages? Some cultures may have another word for toast or not know what toast is.

Now, you might be thinking this is getting too detailed for making a simple toast program. Over the years, software development has gained a reputation of taking too long, costing too much, and not being what the user wants. This reputation came to be because computer programmers often start writing their programs before they have actually thought through their algorithms.

The key ingredients to making successful applications are *design requirements*. Design requirements can be formal and detailed or simple like a list on a piece of paper. Design requirements are important because they help the developer flesh out what the application should and should not do when complete. Design requirements should not be completed in a programmer's vacuum, but should be produced as the result of collaboration between developers, users, and customers.

Another key ingredient to your successful app is the ***user interface*** (UI) design. Apple recommends you spend more than 50 percent of the entire development process focusing on the UI design. The design can be done using simple pencil and paper or using Xcode's storyboard feature to lay out your screen elements. Many software developers start with the UI design, and after laying out all the screen elements and having many users look at paper mock-ups, they write the design requirements from their screen layouts.

■ **Note** If you take anything away from this chapter, let it be the importance of considering design requirements and user interface design before starting software development. This is the most effective (and least expensive) use of time in the software development cycle. Using a pencil and eraser is a lot easier and faster than making changes to code because you didn't have others look at the designs before starting to program.

After you have done your best to flesh out all the design requirements, laid out all the user interface screens, and had the clients or potential customers look at your design and give you feedback, you can begin coding. Once coding begins, design requirements and user interface screens can change, but the changes are typically minor and are easily accommodated by the development process. See Figures 1-1 and 1-2.

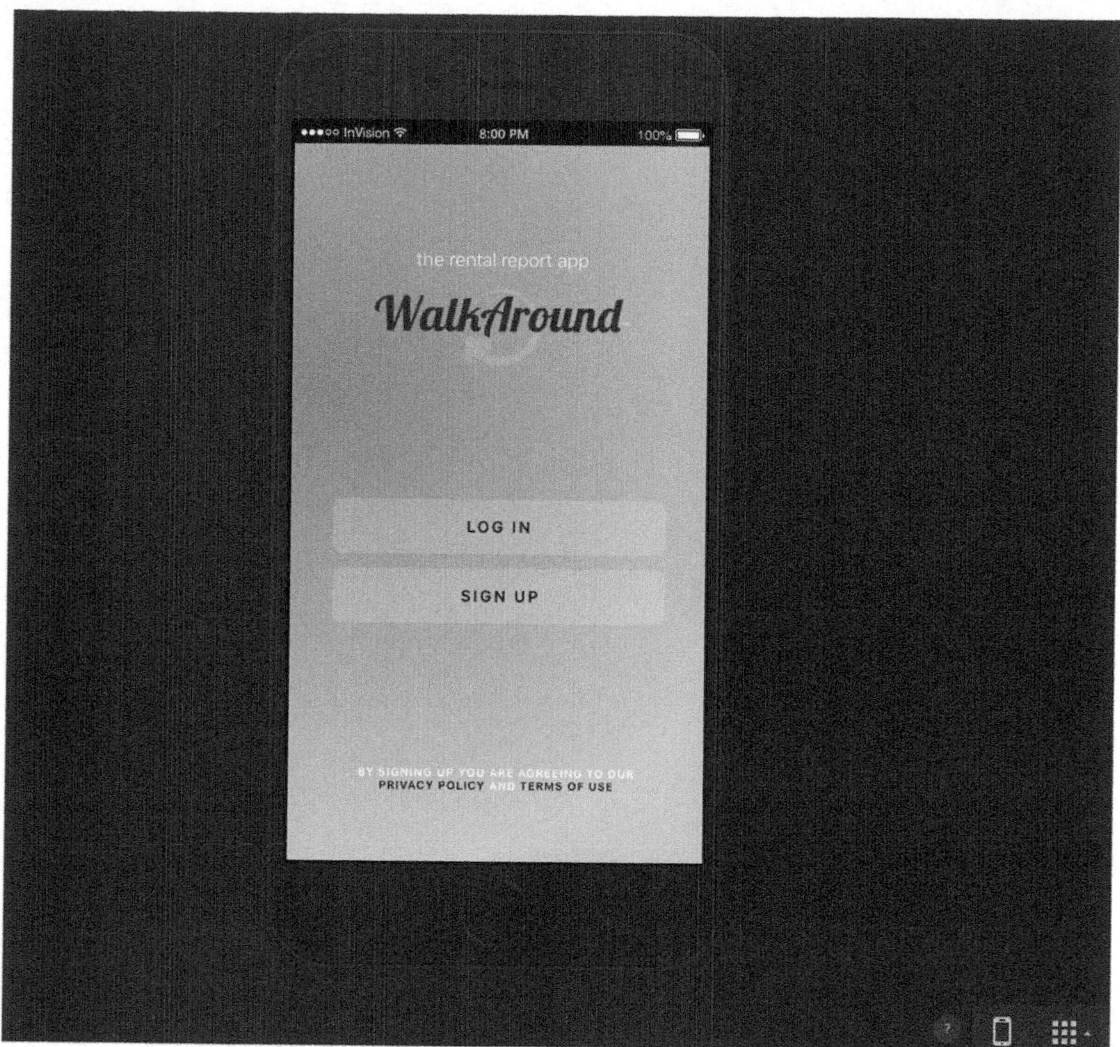

Figure 1-1. *This is a UI mock-up of the Log In screen for an iPhone mobile rental report app before development begins. This UI design mock-up was completed using InVision*

Figure 1-2. *This is the completed iPhone rental report app. This app is called WalkAround*

Figure 1-1 shows a mock-up of a rental report app screen prior to development. Developing mock-up screens along with design requirements forces developers to think through many of the application's usability issues before coding begins. This enables the application development time to be shortened and makes for a better user experience and better reviews on the App Store. Figure 1-2 shows how the view for the rental report app appears when completed. Notice how mock-up tools enable you to model the app to the real thing.

Completing the Development Cycle

Now that you have the design requirements and user interface designs and have written your program, what's next? After programming, you need to make sure your program matches the design requirements and user interface design and ensure that there are no errors. In programming vernacular, errors are called *bugs*. Bugs are undesired results of your programming and must be fixed before the app is released to the App Store. The process of finding bugs in programs and making sure the program meets the design requirements is called ***testing***. Typically, someone who is experienced in software testing methodology and who didn't write the app performs this testing. Software testing is commonly referred to as ***quality assurance*** (QA).

■ **Note** When an application is ready to be submitted to the App Store, Xcode gives the file an `.app` or `.ipa` extension, for example, `appName.app`. That is why iPhone, iPad, and Mac applications are called ***apps***. This book uses *program*, *application*, and *app* to mean the same thing.

During the testing phase, the developer will need to work with the QA staff to determine why the application is not working as designed. The process is called *debugging*. It requires the developer to step through the program to find out why the application is not working as designed. Figure 1-3 shows the complete software development cycle.

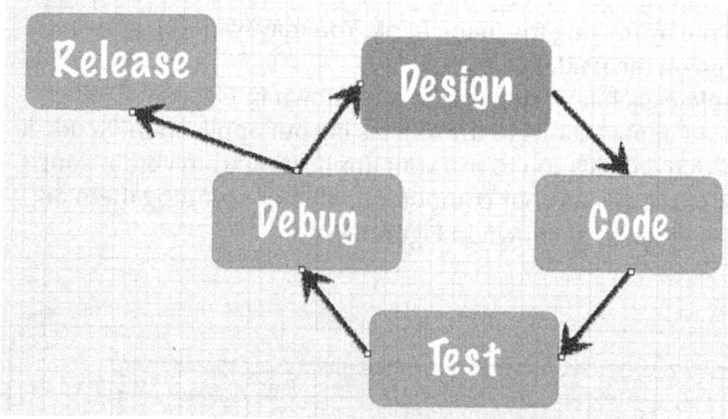

Figure 1-3. *The typical software development cycle*

Frequently during testing and debugging, changes to the requirements (design) must occur to make the application more usable for the customers. After the design requirements and user interface changes are made, the process starts again.

At some point, the application that everyone has been working so hard on must be shipped to the App Store. Many considerations are taken into account as to when in the cycle this happens:

- Cost of development
- Budget
- Stability of the application
- Return on investment

There is always the give-and-take between developers and management. Developers want the app to be perfect, and management wants to start realizing revenue from the investment as soon as possible. If the release date were left up to the developers, the app would likely never ship to the App Store. Developers would continue to tweak the app forever, making it faster, more efficient, and more usable. At some point, however, the code needs to be pried from the developers' hands and uploaded to the App Store so it can do what it was meant to do.

Introducing Object-Oriented Programming

As discussed in detail in the introduction, playgrounds enable you to focus on ***object-oriented programming*** **(OOP)** without having to cover all the Swift programming syntax and complex Xcode development environment in one big step. Instead, you can focus on learning the basic principles of OOP and using those principles quickly to write your first programs.

For decades, developers have been trying to figure out a better way to develop code that is reusable, manageable, and easily maintained over the life of a project. OOP was designed to help achieve code reuse and maintainability while reducing the cost of software development.

OOP can be viewed as a collection of objects in a program. Actions are performed on these objects to accomplish the design requirements.

An ***object*** is anything that can be acted on. For example, an airplane, person, or screen/view on the iPad can all be objects. You may want to act on the plane by making the plane bank. You may want the person to walk or to change the color of the screen of an app on the iPad.

Playgrounds execute your code as you complete each line, such as the one shown in Figure 1-4. When you run your playground applications, the user can apply actions to the objects in your application. Xcode is an ***integrated development environment*** (IDE) that enables you to run your application from within your programming environment. You can test your applications on your computer first before running them on your iOS devices by running the apps in Xcode's simulator, as shown in Figure 1-5.

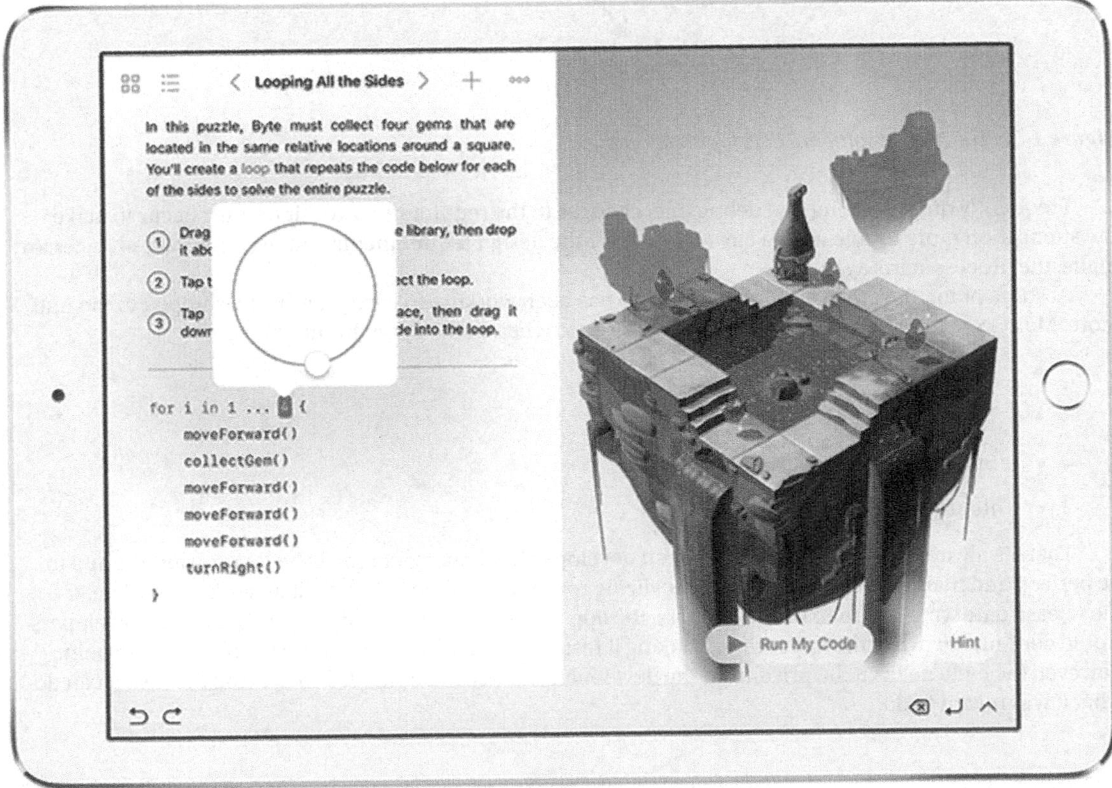

Figure 1-4. *There are multiple objects in this playground view*

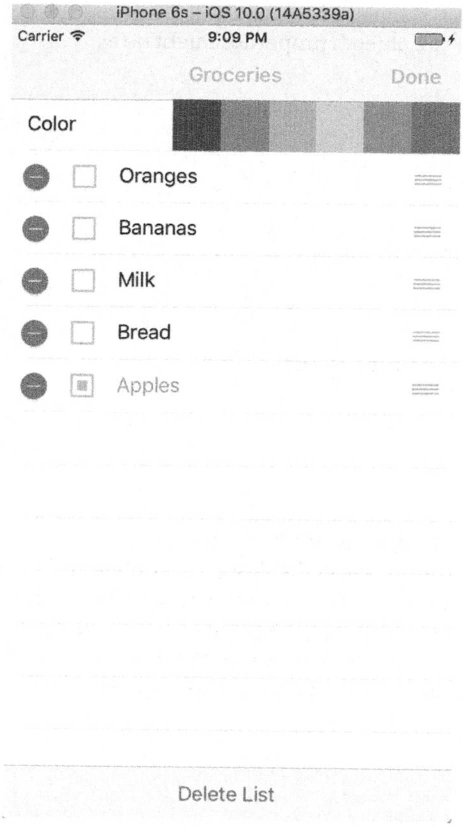

iPhone 6s – iOS 10.0 (14A5339a)
Carrier 9:09 PM
Groceries Done
Color
Oranges
Bananas
Milk
Bread
Apples
Delete List

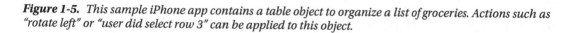

Figure 1-5. *This sample iPhone app contains a table object to organize a list of groceries. Actions such as "rotate left" or "user did select row 3" can be applied to this object.*

Actions that are performed on objects are called ***methods***. Methods manipulate objects to accomplish what you want your app to do. For example, for a `jet` object, you might have the following methods:

```
goUp
goDown
bankLeft
turnOnAfterburners
lowerLandingGear
```

The `table` object in Figure 1-5 is actually called `UITableView` when you use it in a program, and it could have the following methods:

```
numberOfRowsInSection
cellForRowAtIndexPath
canEditRowAtIndexPath
commitEditingStyle
didSelectRowAtIndexPath
```

Most objects have data that describes those objects. This data is defined as *properties*. Each property describes the associated object in a specific way. For example, the jet object's properties might be as follows:

```
altitude = 10,000 feet
heading = North
speed = 500 knots
pitch = 10 degrees
yaw = 20 degrees
latitude = 33.575776
longitude = -111.875766
```

For the UITableView object in Figure 1-5, the following might be the properties:

```
whiteGroundColor = Red
selectedRow = 3
animateView = No
```

An object's properties can be changed at any time when your program is running, when the user interacts with the app, or when the programmer designs the app to accomplish the design requirements. The values stored in the properties of an object at a specific time are collectively called the ***state of an object***.

State is an important concept in computer programming. When teaching students about state, we ask them to go over to a window and find an airplane in the sky. We then ask them to snap their fingers and make up some of the values that the plane's properties might have at that specific time. Those values might be as follows:

```
altitude = 10,000 feet
latitude = 33.575776
longitude = -111.875766
```

Those values represent the *state* of the object at the specific time that they snapped their fingers.

After waiting a couple minutes, we ask the students to find that same plane, snap their fingers again, and record the plane's possible state at that specific point in time.

The values of the properties might then be something like the following:

```
altitude = 10,500 feet
latitude = 33.575665
longitude = -111.875777
```

Notice how the state of the object changes over time.

Working with the Playground Interface

Playgrounds offer a great approach to using the concepts just discussed without all the complexity of learning Xcode and the Swift language at the same time. It takes only a few minutes to familiarize yourself with the playground interface and begin writing a program.

Technically speaking, the playground interface is not a true IDE like you will be using to write your iOS apps, but it is pretty close and much easier to learn in. A true IDE combines code development, user interface layout, debugging tools, documentation, and simulator/console launching for a single application; see Figure 1-6. However, playgrounds offer a similar look, feel, and features to the Xcode IDE you develop apps with.

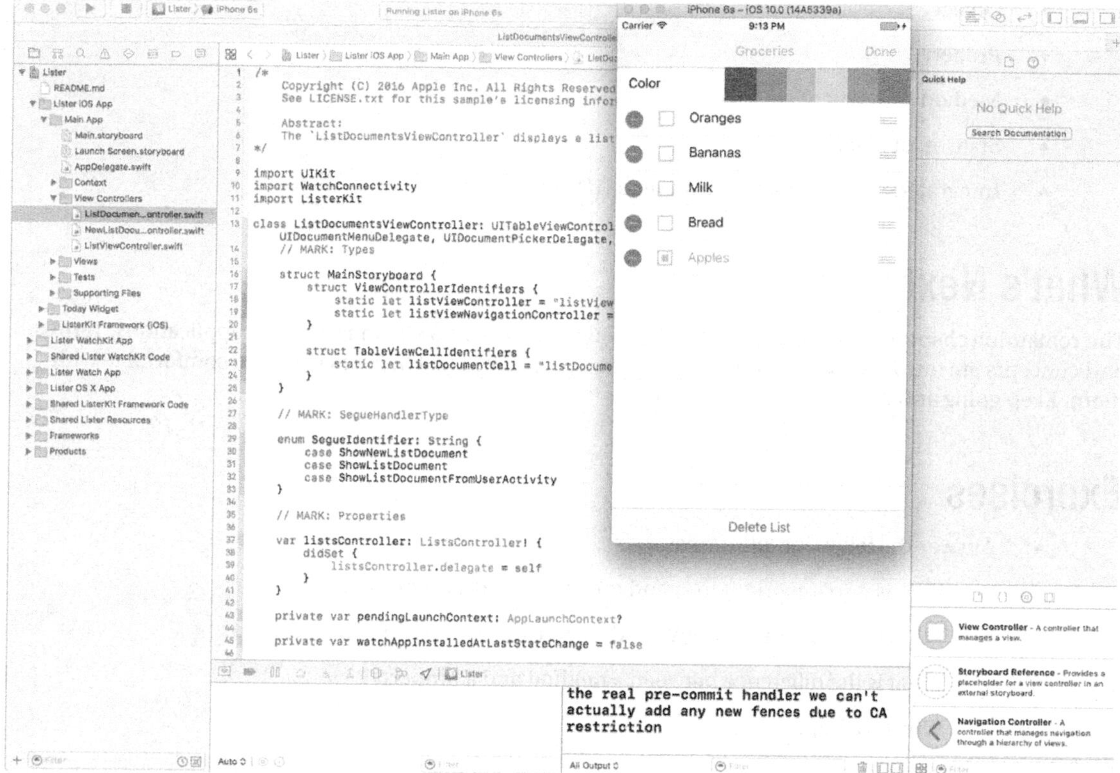

***Figure 1-6.** The Xcode IDE with the iPhone simulator*

In the next chapter, you will go through the playground interface and write your first program.

Summary

Congratulations, you have finished the first chapter of this book. It is important that you have an understanding of the following terms because they will be reinforced throughout this book:

- Computer program
- Algorithm
- Design requirements
- User interface

- Bug
- Quality assurance (QA)
- Debugging
- Object-oriented programming (OOP)
- Object
- Property
- Method
- State of an object
- Integrated development environment (IDE)

What's Next

The remaining chapters provide the information you need to learn Swift and write iOS applications. Terms and concepts are introduced and reinforced over and over so you will begin to get more comfortable with them. Keep going and be patient with yourself.

Exercises

- Answer the following questions:
  - Why is it so important to spend time on your user requirements?
  - What is the difference between design requirements and an algorithm?
  - What is the difference between a method and a property?
  - What is a bug?
  - What is state?
- Write an algorithm for how a soda machine works from the time a coin is inserted until a soda is dispensed. Assume the price of a soda is 80 cents.
- Write the design requirements for an app that will run the soda machine.

CHAPTER 2

Programming Basics

This chapter focuses on the building blocks that are necessary to become a great Swift programmer. This chapter covers how to use the playground user interface, how to write your first Swift program, and how to use the Xcode Integrated Development Environment (IDE).

Note We will introduce you to using playgrounds, which will enable you to program right away without worrying about the complexities of Xcode. We have used this approach teaching Objective-C and Swift, and we know that it helps you learn the concepts quickly, without discouragement, and gives you a great foundation to build upon.

Touring Xcode

Xcode and playgrounds make writing Swift code incredibly simple and fun. Type a line of code, and the result instantly appears immediately. If your code runs a period of time, like a loop or branch, you can watch its progress in the timeline area. When you've completed your code in the playground, it is easy to move your code to a Swift iOS project. With Xcode playgrounds, you can do the following:

- Design or modify an algorithm, observing the results every step of the way
- Create new tests, verifying that they work before promoting them into your test suite

First, you'll need to learn a little more about the Xcode user interface. When you open an Xcode iOS project, you are presented with a screen that looks like Figure 2-1.

G. Bennett and B. Lees, *Swift 3 for Absolute Beginners*, DOI 10.1007/978-1-4842-2331-4_2

Figure 2-1. Xcode Integrated Developer Environment with a Swift project

The Xcode user interface is set up to help you efficiently write your Swift applications. The user interface helps new programmers learn the user interface for an iOS application. You will now explore the major sections of Xcode's IDE workspace and playgrounds.

Exploring the Workspace Window

The workspace window, shown in Figure 2-2, enables you to open and close files, set your application preferences, develop and edit an app, and view the text output and error console.

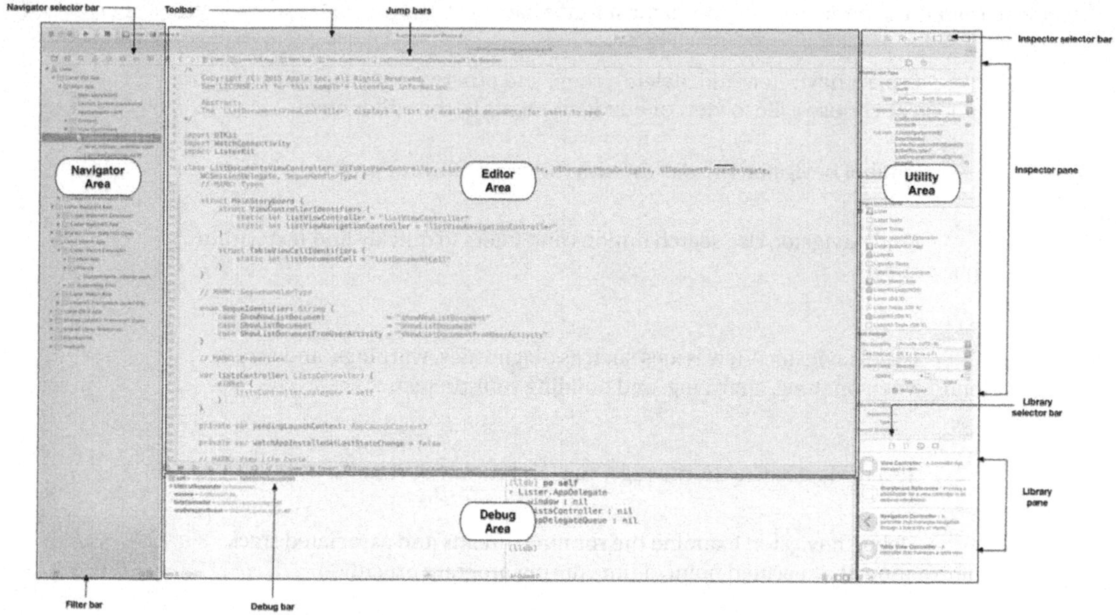

Figure 2-2. *Xcode's workspace window*

The workspace window is your primary interface for creating and managing projects. The workspace window automatically adapts itself to the task at hand, and you can further configure the window to fit your work style. You can open as many workspace windows as you need.

The workspace window has four main areas: Editor, Navigator, Debug, and Utility.

When you select a project file, its contents appear in the Editor area, where Xcode opens the file in the appropriate editor.

You hide or show the other three areas by using buttons in the view selector in the toolbar. These buttons are in the top-right corner of the window.

Clicking this button shows or hides the Navigator area. This is where you view and maneuver through files and other facets of your project.

Clicking this button shows or hides the Debug area. This is where you control program execution and debug code.

Clicking this button shows or hides the Utility area. You use the Utility area for several purposes, most commonly to view and modify attributes of a file and to add ready-made resources to your project.

Navigating Your Workspace

You can access files, symbols, unit tests, diagnostics, and other features of your project from the Navigator area. In the navigator selector bar, you choose the navigator suited to your task. The content area of each navigator gives you access to relevant portions of your project, and each navigator's filter bar allows you to restrict the content that is displayed.

Choose from these options in the navigator selector bar:

Project navigator. Add, delete, group, and otherwise manage files in your project, or choose a file to view or edit its contents in the editor area.

Symbol navigator. Browse the class hierarchy in your project.

Find navigator. Use search options and filters to quickly find text within your project.

Issue navigator. View issues such as diagnostics, warnings, and errors found when opening, analyzing, and building your project.

Test navigator. Create, manage, run, and review unit tests.

Debug navigator. Examine the running threads and associated stack information at a specified point of time during program execution.

Breakpoint navigator. Fine-tune breakpoints by specifying characteristics such as triggering conditions and see all your project's breakpoints in one place.

Report navigator. View the history of your builds.

Editing Your Project Files

Most development work in Xcode occurs in the Editor area, which is the main area that is always visible within the workspace window. The editors you will use most often are as follows:

- *Source editor*: Write and edit Swift source code.
- *Interface Builder*: Graphically create and edit user interface files (see Figure 2-3).
- *Project editor*: View and edit how your apps should be built, such by specifying build options, target architectures, and app entitlements.

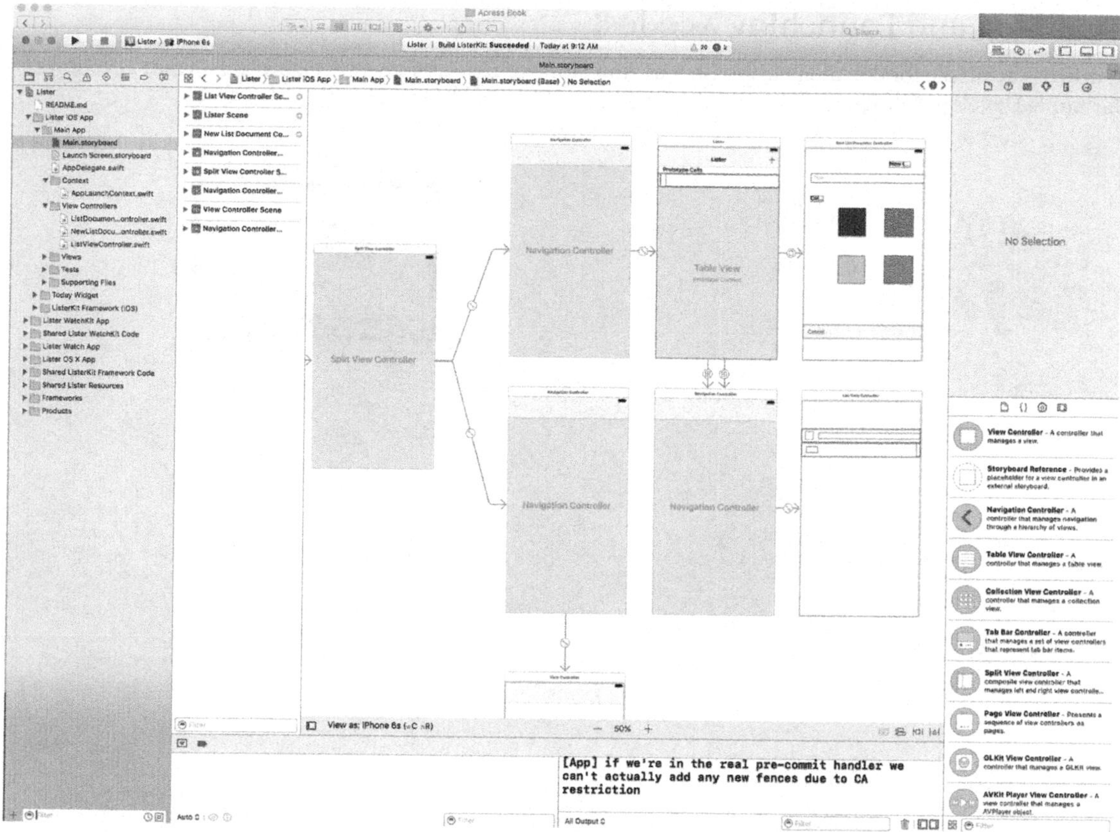

Figure 2-3. *Xcode's Interface Builder showing a storyboard file*

When you select a file, Xcode opens the file in an appropriate editor. In Figure 2-3, the file `Main.storyboard` is selected in the Project navigator, and the file is open in Interface Builder.

The editor offers three controls:

Clicking this button opens the Standard editor. You will see a single editor pane with the contents of the selected file.

Clicking this button opens the Assistant editor. You will see a separate editor pane with content logically related to that in the Standard editor pane.

Clicking this button opens the Version editor. You will see the differences between the selected file in one pane and another version of that same file in a second pane. Used when working with source control.

Creating Your First Swift Playground Program

Now that you have learned a little about Xcode, it's time to write your first Swift playground program and begin to understand the Swift language, Xcode, and some syntax. First, you have to install Xcode.

Installing and Launching Xcode 8

Xcode 8 is available for download from the Mac App Store for free, as shown in Figure 2-4. Figure 2-5 shows the Apple Developer Program.

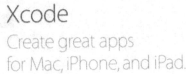

Xcode
Create great apps
for Mac, iPhone, and iPad.

Open

Xcode 4+
Essentials
Xcode includes everything developers need to create great applications for Mac, iPhone, iPad, Apple TV, and Apple Watch. Xcode provides developers a unified workflow for user interface design, coding, testing, and debugging. The Xcode IDE combined with the Swift programming language make developing apps easier and more fun than ever before.
...More
What's New in Version 8.0
Xcode 8 includes Swift 3, and SDKs for iOS 10, watchOS 3, tvOS 10, and macOS Sierra.
...More

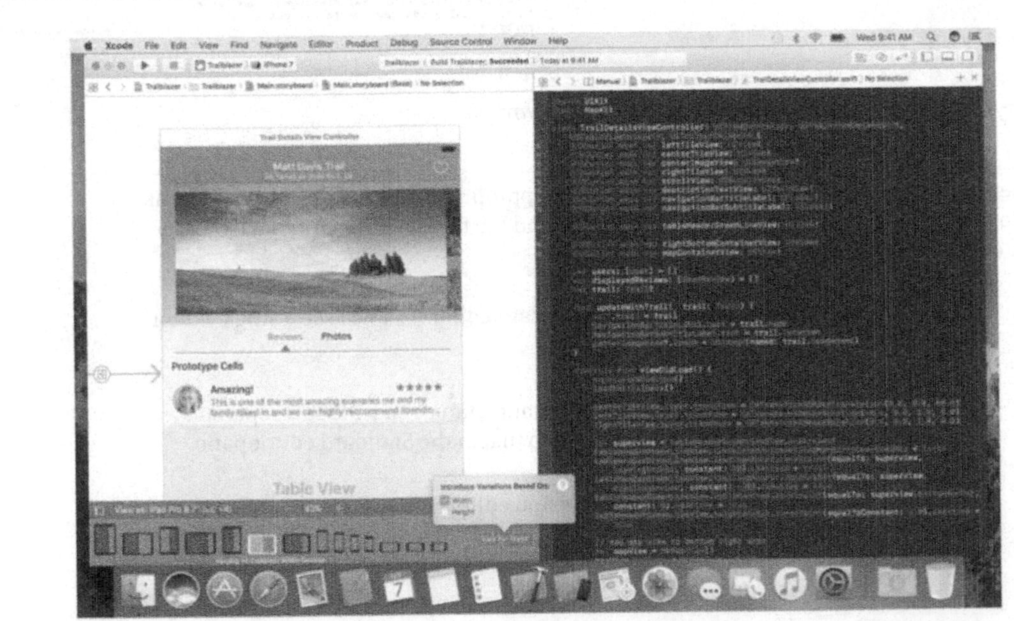

Figure 2-4. *Xcode 8 is available for download from the Mac App Store for free*

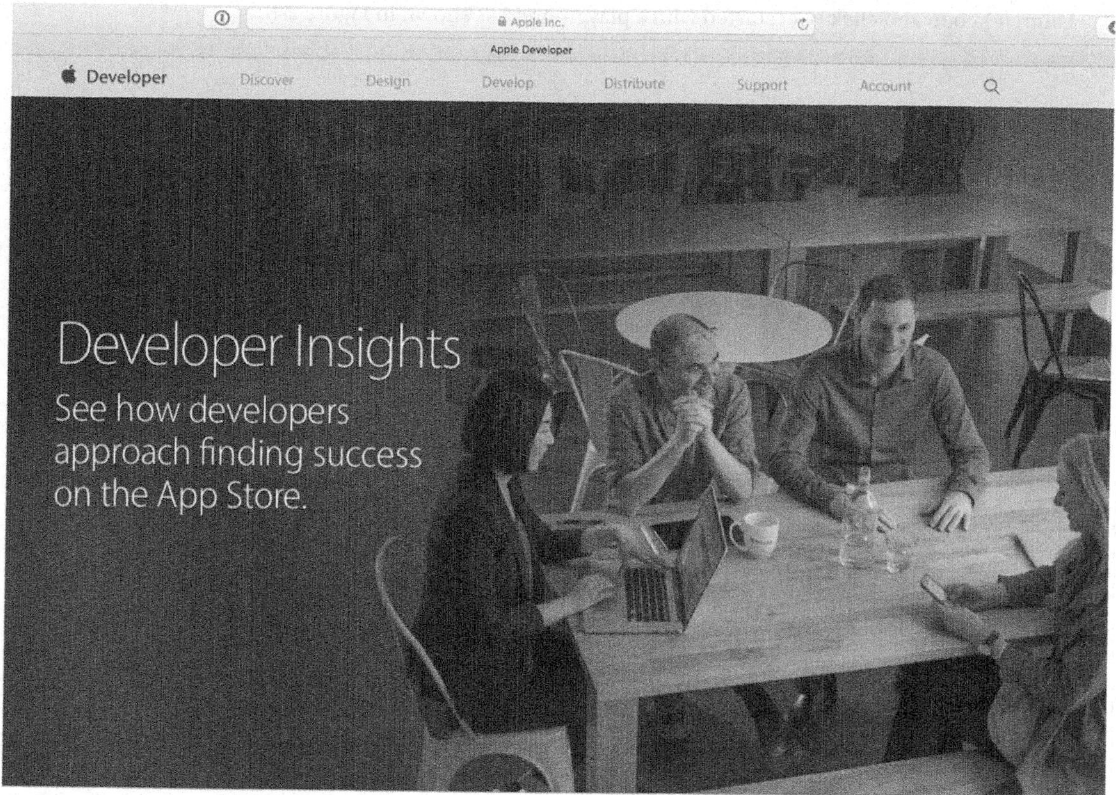

Figure 2-5. *The Apple Developer Program*

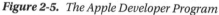

■ **Note** This package has everything you need to write iOS apps. To develop iOS apps, you will need to apply for the Apple Developer Program and pay $99 when you're ready to submit to the App Store. See `http://developer.apple.com`. In 2015, Apple combined the iOS, watchOS, Mac OS X, and Safari developer programs into one program called the *Apple Developer Program*.

Now that you have installed Xcode, let's begin writing a Swift playground.

Launch Xcode and click "Get started with a playground," as shown in Figure 2-6.

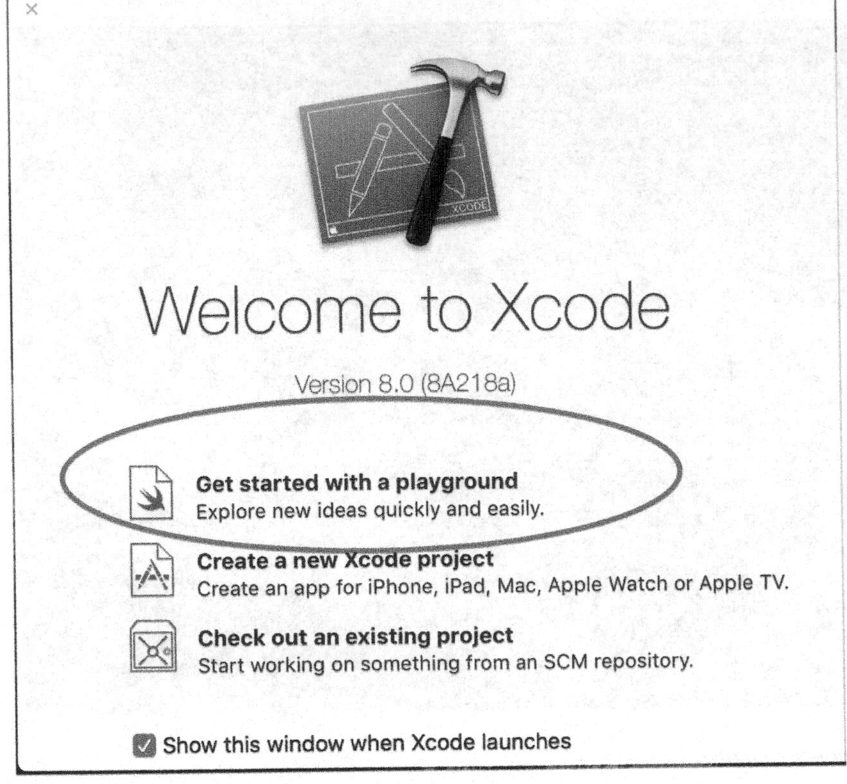

Figure 2-6. *Creating your first Swift playground*

Using Xcode 8

After launching Xcode, follow these steps:

1. Let's name the playground **HelloWorld** and select iOS as the platform, as shown in Figure 2-7. Then click Next and save your app in the folder of your choice.

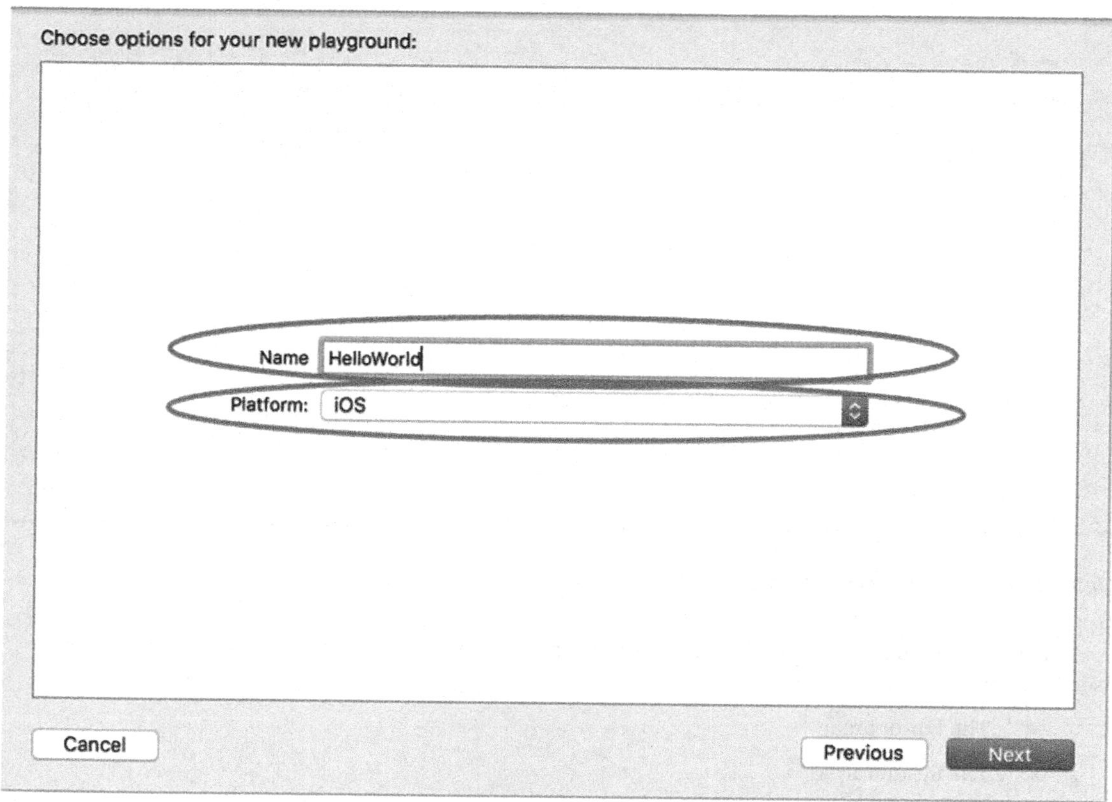

Figure 2-7. *Name your playground **HelloWorld** and select iOS as the platform*

Xcode does a lot of work for you and creates a playground file with code ready for you to use. It also opens your playground file in your Xcode editor so you can start, as shown in Figure 2-8.

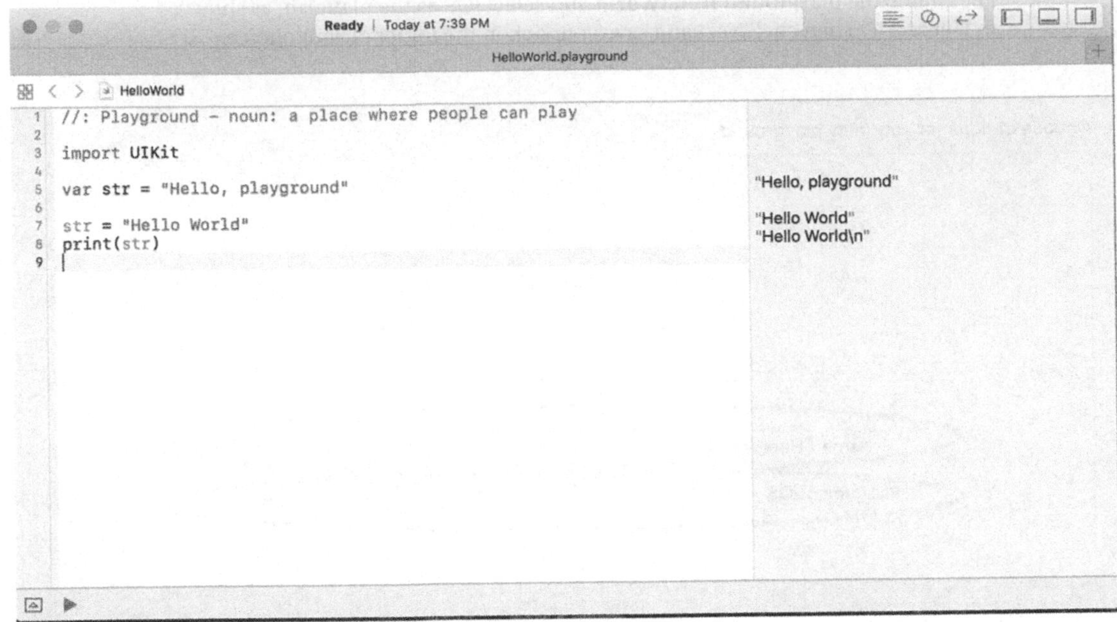
Ready | Today at 7:39 PM
HelloWorld.playground
HelloWorld
//: Playground - noun: a place where people can play
import UIKit
var str = "Hello, playground"
str = "Hello World"
print(str)
"Hello, playground"
"Hello World"
"Hello World\n"

Figure 2-8. *The playground window*

You now need to become familiar with the Xcode playground IDE. Let's look at two of the most often used features:

- The Editor area
- The Results area

Xcode Playground IDE: Editor and Results Areas

The Editor area is the business end of the Xcode playground IDE—where your dreams are turned into reality. It is where you write your code. As you write your code, you will notice it changes color. Sometimes, Xcode will even try to autocomplete words for you. The colors have meanings that will become apparent as you use the IDE. The Editor area is also where you debug your apps.

■ **Note** Even if we've mentioned it already, it is worth saying again: You will learn Swift programming by reading this book, but you will *really* learn Swift by writing and debugging your apps. Debugging is where developers learn and become great developers.

Let's add a line of code to see the power of Swift playgrounds. Add line 6 shown in Figure 2-8. As soon as you enter the line of code, Xcode automatically executes the line and shows the result, "Hello World".

When you write Swift code, everything is important—commas, capitalization, and parentheses. The collection of rules that enable the compiler to compile your code to an executable app is called *syntax*.

Line 5 creates a string variable called `str` and assigns "Hello, playground" to the variable.

Line 6 reassigns "Hello World" to the variable `str`.

Let's create a syntax error by entering line 8 shown in Figure 2-9.

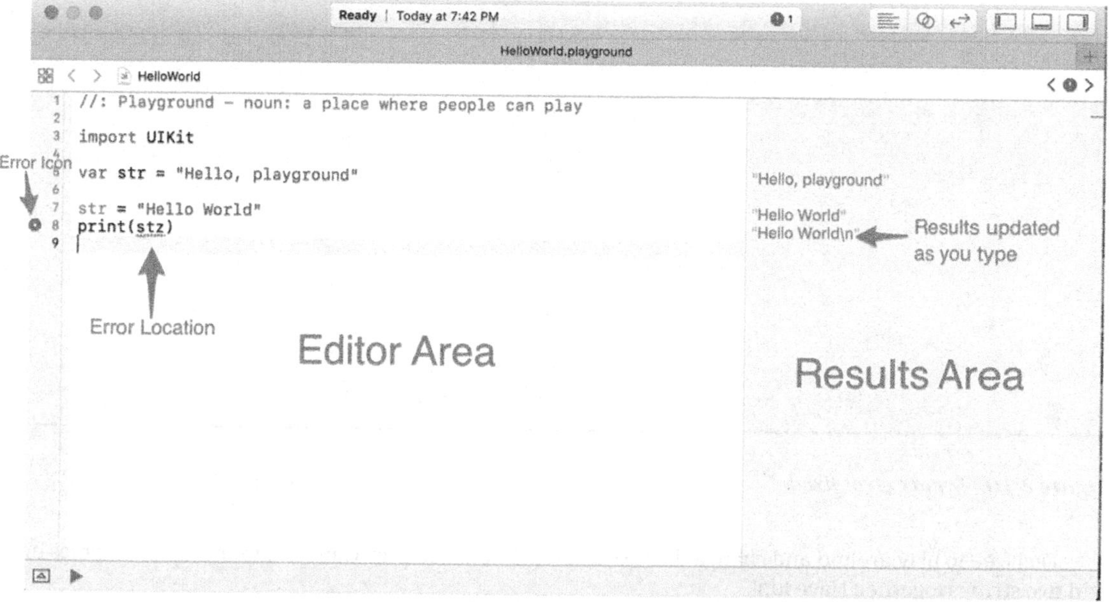

Figure 2-9. *The playground with a syntax error caught by the Swift compiler*

On line 8, `print` is a function that will print the contents of its parameters in the Results area. As you enter code, the Results area automatically updates with the results for each line of code that you entered.

Now, let's fix the app by spelling the *`str`* variable correctly, as shown in Figure 2-10.

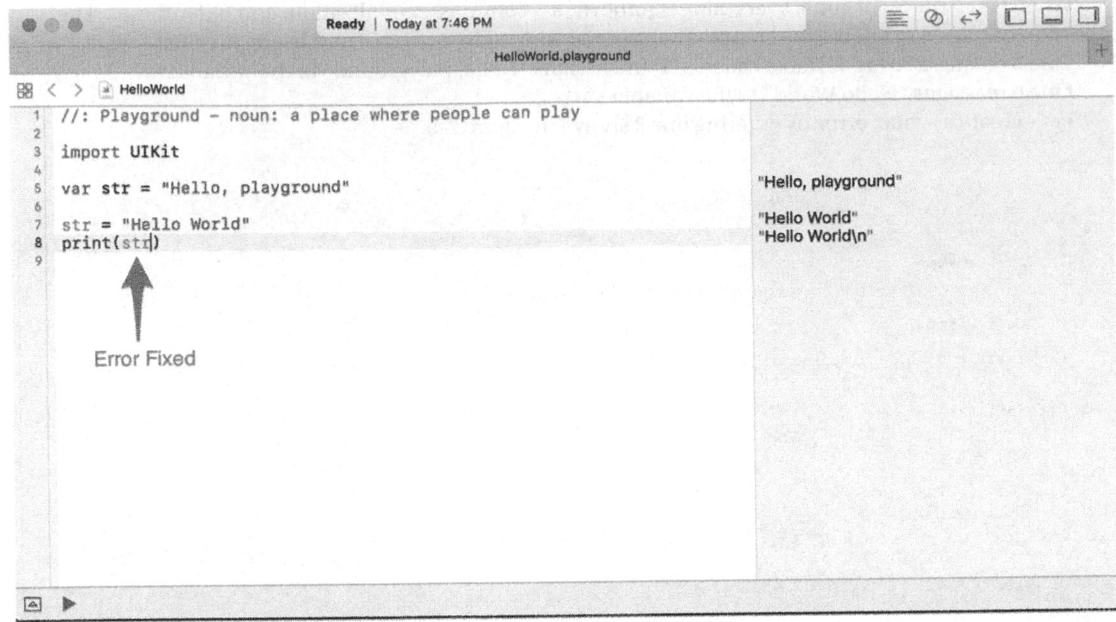

Figure 2-10. *Syntax error fixed*

Feel free to play around and change the text that is printed. You may want to add multiple variables or add two strings together. Have fun!

Summary

In this chapter, you built your first basic Swift playground. We also covered new Xcode terms that are key to your understanding of Swift.

■ **Key to Success** As mentioned in the introduction of the book, you can visit `http://www.xcelme.com/` and click the Free Videos tab to view videos related to this chapter. The videos will help you understand more about Xcode, IDEs, and playgrounds. Also visit `http://forum.xcelme.com/` to ask questions about these concepts.

The concepts that you should understand are as follows:

- Playground
- Editor area
- Results area

EXERCISE

Extend your playground by adding a line of code that prints any text of your choosing.

CHAPTER 3

It's All About the Data

As you probably know, data is stored as zeros and ones in your computer's memory. However, zeros and ones are not very useful to developers or app users, so you need to know how your program uses data and how to work with the data that is stored.

In this chapter, you look at how data is stored on computers and how you can manipulate that data. You then use playgrounds to learn more about data storage.

Numbering Systems Used in Programming

Computers work with information differently than humans do. This section covers the various ways information is stored, tallied, and manipulated by devices such as your iPhone and iPad.

Bits

A *bit* is defined as the basic unit of information used by computers to store and manipulate data. A bit has a value of either **0** or **1**. When computers were first introduced, transistors and microprocessors didn't exist. Data was manipulated and stored by vacuum tubes being turned on or off. If the vacuum tube was on, the value of the bit was 1, and if the vacuum tube was off, the value was 0. The amount of data a computer was able to store and manipulate was directly related to how many vacuum tubes the computer had.

The first recognized computer was called the Electronic Numerical Integrator and Computer (ENIAC). It took up more than 136 square meters and had 18,000 vacuum tubes. It was about as powerful as your handheld calculator.

Today, computers use transistors to store and manipulate data. The power of a computer processor depends on how many transistors are placed on its chip or CPU. Like the vacuum tube, transistors have an off or on state. When the transistor is off, its value is 0. If the transistor is on, its value is 1. At the time of this writing, the A10 processor powers the iPhone 7 and 7S Plus, has a 4-core ARM processor with approximately 3.3 billion transistors, up from 149 million transistors on the A4 and the first iPad. The A10 processor is 120x times faster than the original iPhone. Figure 3-1 shows the processor that was in iPhone 4 and the first iPad.

G. Bennett and B. Lees, *Swift 3 for Absolute Beginners*, DOI 10.1007/978-1-4842-2331-4_3

Figure 3-1. Apple's proprietary A10 processor

Moore's Law

The number of transistors on your iPhone's or iPad's processor is directly related to your device's processing speed, graphics performance, memory capacity, and the sensors (accelerometer, gyroscope) available in the device. The more transistors there are, the more powerful your device is.

In 1965, the cofounder of Intel, Gordon E. Moore, described the trend of transistors in a processor. He observed that the number of transistors in a processor doubled every 18 months from 1958 to 1965 and would likely continue "for at least 18 months." The observation became famously known as Moore's Law and has proven accurate for more than 55 years (see Figure 3-2).

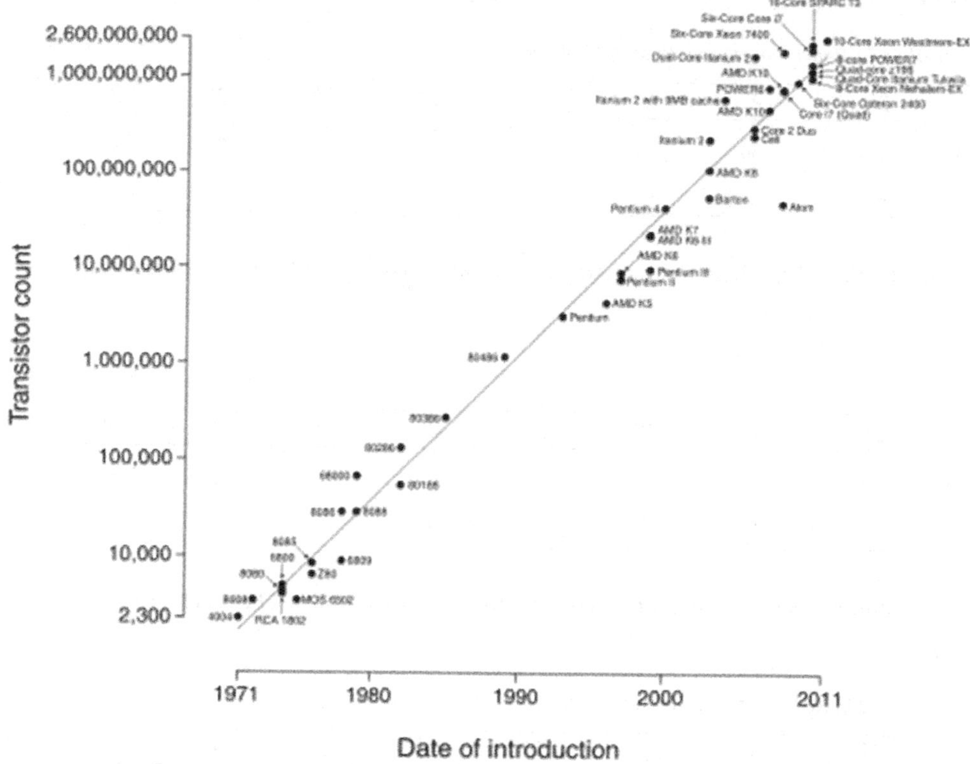

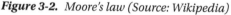

Figure 3-2. *Moore's law (Source: Wikipedia)*

Note There is a downside to Moore's Law, and you have probably felt it in your wallet. The problem with rapidly increasing processing capability is that it renders technology obsolete quickly. So, when your iPhone's two-year cell phone contract is up, the new iPhones on the market will be twice as powerful as the iPhone you had when you signed up. How convenient for everyone!

Bytes

A byte is another unit used to describe information storage on computers. A ***byte*** is composed of eight bits and is a convenient power of two. Whereas a bit can represent up to two different values, a byte can represent up to 2^8, or 256, different values. A byte can contain values from 0 to 255.

Note In Chapter 13, we discuss Base-2, Base-10, and Base-16 number systems in more detail. However, we will introduce these systems in this chapter so you can understand data types.

The ***binary*** number system represents the numerical symbols 0 and 1. To illustrate how the number **71** would be represented in binary, you can use a simple table of eight bits (1 byte), with each bit represented as a power of two. To convert the byte value **01000111** to decimal, simply add up the on bits, as shown in Table 3-1.

Table 3-1. *The Number 71 Represented as a Byte (64 + 4 + 2 + 1)*

Power of 2	2^7	2^6	2^5	2^4	2^3	2^2	2^1	2^0
Value for "**on**" bit	128	64	32	16	8	4	2	1
Actual bit	0	1	0	0	0	1	1	1

To represent the number **22** in binary, turn on the bits that add up to 22, or **00010110**, as shown in Table 3-2.

Table 3-2. *The Number 22 Represented as a Byte (16 + 4 + 2)*

Power of 2	2^7	2^6	2^5	2^4	2^3	2^2	2^1	2^0
Value for "**on**" bit	128	64	32	16	8	4	2	1
Actual bit	0	0	0	1	0	1	1	0

To represent the number **255** in binary, turn on the bits that add up to 255, or **11111111**, as shown in Table 3-3.

Table 3-3. *The Number 255 Represented as a Byte (128 + 64 + 32 + 16 + 8 + 4 + 2 + 1)*

Power of 2	2^7	2^6	2^5	2^4	2^3	2^2	2^1	2^0
Value for "**on**" bit	128	64	32	16	8	4	2	1
Actual bit	1	1	1	1	1	1	1	1

To represent the number **0** in binary, turn on the bits that add up to 0, or **00000000**, as shown in Table 3-4.

Table 3-4. *The Number 0 Represented as a Byte*

Power of 2	2^7	2^6	2^5	2^4	2^3	2^2	2^1	2^0
Value for "**on**" bit	128	64	32	16	8	4	2	1
Actual bit	0	0	0	0	0	0	0	0

3.1.3 Hexadecimal

Often, it will be necessary to represent characters in another format that is recognized by computers, namely, the hexadecimal format. The hex format is simply a "compressed" version of binary, where instead of eight characters used to represent a byte (eight bits), you can use two characters, for example, 00 or 2A or FF. You will encounter hexadecimal numbers when you are debugging your apps. The *hexadecimal* system is a base-16 number system. It uses 16 distinct symbols: 0 to 9 to represent the values 0 to 9 and A to F to represent the values 10 to 15. For example, the hexadecimal number 2AF3 is equal in decimal to $(2 \times 16^3) + (10 \times 16^2) + (15 \times 16^1) + (3 \times 16^0)$, or 10,995. You may want to play with the Mac Calculator application in Programmer mode to see how hex relates to decimal and binary.

Figure 3-3 shows the ASCII table of characters. Because one byte can represent 256 characters, this works well for Western characters. For example, hexadecimal 20 represents a space. Hexadecimal 7D represents a right curly brace (}).You can also see this by playing with the Mac Calculator app in Programmer mode. It can convert the values to ASCII.

Dec	Hx	Oct	Char		Dec	Hx	Oct	Html	Chr	Dec	Hx	Oct	Html	Chr	Dec	Hx	Oct	Html	Chr
0	0	000	NUL	(null)	32	20	040		Space	64	40	100	@	@	96	60	140	`	`
1	1	001	SOH	(start of heading)	33	21	041	!	!	65	41	101	A	A	97	61	141	a	a
2	2	002	STX	(start of text)	34	22	042	"	"	66	42	102	B	B	98	62	142	b	b
3	3	003	ETX	(end of text)	35	23	043	#	#	67	43	103	C	C	99	63	143	c	c
4	4	004	EOT	(end of transmission)	36	24	044	$	$	68	44	104	D	D	100	64	144	d	d
5	5	005	ENQ	(enquiry)	37	25	045	%	%	69	45	105	E	E	101	65	145	e	e
6	6	006	ACK	(acknowledge)	38	26	046	&	&	70	46	106	F	F	102	66	146	f	f
7	7	007	BEL	(bell)	39	27	047	'	'	71	47	107	G	G	103	67	147	g	g
8	8	010	BS	(backspace)	40	28	050	(	(	72	48	110	H	H	104	68	150	h	h
9	9	011	TAB	(horizontal tab)	41	29	051	)	)	73	49	111	I	I	105	69	151	i	i
10	A	012	LF	(NL line feed, new line)	42	2A	052	*	*	74	4A	112	J	J	106	6A	152	j	j
11	B	013	VT	(vertical tab)	43	2B	053	+	+	75	4B	113	K	K	107	6B	153	k	k
12	C	014	FF	(NP form feed, new page)	44	2C	054	,	,	76	4C	114	L	L	108	6C	154	l	l
13	D	015	CR	(carriage return)	45	2D	055	-	-	77	4D	115	M	M	109	6D	155	m	m
14	E	016	SO	(shift out)	46	2E	056	.	.	78	4E	116	N	N	110	6E	156	n	n
15	F	017	SI	(shift in)	47	2F	057	/	/	79	4F	117	O	O	111	6F	157	o	o
16	10	020	DLE	(data link escape)	48	30	060	0	0	80	50	120	P	P	112	70	160	p	p
17	11	021	DC1	(device control 1)	49	31	061	1	1	81	51	121	Q	Q	113	71	161	q	q
18	12	022	DC2	(device control 2)	50	32	062	2	2	82	52	122	R	R	114	72	162	r	r
19	13	023	DC3	(device control 3)	51	33	063	3	3	83	53	123	S	S	115	73	163	s	s
20	14	024	DC4	(device control 4)	52	34	064	4	4	84	54	124	T	T	116	74	164	t	t
21	15	025	NAK	(negative acknowledge)	53	35	065	5	5	85	55	125	U	U	117	75	165	u	u
22	16	026	SYN	(synchronous idle)	54	36	066	6	6	86	56	126	V	V	118	76	166	v	v
23	17	027	ETB	(end of trans. block)	55	37	067	7	7	87	57	127	W	W	119	77	167	w	w
24	18	030	CAN	(cancel)	56	38	070	8	8	88	58	130	X	X	120	78	170	x	x
25	19	031	EM	(end of medium)	57	39	071	9	9	89	59	131	Y	Y	121	79	171	y	y
26	1A	032	SUB	(substitute)	58	3A	072	:	:	90	5A	132	Z	Z	122	7A	172	z	z
27	1B	033	ESC	(escape)	59	3B	073	;	;	91	5B	133	[	[	123	7B	173	{	{
28	1C	034	FS	(file separator)	60	3C	074	<	<	92	5C	134	\	\	124	7C	174			|
29	1D	035	GS	(group separator)	61	3D	075	=	=	93	5D	135	]	]	125	7D	175	}	}
30	1E	036	RS	(record separator)	62	3E	076	>	>	94	5E	136	^	^	126	7E	176	~	~
31	1F	037	US	(unit separator)	63	3F	077	?	?	95	5F	137	_	_	127	7F	177		DEL

Source: www.LookupTables.com

128	Ç	144	É	161	í	177	▒	193	┴	209	╤	225	ß	241	±
129	ü	145	æ	162	ó	178	▓	194	┬	210	╥	226	Γ	242	≥
130	é	146	Æ	163	ú	179	│	195	├	211	╙	227	π	243	≤
131	â	147	ô	164	ñ	180	┤	196	─	212	╘	228	Σ	244	⌠
132	ä	148	ö	165	Ñ	181	╡	197	┼	213	╒	229	σ	245	⌡
133	à	149	ò	166	ª	182	╢	198	╞	214	╓	230	µ	246	÷
134	å	150	û	167	º	183	╖	199	╟	215	╫	231	τ	247	≈
135	ç	151	ù	168	¿	184	╕	200	╚	216	╪	232	Φ	248	°
136	ê	152	_	169	_	185	╣	201	╔	217	┘	233	Θ	249	·
137	ë	153	Ö	170	¬	186	║	202	╩	218	┌	234	Ω	250	·
138	è	154	Ü	171	½	187	╗	203	╦	219	█	235	δ	251	√
139	ï	156	£	172	¼	188	╝	204	╠	220	▄	236	∞	252	_
140	î	157	¥	173	¡	189	╜	205	═	221	▌	237	φ	253	²
141	ì	158	_	174	«	190	╛	206	╬	222	▐	238	ε	254	■
142	Ä	159	ƒ	175	»	191	┐	207	╧	223	▀	239	∩	255	
143	Å	160	á	176	░	192	└	208	╨	224	α	240	≡		

Source: www.LookupTables.com

Figure 3-3. *ASCII characters*

Unicode

Representing characters with a byte worked well for computers until about the 1990s, when the personal computer became widely adopted in non-Western countries where languages have more than 256 characters. Instead of a one-byte character set, Unicode can have up to a four-byte character set.

To facilitate faster adoption, the first 256 code points are identical to the ASCII character table. Unicode can have different character encodings. The most common encoding used for Western text is called UTF-8. The "8" is how many bits are used per character, so it's one byte per character, like ASCII.

As an iPhone developer, you will probably use this character encoding the most.

Data Types

Now that we've discussed how computers store data, we will cover an important concept called ***data types***. Humans can generally just look at data and the context in which it is being used to determine what type of data it is and how it will be used. Computers need to be told how to do this. So, the programmer needs to tell the computer the type of data it is being given. Here's an example: 2 + 2 = 4.

The computer needs to know you want to add two numbers together. In this example, they are integers. You might first believe that adding these numbers is obvious to even the most casual observer, let alone a sophisticated computer. However, it is common for users of iOS apps to store data as a series of characters, not a calculation. For example, a text message might read "Everyone knows that 2 + 2 = 4."

In this case, the example is a series of characters called a ***string***. A data type is simply the declaration to your program that defines the data you want to store. A ***variable*** is used to store your data and is declared with an associated data type. All data is stored in a variable, and the variable has to have a variable type. For example, in Swift, the following are variable declarations with their associated data types:

```
var x: Int = 10
var y: Int = 2
var z: Int = 0
var submarineName: String = "USS Nevada SSBN-733"
```

Data types cannot be mixed with one another. You cannot do the following:

```
z = x + submarineName
```

Mixing data types will cause either compiler warnings or compiler errors, and your app will not run.
Table 3-5 gives examples of the basic data types in Swift.

Table 3-5. *Swift Data Types*

Type	Examples
`Int`	1, 5, 10, 100
`Float` or `Double`	1.0, 2.222, 3.14159
`Bool`	`true`, `false`
`String`	`"Star Wars"`, `"Star Trek"`
`ClassName`	`UIView`, `UILabel`, and so on

Declaring Constants and Variables

Swift constants and variables must be declared before they are used. You declare constants with the `let` keyword and variables with the var keyword. Constants never change during the program, but variables do change during the program.

There are two ways to declare variables: **explicit** and **implicit.**

Here is the syntax for declaring a variable's type **explicitly**:

```
var name: type = value
var firstNumber: Int = 5
```

However, declaring the type is normally optional, and removing the type shortens the code and makes it easier because there is less code to type and maintain.

Here is the syntax for declaring a variable's type **implicitly**:

```
var name = value
var firstNumber = 5
```

You can use `implicit` most of the time because Swift is smart enough to figure out what the variable is by what you assign to it.

If a variable isn't going to change, you should declare it as a ***constant***. Constants never change. Constants start with the keyword `let`, as shown here:

```
let secondNumber = 10
```

To best understand how variables and constants are declared, here are two examples:

```
let maximumNumberOfStudents = 30
var currentNumberOfStudents = 5
```

This code can be read as follows: "Declare a new constant called `maximumNumberOfStudents`, and give it a value of 30. Then, declare a new variable called `currentNumberOfStudents`, and give it an initial value of 5."

In this example, the maximum number of students is declared as a constant because the maximum value never changes. The current number of students is declared as a variable because this value must be incremented or decremented after the student enrollment changes.

Most data you will use in your programs can be classified into four different kinds—Booleans, numbers, strings, and objects. We will discuss how to work with numbers and object data types in the remainder of this chapter. In Chapter 4, we will talk more about Boolean data types when you learn how to write apps with decision making.

■ **Note** *Localizing* your app is the process of writing your app so users can buy and use it in their native language. This process is too advanced for this book, but it is a simple one to complete when you plan from the beginning. Localizing your app greatly expands the total number of potential customers and revenue for your app without your having to rewrite it for each language. Be sure to localize your app. It is not hard to do and can easily double or triple the number of people who buy it. For more information on localizing your app, visit Apple's "Build Apps for the World" site: `https://developer.apple.com/internationalization/`.

Optionals

Swift introduces an important concept called *optionals* that developers need to understand. Even for experienced iOS developers, this concept is new. Optionals are not a hard topic to understand, but they take some time to get used to.

Use optionals when a value may be absent. An optional says the following:

- A variable may or may not have a value assigned to it.

There are times when a constant or variable might not have a value. Listing 3-1 shows an example of the integer initializer called `Int()`, which converts a `String` value to an `Int`.

Listing 3-1. Converting a string to an integer

```
var myString = "42"
let someInteger = Int(myString)
// someInteger is inferred to be of type "Int?", or "optional Int"
```

The constant `someInteger` is assigned the integer value `42.` `someInteger` is also assigned the type of `Int?`. The question mark indicates that it is an optional type, meaning that the variable or constant's value may be absent. See Listing 3-2.

Listing 3-2. Unable to convert a string to an integer

```
1 var myString = "Hello World"
2 let someInteger = Int(myString)
3 // someInteger's value is now absent
```

Line 2 in Listing 3-2 has a problem. It is not possible to convert "Hello World" from a `String` to an `Int`. So, the value of `someInteger` is said to be absent or `nil` because on line 2, `someInteger` is inferred to be an optional `Int`.

■ **Note** Objective-C programmers may have used `nil` to return an object from a method, with `nil` meaning "the absence of a valid object." This works for objects but not well for structures, basic C types, or enumeration values. Objective-C methods typically return a special value, like `NSNotFound`, indicating the absence of a valid object. This assumes that the method's caller knows the special value to test against. Optionals indicate the absence of a value for *any type at all*, without using special constants.

The `Integer Int()` initializer might fail to return a value, so the method returns an *optional* `Int`, rather than an `Int`. Again, the question mark indicates that the value it contains is optional, meaning that it might contain *some* `Int` value, or it may contain *no value at all.* The value is either some `Int` or is nothing at all.

Swift's `nil` is not the same as `nil` in Objective-C. With Objective-C, `nil` is a pointer to a nonexistent object. In Swift, `nil` is not a pointer; it is the absence of a value. Optionals of any type can be set to `nil`, not just object types.

In Chapter 4, you will learn how to "unwrap" optionals and check for the object of a valid object.

Using Variables in Playgrounds

Now that you have learned about data types, let's write your code in a playground that adds two numbers and displays the sum.

1. Open Xcode and select "Get started with a playground," as shown in Figure 3-4.

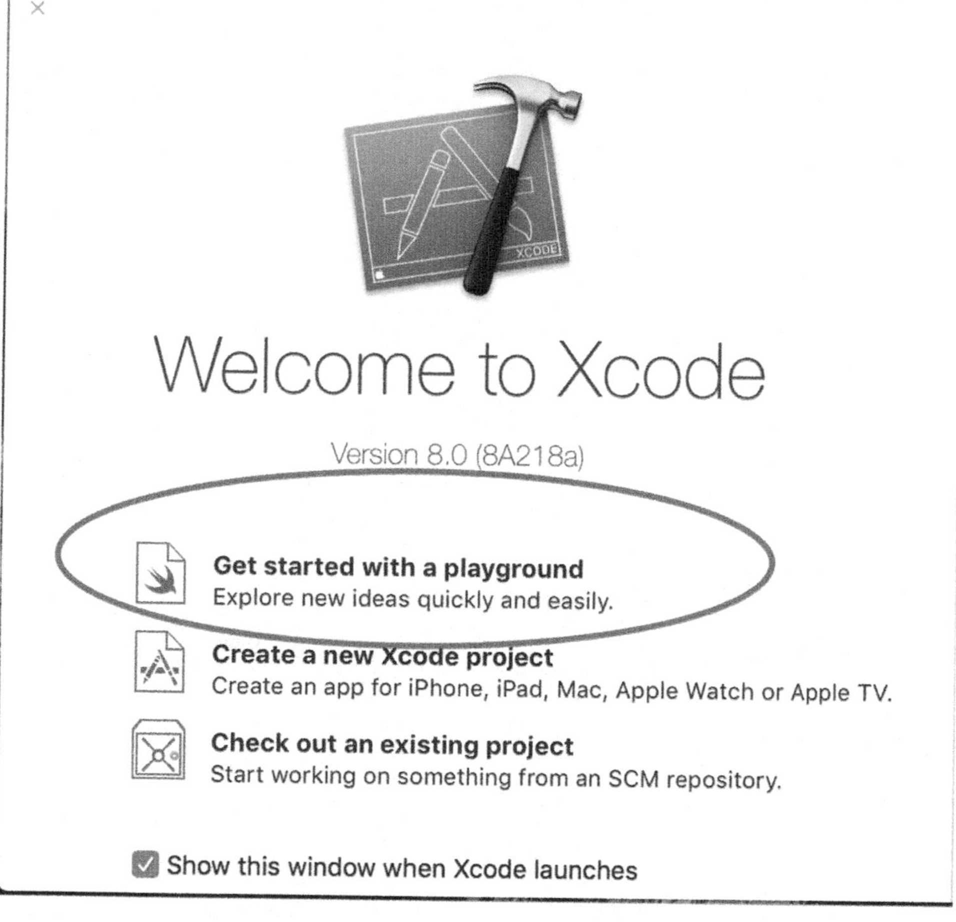

Figure 3-4. Creating a playground

2. Name your playground **DataTypes**, as shown in Figure 3-5. Press Next and select a directory to save your playground.

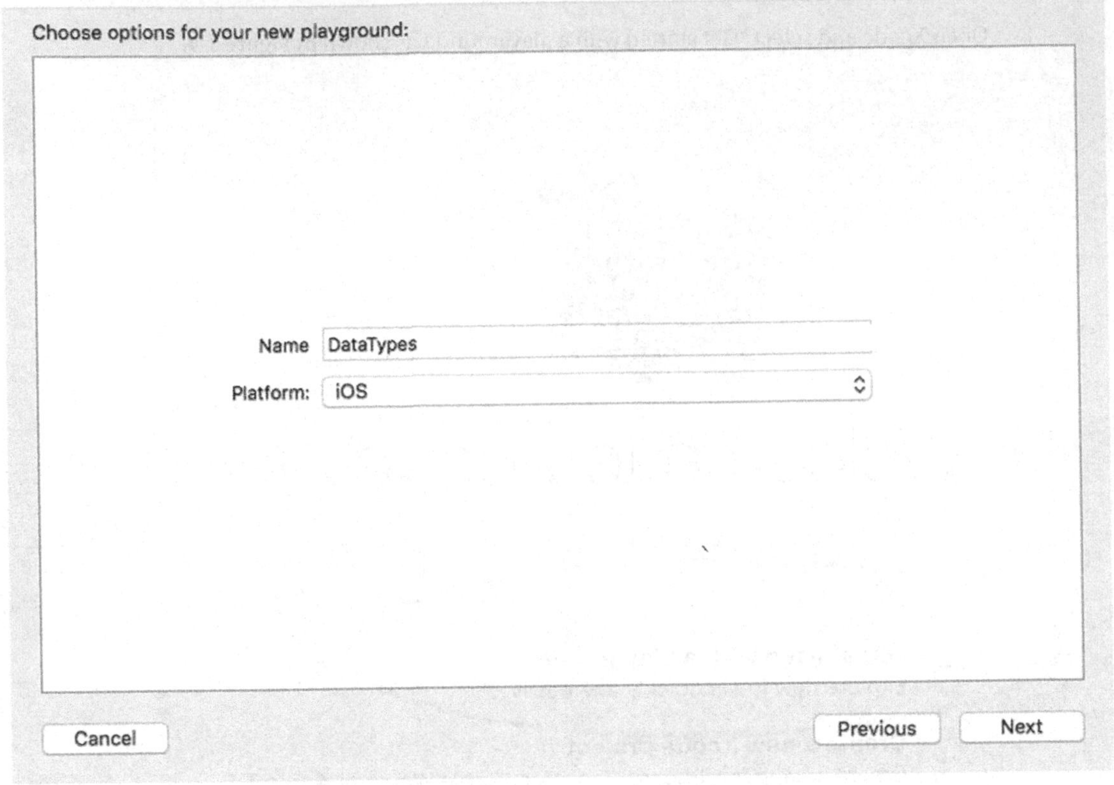

Figure 3-5. Naming your playground

3. When your playground is created, two lines of code are already placed in your code for you, as shown in Figure 3-6.

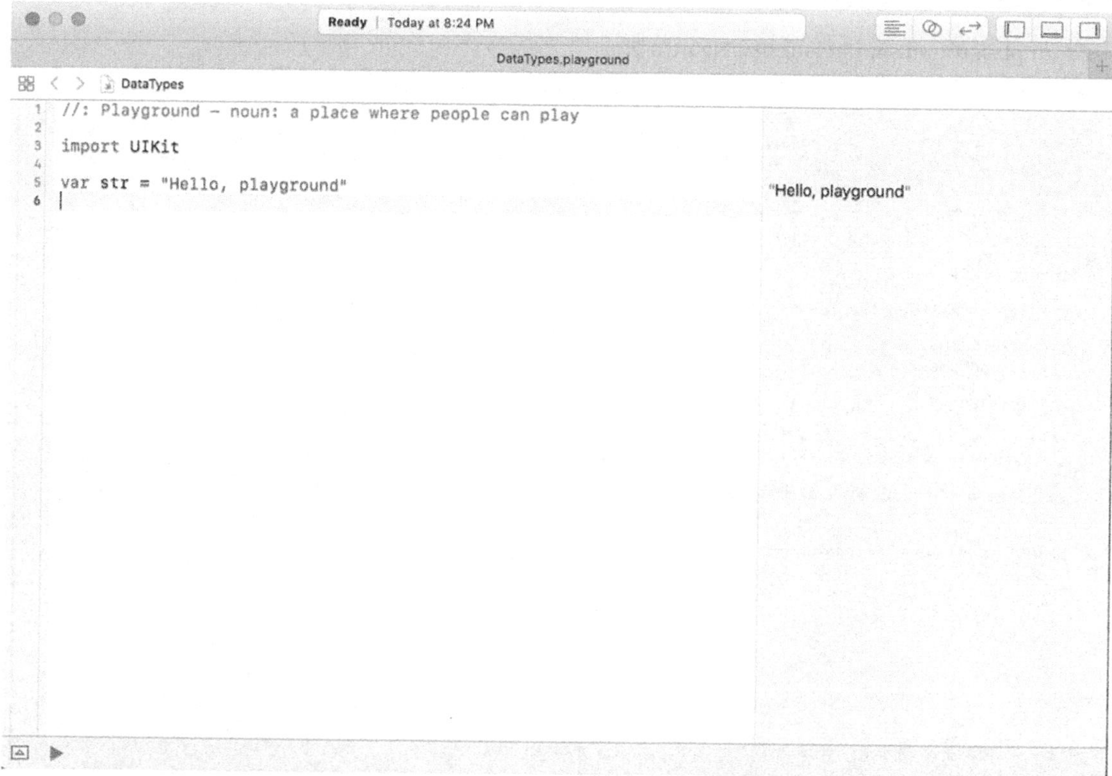

Figure 3-6. *Two lines of code*

4. Add the code to this playground, as shown in Listing 3-3.

Listing 3-3. Playground adding

```
// Playground - noun: a place where people can play

import UIKit

var str = "Hello, playground"

var firstNumber = 2
var secondNumber = 3

var totalSum = firstNumber + secondNumber

firstNumber = firstNumber + 1
secondNumber = secondNumber + 1

```

```
totalSum = firstNumber + secondNumber


print("totalSum = \(totalSum)")
```

Your playground should look like Figure 3-7.

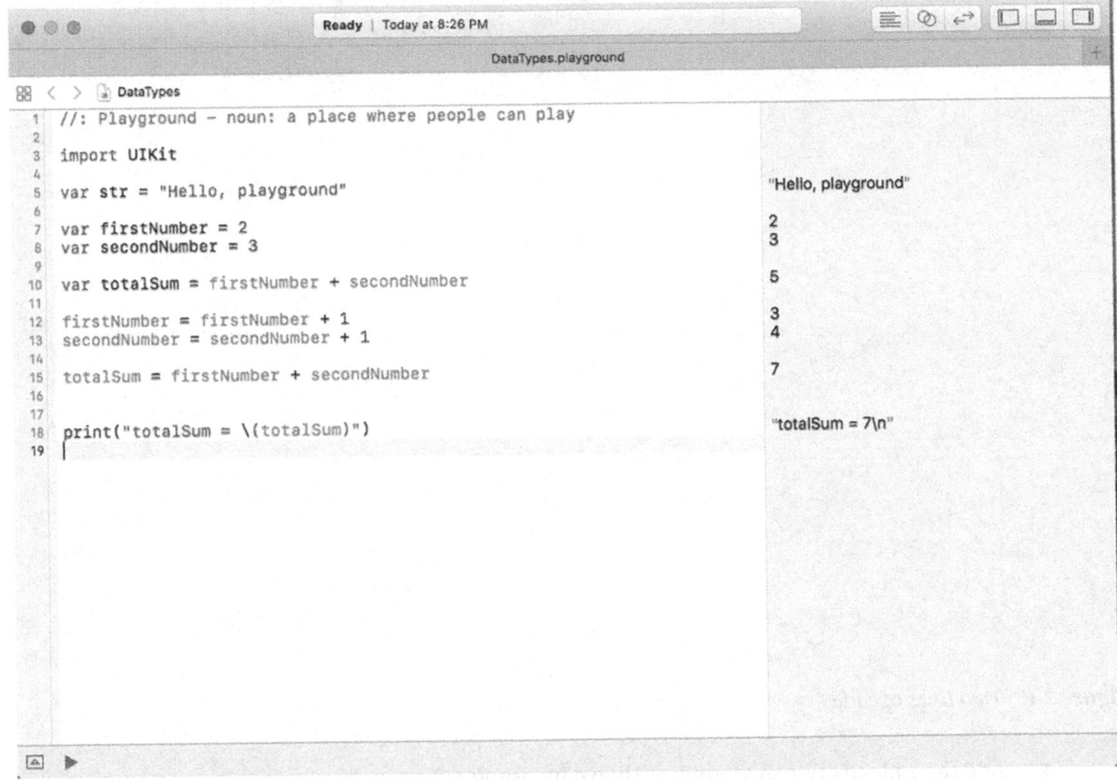

***Figure 3-7.** Playground displaying the results of your Swift app*

One of the neat features of playgrounds is that as you type in your code, Swift executes the line of code as you enter it so you can immediately view the results.

The // used in Swift programming enables programmers to make comments about their code. Comments are not compiled by your applications and are used as notes for the programmer or, more importantly, for programmers who follow the original developer. Comments help both the original developer and later developers understand how the app was developed.

Sometimes, it is necessary for comments to span several lines or just part of a line. This can be accomplished with /* and */. All the text between /* and */ is treated as comments and is not compiled.

`print` is a function that can take one parameter and print its contents.

■ **Note** If your editor doesn't have the same menus or gutter (the left column that contains the line numbers of the program) you saw in the previous screenshots, you can turn these settings in Xcode preferences. You can open Xcode preferences by clicking the Xcode menu in the menu bar and then selecting Preferences. See Figure 3-8.

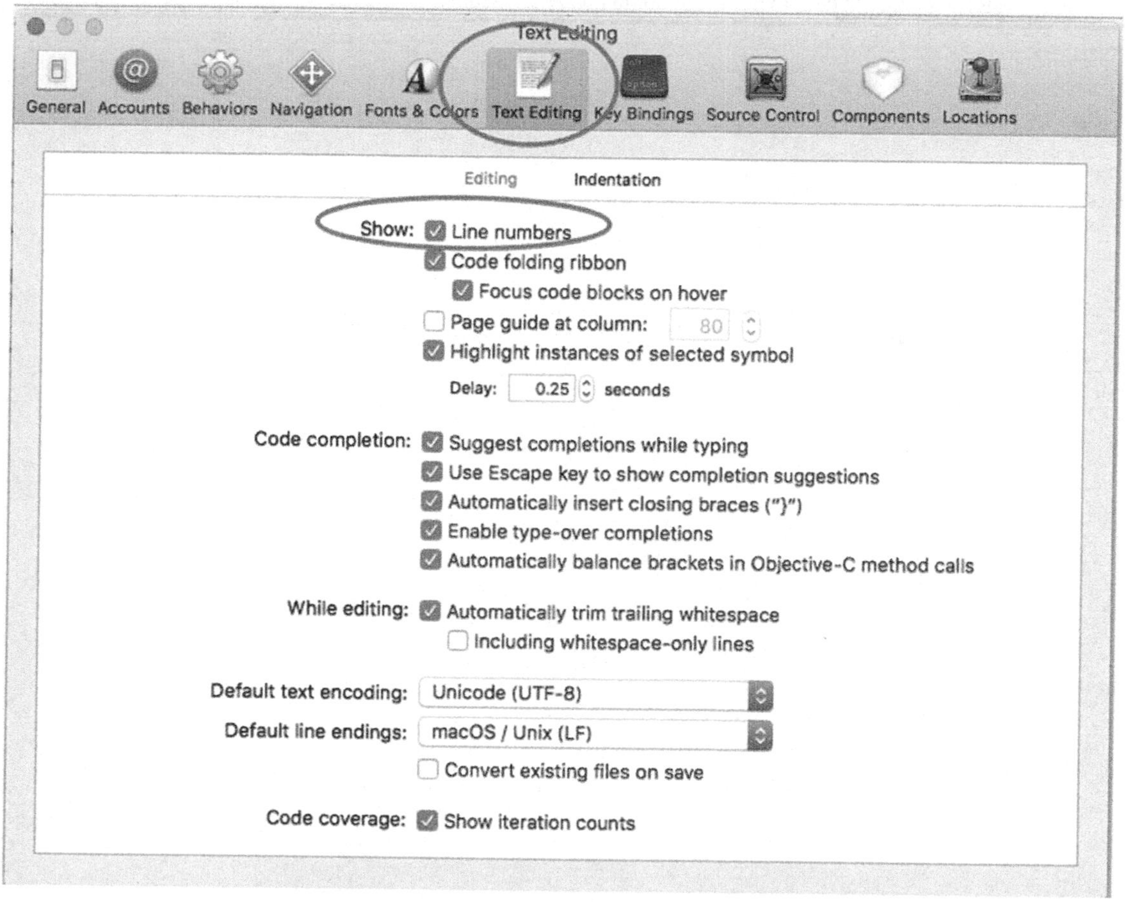

Figure 3-8. *Adding line numbers to the gutter*

Summary

In this chapter, you learned how data is used by your apps. You saw how to initialize variables and how to assign data to them. We explained that when variables are declared, they have a data type associated with them and that only data of the same type can be assigned to variables. The differences between variables and constants were also discussed, and we also introduced optionals.

EXERCISES

- Write code within a Swift playground that multiplies two integers and displays the result.
- Write code within a Swift playground that squares a float. Display the resulting float.
- Write code within a Swift playground that subtracts two floats, with the result being stored as an integer. Note that rounding does not occur.

CHAPTER 4

Making Decisions, Program Flow, and App Design

One of the great things about being an iOS developer is you get to tell your devices exactly what you want them to do and they do it—your devices will do tasks over and over again without getting tired. That's because iOS devices don't care how hard they worked yesterday, and they don't let feelings get in the way. These devices don't need hugs.

There is a downside to being a developer: You have to think of all the possible outcomes when it comes to your apps. Many developers love having this kind of control. They enjoy focusing on the many details of their apps; however, it can be frustrating having to handle so many details. As mentioned in the introduction to this book, there is a price to pay for developing apps, and that price is time. The more time you spend developing and debugging, the better you will get with all the details, and the better your apps will perform. You have to pay this price to become a successful developer.

Computers are black and white; there are no shades of gray. Your devices produce results, many of which are based on true and false conditions.

In this chapter, you learn about computer logic and controlling the flow of your apps. Processing information and arriving at results are at the heart of all apps. Your apps need to process data based on values and conditions. To do this, you need to understand how computers perform logical operations and execute code based on the information your apps have acquired.

Boolean Logic

Boolean logic is a system for logical operations. Boolean logic uses binary operators such as AND and OR and the unary operator NOT to determine whether your conditions have been met. Binary operators take two operands. Unary operators take one operand.

We just introduced a couple of new terms that can sound confusing; however, you probably use Boolean logic every day. Let's look at a couple of examples of Boolean logic with the binary operators AND and OR in a conversation parents sometimes have with their teenage children:

"You can go to the movies tonight if your room is clean AND the dishes are put away."

"You can go to the movies tonight if your room is clean OR the dishes are put away."

Boolean operators' results are either TRUE or FALSE. In Chapter 3, we briefly introduced the Boolean data type. A variable that is defined as Boolean can contain only the values TRUE and FALSE.

```
var seeMovies: Bool = false
```

In the preceding example, the AND operator takes two operands: one to the left and one to the right of the AND. Each operand can be evaluated independently with a TRUE or FALSE.

G. Bennett and B. Lees, *Swift 3 for Absolute Beginners*, DOI 10.1007/978-1-4842-2331-4_4

For an AND operation to yield a TRUE result, both sides of the AND have to be TRUE. In the first example, the teenager has to clean his or her room AND have the dishes done. If either one of the conditions is FALSE, the result is FALSE—no movies for the teenager.

For an OR operation to yield a TRUE result, only one operand has to be TRUE, or both conditions can be TRUE to yield a TRUE result. In the second example, just a clean bedroom would result in the ability to go to the movies.

■ **Note** In Objective-C and other programming languages, Boolean variables can hold integer variables; 0 represents FALSE, and any nonzero value represents TRUE. Swift's strong type checking doesn't allow this. Boolean variables in Swift can be assigned only `true` or `false`.

A NOT statement is a unary operator. It takes just one operand to yield a Boolean result. Here's an example: "You can NOT go to the movies."

This example takes one operand. The NOT operator turns a TRUE operand to a FALSE and a FALSE operand to a TRUE. Here, the result is a FALSE.

AND, OR, and NOT are three common Boolean operators. Occasionally, you need to use more complex operators. XOR, NAND, and NOR are other common operations for iOS developers.

The Boolean operator XOR means *exclusive-or*. An easy way to remember how the XOR operator works is the XOR operator will return a TRUE result ***if only one argument is TRUE, not both.***

Swift does not have these operators built in, but consider that NAND and NOR mean NOT AND and NOT OR. After evaluating the AND or OR argument and the results, simply negate the results.

Truth Tables

You can use a tool to help you evaluate all the Boolean operators called a ***truth table,*** and it is a mathematical table used in logic to evaluate Boolean operators. They are helpful when trying to determine all the possibilities of a Boolean operator. Let's look at some common truth tables for AND, OR, NOT, XOR, NAND, and NOR.

In an AND truth table, there are four possible combinations of TRUE and FALSE.

- TRUE AND TRUE = TRUE
- TRUE AND FALSE = FALSE
- FALSE AND TRUE = FALSE
- FALSE AND FALSE = FALSE

Placing these combinations in a truth table results in Table 4-1.

Table 4-1. *An AND Truth Table*

A	B	A AND B
TRUE	TRUE	TRUE
TRUE	FALSE	FALSE
FALSE	TRUE	FALSE
FALSE	FALSE	FALSE

An AND truth table produces a TRUE result only if both of its operands are TRUE.

Table 4-2 illustrates an OR truth table and all possible operands.

Table 4-2. *An OR Truth Table*

A	B	A OR B
TRUE	TRUE	TRUE
TRUE	FALSE	TRUE
FALSE	TRUE	TRUE
FALSE	FALSE	FALSE

An OR truth table produces a TRUE result if one or both of its operands are TRUE.

Table 4-3 illustrates a NOT truth table and all possible operands.

Table 4-3. *A NOT Truth Table*

A	NOT A
TRUE	FALSE
FALSE	TRUE

A NOT *flips the bit* or negates the original operand's Boolean value.

Table 4-4 illustrates an XOR (or exclusive-or) truth table and all possible operands.

Table 4-4. *An XOR Truth Table*

A	B	A XOR B
TRUE	TRUE	FALSE
TRUE	FALSE	TRUE
FALSE	TRUE	TRUE
FALSE	FALSE	FALSE

The operator XOR yields a TRUE result if only one of the operands is TRUE.

Table 4-5 illustrates a NAND truth table and all possible operands.

Table 4-5. *A NAND Truth Table*

A	B	A NAND B
TRUE	TRUE	FALSE
TRUE	FALSE	TRUE
FALSE	TRUE	TRUE
FALSE	FALSE	TRUE

Table 4-6 illustrates a NOR truth table and all possible operands.

Table 4-6. *A NOR Truth Table*

A	B	A NOR B
TRUE	TRUE	FALSE
TRUE	FALSE	FALSE
FALSE	TRUE	FALSE
FALSE	FALSE	TRUE

The easiest way to look at the NAND and NOR operators is to simply negate the results from the AND and OR truth tables, respectively.

Comparison Operators

In software development, you can compare different data items using ***comparison operators.*** These operators produce a logical TRUE or FALSE result. Table 4-7 shows the list of comparison operators.

Table 4-7. *Comparison Operators*

Operator	Definition
>	Greater than
<	Less than
>=	Greater than or equal to
<=	Less than or equal to
==	Exactly equal to
!=	Not equal to

■ **Note** If you're constantly forgetting which way the greater than and less than signs go, use a crutch we learned in grade school: If the greater than and less than signs represent the mouth of an alligator, the alligator always eats the bigger value. It may sound silly, but it works.

Designing Apps

Now that we've introduced Boolean logic and comparison operators, you can start designing your apps. Sometimes it's important to express all or parts of your apps to others without having to write the actual code.

Writing pseudocode helps a developer think out loud and brainstorm with other developers regarding sections of code that are of concern. This helps to analyze problems and possible solutions before coding begins.

Pseudocode

Pseudocode refers to writing code that is a high-level description of an algorithm you are trying to solve. Pseudocode does not contain the necessary programming syntax for coding; however, it does express the algorithm that is necessary to solve the problem at hand.

Pseudocode can be written by hand on paper (or a whiteboard) or typed on a computer.

Using pseudocode, you can apply what you know about Boolean data types, truth tables, and comparison operators. Refer to Listing 4-1 for some pseudocode examples.

■ **Note** Pseudocode is for expressing and teaching coding ideas. Pseudocode will not execute!

Listing 4-1. Pseudocode Examples Using Conditional Operators in if-then-else Code

```
x = 5
y = 6
isComplete = TRUE

if  x < y
{
    // in this example, x is less than 6
    do stuff
}
else
{
     do other stuff
}

if isComplete == TRUE
{
     // in this example, isComplete is equal to TRUE
     do stuff
}
else
{
     do other stuff
}

// another way to check isComplete == TRUE
if isComplete
{
     // in this example, isComplete is TRUE
     do stuff
}

// two ways to check if a value is false
if isComplete == FALSE
{
     do stuff
}
```

```
else
{
     // in this example, isComplete is TRUE so the else block will be executed
     do other stuff
}

// another way to check isComplete == FALSE
if !isComplete
{
     do stuff
}
else
{
     // in this example,  isComplete is TRUE so the else block will be executed
     do other stuff
}
```

Note that ! switches the value of the Boolean it's applied to, so using ! makes a TRUE value into a FALSE and makes a FALSE value into a TRUE. This is the Logical NOT operator in Swift.

Often, it is necessary to combine your comparison tests. A compound relationship test is one or more simple relationship tests joined by either && or || (two pipe characters).

&& and || are the logical AND and logical OR, respectively in Swift. The **pseudocode** in Listing 4-2 illustrates logical AND and logical OR operators.

Listing 4-2. Using && and || Logical Operators Pseudocode

```
x = 5
y = 6
isComplete = TRUE

// using the logical AND
if x < y && isComplete == TRUE
{
    // in this example, x is less than 6 and isComplete == TRUE
    do stuff
}

if x < y || isComplete == FALSE
{
    // in this example, x is less than 6.
    // Only one operand has to be TRUE for an OR to result in a TRUE.
    // See Table 4-2 A OR Truth Table
    do stuff
}

// another way to test for TRUE
if x < y && isComplete
{
    // in this example, x is less than 6 and isComplete == TRUE
    do stuff
}
```

```
// another way to test for FALSE
if x < y && !isComplete
{
    do stuff
}
else
{
     // isComplete == TRUE
     do other stuff
}
```

Optionals and Forced Unwrapping

Chapter 3 introduced optionals. Optionals are variables that might not contain a value. Since optionals may not contain a value, you need to check for that before you access them.

You start by using an `if` statement to determine whether the optional contains a value by comparing the optional against `nil`. If the optional has a value, it is considered to be "not equal to" `nil`, as shown in Listing 4-3.

Line 4 in Listing 4-3 checks to see whether the optional variable is not equal to `nil`. In this example, the `someInteger` value is absent, and it is equal to `nil`, so line 8 code is executed.

Listing 4-3. Checking Whether an Optional Has a Value

```
1 var myString = "Hello world"
2 let someInteger = Int(myString)
3 // someInteger's value is now absent
4 if someInteger != nil {
5     print("someInteger contains an integer value.")
6 }
7 else {
8     print("someInteger doesn't contain an integer value.")
9 }
```

Now that you have added a check to make sure your optional does or doesn't contain a value, you can access its value by adding an exclamation mark (`!`) to the end of the optional's name. The `!` means you have checked to ensure the optional variable has a value and use it. This is called *forced unwrapping* of the optional's value. See Listing 4-4.

Listing 4-4. Forced Unwrapping

```
var myString = "42"
let someInteger = Int(myString)
// someInteger contains a value
if someInteger != nil {
    print("someInteger contains a value. Here it is: \(someInteger!)")
}
else {
    print("someInteger doesn't contain an integer value.")
}
```

■ **Note** Displaying the contents of a variable in a `print` function is done with `\()`.

Optional Binding

You can find out whether an optional contains a value and, if so, assign a temporary constant or variable to that value in a single action. (See Listing 4-5.) This is called *optional binding*. Optional binding can be used with `if` and `while` statements to determine whether an optional has a value and, if so, extract the value to a constant or variable.

Listing 4-5. Optional Binding Syntax to a Constant

```
let someOptional: String? = "hello world"
if let constantName = someOptional {
    print("constantName contains a value, Here it is: \(constantName)")
}
```

If you want to assign the optional to a variable so you can manipulate that variable, you can assign the optional to a `var`, as shown in Listing 4-6.

Listing 4-6. Optional Binding Syntax to a Variable

```
let someOptional: String? = "hello world"
if var variableName = someOptional {
    print("variableName contains a value, Here it is: \(variableName)")
    }
```

Notice in Listings 4-5 and 4-6 that you didn't need to use the `!`. If the conversion was successful, the variable or constant was initialized with the value contained within the optional, so the ! was not necessary.

It may be confusing that the Logical NOT operator and the process of forced unwrapping occur at the same time since they both use the ! character. The Logical NOT operator is located before a variable or constant, and the forced unwrapping operator is located after an optional constant or variable.

Implicitly Unwrapped Optionals

There are instances after the value is first set when you know that an optional will always have a value. In these instances, it's useful to remove the need to check and unwrap an optional every time it needs to be accessed. These kinds of optionals are called *implicitly unwrapped optionals*.

Because of the program's structure, you know that the optional has a value, so you can give permission for the optional to be safely unwrapped whenever it needs to be accessed. The ! is not needed every time you use it; instead, you place an ! after the optional's type when you declare it. Listing 4-7 shows the comparison between an optional `String` and an implicitly unwrapped optional `String`.

Listing 4-7. Comparison of an Optional String and an Implicitly Unwrapped Optional String

```
var optionalString: String? = "My optional string."
var forcedUnWrappedString: String = optionalString! // requires an !

var nextOptionalString: String! = "An implicitly unwrapped optional."
var implicitUnwrappedString: String = nextOptionalString // no need for an !
```

Flowcharting

After the design requirements are finalized, you can create pseudocode sections of your app to solve complex development issues. ***Flowcharting*** is a common method of diagramming an algorithm. An algorithm is represented as different types of boxes connected by lines and arrows. Developers often use flowcharting to express code visually, as shown in Figure 4-1.

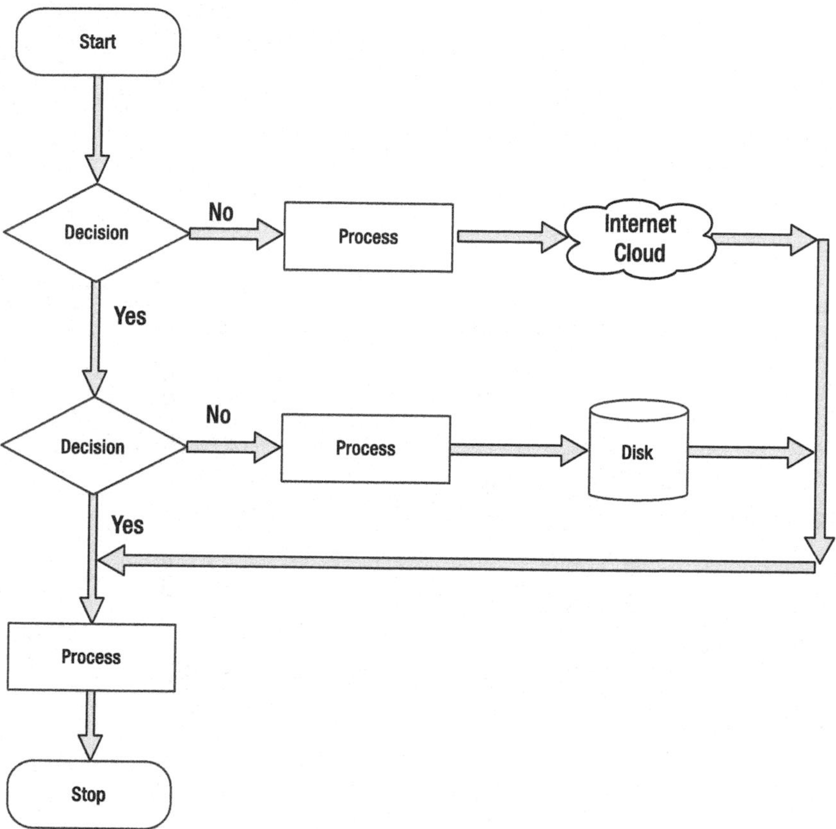

Figure 4-1. *Sample flowchart showing common figures and their associated names*

Flowcharts should always have a start and a stop. Branches should never come to an end without a stop. This helps developers make sure all of the branches in their code are accounted for and that they cleanly stop execution.

Designing and Flowcharting an Example App

We have covered a lot of information about decision-making and program flow. It's time to do what programmers do best: write apps!

The app you have been assigned to write generates a random number between 0 and 100 and asks the user to guess the number. Users have to do this until the number is guessed. When users guess the correct answer, they will be asked if they want to play again.

The App's Design

Using your design requirements, you can make a flowchart for your app. See Figure 4-2.

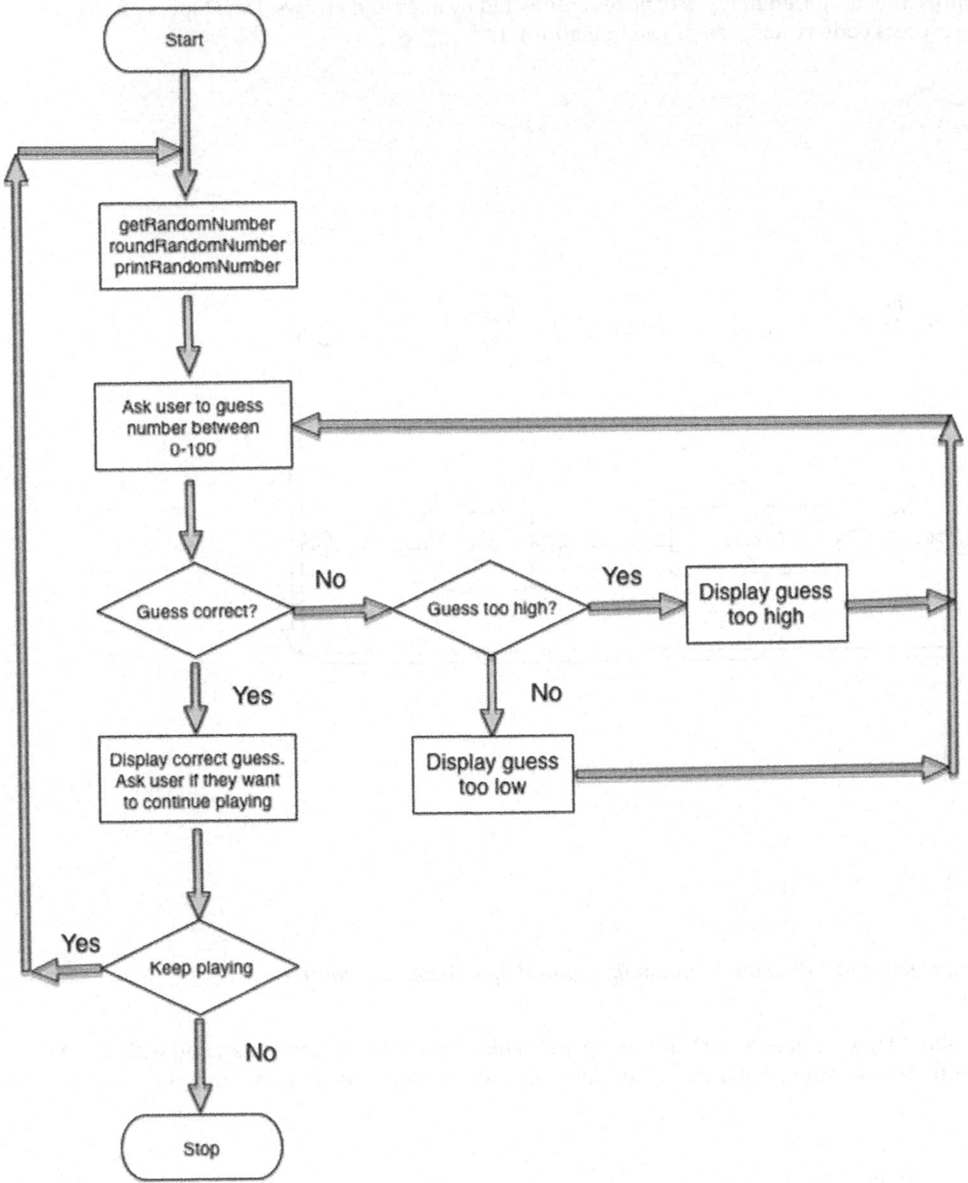

Figure 4-2. *Flowchart for guessing a random number app*

Reviewing Figure 4-2, you'll notice that as you approach the end of a block of logic in your flowchart, there are arrows that go back to a previous section and repeat that section until some condition is met. This is called ***looping***. It enables you to repeat sections of programming logic—without having to rewrite those sections of code over—until a condition is met.

Using Loops to Repeat Program Statements

A ***loop*** is a sequence of program statements that is specified once but can be repeated several times in succession. A loop can repeat a specified number of times (count-controlled) or until some condition (condition-controlled) occurs.

In this section, you'll learn about count-controlled loops and condition-controlled loops. You will also learn how to control your loops with Boolean logic.

Count-Controlled Loops

A count-controlled loop repeats a specified number of times. In Swift, this is a **for loop**. A for loop has a counter variable, which enables the developer to specify the number of times the loop will be executed. See Listing 4-8.

Listing 4-8. A Count-Controlled Loop

```
for i in 0..<10 {
    print(i)
}}
//....continue
```

The loop in Listing 4-8 will loop ten times. The variable i starts at zero and increments at the end of the } by one. The incrementing is done by the i++ in the for statement; i++ is equivalent to i = i + 1. Then i is incremented by one to ten and checked to see whether it is less than ten. This for loop will exit when i = 10 and the } is reached.

■ **Note** It is common for developers to confuse the number of times they think their loops will repeat. If the loop started at 1 in Listing 4-8, the loop would repeat nine times instead of ten.

You use the for-in loop to iterate over collections of items, such as ranges of numbers, items in an array, or characters in a string.

Listing 4-9 prints a few entries in the ten times table.

Listing 4-9. Counter Variable Initialized in the for Loop Declaration

```
for index in 1...10 {
    print("\(index) times 10 is \(index * 10)")
}
//....continue
```

Condition-Controlled Loops

Swift has the ability to repeat a loop until some condition changes. You may want to repeat a section of your code until a false condition is reached with one of your variables. This type of loop is called a while loop. A while loop is a control flow statement that repeats based on a given Boolean condition. You can think of a while loop as a repeating if statement. See Listing 4-10.

Listing 4-10. A Swift while Loop Repeating

```
var isTrue = true
while isTrue
{
    // do something
    isTrue = false // a condition occurs that sometimes sets isTrue to FALSE
}
//....continue
```

The `while` loop in Listing 4-10 first checks whether the variable `isTrue` is `true`—which it is—so the `{loop body}` is entered where the code is executed. Eventually, some condition is reached that causes `isTrue` to become `false`. After completing all the code in the loop body, the condition (`isTrue`) is checked once more, and the loop is repeated. This process is repeated until the variable `isTrue` is set to `false`.

Infinite Loops

An infinite loop repeats endlessly, either because of the loop not having a condition that causes termination or because of the loop having a terminating condition that can never be met.

Generally, infinite loops can cause apps to become unresponsive. They are the result of a side effect of a bug in either the code or the logic.

Listing 4-11 is an example of an infinite loop caused by a terminating condition that can never be met. The variable x will be checked with each iteration through the `while` loop but will never be equal to 5. The variable x will always be an even number because it was initialized to zero and incremented by two in the loop. This will cause the loop to repeat endlessly. See Listing 4-12.

Listing 4-11. An Example of an Infinite Loop

```
var x = 0
while x != 5
{
    // do something
    x = x + 2
}
//....continue
```

Listing 4-12. An Example of an Infinite Loop Caused by a Terminating Condition That Can Never Be Met

```
while true
{
    // do something forever
}
//....continue
```

Coding the Example App in Swift

Using your requirements and what you learned, try writing your random number generator in Swift.

To program this app, you have to leave the playground and do this as a Mac Console app. Unfortunately, at this time, a playground doesn't enable you to interact with a running app, so you can't capture keyboard input.

■ **Note** You can download the complete random number generator app at `http://forum.xcelme.com`. The code is the topic of Chapter 4.

Your Swift app will run from the command line because it asks the user to guess a random number.

1. Open Xcode and start a new project. Choose the Command Line Tool project. See Figure 4-3.

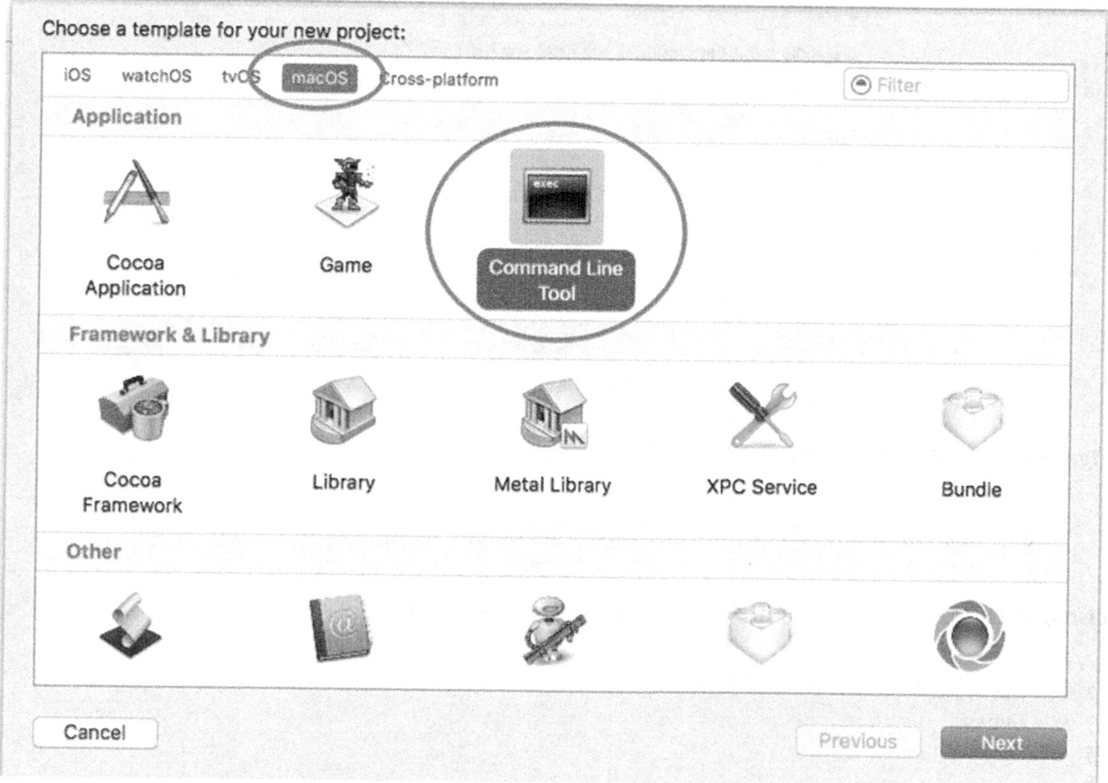

Figure 4-3. *Starting a new Command Line Tool project*

2. Call your project **RandomNumber** (see Figure 4-4). Ensure that the Language drop-down is Swift. Save the project anywhere you prefer on your hard drive.

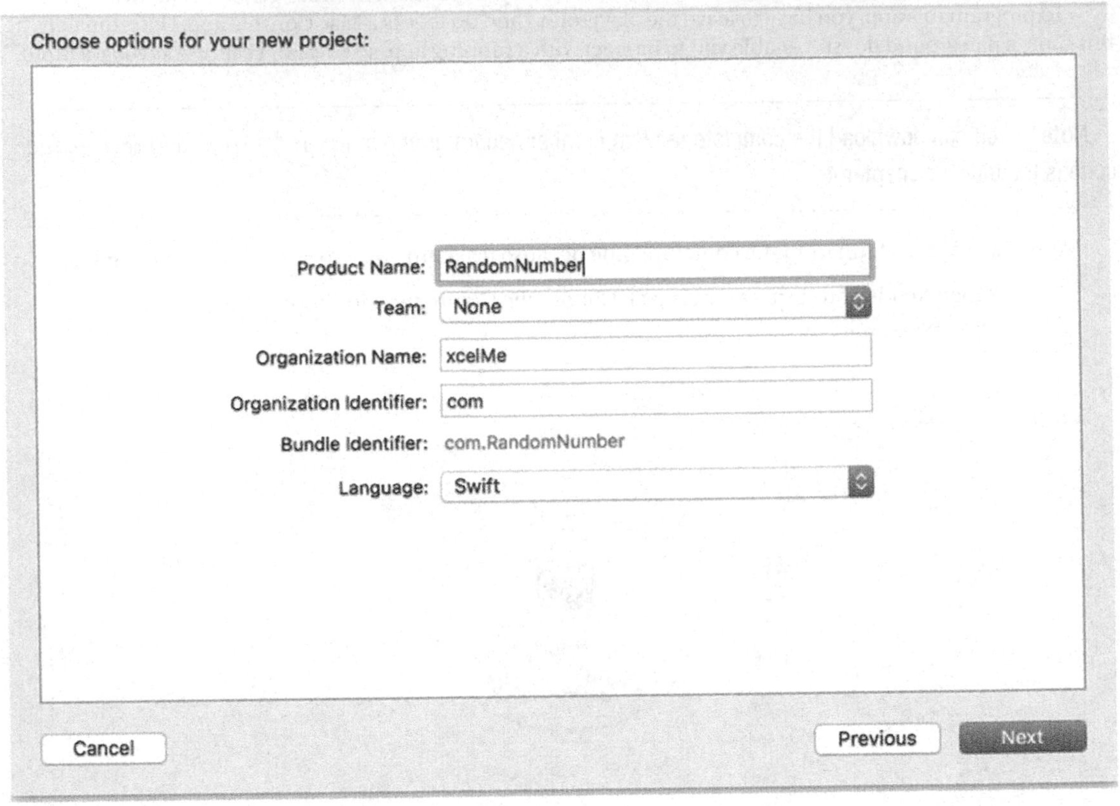

Choose options for your new project:

Product Name: RandomNumber
Team: None
Organization Name: xcelMe
Organization Identifier: com
Bundle Identifier: com.RandomNumber
Language: Swift

Cancel   Previous   Next

Figure 4-4. *Project options for RandomNumber*

3. Open the `main.swift` file. Write the code in Listing 4-13.

Listing 4-13. Source Code for Your Random Number Generator App

```
//
//  main.swift
//  Guess


import Foundation

var randomNumber = 1
var userGuess: Int? = 1
var continueGuessing = true
var keepPlaying = true
var input = ""

```

```
14 while keepPlaying {
15     randomNumber = Int(arc4random_uniform(101)) //get a random number between 0-100
16     print("The random number to guess is: \(randomNumber)")
17     while continueGuessing {
18         print("Pick a number between 0 and 100.")
19         input = NSString(data: FileHandle.standardInput.availableData, encoding:String.
Encoding.utf8.rawValue)! as String // get keyboard input
20         input = input.replacingOccurrences(of: "\n", with: "", options: NSString.
CompareOptions.literal, range: nil) // strip off the \n
21         userGuess = Int(input)
22         if userGuess == randomNumber {
23             continueGuessing = false
24             print("Correct number!")
25         }
26             //nested if statement
27         else if userGuess! > randomNumber {
28             // user guessed too high
29             print("Your guess is too high")
30         }
31         else{
32             // no reason to check if userGuess < randomNumber. It has to be.
33             print("Your guess is too low")
34         }
35     }
36     print ("Play Again? Y or N")
37     input = NSString(data: FileHandle.standardInput.availableData, encoding:String.
Encoding.utf8.rawValue)! as String
38     input = input.replacingOccurrences(of: "\n", with: "", options: NSString.
CompareOptions.literal, range: nil)
39
40     if input == "N" || input == "n" {
41         keepPlaying = false
42     }
43     continueGuessing = true
44 }
```

In Listing 4-13, there is new code that we haven't discussed before. The first new line of code (line 15) is as follows:

```
randomNumber = Int(arc4random_uniform(101))
```

This line will produce a random number between 0 and 100. `arc4random_uniform()` is a function that returns a random number.

The next line of new code is on line 19:

```
19         input = NSString(data: FileHandle.standardInput.availableData,
encoding:String.Encoding.utf8.rawValue)! as String // get keyboard input
```

This enables you to get keyboard input for the user. We will talk about this syntax in later chapters.

The next new line of code is on line 21:

```
userGuess = Int(input)
```

Int takes a string initializer and converts it to an integer.

Nested if Statements and else if Statements

Sometimes, it is necessary to nest if statements. This means that you need to have if statements nested inside an existing if statement. Additionally, it is sometimes necessary to have a comparison as the first step in the else section of the if statement. This is called an else if statement (recall line 27 in Listing 4-13).

```
else if userGuess! > randomNumber
```

Removing Extra Characters

Line 20 in Listing 4-13 is as follows:

```
input = input.replacingOccurrences(of: "\n", with: "", options:
NSString.CompareOptions.literal, range: nil) // strip off the \n
```

Reading keyboard input can be difficult. In this case, it leaves a remnant at the end of your string, \n, and you need to remove it. This is a *newline* character that is generated when the users press the Return key on their keyboards.

Improving the Code Through Refactoring

Often, after you get your code to work, you examine the code and find more efficient ways to write it. The process of rewriting your code to make it more efficient, maintainable, and readable is called ***code refactoring***.

As you review your code in Swift, you will often notice that you can eliminate some unnecessary code.

■ **Note** As developers, we have found that the best line of code is the line that you don't have to write—less code means less to debug and maintain.

Running the App

To run your app, click the Play button at the top left of your screen in your Swift project. See Figure 4-5.

■ **Note** If you're not seeing the output console when you run your app, make sure you have selected the same options at the top-right and bottom-right corners of the editor (choose View > Debug Area > Activate Console). See Figure 4-5.

```
//
//  main.swift
//  Guess


import Foundation

var randomNumber = 1
var userGuess:Int? = 1
var continueGuessing = true
var keepPlaying = true
var input = ""

while keepPlaying {
    randomNumber = Int(arc4random_uniform(101)) //get a random number between 0-100
    print("The random number to guess is: \(randomNumber)")
    while continueGuessing {
        print ("Pick a number between 0 and 100. ")
        input = NSString(data: FileHandle.standardInput.availableData, encoding:String.Encoding.utf8.rawValue)! as String //get keyboard input
        input = input.replacingOccurrences(of: "\n", with: "", options: NSString.CompareOptions.literal, range: nil) //strip off the /n
        userGuess = Int(input)
        if userGuess == randomNumber {
            continueGuessing = false
            print("Correct number!")
        }
            //nested if statement
        else if userGuess! > randomNumber{
            //user guessed too high
            print("Your guess is too high")
        }
        else{
            // no reason to check if userGuess < randomNumber. It has to be.
            print("Your guess is too low")
        }
    }
    print ("Play Again? Y or N")
    input = NSString(data: FileHandle.standardInput.availableData, encoding:String.Encoding.utf8.rawValue)! as String
    input = input.replacingOccurrences(of: "\n", with: "", options: NSString.CompareOptions.literal, range: nil)

    if input == "N" || input == "n"{
        keepPlaying = false
    }
    continueGuessing = true
}
```

```
Your guess is too high
Pick a number between 0 and 100.
34
Your guess is too low
Pick a number between 0 and 100.
36
```

Figure 4-5. *The console output of the Swift random number generator app*

Design Requirements

As discussed in Chapter 1, the most expensive process in the software development life cycle is writing code. The least expensive process in the software development life cycle is gathering the requirements for your application; yet, this latter process is the most overlooked and least used in software development.

Design requirements usually begin by asking clients, customers, and/or stakeholders how the application should work and what problems it should solve.

With respect to apps, requirements can include long or short narrative descriptions, screen mock-ups, and formulas. It is far easier to open your word processor and change the requirements and screen mock-ups before coding begins than it is to modify an iOS app. The following is the design requirement for one view of an iPhone mobile banking app:

- ***View:*** Accounts view.
- Description: Displays the list of accounts the user has. The list of accounts will be in the following sections: Business Accounts, Personal Accounts and Car Loans, IRA, and Home Equity Loans.
- ***Cells:*** Each cell will contain the account name, the last four digits of the account, the available balance, and the present balance.

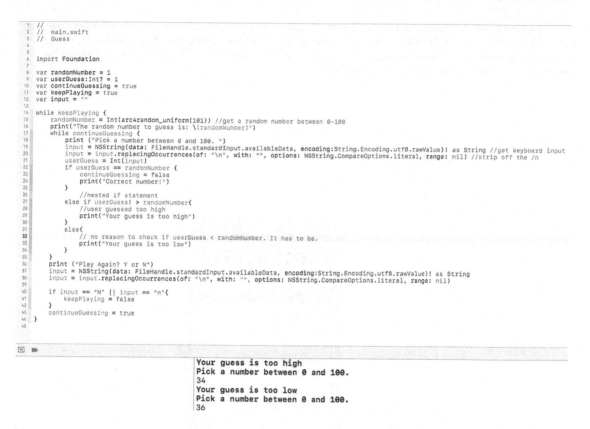

A picture is worth a thousand words. Screen mock-ups are helpful to developers and users because they can show how the views will look when they are completed. There are many tools that can quickly design mock-ups; one of these tools is OmniGraffle. See Figure 4-6 for an example of a screen mock-up used for design requirements generated by OmniGraffle.

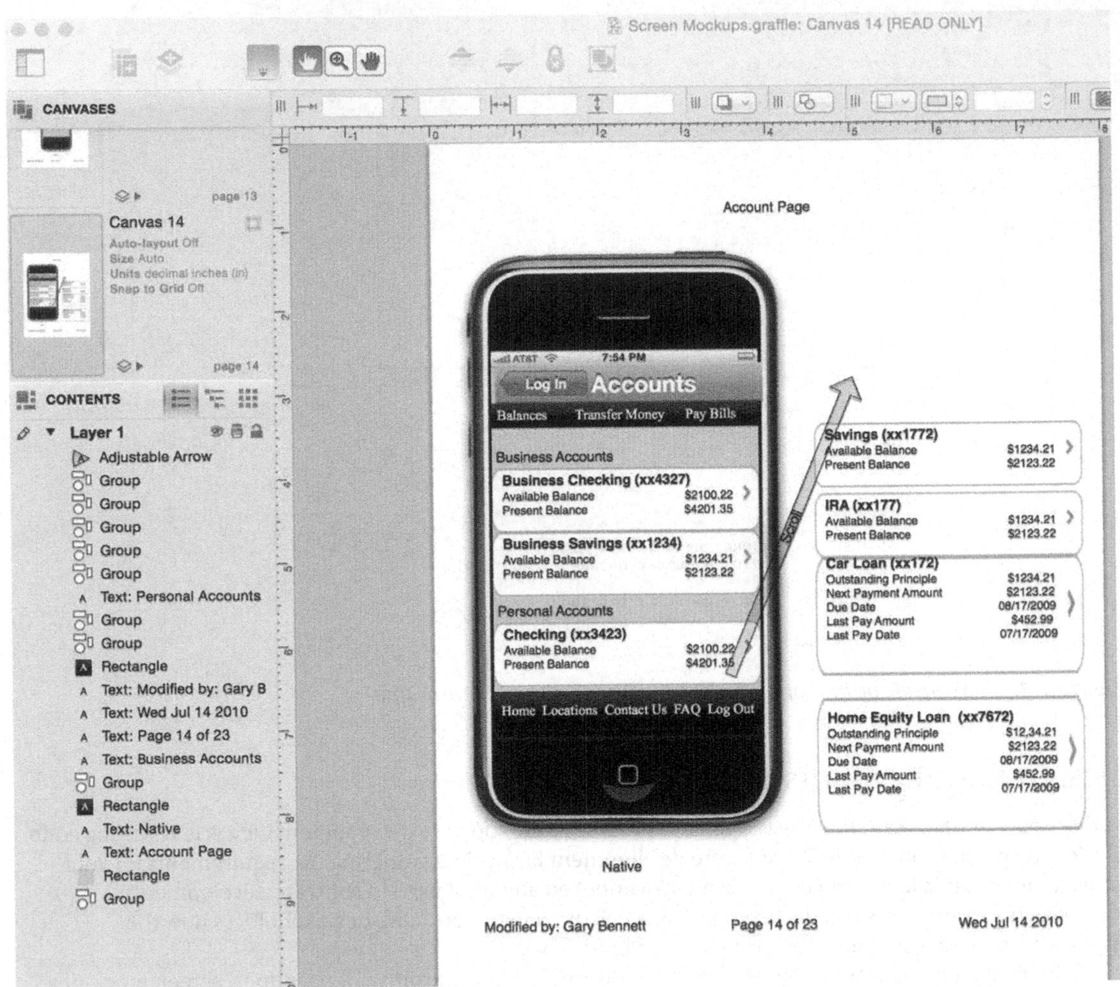

Figure 4-6. *Screen mock-up for a mobile banking app using OmniGraffle and the Ultimate iPhone Stencil plug-in. This mock-up was done for the original Woodforest Banking app in 2010*

Many developers believe that design requirements take too long and are unnecessary. This is not the case. There is a lot of information presented on the Accounts screen in Figure 4-6. Many business rules can determine how information is displayed to the users, along with all of the error handling when things go bad. When designing your app, working with all the business stakeholders at the beginning of the development process is critical to getting it right the first time.

Figure 4-7 is an example of all stakeholders being involved in your app's development. Having all stakeholders involved in every view from the beginning will eliminate multiple rewrites and application bugs.

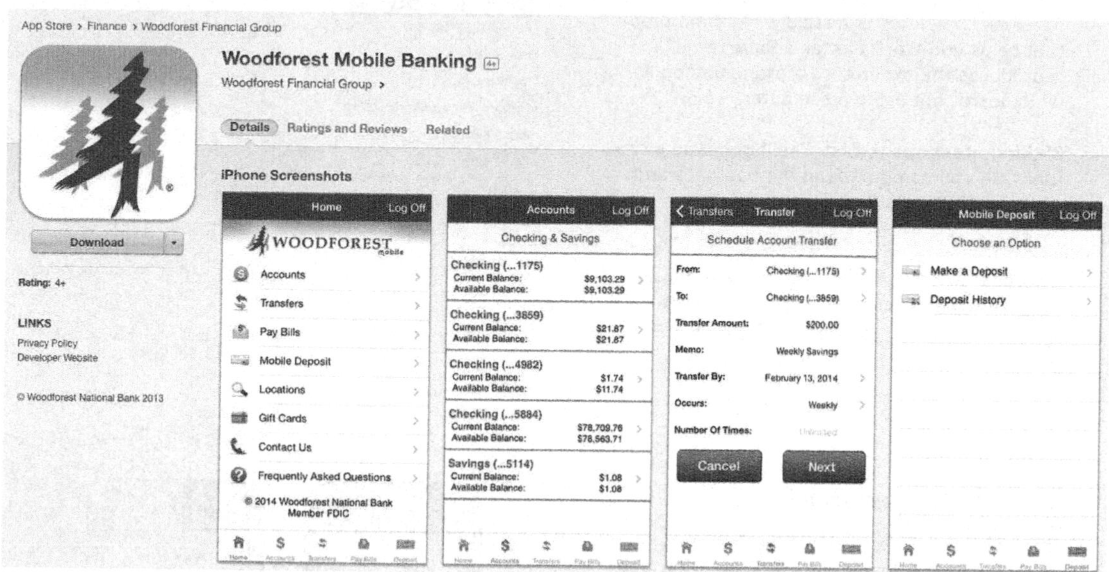

Figure 4-7. *Woodforest Mobile Banking app as it appeared on the App Store in 2015; compare this with the app requirements Accounts screen in Figure 4-6*

Additionally, Apple recommends that developers spend at least 50 percent of their development time on the user interface's design and development.

Balsamiq also has great tools for laying out your iOS app's look. See Figure 4-8.

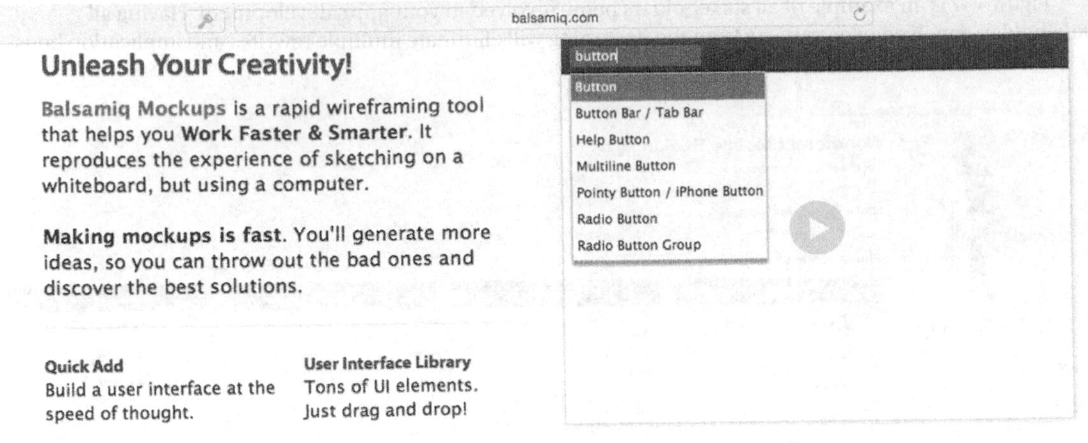

balsamiq.com
Unleash Your Creativity!
Balsamiq Mockups is a rapid wireframing tool that helps you Work Faster & Smarter. It reproduces the experience of sketching on a whiteboard, but using a computer.
Making mockups is fast. You'll generate more ideas, so you can throw out the bad ones and discover the best solutions.
Quick Add
Build a user interface at the speed of thought.
User Interface Library
Tons of UI elements. Just drag and drop!
button
Button
Button Bar / Tab Bar
Help Button
Multiline Button
Pointy Button / iPhone Button
Radio Button
Radio Button Group

Get Honest Feedback
Improve your designs by getting immediate and meaningful feedback. Sketch-style wireframes help focus the conversation on content and interaction, not minute details (those can come later).
Sketch-Style Controls
They look like sketches on purpose! It encourages brainstorming.
Clean Wireframes Option
Need to present your work? Switch to the clean wireframe skin!

Figure 4-8. *Balsamiq.com web site for creating wireframe mock-ups*

Summary

This chapter covered a lot of important information on how to control your applications; program flow and decision-making are essential to every iOS app. Make sure you have completed the Swift example in this chapter. You might review these examples and think you understand everything without having to write this app. This will be a fatal mistake that will prevent you from becoming a successful iOS developer. You must spend time coding this example. Developers learn by doing, not by reading.

The terms in this chapter are important. You should be able to describe the following:

- AND
- OR
- XOR
- NAND

- NOR
- NOT
- Truth tables
- Negation
- All comparison operators
- Application requirement
- Logical AND (&&)
- Logical OR (||)
- Optionals and forced unwrapping
- Optional binding
- Implicitly unwrapped optionals
- Flowchart
- Loop
- Count-controlled loops
- For loop
- Condition-controlled loops
- Infinite loops
- `while` loops
- Nested `if` statements
- Code refactoring

EXERCISES

- Extend the random number generator app to print to the console how many times the user guessed before guessing the correct random number.
- Extend the random number generator app to print to the console how many times the user played the app. Print this value to the console when the user quits the app.

CHAPTER 5

Object-Oriented Programming with Swift

Over the past 15 years, the programming world focused on the development paradigm of object-oriented programming (OOP). Most modern development environments and languages implement OOP. Put simply, OOP forms the basis of everything you develop today.

You may be asking yourself why we waited until Chapter 5 to present OOP using Swift if it is the primary development style of today. The simple answer is that it is not an easy concept for new developers. This chapter will go into detail about the different aspects of OOP and how they affect your development.

Implementing OOP into your applications correctly will take some front-end planning, but you will save yourself a lot of time throughout the life of your projects. OOP has changed the way development is done. In this chapter, you will learn what OOP is. OOP was initially discussed in the first chapter of this book, but this chapter will go into more detail about it. You will revisit what objects are and how they relate to physical objects you find in the world. You will look into what classes are and how they relate to objects. You will also learn the steps you need to take when planning your classes and some visual tools you can use to accomplish these steps. When you have read this chapter and have worked through the exercises, you will have a better understanding of what OOP is and why it is necessary for you as a developer.

At first, objects and object-oriented programming may seem difficult to understand, but the hope is that as you progress through this chapter, they will begin to make sense.

The Object

As discussed in Chapter 1, OOP is based on objects. Some of the discussion about objects will be a review, but it will also go into more depth. An *object* is anything that can be acted upon. To better understand what a programming object is, you will first look at some items in the physical world around you. A physical object can be anything around you that you can touch or feel. Take, for example, a television. Some characteristics of a television include type (plasma, LCD, or CRT), size (40 inches), brand (Sony or Vizio), weight, and cost. Televisions also have functions. They can be turned on or off. You can change the channel, adjust the volume, and change the brightness.

Some of these characteristics and functions are unique to televisions, and some are not. For example, a couch in your house would probably not have the same characteristics as a television. You would want different information about a couch, such as material type, seating capability, and color. A couch might have only a few functions, such as converting to a bed or reclining.

Now let's talk specifically about objects as they relate to programming. An object is a specific item. It can describe something physical like a book, or it could be something such as a window for your application. Objects have properties and methods. Properties describe certain things about an object such as location, color, or name. Conversely, methods describe actions the object can perform such as close or recalculate.

G. Bennett and B. Lees, *Swift 3 for Absolute Beginners*, DOI 10.1007/978-1-4842-2331-4_5

In this example, a TV object would have type, size, and brand properties, while a Couch object would have properties such as color, material, and comfort level. In programming terms, a property is a variable that is part of an object. For example, a TV would use a string variable to store the brand and an integer to store the height.

Objects also have commands the programmer can use to control them. The commands are called *methods*. Methods are the way that other objects interact with a certain object. For example, with the television, a method would be any of the buttons on the remote control. Each of those buttons represents a way you can interact with your television. Methods can and often are used to change the values of properties, but methods do not store any values themselves.

As described in Chapter 1, objects have a *state*, which is basically a snapshot of an object at any given point in time. A state would be the values of all the properties at a specific time.

In previous chapters, you saw the example of the bookstore. A bookstore contains many different objects. It contains book objects that have properties such as title, author, page count, and publisher. It also contains magazines with properties such as title, issue, genre, and publisher. A bookstore also has some nontangible objects such as a sale. A sale object would contain information about the books purchased, the customer, the amount paid, and the payment type. A sale object might also have some methods that calculate tax, print the receipt, or void the sale. A sale object does not represent a tangible object, but it is still an object and is necessary for creating an effective bookstore.

Because the object is the basis of OOP, it is important to understand objects and how to interact with them. You will spend the rest of the chapter learning about objects and some of their characteristics.

What Is a Class?

We cannot discuss OOP without discussing what a class is. A class defines which properties and methods an object will have. A class is basically a cookie cutter that can be used to create objects that have similar characteristics. All objects of a certain class will have the same properties and the same methods. The values of those properties will change from object to object.

A class is similar to a species in the animal world. A species is not an individual animal, but it does describe many similar characteristics of the animal. To understand classes more, let's look at an example of classes in nature. The Dog class has many properties that all dogs have in common. For example, a dog may have a name, an age, an owner, and a favorite activity. An object that is of a certain class is called an *instance* of that class. If you look at Figure 5-1, you can see the difference between the class and the actual objects that are instances of the class. For example, Lassie is an instance of the Dog class. In Figure 5-1, you can see a Dog class that has four properties (Breed, Age, Owner, and Favorite Activity). In real life, a dog will have many more properties, but these four are for this demonstration.

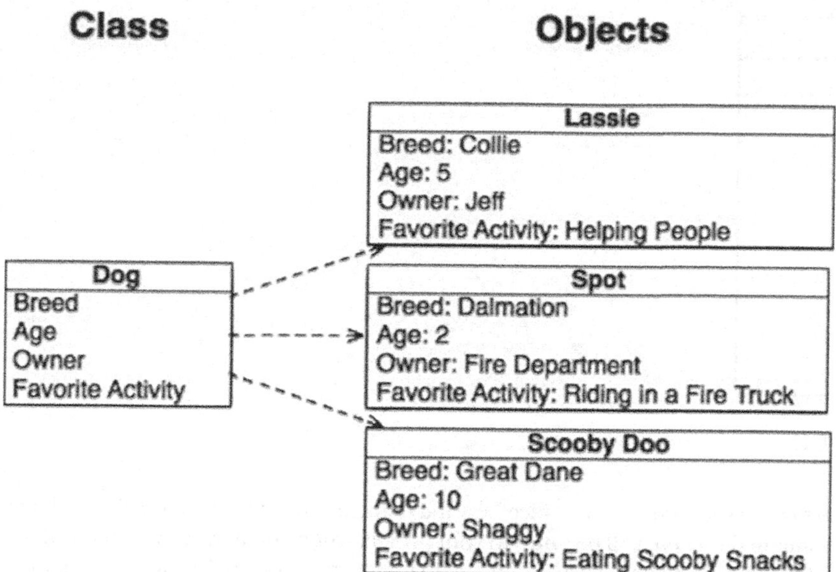

Figure 5-1. *An example of a class and its individual objects*

Planning Classes

Planning your classes is one of the most important steps in your development process. While it is possible to go back and add properties and methods after the fact (and you will definitely need to do this), it is important that you know which classes are going to be used in your application and which basic properties and methods they will have. Spending time planning your different classes is important at the beginning of the process.

Planning Properties

Let's look at the bookstore example and some of the classes you need to create. First, it is important to create a `Bookstore` class. A `Bookstore` class contains the blueprint of the information each `Bookstore` object stores, such as the bookstore's name, address, phone number, and logo (see Figure 5-2). Placing this information in a class rather than hard-coding it in your application will allow you to easily make changes to this information in the future. You will learn the reasons for using OOP methodologies later in this chapter. Also, if your bookstore becomes a huge success and you decide to open another one, you will be prepared because you can create another object of class `Bookstore`.

Bookstore
Name
Address1
Address2
City
State
Zip
Phone Number
Logo

Figure 5-2. *The Bookstore class*

Let's also plan a `Customer` class (see Figure 5-3). Notice how the name has been broken into `First Name` and `Last Name`. This is important to do. There will be times in your project when you may want to use only the first name of a customer, and it would be hard to separate the first name from the last if you didn't plan ahead. Let's say you want to send a letter to a customer letting them know about an upcoming sale. You do not want your greeting to say, "Dear John Doe." It would look much more personal to say, "Dear John."

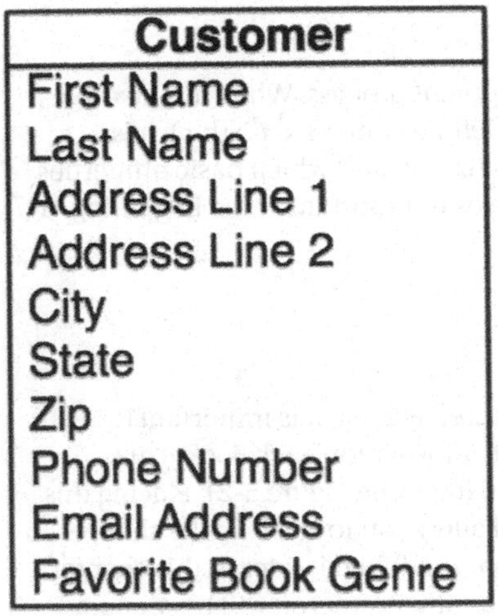

Customer
First Name
Last Name
Address Line 1
Address Line 2
City
State
Zip
Phone Number
Email Address
Favorite Book Genre

Figure 5-3. *The Customer class*

You will also notice how the address is broken into its different parts instead of grouping it all together. The `Address Line 1`, `Address Line 2`, `City`, `State`, and `Zip` are separate. This is important and will be usedin your application. Let's go back to the letter you want to send to customers about an upcoming sale. You might not want to send it to all of the customers who live in different states. By separating the address, you can easily filter out those customers you do not want to include in your mailings.

We have also added the attribute of `Favorite Book Genre` to the `Customer` class. We added this to show you how you can keep many different types of information in each class. This field may come in handy if you have a new mystery title coming out and you want to send an e-mail alerting customers who are especially interested in mysteries. By storing this type of information, you will be able to specifically target different portions of your customer base.

A Book class is also necessary to create the bookstore (see Figure 5-4). You will store information about the book such as author, publisher, genre, page count, and edition number (in case there are multiple editions). The Book class will also have the price for the book.

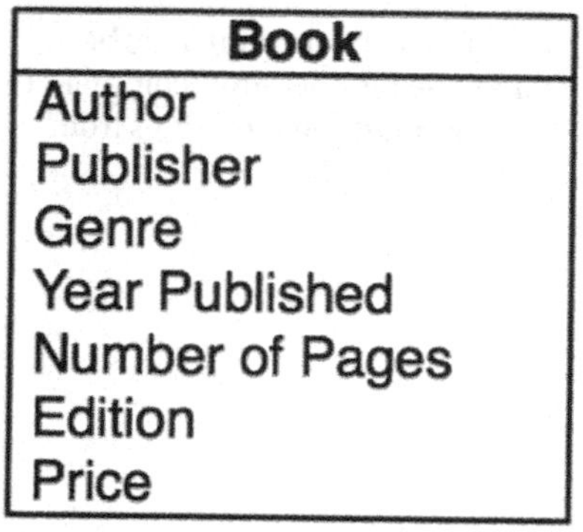

Book
Author Publisher Genre Year Published Number of Pages Edition Price

Figure 5-4. The Book class

You can add another class called `Sale` (see Figure 5-5). This class is more abstract than the other classes discussed because it does not describe a tangible object. You will notice how we have added a reference to a customer and a book to the `Sale` class. Because the `Sale` class will track sales of books, you need to know which book was sold and to which customer.

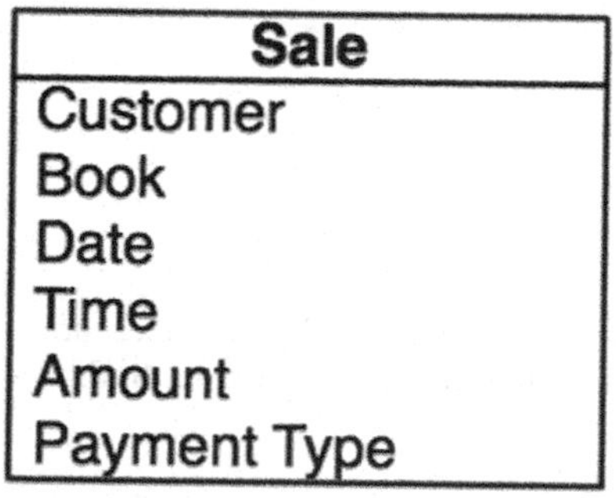

Sale
Customer Book Date Time Amount Payment Type

Figure 5-5. The Sale class

Now that you know the properties of the classes, you need to look at some methods that each of the classes will have.

Planning Methods

You will not add all of the methods now, but the more planning you can do at the beginning, the easier it will be for you later. Not all of your classes will have many methods. Some may not have any methods at all.

■ **Note** When planning your methods, remember to have them focus on a specific task. The more specific the method, the more likely it is that it can be reused.

For the time being, you will not add any methods to the `Book` class or the `Bookstore` class. You will focus on your other two classes.

For the `Customer` class, you will add methods to list the purchase history of that client. There may be other methods that you will need to add in the future, but you will add just that one for now. Your completed `Customer` class diagram should look like Figure 5-6. The line near the bottom separates the properties from the methods.

Customer
First Name Last Name Address Line 1 Address Line 2 City State Zip Phone Number Email Address Favorite Book Genre
List Purchase History

Figure 5-6. *The completed Customer class*

For the `Sale` class, we have added three methods. We added `Charge Credit Card`, `Print Invoice`, and `Checkout` (see Figure 5-7). For the time being, you do not need to know how to implement these methods, but you need to know that you are planning on adding them to your class.

Sale
Customer Book Date Time Amount Payment Type
Charge Credit Card Print Invoice Checkout

Figure 5-7. *The completed Sale class*

Now that you have finished mapping out the classes and the methods you are going to add to them, you have the beginnings of a Unified Modeling Language (UML) diagram. Basically, this is a diagram used by developers to plan their classes, properties, and methods. Starting your development process by creating such a diagram will help you significantly in the long run. An in-depth discussion of UML diagrams is beyond the scope of this book. If you would like more information about this subject, `smartdraw.com` has a great in-depth overview of them; see `http://www.smartdraw.com/uml-diagram/`. Omnigroup (`www.omnigroup.com`) provides a great UML diagram program for macOS called Omnigraffle.

Figure 5-8 shows the complete diagram.

Bookstore
Name Address1 Address2 City State Zip Phone Number Logo

Sale
Customer Book Date Time Amount Payment Type
Charge Credit Card Print Invoice Checkout

Book
Author Publisher Genre Year Published Number of Pages Edition Price

Customer
First Name Last Name Address Line 1 Address Line 2 City State Zip Phone Number Email Address Favorite Book Genre
List Purchase History

Figure 5-8. *The completed UML diagram for the bookstore*

Implementing the Classes

Now that you understand the objects you are going to be creating, you need to create your first object. To do so, you will start with a new project.

1. Launch Xcode. Select File ➤ New ➤ Project.
2. Select iOS on the top menu. On the right side, select Master-Detail Application. For what you are doing in this chapter, you could have selected any of the application types (see Figure 5-9). Click Next.

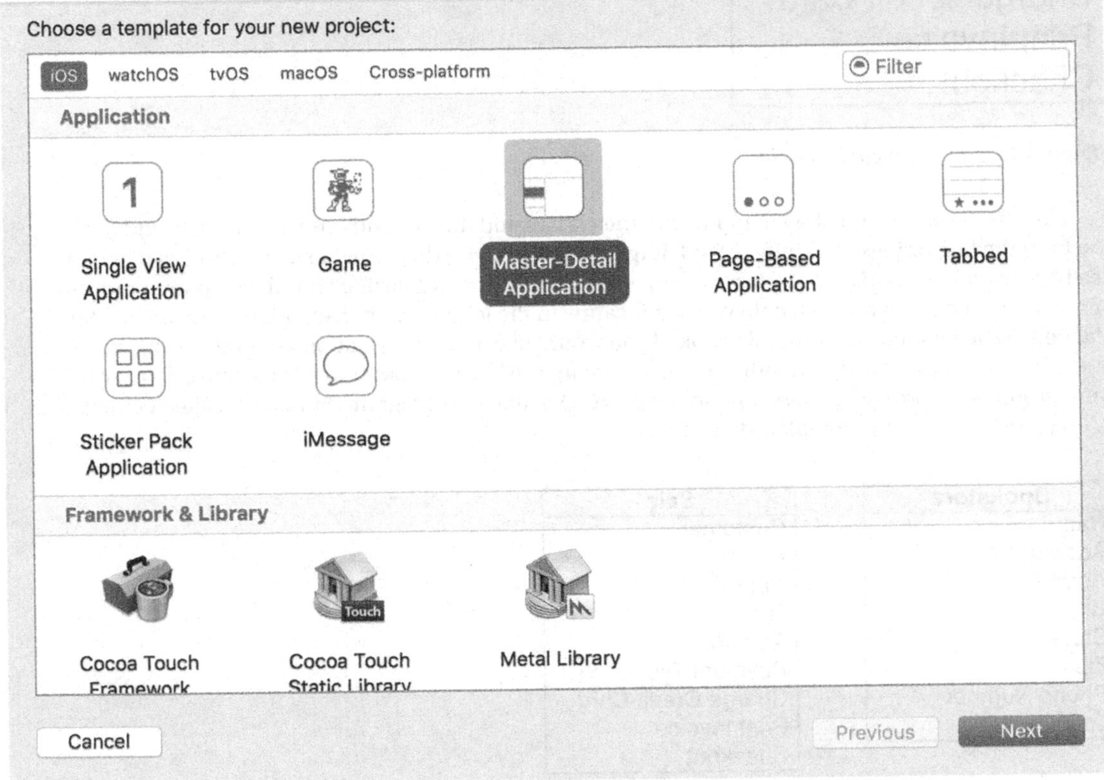

Figure 5-9. Creating a new project

3. Enter a product name for your project. We will use the name of `BookStore`. You will also have to enter a company name and a company identifier. The company identifier is usually `com.companyname` (that is, `com.innovativeware`). Leave the checkboxes on this screen as they appear by default. You will not be worrying about Core Data right now; it's discussed in Chapter 11. Also, leave the current language selection set to Swift. Click Next to select a location to save your project and then save your project.
4. Select the `BookStore` project from the Project navigator on the left side of the screen (see Figure 5-10). This is where the majority of your code will reside.

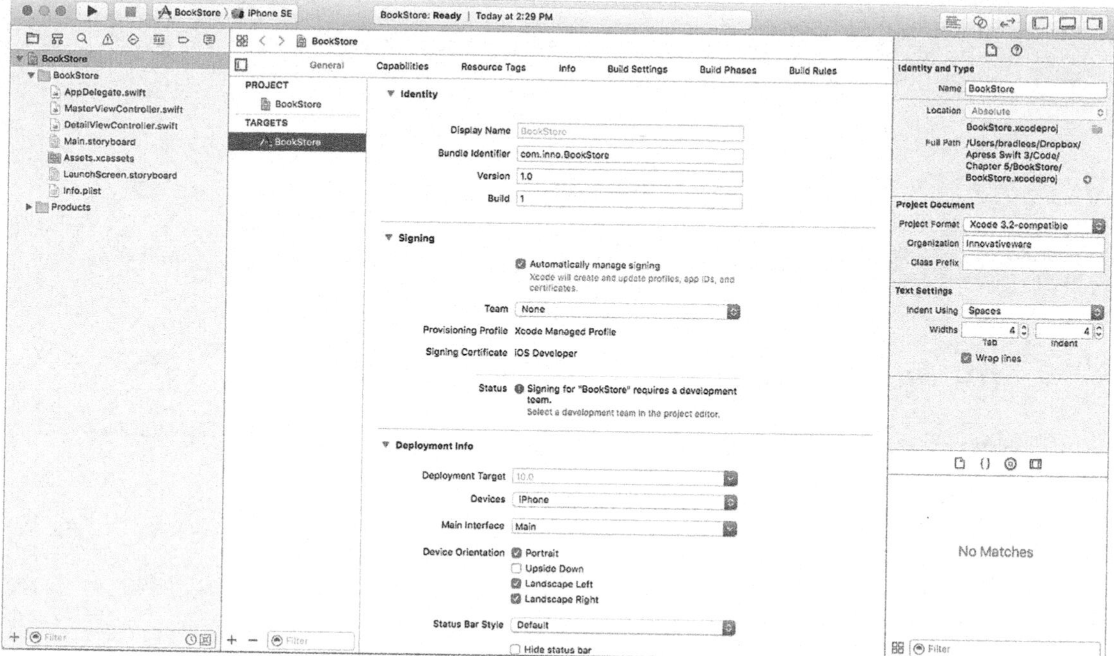

Figure 5-10. *Selecting the BookStore project*

5. Select File ➤ New ➤ File.
6. From the pop-up window, make sure iOS is selected at the top and then click the Cocoa Touch Class on the bottom (see Figure 5-11). Then click Next.

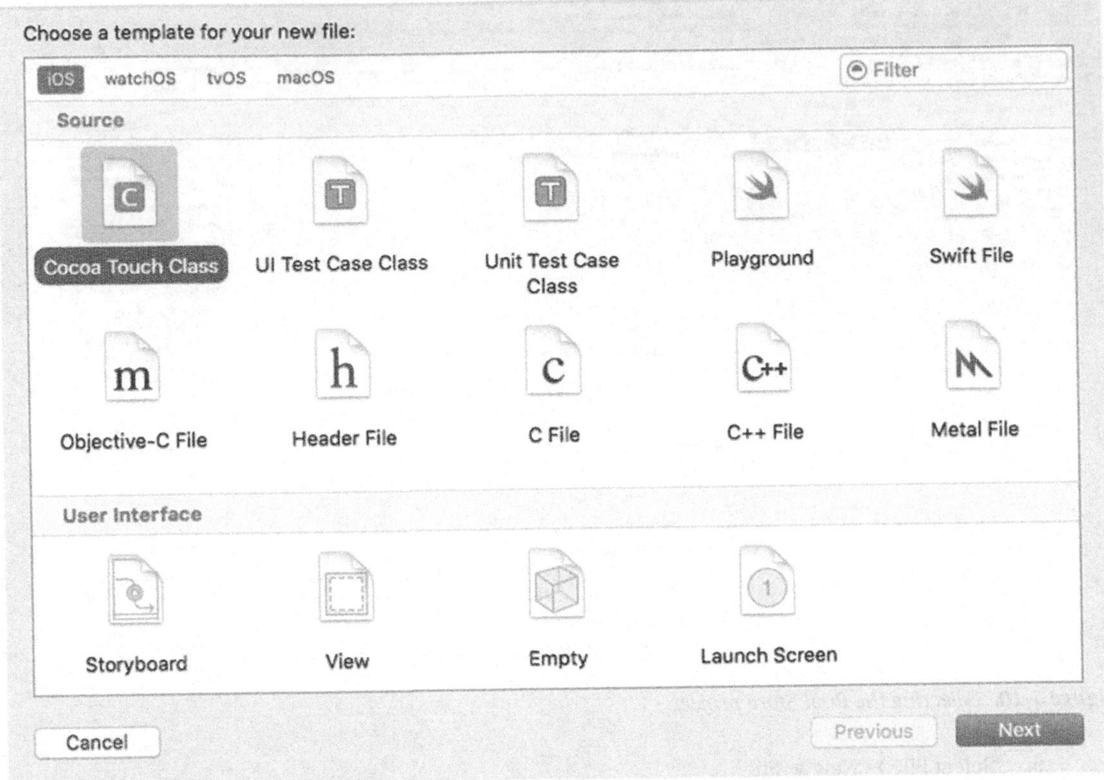

Figure 5-11. Creating a new Swift class file

7. You will now be given the opportunity to name your class (see Figure 5-12). For this exercise, you will create the `Customer` class. Again, make sure the Language is set to Swift. Click Next and save the file in the default location.

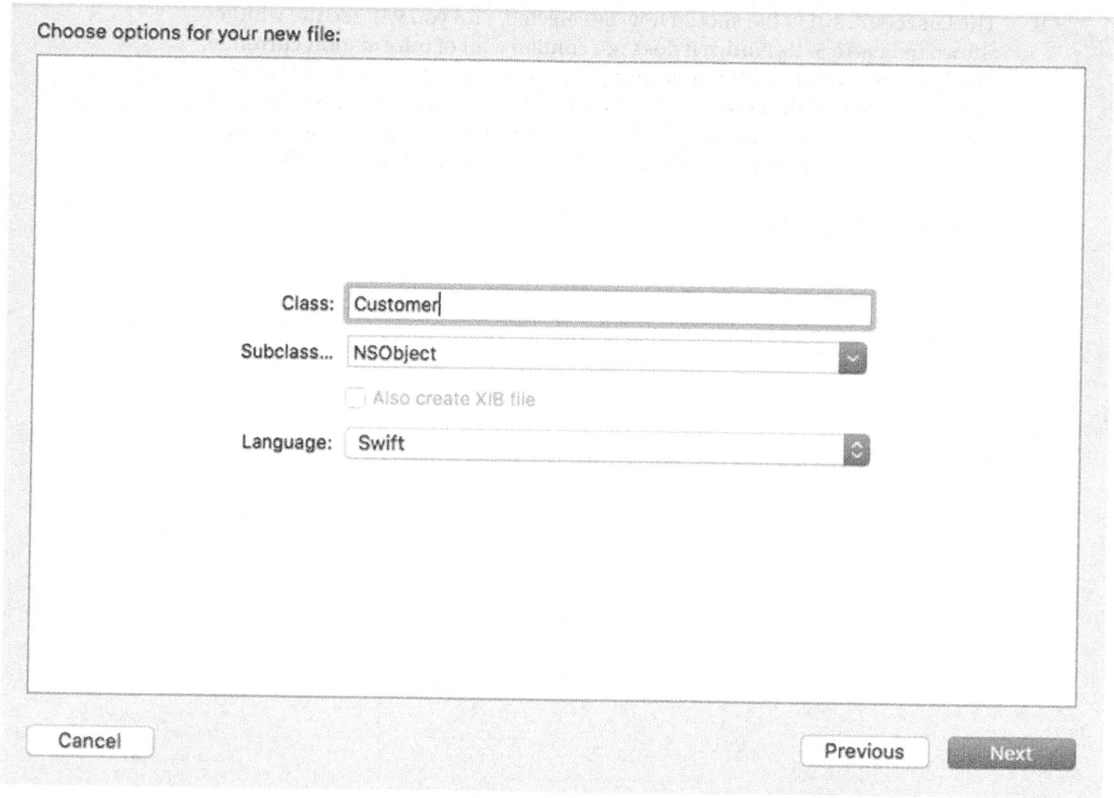

Figure 5-12. *Creating the file*

■ **Note** For ease of use and for understanding your code, remember that class names should always be capitalized in Swift. Object names should always start lowercase. For example, `Book` would be an appropriate name for a class, and `book` would be a great name for an object based on the `Book` class. For a two-word object, such as the book's author, an appropriate name would be `bookAuthor`. This type of capitalization is called *lower camel case*.

---

8. Now look in your main project folder; you should have a new file. It is called `Customer.swift`.

■ **Note** If you had created a class in Objective-C, `Customer.h` and `Customer.m` files would have been created. The `.h` file is the header file that contains information about your class. The header file lists all of the properties and methods in your class, but it does actually contain the code related to them. The `.m` file is the implementation file, which is where you write the code for your methods. In Swift, the entire class is contained in a single file.

---

9. The `Customer.swift` file should now be selected, and you will see the window shown in Figure 5-13. Notice it does not contain a lot of information currently. The first part, with the double slashes (//), consists of comments and is not considered part of the code. Comments allow you to tell those who might read your code what each portion of code is meant to accomplish. The second part of the file is your new Customer class. The new class declaration is as follows:

```
class Customer: NSObject {
}
```

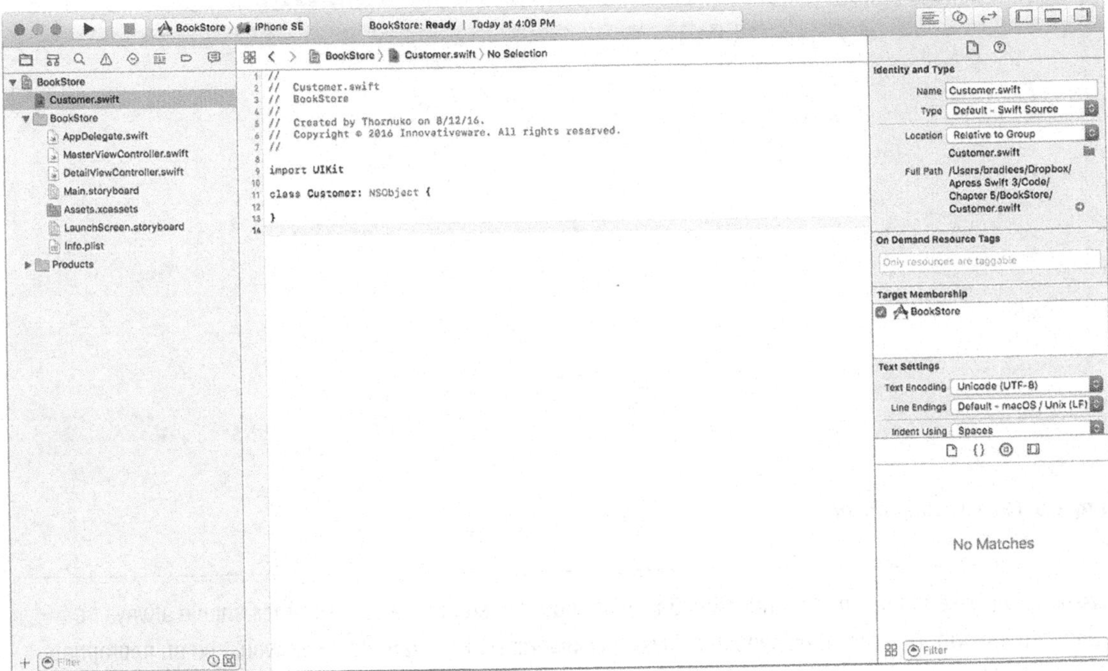

Figure 5-13. *Your empty Customer class*

■ **Note** In Swift, a class does not need to be in its own file. Many classes can be defined in a single Swift file, but this can be difficult to maintain when your project contains a lot of classes. It is usually cleaner and more organized to have a separate file for each class.

Now let's transfer the properties from the UML diagram to the actual class.

■ **Tip** Properties should always start with a lowercase letter. There can be no spaces in a property name.

For the first property, First Name, add this line to your file:

```
var firstName = ""
```

This creates an object in your class called `firstName`. Notice you did not tell Swift what type of property `firstName` is. In Swift, you can declare a property and not specify the type, and a property can be assigned a type based on the value we initially assign it. By giving the property an initial value of "", you tell the Swift compiler to make `firstName` a String. In Swift, all non-optional properties require a default value either when they are declared or in the class initializer. We will discuss optionals later in this book.

■ Note In Objective-C, all properties are required to declare a type. For example, to create the same `firstName` property, you would use the following code:

```
NSString *firstName;
```

This declares an `NSString` with the name `firstName`. In Swift, you can declare only a variable and allow the system to determine the type.

Since all of the properties will be vars, you just need to repeat the same procedure for the other ones. When that is complete, your Swift file should look like Figure 5-14.

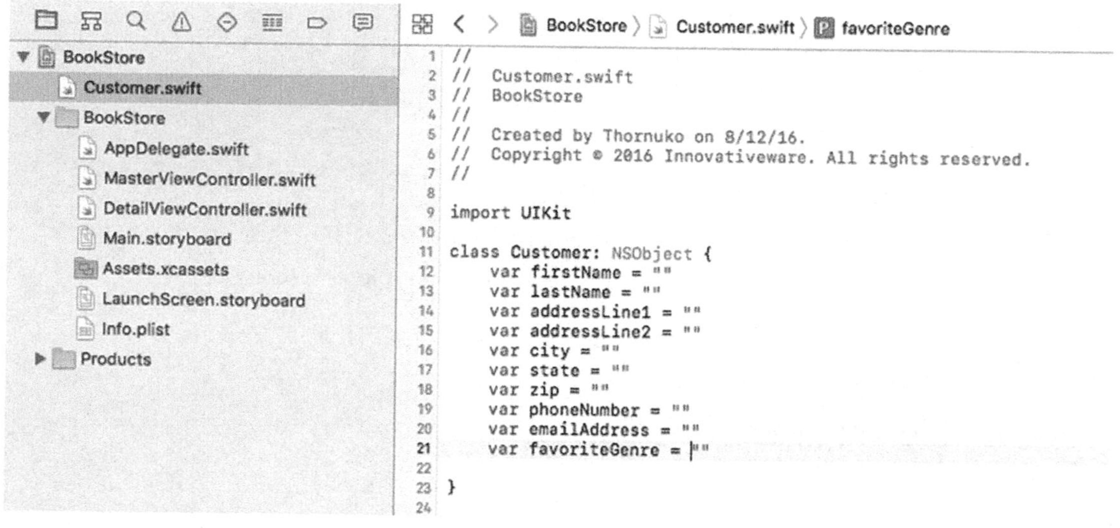

Figure 5-14. *The Customer class interface with properties*

Now that the class declaration is complete, you will need to add your method. Methods should be contained in the same class file and location as the properties. You will add a new method that returns an array. This code will look like the following:

```
func listPurchaseHistory() -> [String] {
    return ["Purchase 1", "Purchase 2"]
}
```

This code might seem a little confusing. The empty parentheses tell the compiler that you are not passing any parameters to the method. The -> tells the system what you return from your method. [String] tells you that you are returning an array of strings. In the final version, you will actually want to return purchase objects, but you are using String for now. This code will not yet compile because you do not return an array, so you added a return of a simple array. That is all that needs to be done in the Swift file to create the class. Figure 5-15 shows the final Swift file.

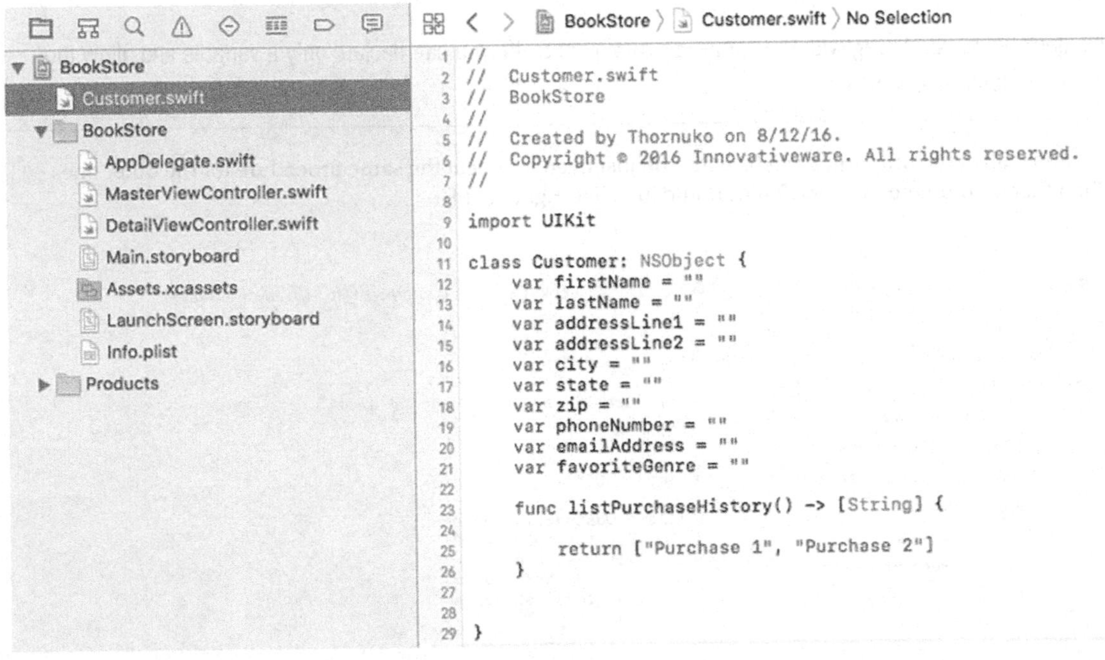

Figure 5-15. *The finished Customer class Swift file*

Inheritance

Another major quality of OOP is inheritance. Inheritance in programming is similar to genetic inheritance. You might have inherited your eye color from your mother or hair color from your father, or vice versa. Classes can, in a similar way, inherit properties and methods from their parent classes, but unlike genetics, you do not inherit the values of those properties. In OOP, a parent class is called a *superclass*, and a child class is called a *subclass*.

■ **Note** In Swift, there is no superclass unless specifically stated.

You could, for example, create a class of printed materials and use subclasses for books, magazines, and newspapers. Printed materials can have many things in common, so you could define properties in the superclass of printed materials and not have to redundantly define them in each individual class. By doing this, you further reduce the amount of redundant code that is necessary for you to write and debug.

In Figure 5-16, you will see a layout for the properties of a `Printed Material` superclass and how that will affect the subclasses of Book, `Magazine`, and `Newspaper`. The properties of the `Printed Material` class will be inherited by the subclasses, so there is no need to define them explicitly in the class. You will notice that the Book class now has significantly fewer properties. By using a superclass, you will significantly reduce the amount of redundant code in your programs.

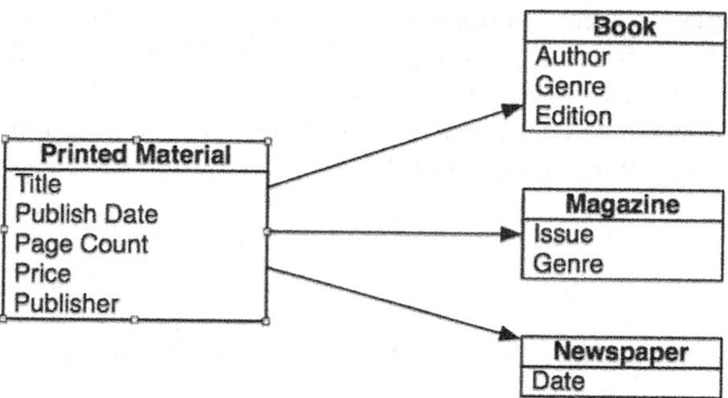

Figure 5-16. *Properties of the super- and subclasses*

Why Use OOP?

Throughout this chapter, we have discussed what OOP is and have even discussed how to create classes and objects. However, it's also important to discuss why you want to use OOP principles in your development.

If you take a look at the popular programming languages of the day, all of them use the OOP principles to a certain extent. Swift, Objective-C, C++, Visual Basic, C#, and Java all require the programmer to understand classes and objects to successfully develop in those languages. In order to become a developer in today's world, you need to understand OOP. But why use it?

OOP Is Everywhere

Just about any development you choose to do today will require you to understand object-oriented principles. On macOS and in iOS, everything you interact with will be an object. For example, simple windows, buttons, and text boxes are all objects and have properties and methods. If you want to be a successful programmer, you need to understand OOP.

Eliminate Redundant Code

By using objects, you can reduce the amount of code you have to retype. If you write code to print a receipt when a customer checks out, you will want that same code available when you need to reprint a receipt. If you placed your code to print the receipt in the `Sale` class, you will not have to rewrite this code again.

This not only saves you time but often helps you eliminate mistakes. If you do not use OOP and there is a change to the invoice (even something as simple as a graphic change), you have to make sure you make the change in your desktop and mobile applications. If you miss one of them, you run the risk of having the two interfaces behave differently.

Ease of Debugging

By having all of the code relating to a book in one class, you know where to look when there is a problem with the book. This may not sound like such a big deal for a little application, but when your application gets to hundreds of thousands or even millions of lines of code, it will save you a lot of time.

Ease of Replacement

If you place all of your code in a class, then as things change in your application, you can change out classes and give your new class completely different functionality. However, the modified class can still interact with the rest of the application in the same way as your current class. This is similar to car parts. If you want to replace a muffler on a car, you do not need to get a new car. If you have code related to your invoice scattered all over the place, it makes it much more difficult to change items about a class.

Advanced Topics

We have discussed the basics of OOP throughout this chapter, but there are some other topics that are important to your understanding.

Interface

As discussed in this chapter, the way the other objects interact with a class is with methods. In Swift, you can set access levels on your methods. Declaring a method `private` will make it accessible only to objects derived from it. By default, Swift methods are internal and can be accessed by any object or method in the current module. This is often called the *interface* because it tells other objects how they can interact with your objects. Implementing a standard interface throughout your application will allow your code to interact with different objects in similar ways. This will significantly reduce the amount of object-specific code you need to write.

Polymorphism

Polymorphism is the ability of an object of one class to appear and be used as an object of another class. This is usually done by creating methods and properties that are similar to those of another class. A great example of polymorphism that you have been using is the bookstore. In the bookstore, you have three similar classes: `Book`, `Magazine`, and `Newspaper`. If you wanted to have a big sale for your entire inventory, you could go through all of the books and mark them down. Then you could go through all of the magazines and mark them down and then go through all of the newspapers and mark them down. That would be more work than you would need to do. It would be better to make sure all of the classes have a markdown method. Then you could call that on all of the objects without needing to know which class they were as long as they were subclasses of a class that contained the methods needed. This would save a bunch of time and coding.

As you are planning your classes, look for similarities and for methods that might apply to more than one type of class. This will save you time and speed up your application in the long run.

Summary

You've finally reached the end of the chapter! Here is a summary of the things that were covered:

- *Object-oriented programming (OOP):* You learned about the importance of OOP and the reasons why all modern code should use this methodology.
- *Objects*: You learned about OOP objects and how they correspond to real-world objects. You also learned about abstract objects that do not correspond to real-world objects.
- *Classes:* You learned that a class determines the types of data (properties) and the methods that each object will have. Every object needs to have a class. It is the blueprint for the object.
- *Creating a class:* You learned how to map out the properties and methods of your classes.
- *Creating a class file:* You used Xcode to create a class file.
- *Editing a file:* You edited the Swift file to add your properties and methods.

EXERCISES

- Try creating the class files for the rest of the classes you mapped out.
- Map out an `Author` class. Choose the kind of information you would need to store about an author.

For the daring and advanced:

- Try creating a superclass called `PrintedMaterial` Map out the properties that a class might have.
- Create classes for the other types of printed materials a store might carry.

CHAPTER 6

Learning Swift and Xcode

For the most part, all programming languages perform the typical tasks any computer needs to do—store information, compare information, make decisions about that information, and perform some action based on those decisions. The Swift language makes these tasks easier to understand and accomplish. The real trick with Swift (actually, the trick with most programming languages) is to understand the symbols and keywords used to accomplish those tasks. This chapter continues the examination of Swift and Xcode so you can become even more familiar with them.

A Newcomer

As you may know, Swift has not been around for long. Development of the Swift language began about four years ago by Chris Lattner, and on September 9, 2014, Swift 1.0 was officially released. Swift borrows many ideas from Objective-C, but it also incorporates many features used by modern programming languages. Swift was designed from the ground up to be accessible to the average programmer.

Currently, there are two main types of programming languages. Compiled languages such as Objective-C and C++ are known for being rigid and requiring certain syntax. Compiled languages are also significantly faster in execution. Interpreted languages, such as Ruby, PHP, and Python, are known for being easier to learn and code but slower in their execution. Swift is a language that bridges the gap between the two. Swift incorporates the flexibility that makes interpreted languages so popular with the performance required for demanding applications and games. In fact, Apple claims that Swift applications will perform faster than those written in Objective-C. In some of Apple's tests, Swift performed almost four times faster than Python and 40 percent faster than Objective-C.

Understanding the Language Symbols

Understanding symbols is a basic part of any programming language. Symbols are punctuation used to portray specific meanings in source code. Understanding the symbols of a language is required to be able to use the language. Here are some of the symbols and language constructs used in Swift, most of which you've already encountered in one way or another:

- {: This is the *begin* brace. It's used to start what's commonly referred to as a ***block*** of code. Blocks are used to define and surround a section of code and define its scope.
- }: This is the *end* brace. It's used to end a block of code. Wherever there is a begin brace ({), there must always be an accompanying end brace (}).

G. Bennett and B. Lees, *Swift 3 for Absolute Beginners*, DOI 10.1007/978-1-4842-2331-4_6

- `[ ]`: These are the open and close brackets. They are used in the declaration and consumption of arrays.
- `func methodName() -> String`: This is how a Swift function is defined. The word `methodName`, of course, can represent any name. The word `String` can also change. It represents what type of information the method returns. In this example, `String` indicates the method will return a string, or a group of characters (data types were introduced in Chapter 3 and will be covered in more depth in later chapters). This will be discussed in more depth later in the chapter.

Figure 6-1 shows an example of Swift code.

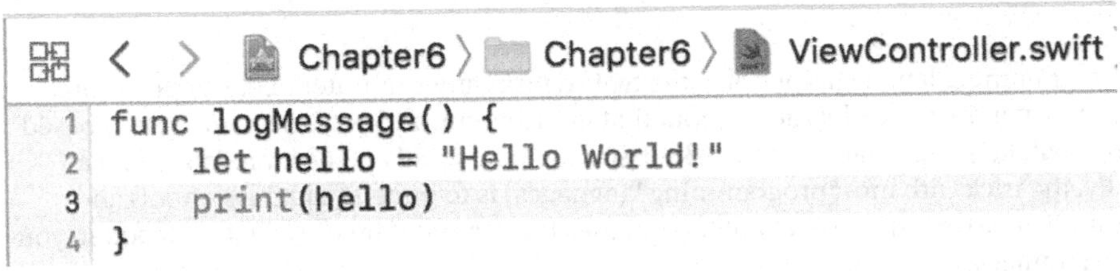

Chapter6 〉 Chapter6 〉 ViewController.swift

```
1 func logMessage() {
2     let hello = "Hello World!"
3     print(hello)
4 }
```

Figure 6-1. *Example of Swift code*

Line 1 represents a Swift function. The empty parentheses, `()`, indicate that this function does not receive any variables. The fact that the parentheses are not followed by `->` signifies that this function does not return any type of data and, if invoked, would not return a value to the caller.

The end of line 1 and line 4 are the braces that define a block of code. This block is what defines the method. Every method has at least one block.

Line 2 creates a constant named `hello`. As you learned in previous chapters, a constant is a value that cannot change. The value of the constant `hello` is assigned "Hello World!" Because you assign `hello` to a `String` value, `hello` becomes a `String` and can use any method related to `Strings` (recall that you first saw strings in Chapter 3). Line 3 could be rewritten as follows:

```
let hello: String = "Hello World!"
```

Line 3 is a call to the `print` function. You pass the object to the method in order to print the `hello` `String` object.

Although it does look a little cryptic to someone who is just learning Swift, the simple and terse syntax doesn't take too much time to learn.

Implementing Objects in Swift

Swift was built from the ground up to be object-oriented. It incorporates the best parts of Objective-C without the constraints of being compatible with C. It also takes some of the best features of a scripted language. The following are some of the concepts that make Swift object-oriented. Don't worry if some of these terms seem unfamiliar; they will be discussed in later chapters (Chapters 7 and 8 cover the basics).

- Pretty much everything is an *object.*
- Objects contain ***instance*** variables.
- Objects and instance variables have a defined *scope.*
- Classes hide an object's *implementation.*

■ **Note** As you saw in Chapter 5, the term ***class*** is used to represent, generically, the definition or type of an object. An ***object*** is created from the class. For example, an SUV is a *class* of vehicle. A class is a blueprint of sorts. A factory builds SUVs. The results are SUV objects that people drive. You can't drive a *class*, but you can drive an *object* built from a class.

So, how do these concepts translate to Swift? Swift is flexible in the implementation of classes.

■ **Note** Even though in Swift a single file may contain many different classes, a programmer will want to separate the code into different files to make access easier.

Let's look at a complete definition of a Swift class called `HelloWorld` (Figure 6-2).

```
1  import Foundation
2
3
4  class HelloWorld {
5
6      func logMessage() {
7          let hello = "Hello World!"
8          print(hello)
9      }
10
11 }
12
```

Figure 6-2. *HelloWorld class*

In Figure 6-2, a class called `HelloWorld` is being defined. This class has only one method defined: `logMessage`. What do all these strange symbols mean? Using the line numbers as a reference, you can review this code line by line.

Line 1 contains a compiler directive, `import Foundation`. For this little program to know about certain other objects, you need to have the compiler read other interface files. In this case, the `Foundation` file defines the objects and interfaces to the **Foundation framework**. This framework contains the definition of most non-user-interface base classes of the iOS and macOS systems. You will not be using any Foundation framework-specific objects in this example, but it is a default part of any new Swift file.

The actual start of the object is on line 4, as follows:

```
class HelloWorld {
```

`HelloWorld` is the class. If you wanted `HelloWorld` to be a subclass of a logging class you had created, such as `LogFile`, you would change the declaration as follows:

```
class HelloWorld: LogFile  {
```

Line 6 contains a method definition for this object, as follows:

```
func logMessage() {
```

When you're defining a method, you must decide whether you want the method to be a type or an instance method. In the case of the `HelloWorld` object, you are using the default method type, which is an instance. This method can only be used *after* an object is created. If the word class is added before the `func`, the method can be used *before* an object is created, but you will not have access to properties in the object. If you changed `logMessage` to a type method, it would be as follows:

```
class func logMessage() {
```

Lines 7 and 8 contain the body of the method. You learned about the details of the statements earlier in the chapter.

That's the complete description of class `HelloWorld`; there's not a whole lot here. More complicated objects simply have more methods and more properties.

But wait, there is more. Now that you have a new Swift class defined, how is it used? Figure 6-3 shows another piece of code that uses the newly created class.

```
let myHelloWorld = HelloWorld()
myHelloWorld.logMessage()
```

Figure 6-3. *Calling a Swift method*

The first line defines a constant called `myHelloWorld`. It then assigns the constant to an instance of the `HelloWorld` class. The second line simply calls the `logMessage` method of the `myHelloWorld` object. Those who have spent time in Objective-C will quickly see how much shorter and efficient both the class declaration and the object creation are in Swift.

■ **Note** Instantiation makes a class a real object in the computer's memory. A class by itself is not really usable until there is an instance of it. Using the SUV example, an SUV means nothing until a factory builds one (instantiates the class). Only then can the SUV be used.

■ **Note** Method calls can also accept multiple arguments. Consider, for example, `myCarObject.switchRadioBandTo(FM, 104.7)`. The method here would be `switchRadioBandTo`. The two arguments are contained in the parentheses. Being consistent in naming methods is critical.

Writing Another Program in Xcode

When you first open Xcode, you'll be presented with a Welcome to Xcode screen. This screen provides some nice shortcuts to access recently used Xcode projects. Until you are more comfortable with Xcode, keep the "Show this window when Xcode launches" check box selected.

Creating the Project

You are going to start a new project, so click the "Create a new Xcode project" icon. Whenever you want to start a new iOS or macOS application, library, or anything else, use this icon. Once a project has been started and saved, the project will appear in the Recent list on the right of the display.

For this Xcode project, you will choose something simple. Make sure the iOS Application is selected. Then select Single View Application, as shown in Figure 6-4. Then simply click the Next button.

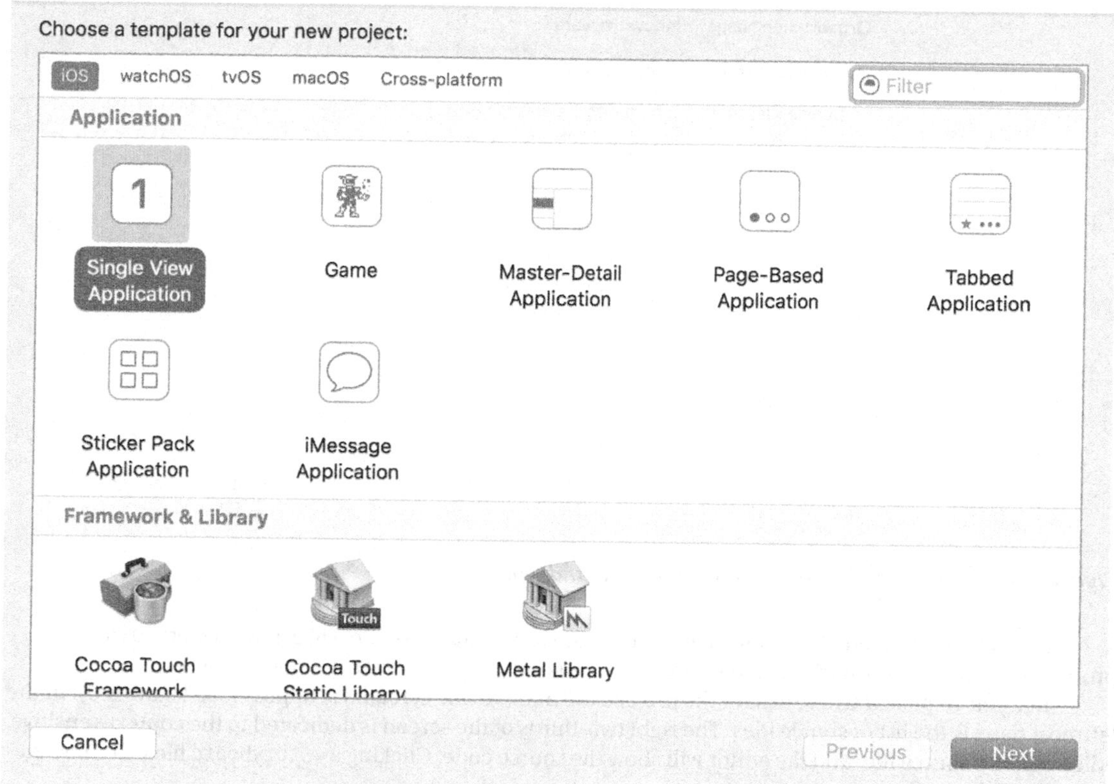

Figure 6-4. *Choosing a new project from a list of templates*

There are several types of templates. These templates make it easier to start a project from scratch in that they provide a starting point by automatically creating simple source files.

Once you've chosen the template and clicked the Next button, Xcode presents you with a dialog box asking for the project's name and some other information, as shown in Figure 6-5. Type a product name of `Chapter6`. The organization identifier needs to have some value, so we used `com.innovativeware`. Also make sure the Devices drop-down is set to iPhone. If you are planning on running this app on an actual iOS device or submitting it to the App store, you will need to select your team from the drop-down. If you do not select it now, it can be added to the project later.

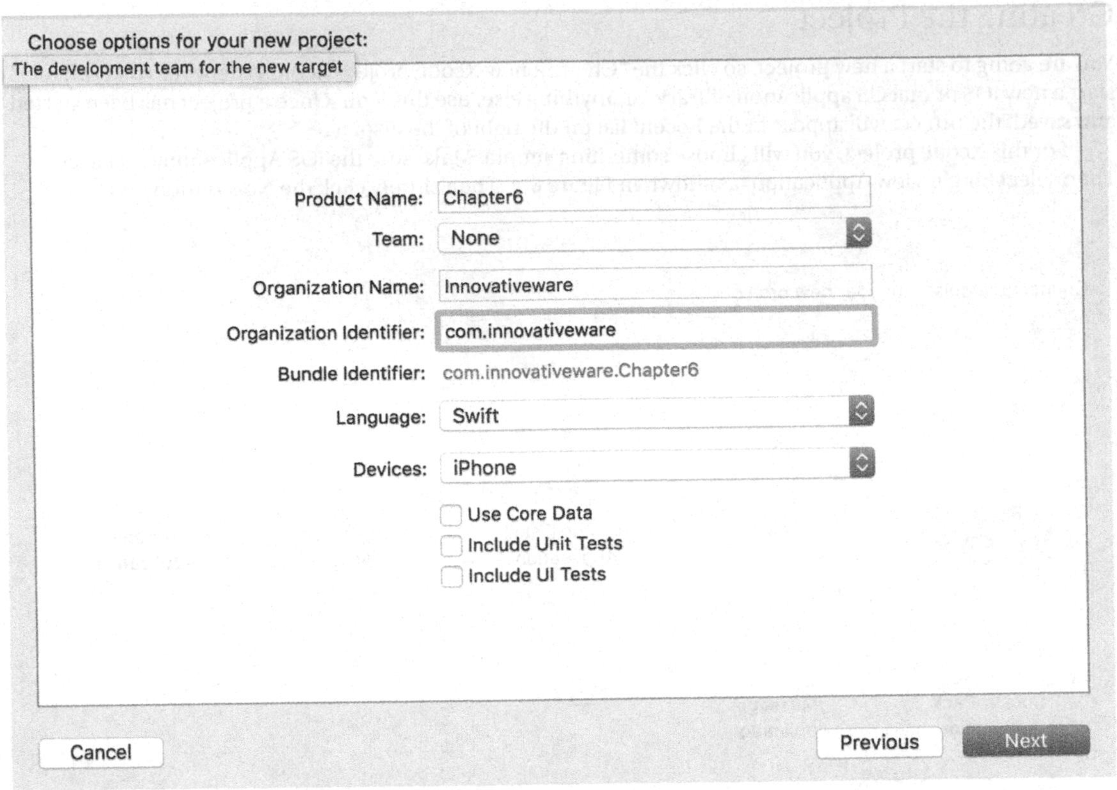

Figure 6-5. *Setting up the product name, company, and type*

Once you've supplied all the information, click the Next button. Xcode will ask you where to save the project. You can save it anywhere, but the desktop is a good choice because it's always visible.

Once you've picked where to save the project, the main Xcode screen will appear (see Figure 6-6). In the leftmost pane is the list of source files. The right two-thirds of the screen is dedicated to the context-sensitive editor. Click a source file, and the editor will show the source code. Clicking a `.storyboard` file will show the Screen Interface editor.

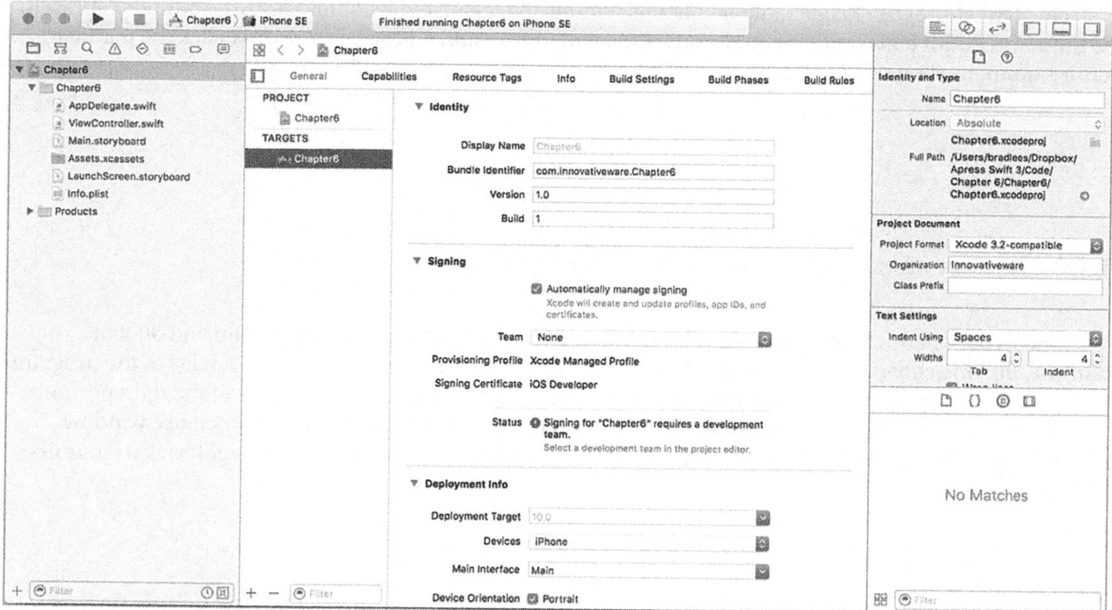

Figure 6-6. *The Xcode 8 main screen*

The first app is going to be simple. This iPhone app will contain a button. When the button is clicked, your name will appear on the screen. So, let's start by first looking more closely at some of the stub source code that Xcode built for you. The nice thing about Xcode is that it will create a stub application that will execute without any modification. Before you start adding code, let's look at the main toolbar of Xcode, as shown in Figure 6-7.

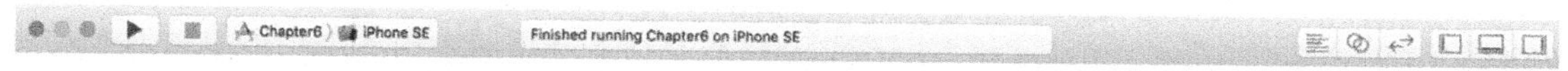

Figure 6-7. *The Xcode 8 toolbar*

At first glance, there are three distinct areas of the toolbar. The left area is used to run and debug the application. The middle area displays status as a summary of compiler errors and warnings. The far-right area contains a series of buttons that customize the editing view.

As shown in Figure 6-8, the left portion of the toolbar contains a *Play* button that will compile and run the application. If the application is running, the Stop button will not be grayed out. Since it's grayed out, you know the application is not running. The *scheme selection* can be left alone for now. Schemes will be discussed in more detail in Chapter 13.

Figure 6-8. *Close-up of the left portion of the Xcode toolbar*

The right side of the Xcode toolbar contains buttons that change the editor. The three buttons represent the Standard editor (selected), the Assistant editor, and the Version editor. For now, just click the Standard editor button, as shown in Figure 6-9.

***Figure 6-9.** Close-up of the right portion of the Xcode toolbar*

Next to the editor choices are a set of View buttons. These buttons can be toggled on and off. For example, the one chosen in Figure 6-10 represents the current view shown in Figure 6-7, a list of the program files on the left third of the screen, the main editor in the middle third, and the Utilities in the right portion of the screen. Any combination, or none, can be chosen to help customize the main workspace window. The last button opens the Utilities area. Chapter 13 discusses this button. For now, let's get back to your first iPhone app.

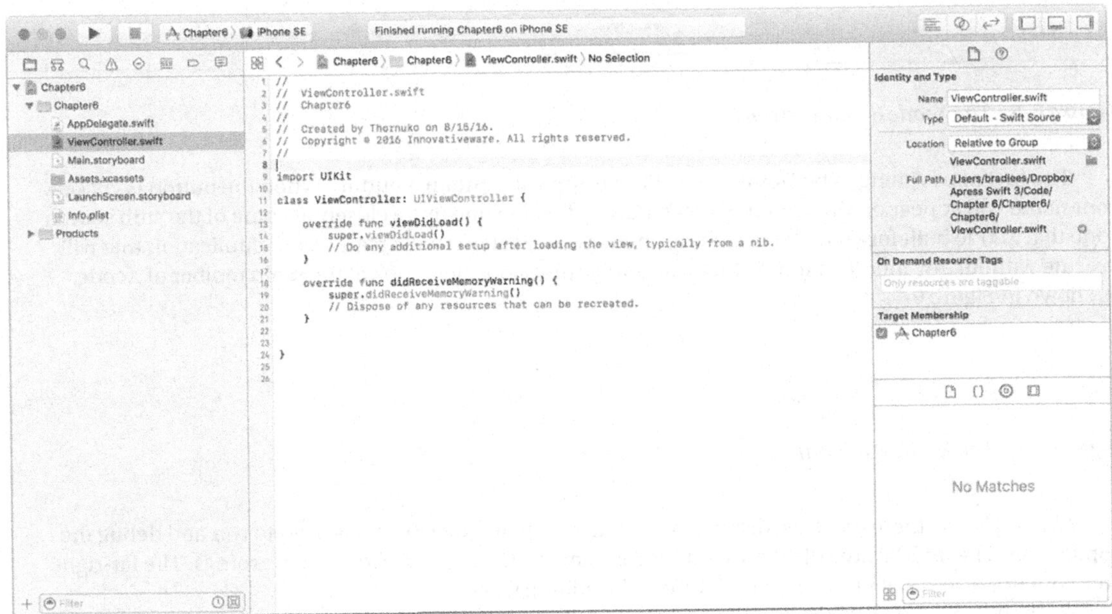

***Figure 6-10.** Looking at the source code in the Xcode editor*

Click the `ViewController.swift` file, as shown in Figure 6-10. The editor shows some Swift code that defines a `ViewController` class.

You will notice two functions in the code. `viewDidLoad` is called immediately after a view is loaded and can be used for setting up the view. This is a good place to put code that sets up labels, buttons, colors, and so on. `didReceiveMemoryWarning` is called when your application is getting low on memory. You can use this function to decrease the amount of memory required by your application.

■ **Note** For now, you're simply going to add a few lines of code and see what they do. It's not expected that you understand what this code means right now. What's important is simply going through the motions to become more familiar with Xcode. Chapter 7 goes into more depth about what makes up a Swift program, and Chapter 10 goes into more depth about building an iPhone interface.

Next, you'll add a few lines of code into this file, as shown in Figure 6-11. Line 13 defines an iPhone label on the screen where you can put some text. Line 15 defines the method showName. You'll be calling this method in order to populate the iPhone label. A label is nothing more than an area on the screen where you can put some text information.

```
1  //
2  //  ViewController.swift
3  //  Chapter6
4  //
5  //  Created by Thornuko on 8/15/16.
6  //  Copyright © 2016 Innovativeware. All rights reserved.
7  //
8
9  import UIKit
10
11 class ViewController: UIViewController {
12
13     @IBOutlet weak var nameLabel: UILabel!
14
15     @IBAction func showName(sender: AnyObject) {
16         nameLabel.text = "My Name is Brad!"
17     }
18
19     override func viewDidLoad() {
20         super.viewDidLoad()
21         // Do any additional setup after loading the view, typically from a nib.
22     }
23
24     override func didReceiveMemoryWarning() {
25         super.didReceiveMemoryWarning()
26         // Dispose of any resources that can be recreated.
27     }
28
29
30 }
31
32
```

Figure 6-11. *Code added to the ViewController.swift file*

■ **Caution** Type the code exactly as shown in the example, including case. For instance, `UILabel` can't be `uilabel` or `UILABEL`. Swift is a case-sensitive language, so `UILabel` is completely different from `uilabel`.

You will notice that the code you added has `@IBOutlet` and `@IBAction` in front of them. These attributes are necessary when connecting objects with the interface designer. `IBOutlet` allows you to control an interface object with code. `IBAction` allows you to execute code when something happens in the interface such as tapping a button.

■ **Note** `IBOutlet` and `IBAction` both start with `IB`, which is an acronym from Interface Builder. Interface Builder was the tool used by NeXT and then Apple for building user interfaces.

You now have the necessary code in place, but you don't yet have an interface on the iPhone. Next, you're going to edit the interface and add two interface objects to your app.

To edit the iPhone's interface, you need to click the `Main.storyboard` file once. The `.storyboard` file contains all the information about a single window or view. Xcode 8 also supports `.xib` (pronounced *zib*) files.

■ **Note** Each `.xib` file represents one screen on an iPhone or iPad. Apps that have multiple views will have multiple `.xib` files, but many different views can be stored in each storyboard file.

You will use Xcode's interface editor to *connect* a UI object, such as a `Label` object, to the code you just created. Connecting is as easy as clicking and dragging.

Click the last view button in the upper-right part of the screen, as shown in Figure 6-12. This opens the Utilities view for the interface. Among other things, this Utilities view shows you the various interface objects you can use in your app. You're going to be concerned with only the right-most objects: `Button` and `Label`. Figure 6-13 shows the Object Library. There are other libraries available, but for now you will be using only the third one from the left.

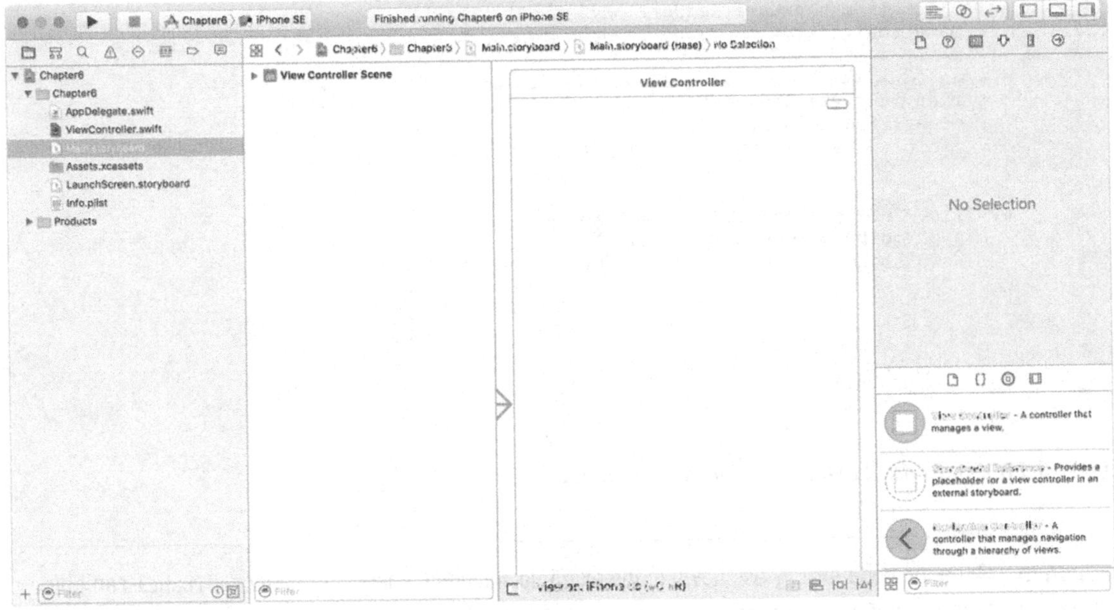

Figure 6-12. *The iPhone interface you're going to modify*

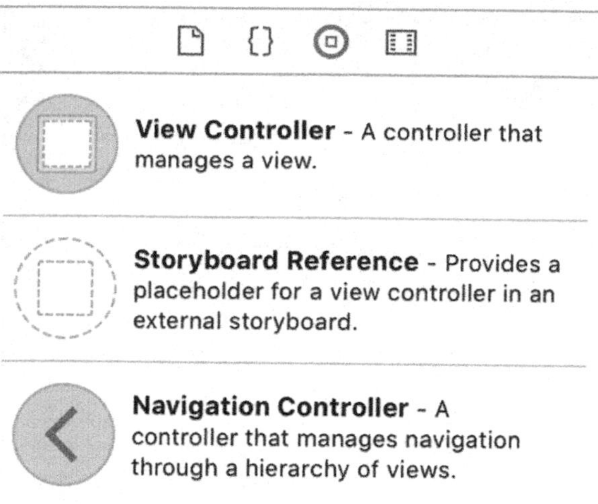
View Controller - A controller that manages a view.
Storyboard Reference - Provides a placeholder for a view controller in an external storyboard.
Navigation Controller - A controller that manages navigation through a hierarchy of views.

Figure 6-13. *The Object Library*

The first step is to click the `Button` object in the Utilities window. Next, drag the object to the iPhone view, as shown in Figure 6-14. Don't worry; dragging the object doesn't remove it from the list of objects in the Utilities view. Dragging it creates a new copy of that object on the iPhone interface.

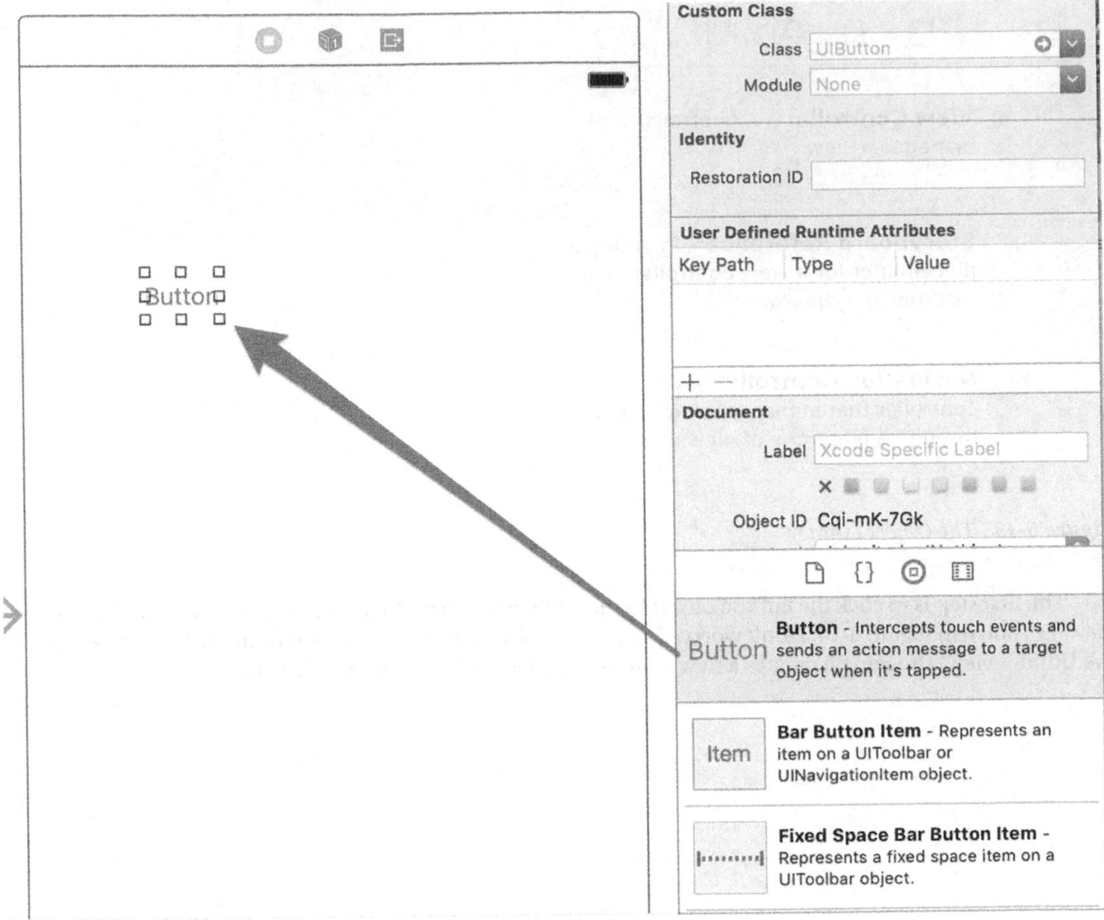

Figure 6-14. *Moving a Button object onto the iPhone view*

Next, double-click the `Button` object that was just added to the iPhone interface. This allows you to change the title of the button, such as to `Name`, as shown in Figure 6-15. Many different interface objects work just like this. Simply double-click, and the title of the object can be changed. This can also be done in the actual code, but it's much simpler to do in Interface Builder.

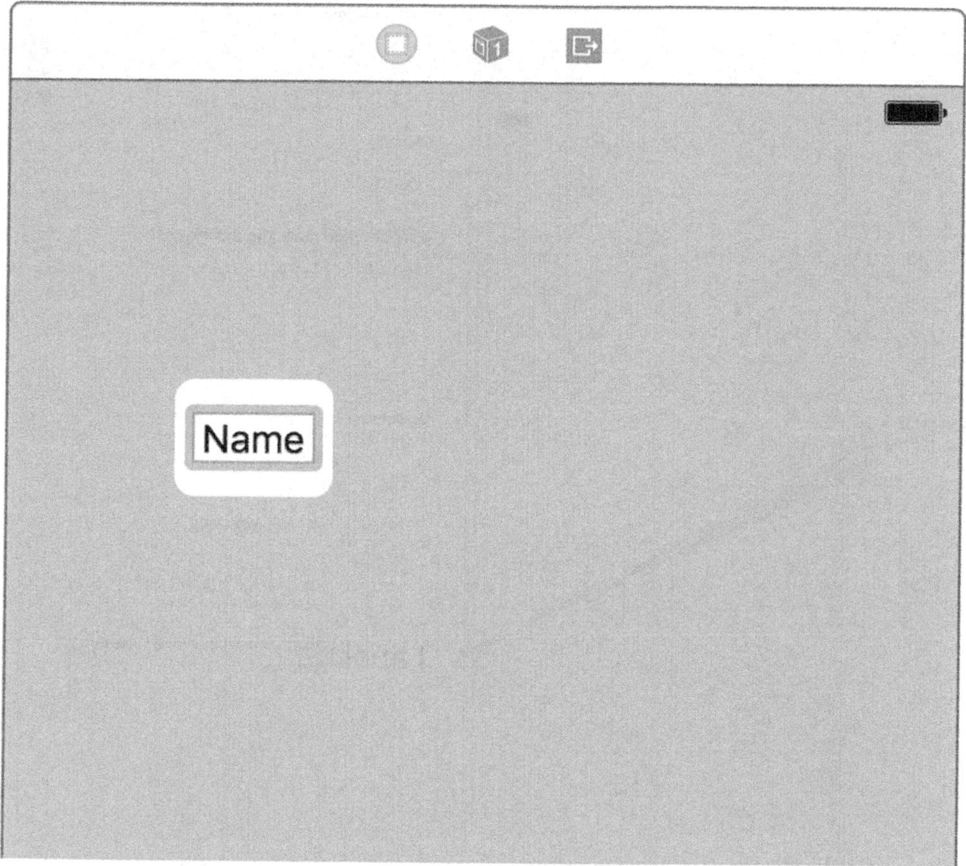

Figure 6-15. *Modifying the Button object's title*

Once the title has been changed, drag a `Label` object to right below the button, as shown in Figure 6-16.

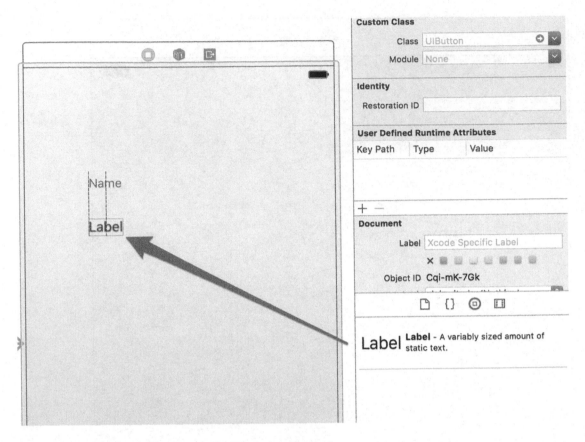

Figure 6-16. Adding a Label object to the iPhone interface

For now, you can leave the label's text as "Label" since this makes it easy to find on the interface. If you clear the label's text, the object will still be there, but there is nothing visible to click in order to select it. Expand the size of the label by dragging the center white square to the right, as shown in Figure 6-17.

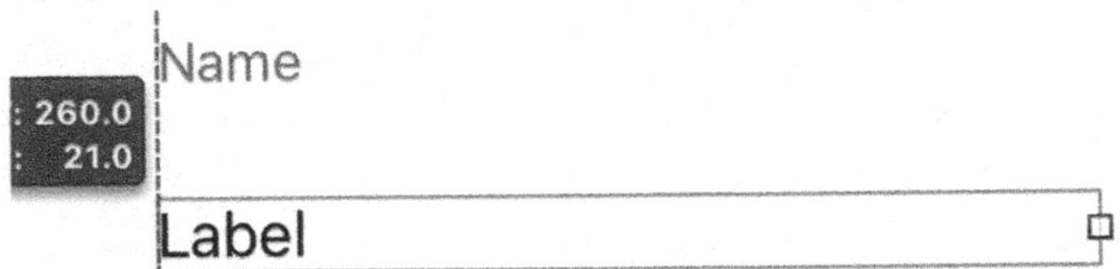

Figure 6-17. Expanding the label's size

Now that you have a button and the label, you can connect these visual objects to your program. Start by right-clicking (or Control-clicking) the Button control. This brings up a connection menu, as shown in Figure 6-18.

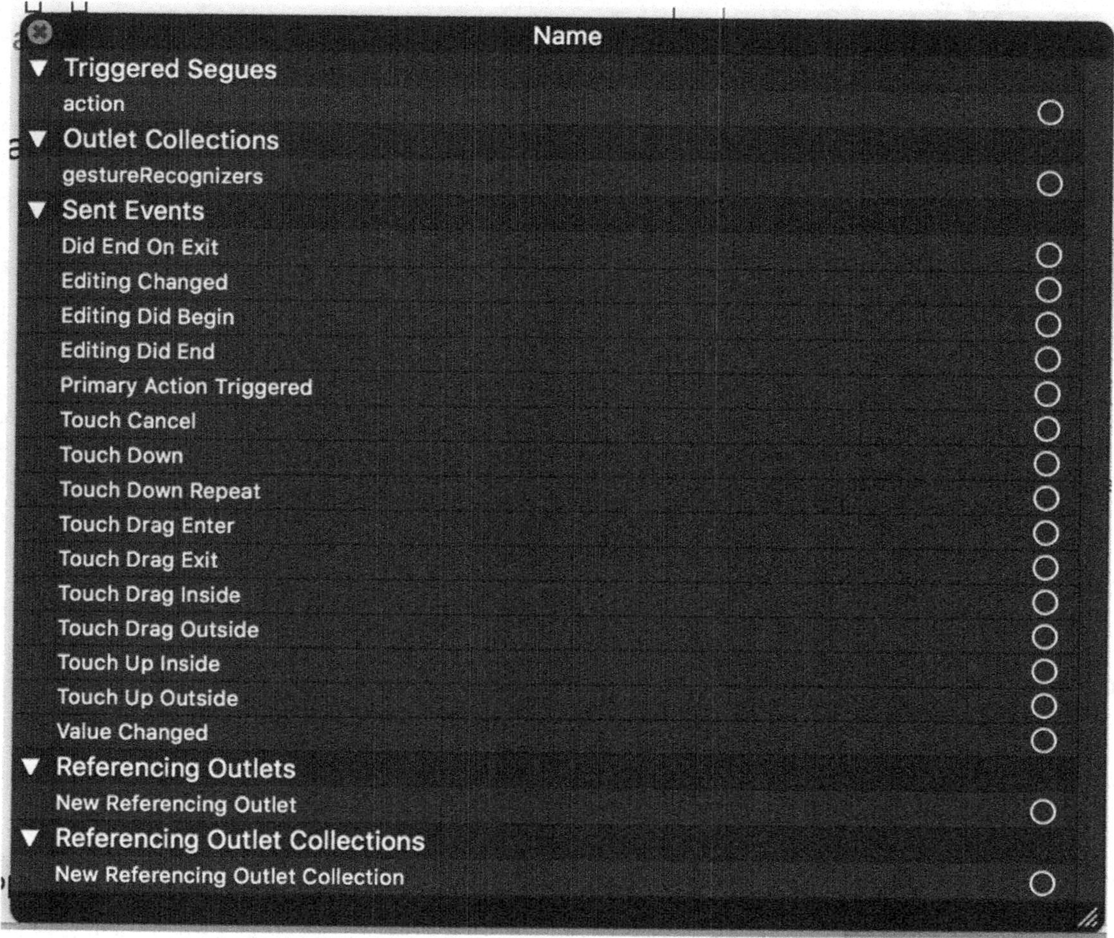

Figure 6-18. *Connection menu for the Button object*

Next, click and drag from the Touch Up Inside connection circle to the View Controller icon, as shown in Figure 6-19. Touch Up Inside means the user clicked *inside* the `Button` object. Dragging the connection to the View Controller connects the Touch Up Inside event to the `ViewController` object. This causes the object to be notified whenever the `Button` object is clicked.

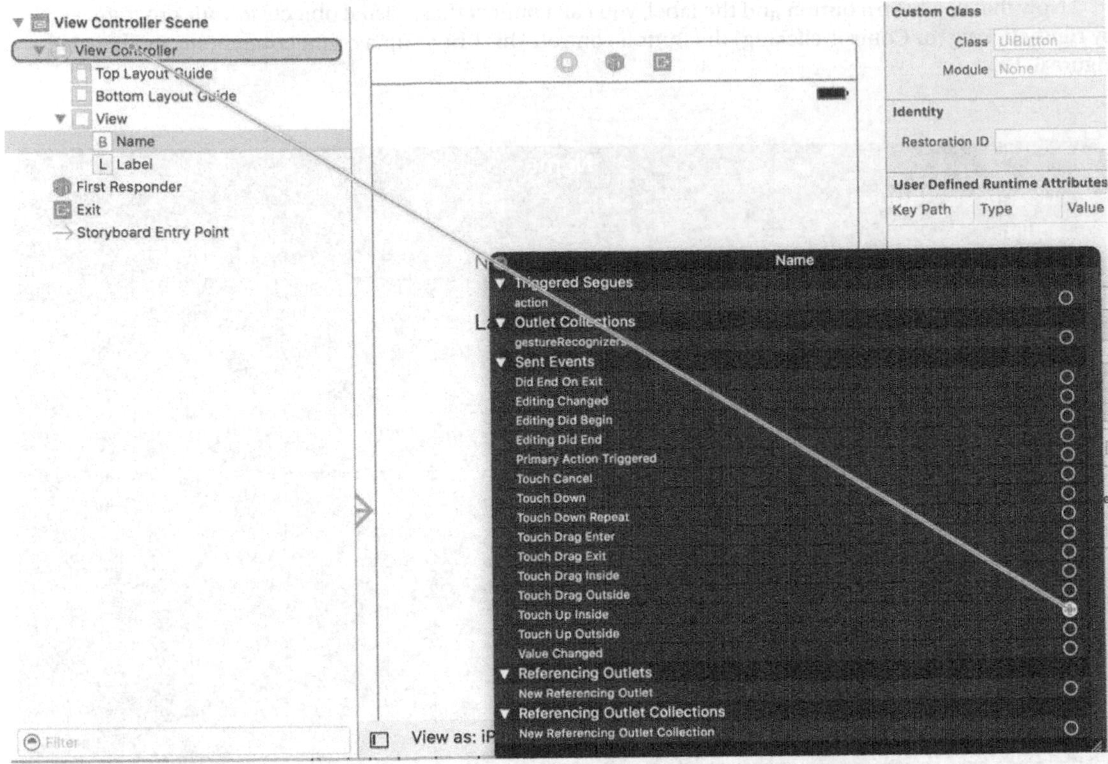

Figure 6-19. *Connecting the Touch Up Inside event to the object*

Once the connection is dropped, a list of methods that can be used in your connection is displayed, as shown in Figure 6-20. In this example, there is only one method, `showName:`. Selecting the `showName:` method connects the Touch Up Inside event to the object.

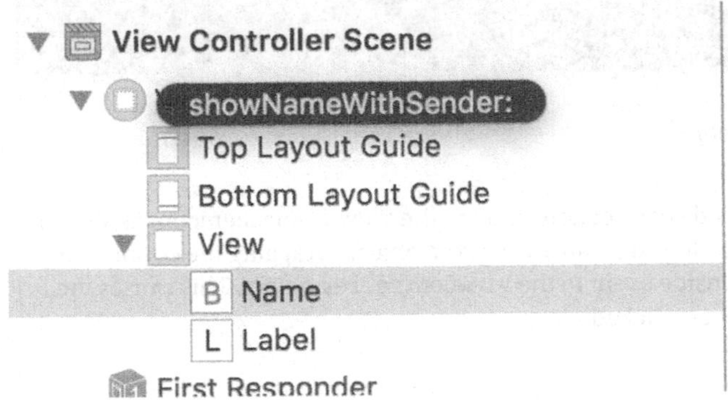

Figure 6-20. *Selecting the method to handle the Touch Up Inside event*

Once the connection has been made, the details are shown on the button's connection menu, as shown in Figure 6-21.

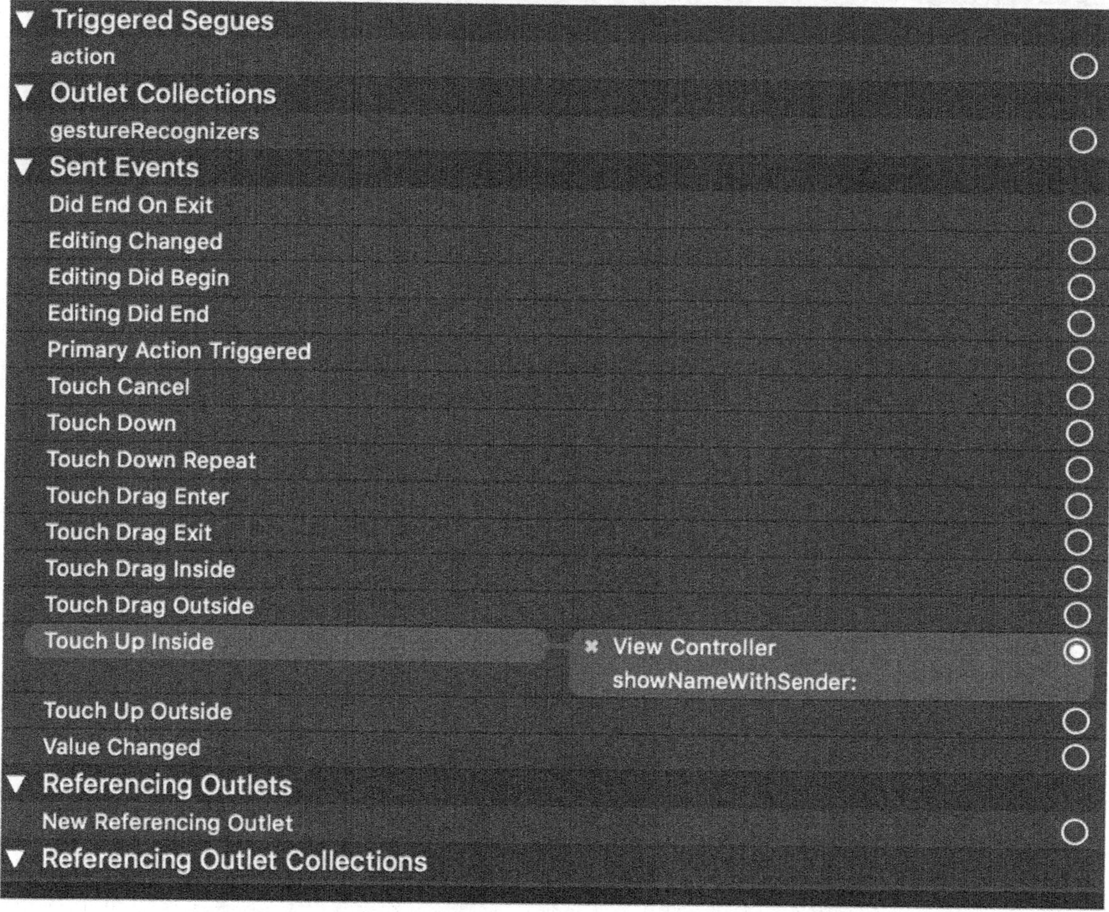

Figure 6-21. *The connection is now complete*

Next, you create a connection for the `Label` object. In this case, you don't care about the Label events; instead, you want to connect the `ViewController`'s `nameLabel` outlet to the object on the iPhone interface. This connection basically tells the object that the label you want to set text on is on the iPhone interface.

Start by right-clicking the `Label` object on the iPhone interface. This brings up the connection menu for the `Label` object, as shown in Figure 6-22. There are not as many options for a `Label` object as there were for the `Button` object.

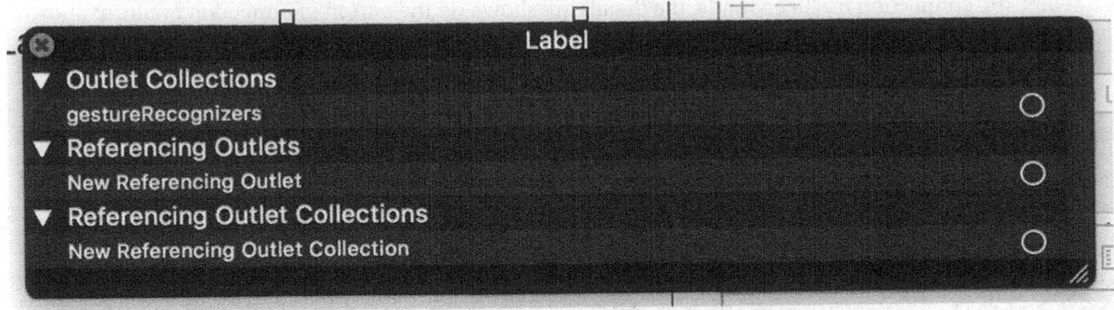

Figure 6-22. *Connection menu for the Label object*

As mentioned, you are not here to connect an event. Instead, you connect what's referred to as a *referencing outlet*. This connects a screen object to a variable in your `ViewController` object. Just like with the button, you should drag the connection to the View Controller icon, as shown in Figure 6-23.

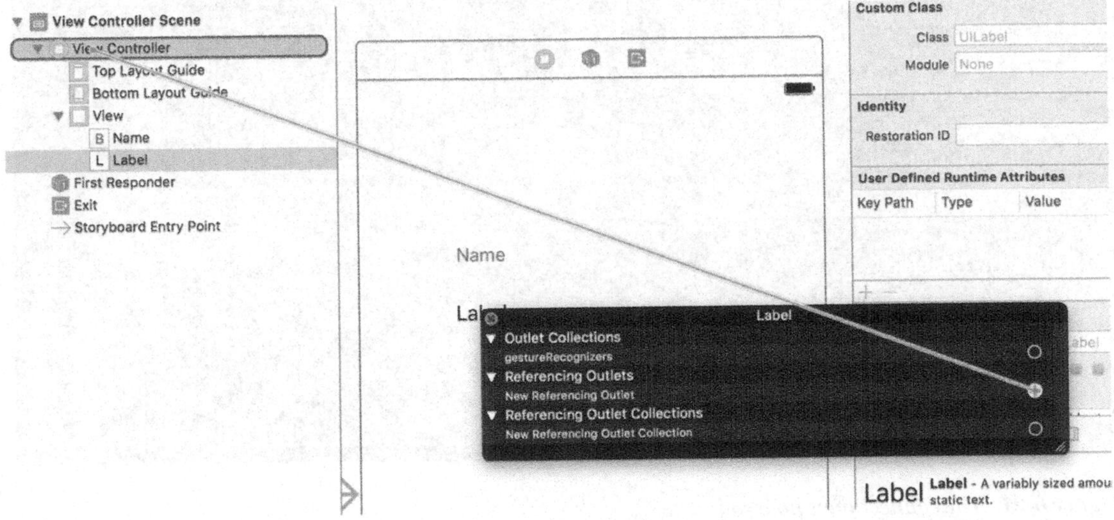

Figure 6-23. *Connecting the referencing outlet to the object*

Once the connection is dropped on the View Controller icon, a list of outlets in your `ViewController` object will be displayed, as shown in Figure 6-24. Of the two choices, you want to choose `nameLabel`. This is the name of the variable in the `ViewController` object you are using.

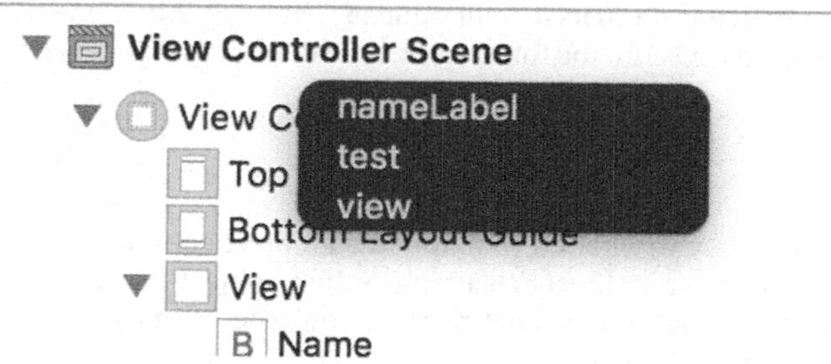

Figure 6-24. Selecting the object's variable to complete the connection

Once you've chosen `nameLabel`, you're ready to run your program. Click the Run button (which looks like a Play button) at the top-left corner of the Xcode window (see Figure 6-8). This will automatically save your files and start the application in the iPhone Simulator, as shown in Figure 6-25.

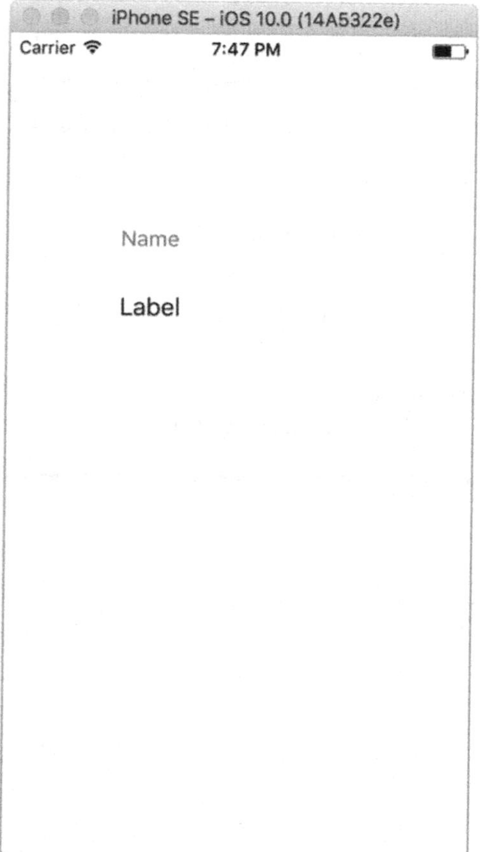

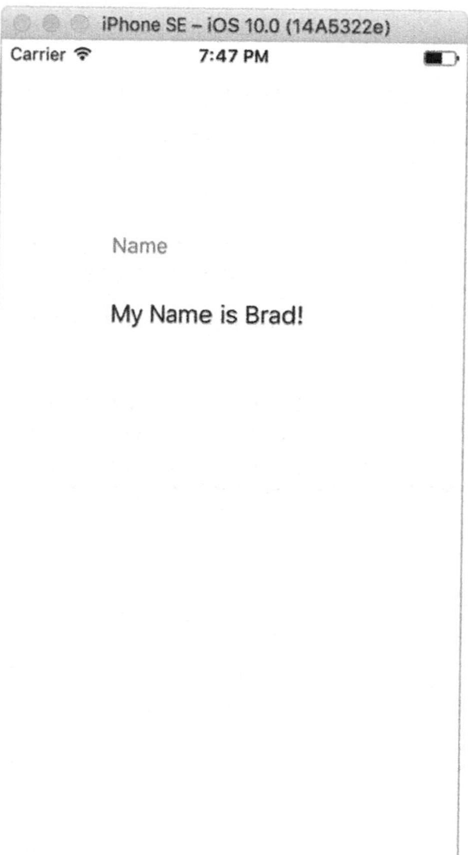

Figure 6-25. The app running, before and after the button is clicked

By clicking the Name button, the label's text will change from its default value of "Label" to "My Name is Brad!" or whatever value you entered. If you want to, go back into the interface and clear the default label text.

Summary

The examples in this chapter were simple, but ideally they've whetted your appetite for more complex applications using Swift and Xcode. In later chapters, you can expect to learn more about object-oriented programming and more about what Swift can do. Pat yourself on the back because you've learned a lot already. Here is a summary of the topics discussed in this chapter:

- The origins and brief history of the Swift language
- Some common language symbols used in Swift
- A Swift class example
- Using Xcode a bit more, including discussing the `HelloWorld.swift` source file
- Connecting visual interface objects with methods and variables in your application object

EXERCISES

- Clear the default text of "Label" in the program and re-run the example.
- Change the size of the `Label` object on the interface to be smaller in width. How does that affect your text message?
- Delete the referencing outlet connection of the label and rerun the project. What happens?
- If you think you have the hang of this, add a new button and label to the `ViewController` object and to the interface. Change the label from displaying your name to displaying something else.

CHAPTER 7

Swift Classes, Objects, and Methods

If you haven't already read Chapter 6, please do so before reading this chapter because it provides a great introduction to some of the basics of Swift. This chapter builds on that foundation. By the end of this chapter, you can expect to have a greater understanding of the Swift language and how to use the basics to write simple programs. The best way to learn is to take small programs and write (or rewrite) them in Swift just to see how the language works.

This chapter covers what composes a Swift class and how to interact with Swift objects via methods. It uses a simple radio station class as an example of how a Swift class is written. This will impart an understanding of how to use a Swift class. This chapter also teaches you how to formulate a design for objects that are needed to solve a problem. The chapter touches on how to create custom objects, as well as how to use existing objects provided in the foundation classes.

This chapter expands on Chapter 6's topics and introduces some of the concepts described in detail in Chapter 8.

Creating a Swift Class

Classes are simple to create in Swift. Generally, a class will be contained in its own file, but a single file can hold many classes if desired.

Here is a sample of the first line from a class's declaration:

```
class RadioStation
```

Here, the class name is `RadioStation`. Swift classes, by default, do not inherit from a superclass. If you want to make your Swift class inherit from another class, you can do this like so:

```
class RadioStation: Station
```

In this example, `RadioStation` is now a subclass of `Station` and will inherit all of the properties and methods of `Station`. Listing 7-1 shows the full definition of a class.

G. Bennett and B. Lees, *Swift 3 for Absolute Beginners*, DOI 10.1007/978-1-4842-2331-4_7

Listing 7-1. A Swift Class

```
1 import UIKit
2
3 class RadioStation: Station {
4
5     var name: String
6     var frequency: Double
7
8     override init() {
9         name = "Default"
10        frequency = 100
11    }
12
13    class func minAMFrequency() -> Double {
14        return 520.0
15    }
16
17    class func maxAMFrequency() -> Double {
18        return 1610.0
19    }
20
21    class func minFMFrequency() -> Double {
22        return 88.3
23    }
24
25    class func maxFMFrequency() -> Double {
26        return 107.9
27    }
28
29    func band() -> Int {
30        if frequency >= RadioStation.minFMFrequency() && frequency <=
          RadioStation.maxFMFrequency() {
31            return 1 //FM
32        } else {
33            return 0 //AM
34        }
35    }
36
37 }
```

Instance Variables

Listing 7-1 shows a sample class with two different properties: `name` and `frequency`. Line 1 imports the `UIKit` class definitions (more on that in a bit). Line 3 starts the definition of the class by defining its name (sometimes called the *type*). Lines 5 and 6 define the properties for the `RadioStation` class.

Whenever the `RadioStation` class is instantiated, the resulting `RadioStation` object has access to these properties, which are only for specific instances. If there are ten `RadioStation` objects, each object has its own variables independent of the other objects. This is also referred to as *scope*, in that the object's variables are within the scope of each object.

Methods

Almost every object has methods. In Swift, the common concept to interact with an object is calling a method on an object, like so:

```
myStation.band()
```

The preceding line will call a method named band on an instance of the `RadioStation` class object.

Methods can also have parameters passed along with them. Why pass parameters? Parameters are passed for several reasons. First (and most common), the range of possibilities is too large to write as separate methods. Second, the data you need to store in your object is variable—like a radio station's name. In the following example, you will see that it isn't practical to write a method for every possible radio frequency; instead, the frequency is passed as a parameter. The same applies to the station name.

```
myStation.setFrequency(104.7)
```

The method name is `setFrequency`. Method calls can have several parameters, as the following example illustrates:

```
myStation = RadioStation.init(name: "KZZP", frequency: 104.7)
```

In the preceding example, the method call consists of two parameters: the station name and its frequency. What's interesting about Swift relative to other languages is that the methods are essentially named parameters. If this were a C++ or Java program, the call would be as follows:

```
myObject = new RadioStation("KZZP", 104.7)
```

While a `RadioStation` object's parameters might seem obvious, having named parameters can be a bonus because they more or less state what the parameters are used for or what they do.

Using Type methods

A class doesn't always have to be instantiated to be used. In some cases, classes have methods that can actually perform some simple operations and return values before a class is instantiated. These methods are called *type methods*. In Listing 7-1, the method names that start with `class` are type methods.

Type methods have limitations. One of their biggest limitations is that none of the instance variables can be used. Being unable to use instance variables makes sense since you haven't instantiated anything. A type method can have its own local variables within the method itself but can't use any of the variables defined as instance variables.

A call to a type method would look like this:

```
RadioStation.minAMFrequency.()
```

Notice that the call is similar to how a method is called on an instantiated object. The big difference is that instead of an instance variable, the *class name* is used. Type methods are used quite extensively in the macOS and iOS frameworks. They are used mostly for returning some fixed or well-known type of value or to return a new instance of an object. These types of type methods are referred to as *initializers*. Here are some initializer method examples:

```
1.  Date.timeIntervalSinceReferenceDate          // Returns a number
2.  String(format:"http://%@", "1000")           // Returns a new String object
3.  Dictionary<String, String>()                 // Returns a new Dictionary object.
```

All of the preceding messages are type methods being called.

Line 1 simply returns a value that represents the number of seconds since January 1, 2001, which is the reference date.

Line 2 returns a new `String` object that has been formatted and has a value of `http://1000`.

Line 3 is a form that is commonly used because it actually allocates a new object. Typically, the line is not used by itself, but in a line like this:

```
var myDict = Dictionary<String, String>()
```

So, when would you use a type method? As a general rule, if the method returns information that is *not* specific to any particular instance of the class, make the method a type method. For example, the `minAMFrequency` in the preceding example would be the same for all instances of any `RadioStation`.

`object–this` is a great candidate for a type method. However, the station's name or its assigned frequency would be different for each instance of the class. These should not (and indeed could not) be type methods. The reason for this is that type methods cannot use any of the instance variables defined by the class.

Using Instance Methods

Instance methods (lines 29 to 35 in Listing 7-1) are available only once a class has been instantiated. Here's an example:

```
1   var myStation: RadioStation          // This declares a variable to hold the RadioStation object.
2   myStation = RadioStation()           // This creates a new RadioStation object.
3   var band = myStation.band()          // This method returns the Band of the RadioStation.
```

Line 3 calls a method on the `RadioStation` object. The method band returns a 1 for FM and a 0 for AM. An instance method is any method that does not contain the class declaration before it.

Using Your New Class

You've created a simple `RadioStation` class, but by itself it doesn't accomplish a whole lot. In this section, you will create the `Radio` class and have it maintain a list of `RadioStation` classes.

Creating Your Project

Let's start Xcode and create a new project named `RadioStations`.

1. Launch Xcode and select "Create a new Xcode project."
2. Make sure you choose an iOS application and select the Single View Application template, as shown in Figure 7-1.

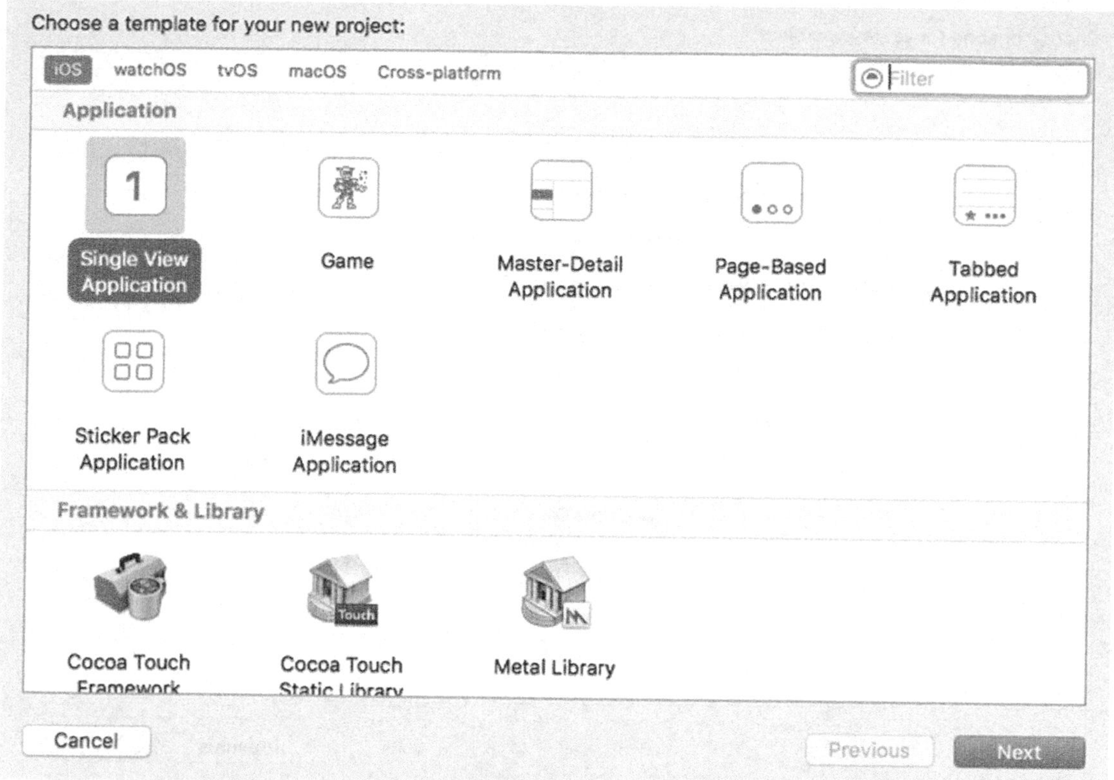

Figure 7-1. *Selecting a template in the new project window*

3. Once you've selected the template, click the Next button.
4. Set the product name (application name) to `RadioStations`.
5. Set the company identifier (a pretend company will do) and set the device family to iPhone (as shown in Figure 7-2). Make sure Swift is selected in the Language drop-down list.

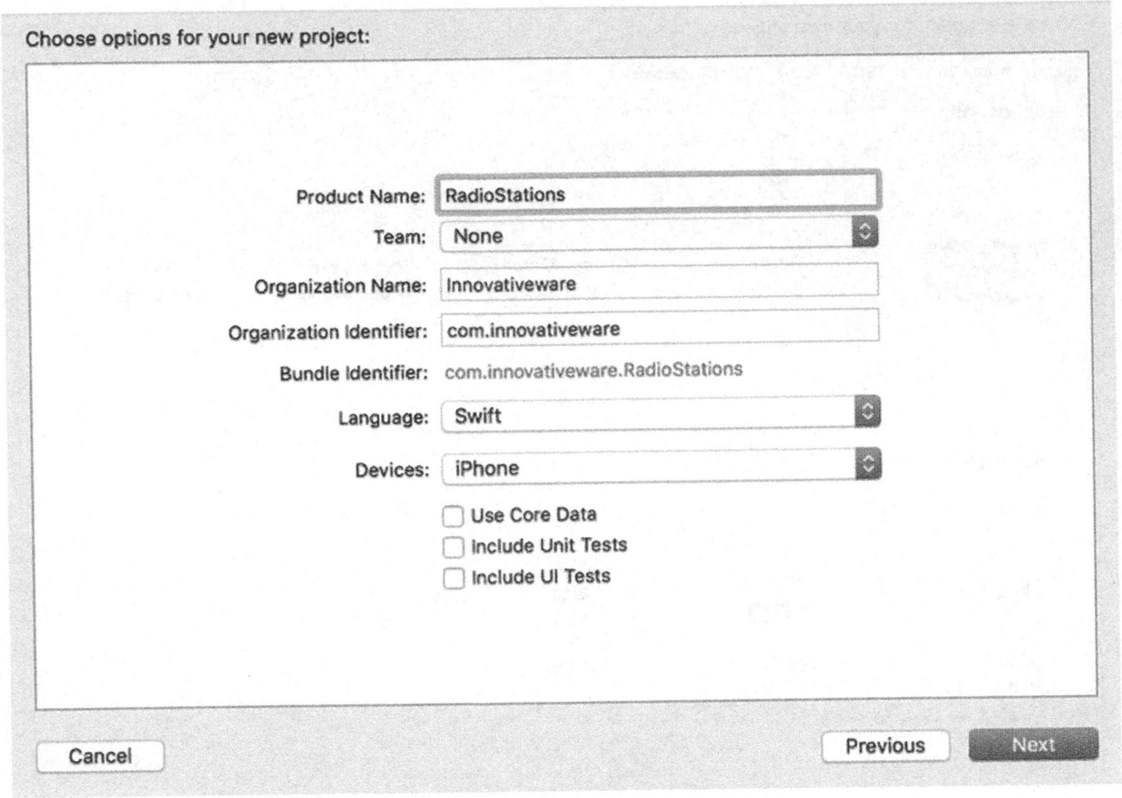

Figure 7-2. *Naming the new iPhone application*

6. Click the Next button, and Xcode will ask you where you want to save your new project. You can save the project on your desktop or anywhere in your home folder. Once you've made your choice, simply click the Create button.

7. Once you've clicked the Create button, the Xcode workspace window should be visible, as shown in Figure 7-3.

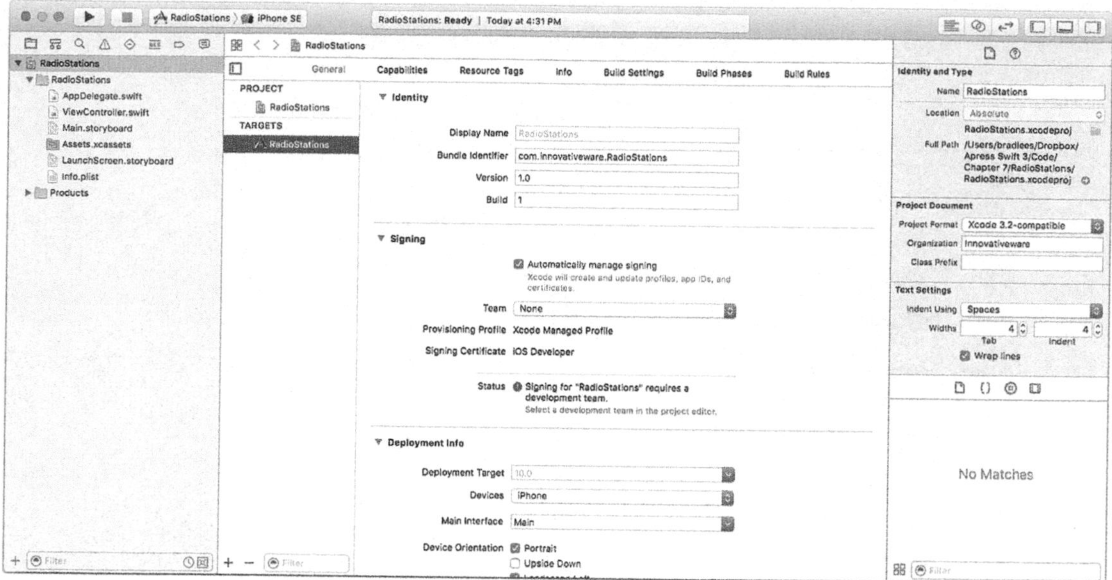

Figure 7-3. *The workspace window in Xcode*

Adding Objects

Now you can add your new objects.

1. First, create your `RadioStation` object. Right-click the RadioStations project and select New File (as shown in Figure 7-4).

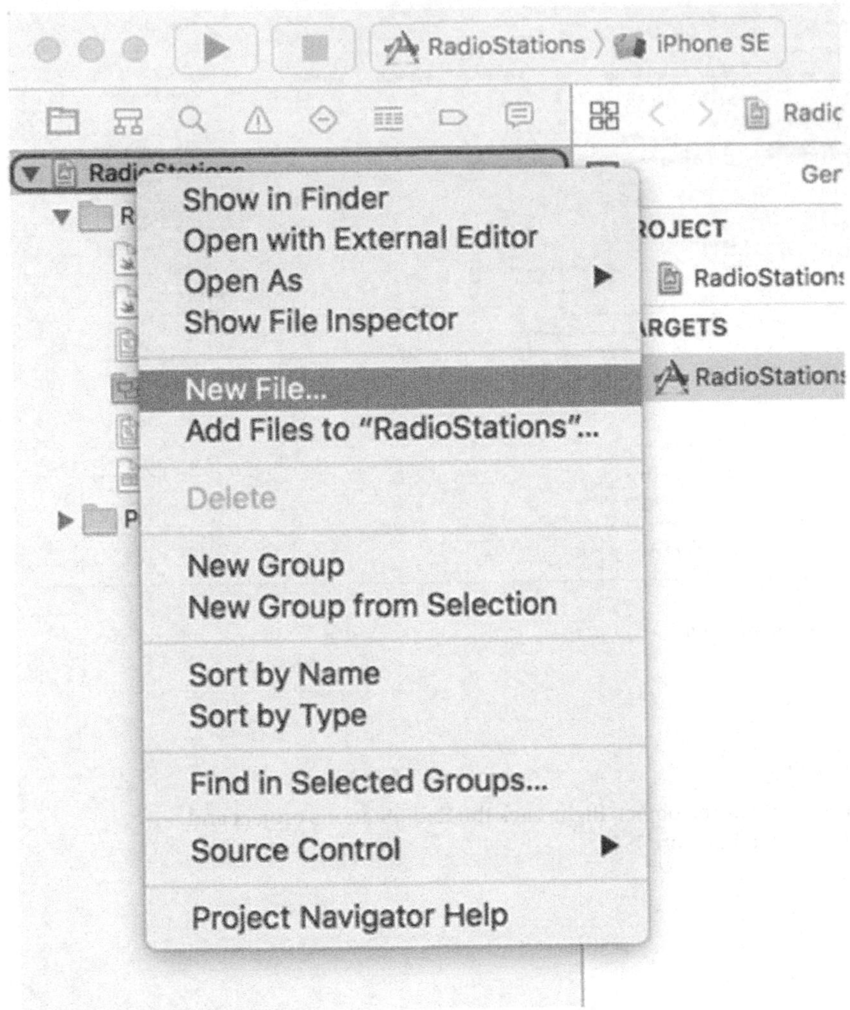

Figure 7-4. *Adding a new file*

2. The next screen, shown in Figure 7-5, asks for the new file type. Simply choose Cocoa Touch Class from the Source group, and then click Next.

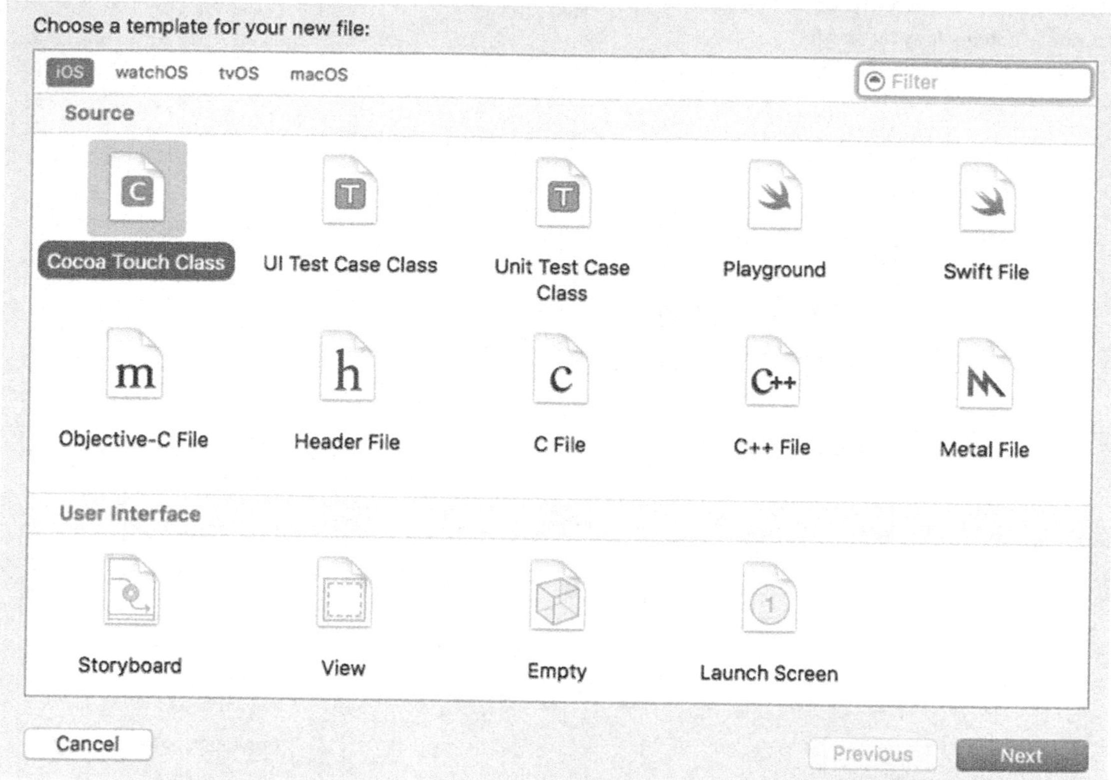

Figure 7-5. *Selecting the new file type*

3. The following screen will ask you the name of the class. Enter `RadioStation`. Keep Subclass set to NSObject and make sure Language is set to Swift. See Figure 7-6

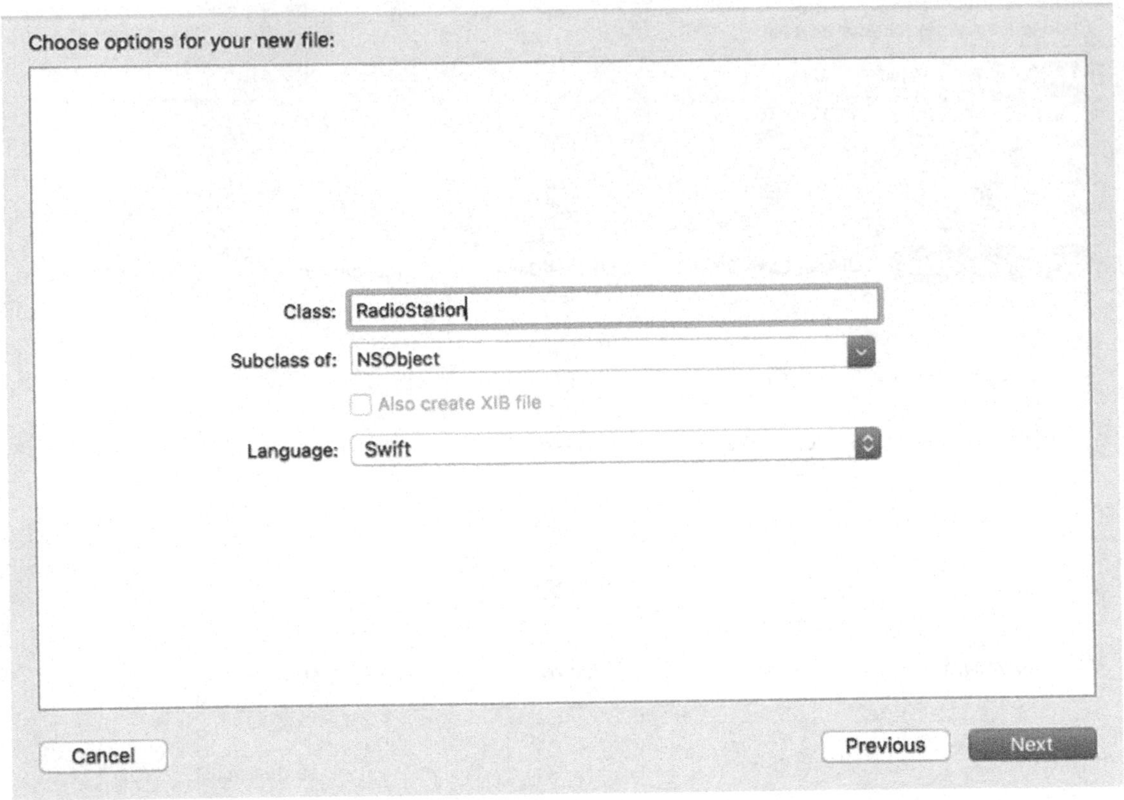

Figure 7-6. *Naming the New Class*

4. The next screen asks you the location to save the newly created file. Simply click the Create button since the location in which Xcode chooses to save the files is within the current project.

5. Your project window should now look like Figure 7-7. Click the `RadioStation.swift` file. Notice that the stub of your new `RadioStation` class is already present. Now, fill in the empty class so it looks like Listing 7-1, your `RadioStation` Swift file.

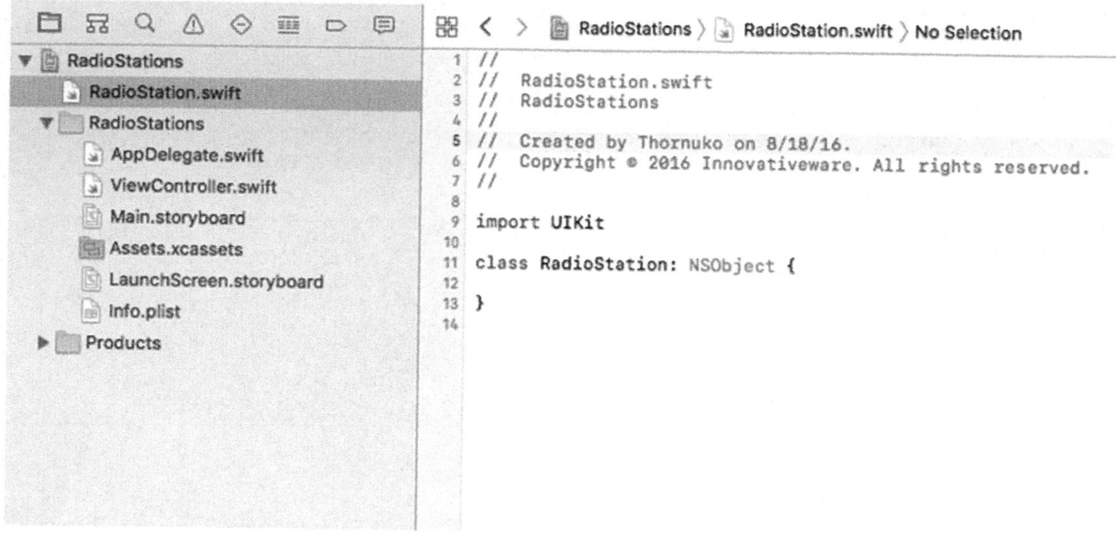

Figure 7-7. *Your newly created file in the workspace window*

Writing the Class

Now that you have created your project and your new `RadioStation.swift` file, you are ready to begin creating your class.

1. The class file you'll use here is the same one you used at the beginning of this chapter, and it will work perfectly for the radio station application. Click the `RadioStation.swift` file, and enter the code in your class, as shown in Figure 7-8.

```
//
//  RadioStation.swift
//  RadioStations
//
//  Created by Thornuko on 8/18/16.
//  Copyright © 2016 Innovativeware. All rights reserved.
//

import UIKit

class RadioStation: NSObject {

    var name: String
    var frequency: Double

    override init() {
        name="Default"
        frequency=100
    }

    class func minAMFrequency() -> Double {
        return 520.0
    }

    class func maxAMFrequency() -> Double {
        return 1610.0
    }

    class func minFMFrequency() -> Double {
        return 88.3
    }

    class func maxFMFrequency() -> Double {
        return 107.9
    }

    func band() -> Int {
        if frequency >= RadioStation.minFMFrequency()  &&
            frequency <= RadioStation.maxFMFrequency() {
            return 1 //FM
        } else {
            return 0 //AM
        }
    }

}
```

Figure 7-8. The RadioStation class file

We will come back to a few items in Figure 7-8 and explain them further in a moment; however, with the `RadioStation` class defined, you can now write the code that will actually use it.

2. Click the `ViewController.swift` file. You'll need to define a few variables for this class to use, as shown in Figure 7-9.

```
//
//  ViewController.swift
//  RadioStations
//
//  Created by Thornuko on 8/18/16.
//  Copyright © 2016 Innovativeware. All rights reserved.
//

import UIKit

class ViewController: UIViewController {

    @IBOutlet var stationName: UILabel!
    @IBOutlet var stationFrequency: UILabel!
    @IBOutlet var stationBand: UILabel!

    var myStation: RadioStation

    required init?(coder aDecoder: NSCoder) {
        myStation = RadioStation()
        myStation.frequency = 102.5
        myStation.name = "KNIX"
        super.init(coder: aDecoder)
    }

    override func viewDidLoad() {
        super.viewDidLoad()
        // Do any additional setup after loading the view, typically from a nib.
    }

    override func didReceiveMemoryWarning() {
        super.didReceiveMemoryWarning()
        // Dispose of any resources that can be recreated.
    }


}
```

Figure 7-9. *Adding a RadioStation object to the View Controller*

Lines 13 to 15 are going to be used by your iOS interface to show some values on the screen (more on these later). Line 17 defines the variable `myStation` of type `RadioStation`. Lines 19 to 24 contain the required `init` method. In Swift, classes do not require an initializer method, but it is a good place to set the default values of your object. This method sets up the variables used in that class. Also, don't forget to include the curly braces ({ ... }).

Creating the User Interface

Next, the main window has to be set up in order to display your station information.

1. Click the `Main.storyboard` file. This file produces the main iPhone screen. Click the Object Library icon, as shown in Figure 7-10.

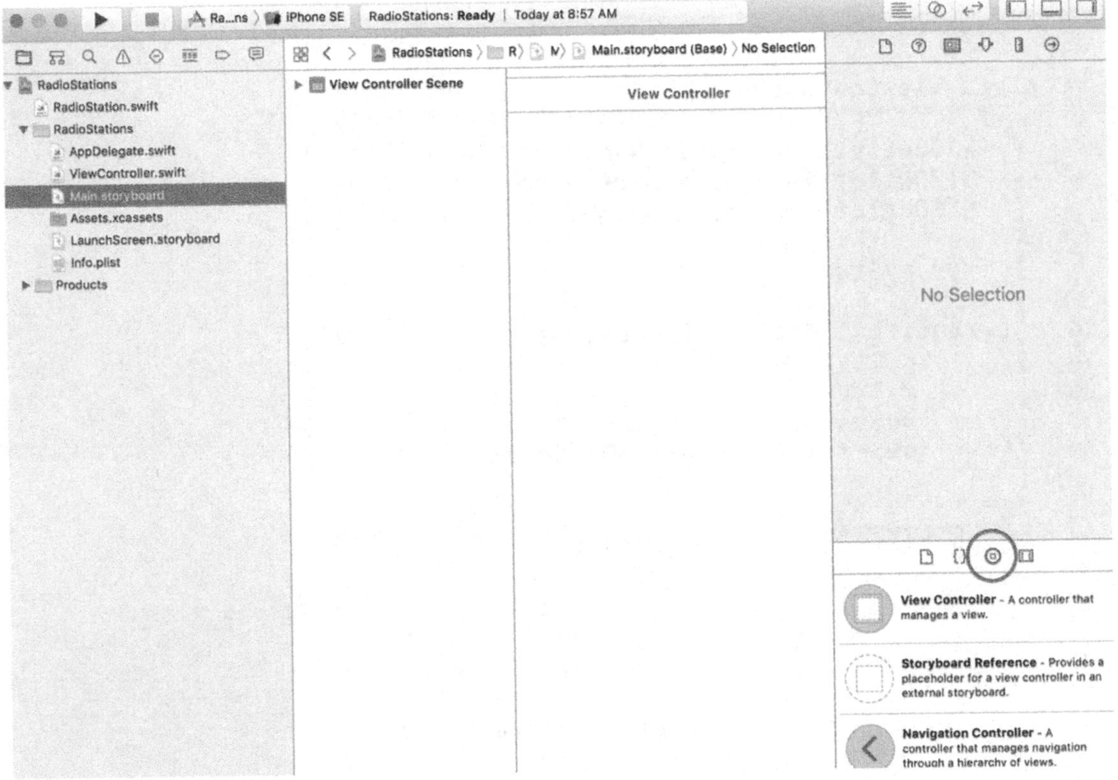

Figure 7-10. *Adding a Label object to your iPhone screen*

2. Drag and drop three `Label` objects onto the screen, as shown in Figure 7-11. The labels can be aligned in any manner, or as shown in Figure 7-11.

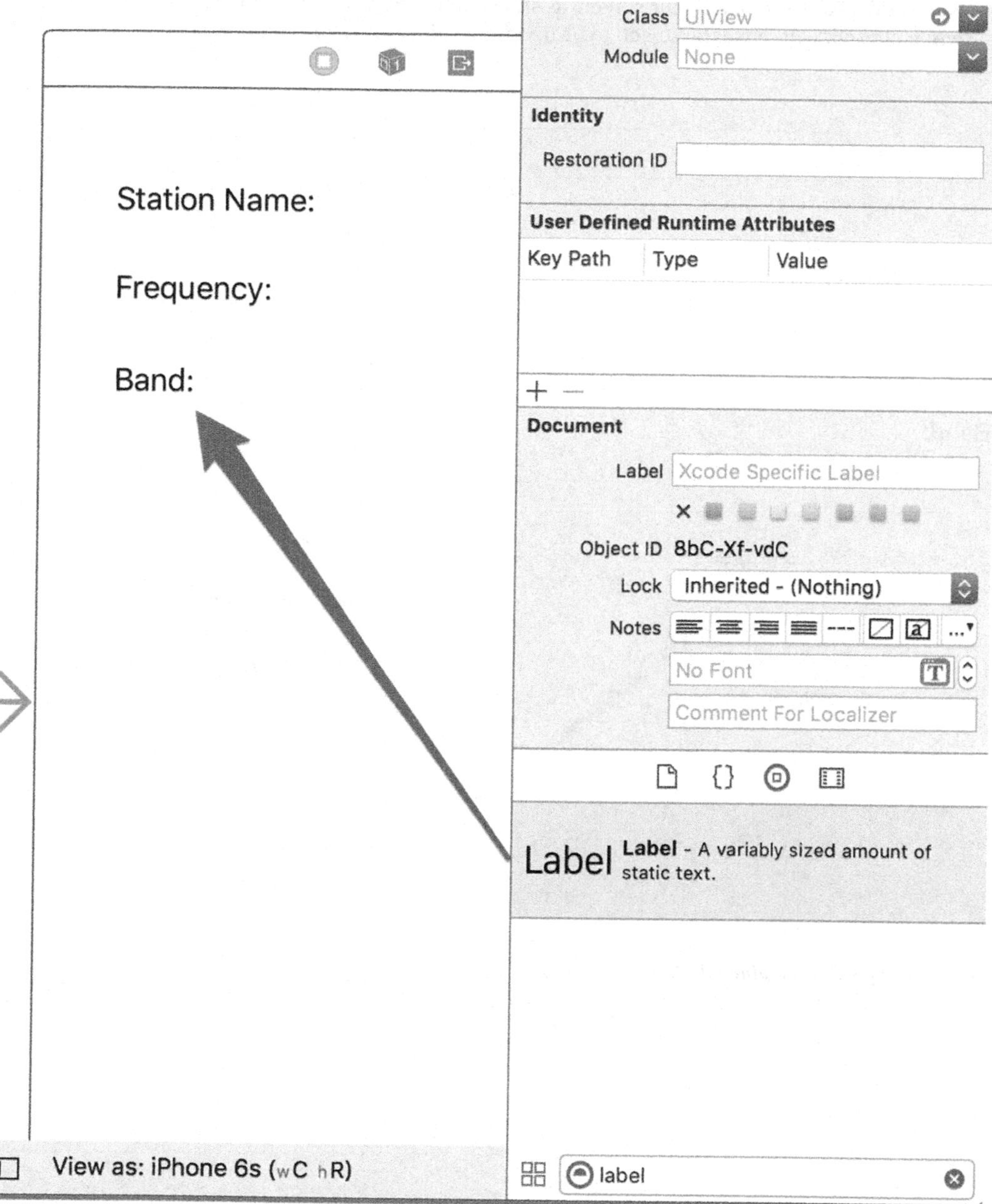

Figure 7-11. *All three Label objects on the iPhone screen*

3. You're going to need space, however. Once the Label objects are on the iPhone screen, double-click each Label object in order to change its text so that the iPhone screen looks something like Figure 7-11.

4. Next, add a Button object to the screen, as shown in Figure 7-12. This button, when clicked, will cause the screen to be updated with your radio station information.

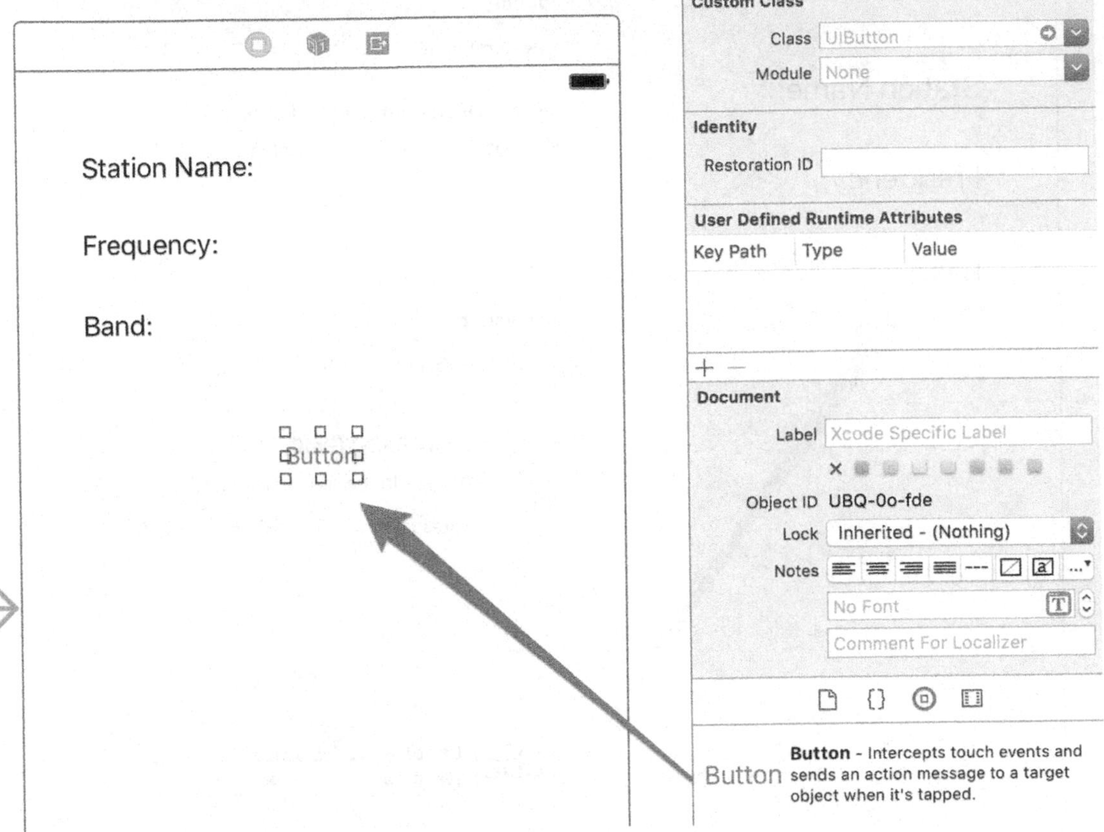

Figure 7-12. Adding a Button object to the screen

5. Just like with the *Label* object, simply double-click the `Button` object in order to change its title to My Station. The button should automatically resize to fit the new title.

6. Next, you need to add the Label fields that will hold the radio station information. These fields are situated just after the existing `Label` objects. Figure 7-13 shows the placement of the first label. Once the `Label` object is placed, it needs to be resized so that it can show more text, as shown in Figure 7-14.

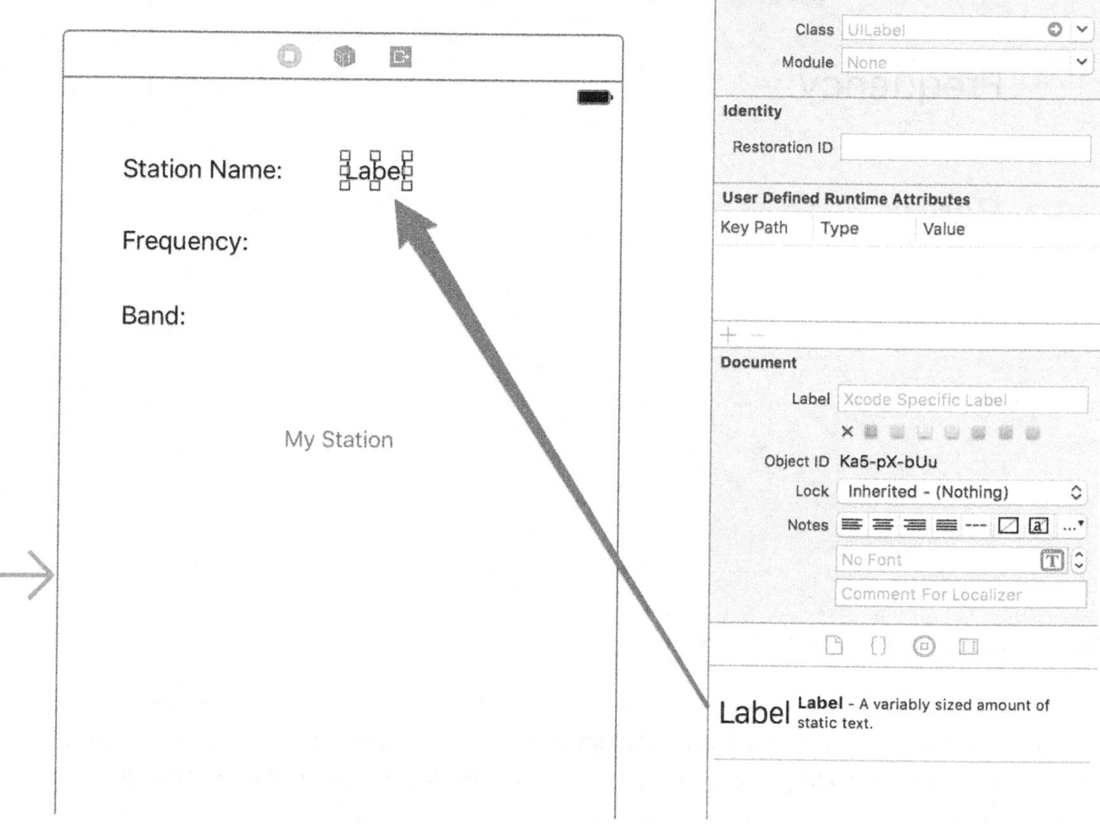

Figure 7-13. *Adding another Label object*

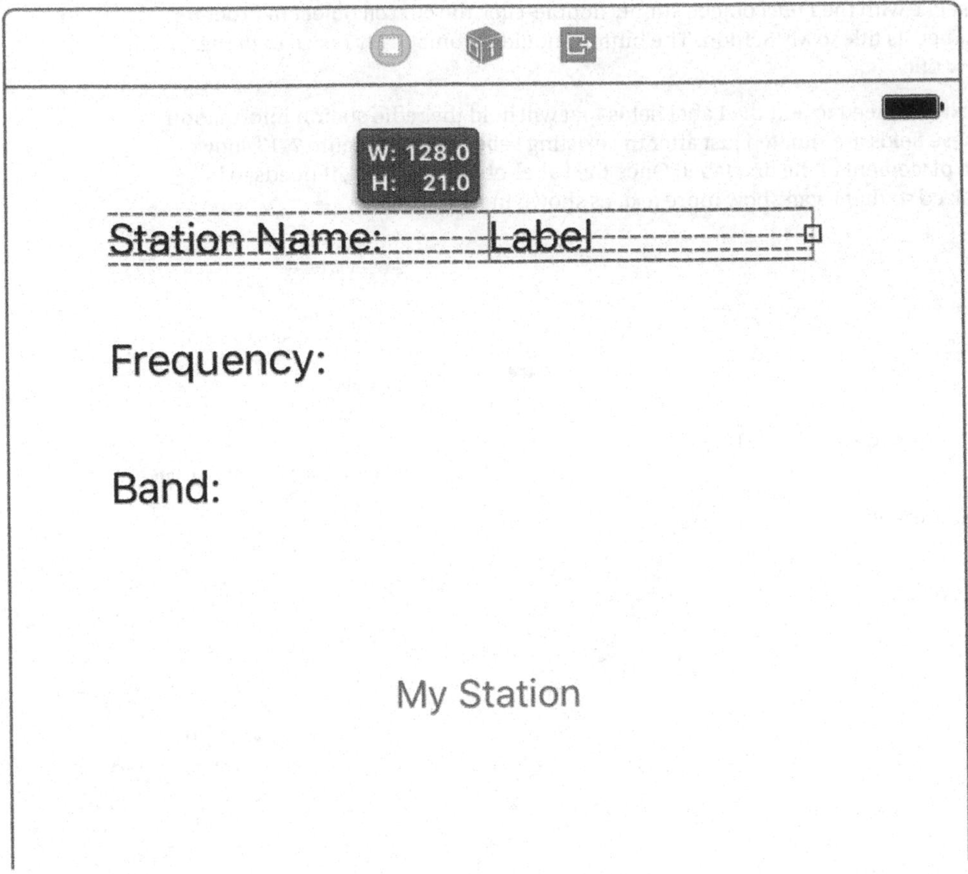

__Figure 7-14.__ Stretching the Label object

■ **Note** Stretching the `Label` object allows the Label's text to contain a reasonably long string. If you didn't resize the `Label` object, the text would be cut off (since it wouldn't fit), or the font size would get smaller.[1]

---

[1]By using either code or Interface Builder, you can customize how the `Label` object reacts to text that is too large to fit. The behavior described is based on typical defaults for the `Label` object.

7. Repeat adding and sizing a `Label` object next to the existing Frequency and Band Labels, as shown in Figure 7-15. It's okay to leave the default text of the label set to "Label" for now.

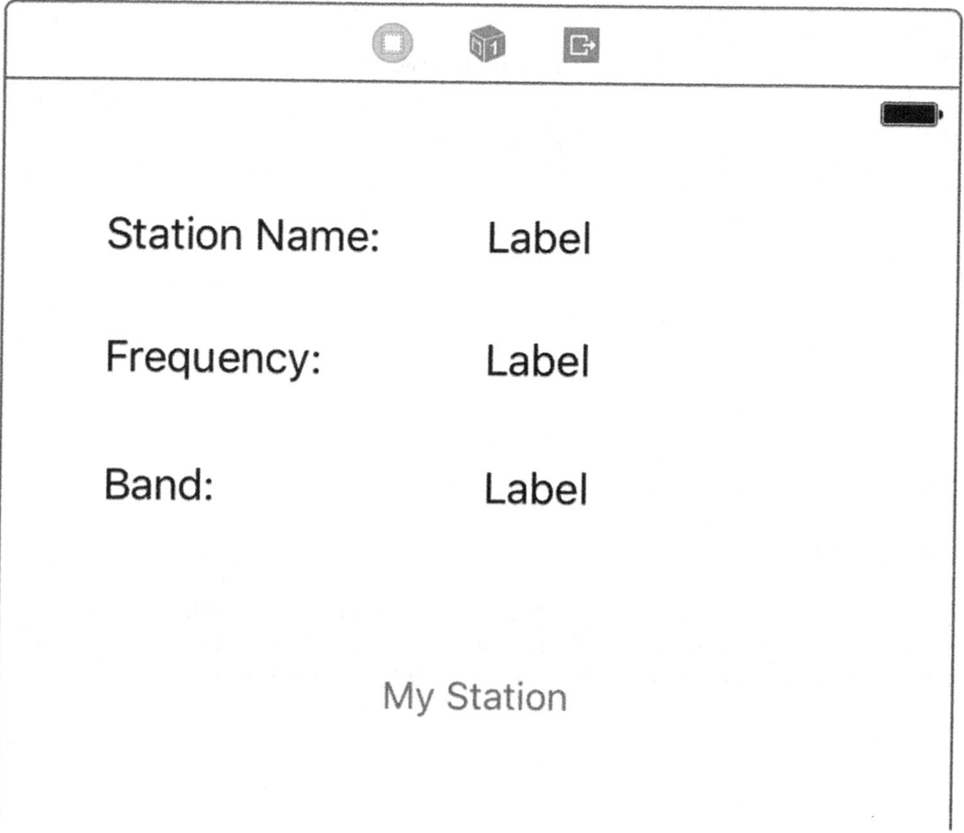

Figure 7-15. *Adding another Label object*

Hooking Up the Code

Now that all the user interface objects are in place, you can begin to hook up these interface elements to the variables in your program. As you saw in Chapter 6, you do this by *connecting* the user interface objects with the objects in your program.

1. Start by connecting the Label object to the right of Station Name to your variable, as shown in Figure 7-16. Right-click (or Control-click) the View Controller object and drag it to the `Label` object next to the Station Name text to bring up the list of outlets.

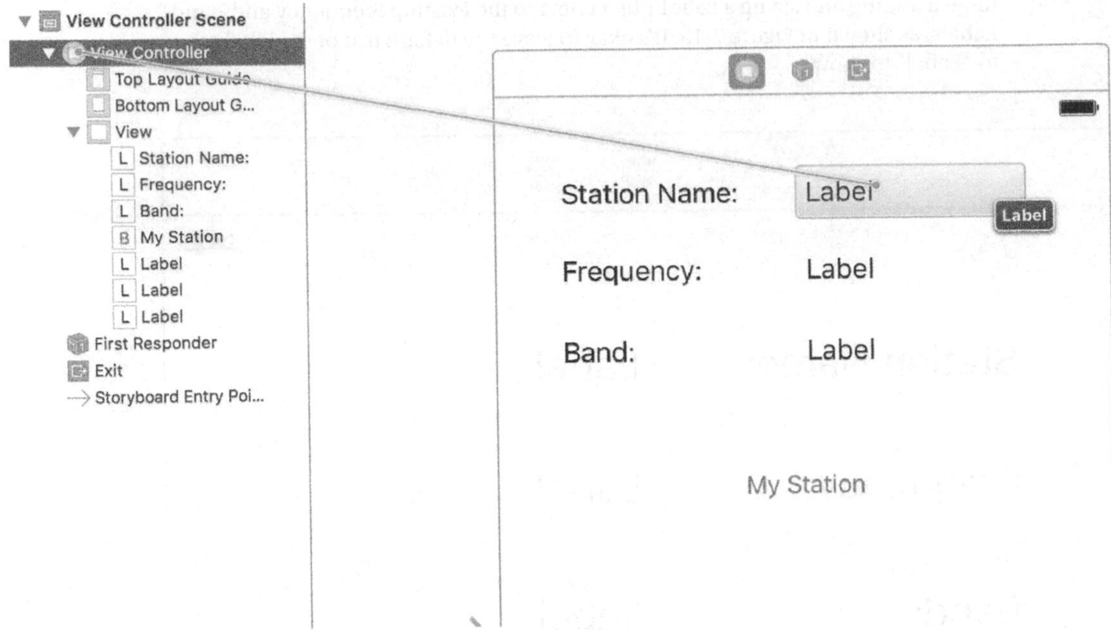

Figure 7-16. Creating a connection

2. When the connection is dropped from the View Controller icon, another small menu will be shown. Click the property name that you want to display in this `Label` object—in this case, you want the `stationName` property, as shown in Figure 7-17.

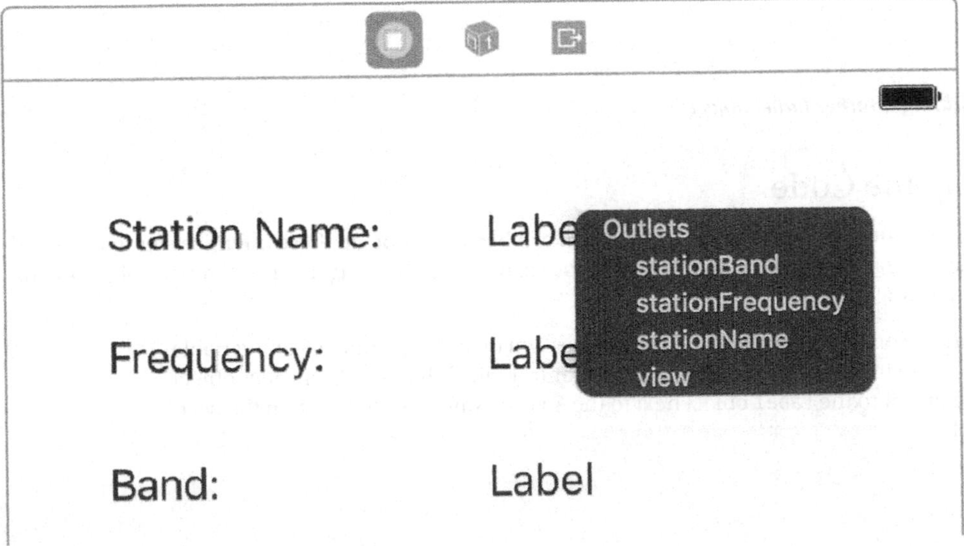

Figure 7-17. Connecting the Label to your stationName variable

3. Now, the interface `Label` object is *connected* to the `stationName` property. Whenever you set the property's value, the screen will also be updated. Repeat the previous connection steps for Frequency and Band.

To hook up your button, you need a method in the `ViewController` class to handle this. You could go to the `ViewController.swift` file and add it there. There is also a shortcut to adding `@IBOutlet` properties and `@IBAction` methods. On the right side of the Xcode toolbar, click the Assistant Editor icon shown in Figure 7-18. (It looks like two circles.)

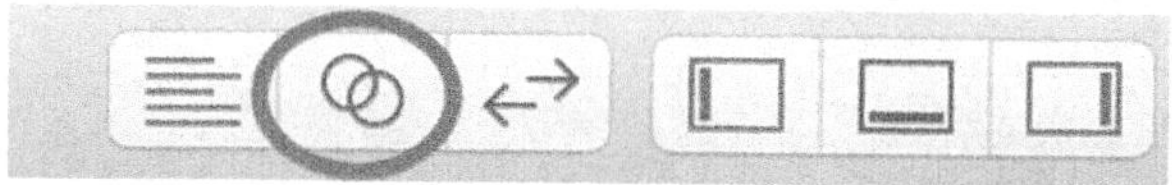

Figure 7-18. *The Assistant Editor icon*

After clicking the Assistant Editor icon, a second window will pop open showing the `ViewController` source. Right-click (or Controller-click) and drag the button to the code window, as shown in Figure 7-19.

Station Name: Label

Frequency: Label

Band: Label

My Station

```
//
//  ViewController.swift
//  RadioStations
//
//  Created by Thornuko on 8/18/16.
//  Copyright © 2016 Innovativeware. All rights
    reserved.
//

import UIKit

class ViewController: UIViewController {

    @IBOutlet var stationName: UILabel!
    @IBOutlet var stationFrequency: UILabel!
    @IBOutlet var stationBand: UILabel!

    var myStation: RadioStation

    required init?(coder aDecoder: NSCoder) {
        myStation = RadioStation()
        myStation.frequency = 102.5
        myStation.name = "KNIX"
        super.init(coder: aDecoder)
    }

    override func viewDidLoad() {
        super.viewDidLoad()
        // Do any additional setup after loading the
            view, typically from a nib.
    }

    override func didReceiveMemoryWarning() {
        super.didReceiveMemoryWarning()
        // Dispose of any resources that can be
            recreated.
    }

}
```

Insert Outlet, Action, or Outlet Collection

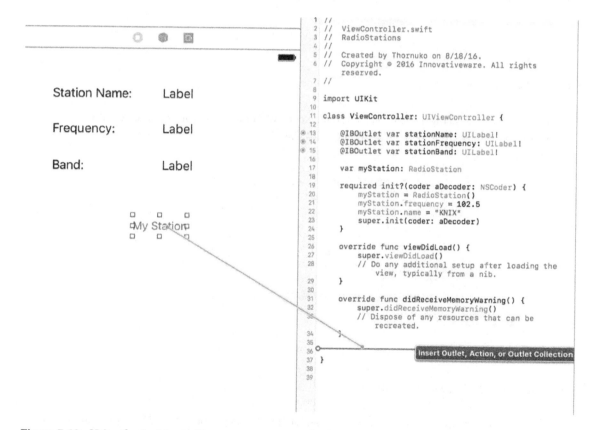

Figure 7-19. *Using the Assistant editor to create your method*

4. When you release the mouse, a little window will pop up, as shown in Figure 7-20.

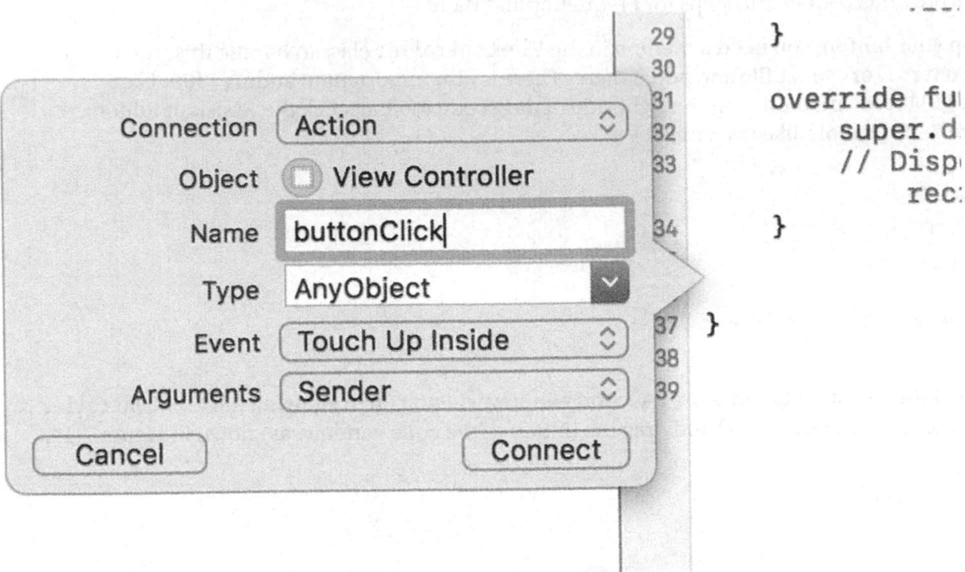

Figure 7-20. *Creating the action*

Select Action and set the name to `buttonClick`. Xcode will now create your method for you. Finish your method by adding the code shown in Figure 7-21.

```
36      @IBAction func buttonClick(_ sender: AnyObject) {
37          stationName.text = myStation.name
38          stationFrequency.text = String(format: "%.1f", myStation.
                frequency)
39
40          if myStation.band() == 1 {
41              stationBand.text = "FM"
42          } else {
43              stationBand.text = "AM"
44          }
45      }
46
47  }
```

Figure 7-21. *Finished buttonClick method*

Let's walk through the code you just added. First, on line 36, you'll notice the `IBAction` attribute. This lets Xcode know that this method can be called as a result of an action. So, when you go to connect an action to your application, you will see this method.

Lines 37 and 38 both set the text fields to the values found in your `RadioStation` class. Line 37 is as follows:

```
stationName.text = myStation.name
```

The `stationName` variable is what you just connected to the user interface `Label` object, and `myStation.name` is used to return the name of the station.

Line 38 effectively does the same thing as line 37, but you have to first convert the double value (the station's frequency) to a `String`. The `"%.1f"` means that you convert a floating-point value and should see only one digit after the decimal point.

Lines 40 to 44 make use of both the instance variables and the type methods of the `RadioStation` class. Here, you simply call the method `band()` on the `myStation` object. If so, the station is an FM station and `band()` will return a 1; otherwise, assume it's the AM band. Lines 41 and 43 show the band value on the screen.

■ **Note** The Button sends the Touch Up Inside event whenever a user touches the inside of the button and then releases—not until the user lifts their finger is the event actually sent.

Running the Program

Once the connection has been made, you're ready to run and test your program! To do this, simply click the Play button at the top left of the Xcode window, as shown in Figure 7-22.

Figure 7-22. *Click the Play button to run your program*

If there are no compile errors, the iPhone Simulator should come up, and you should see your application. Simply click the My Station button, and the radio station information will be displayed, as shown in Figure 7-23.

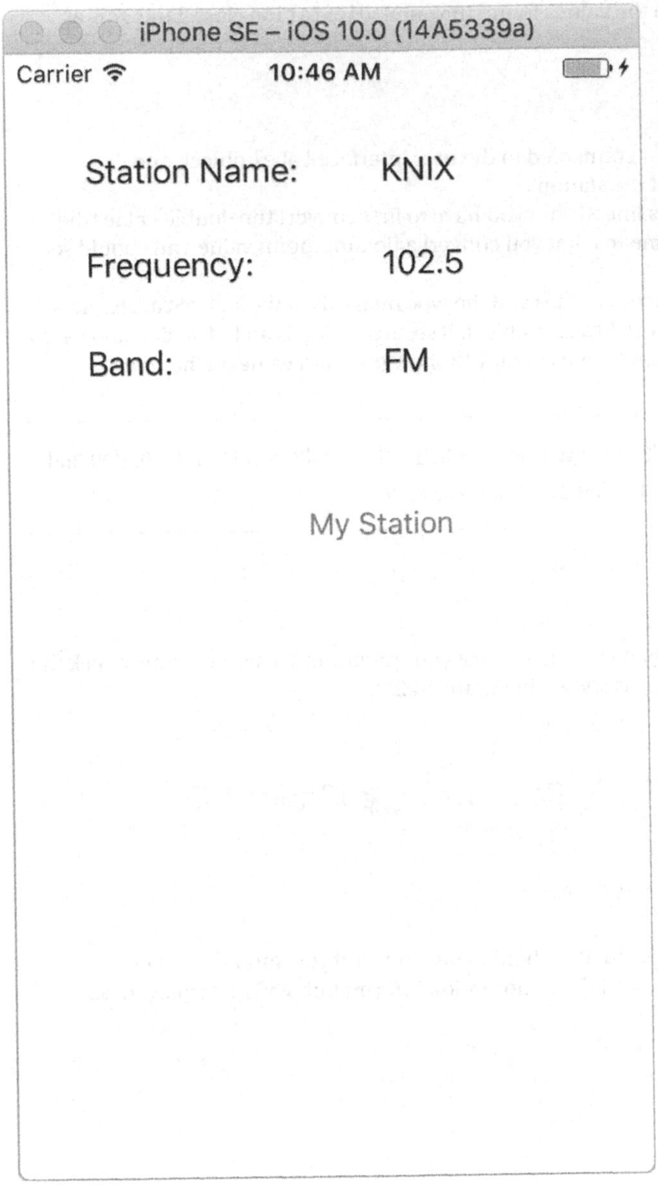

Figure 7-23. *Showing your radio station information*

If things don't quite look or work right, retrace your steps and make sure all the code and connections described in this chapter are in place.

Taking Type methods to the Next Level

In your program, you haven't taken advantage of all the type methods for `RadioStation`, but this chapter does describe what a type method is and how it is used. Use that knowledge to try a few of the exercises mentioned at the end of this chapter. Just play around with this simple working program by adding or changing class or instance methods to get an idea of how they work.

Accessing the Xcode Documentation

There is a wealth of information provided in the Xcode developer documentation. When Xcode is opened, select Help ➤ Documentation and API Reference (see Figure 7-24) to open the Documentation window.

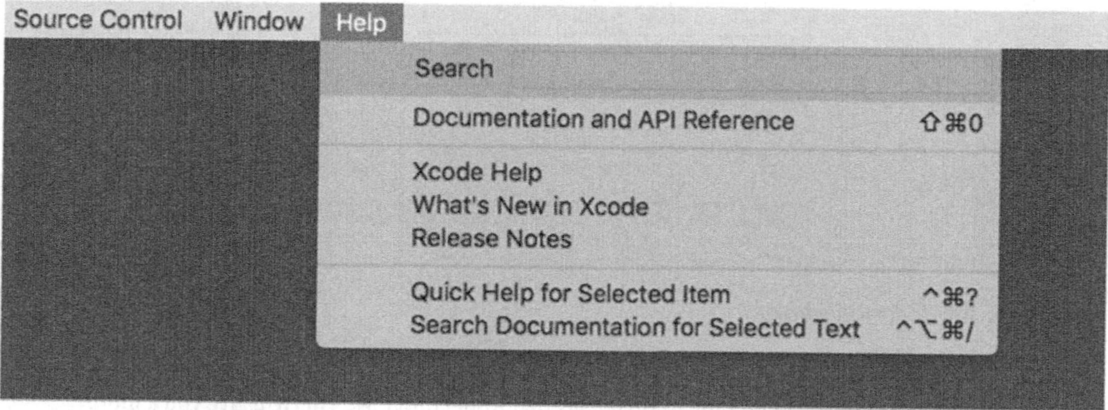

Figure 7-24. *The Xcode Help menu*

Once it's opened, the search window can be used to look up any of the Swift classes you've used in this chapter, including the `String` class documentation, as shown in Figure 7-25.

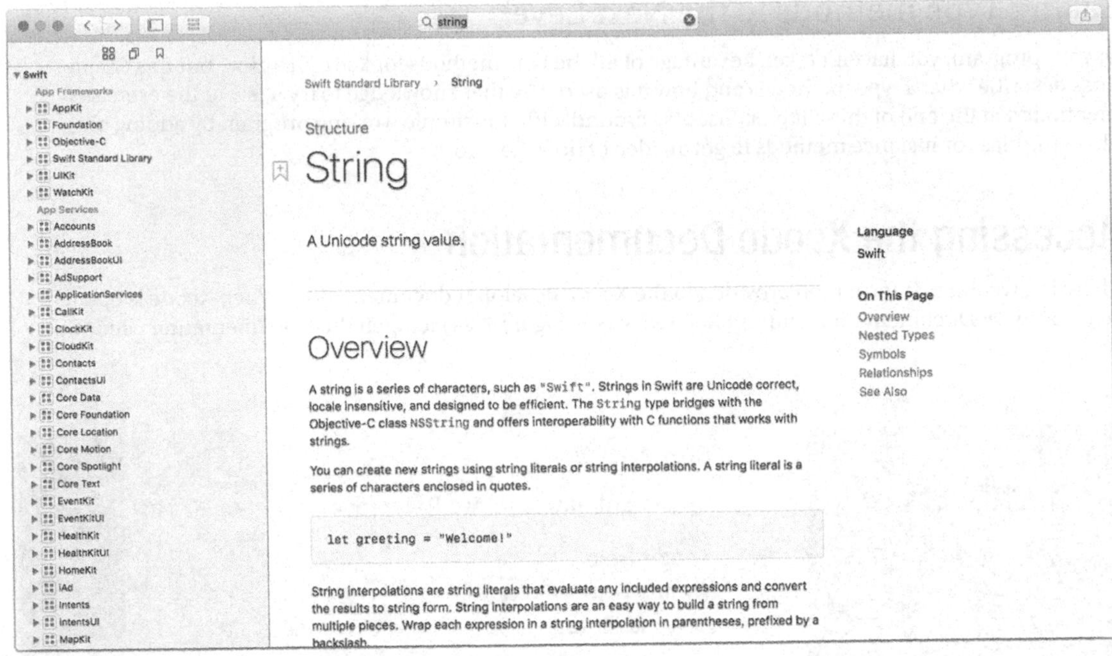

Figure 7-25. *Xcode documentation*

There are several different things to discover about the `String` class shown in Figure 7-25. Go through the documentation and the various companion guides that Apple provides. This will give you a more thorough understanding of the various classes and the various methods supported by them.

Summary

Once again, congratulate yourself for being able to single-handedly stuff your brain with a lot of information! Here is a summary of what was covered in this chapter:

- Swift classes review
  - Type methods
  - Instance methods
- Creating a class
  - Limitations of using type methods vs. instance methods
  - Initializing the class and making use of the instance variables
- Making use of your new `RadioStation` object
  - Building an iPhone app that uses your new object
  - Connecting interface classes to properties
  - Connecting user interface events to methods in your class

EXERCISES

- Change the code that creates your `RadioStation` class and make the station's name much longer than what can appear on the screen. What happens?
- Change the current button and add a new button. Label the buttons FM and AM. If the user clicks the FM button, show an FM station. If the user clicks the AM button, display an AM station. (Hint: you'll need to add a second `RadioStation` object to the `ViewController.swift` file.)
- Clean up the interface a little by making sure that the user doesn't see the text "Label" when the iPhone application first starts.
    - Fix the issue by using the interface tool.
    - How could you fix this by adding code to the application instead?
- Add more validation to the `@IBAction func buttonClick(_ sender: AnyObject)` method. Right now, it validates FM ranges, but not AM ranges. Fix the code so that it also validates an AM range.
    - If the radio station frequency is out of bounds, use the existing labels to display some type of error message.

CHAPTER 8

Programming Basics in Swift

Swift is an elegant language. It mixes the efficiency of a compiled language with the flexibility and modern features of many scripting languages.

This chapter introduces some of the more common concepts in Swift, such as properties and collection classes. It also shows how properties are used from within Xcode when dealing with user interface elements. This sounds like a lot to accomplish, but Swift, the Foundation framework, and the Xcode tool provide a wealth of objects and methods and a way to build applications with ease.

Using let vs. var

If you have spent much time with Swift, you have seen the word `var` appear before variable declarations. You may also have seen `let` before other declarations. The word `var` is used to define a variable, while the word `let` is used to define a constant. This means that if you declare a value with `let`, you will not be able to change the value. The following code defines a constant:

```
let myName = "Brad"
```

Once you define a constant, you cannot change the value.

Caution Xcode 8 will now warn you if you declare a variable and never change its value. It will recommend using `let` instead of `var`.

```
myName = "John"
```

This will give you an error. If you want to create a mutable or changeable variable, you need to use `var`. For example, you can do the following:

```
var myName = "Brad"

myName = "John"
```

This will not give you any errors because `myName` is now a variable. This does not relate to only `Strings` and `Ints`, but it can also be used with collections and other objects.

Variables give you more flexibility, so why would anyone ever want to use a constant? The quick answer is performance. If you know that you have a value that will not change, the compiler can optimize that value as a constant.

G. Bennett and B. Lees, *Swift 3 for Absolute Beginners*, DOI 10.1007/978-1-4842-2331-4_8

Understanding Collections

Understanding collections is a fundamental part of learning Swift. In fact, collection objects are fundamental constructs of nearly every modern object-oriented language library (sometimes they are referred to as *containers*). Simply put, a *collection* is a type of class that can hold and manage other objects. The whole purpose of a collection is that it provides a common way to store and retrieve objects efficiently.

There are several types of collections. While they all fulfill the same purpose of being able to hold other objects, they differ mostly in the way objects are retrieved. The most common collections used in Swift are the Array and the Dictionary.

Both of these collections can be created as constants or regular variables. If you create a collection as a constant, you must fill it with the objects at the time of creation. It cannot be modified after that point.

Using Arrays

The `Array` class is like any other collection in that it allows the programmer to manage a group of objects. An array is an *ordered* collection, which means that objects are entered in an array in a certain order and retrieved in the same order.

■ **Note** There are some methods for working with arrays that allow you to change the order of the objects or to add an object at a specific location in the array.

The `Array` class allows an object to be retrieved by its *index* in the array. An index is the numeric position that an object would occupy in the array. For example, if there are three elements in the array, the objects can be referenced with indexes from 0 to 2. Like with most things in Swift and other programming languages, indexes start at 0, not 1. See Listing 8-1.

Listing 8-1. Accessing Objects in an Array

```
var myArray: [String] = ["One", "Two", "Three"]
print (myArray[0])
print (myArray[1])
print (myArray[2])
```

As you can see, objects in the array can be retrieved via their index. The indexes start at 0 and can't exceed the size of the array minus 1. You can easily calculate the size of the array by sending a `count` message to the `Array` object, as shown here:

```
var entries = myArray.count
```

In fact, every collection type, including `Array` and `Dictionary`, will respond to the `count` message.

Adding items to the end of an array is simple. You can just call the append method on the array. See Listing 8-2.

Listing 8-2. Adding Objects to an Array

```
var myArray: [String] = ["One", "Two", "Three"]
myArray.append("Four")
myArray.append("Five")
myArray.append("Six")
```

Swift provides you with many different methods for adding items to an array. If you want to add multiple objects to an array, you can use the standard += (often called *plus equals*) operator. Listing 8-3 creates an array and then adds three more `String` objects to the array on line 2. Notice the new values are in brackets instead of parentheses.

Listing 8-3. Adding Multiple Objects to an Array

```
1    var myArray: [String] = ["One", "Two", "Three"]
2    myArray += ["Four", "Five", "Six"]
```

As discussed earlier, an array is actually ordered. The order of the objects in your array is important. There may be times where you need to add an item at a certain position in the array. You can accomplish this with the `insert(at:)` method, as shown in Listing 8-4.

Listing 8-4. Adding a String to the Beginning of an Array

```
var myArray: [String] = ["Two", "Three"]
myArray.insert("One", at: 0)
```

The array now contains One, Two, Three.

Accessing items in an array is simple. You can use standard square brackets to access an object at a certain position. For example, `myArray[0]` would give you the first object in the array. If you want to loop through each of the items in the array, you can use something called *fast enumeration* or *For-In Loops*. Listing 8-5 is an example of fast enumeration.

Listing 8-5. Fast Enumeration

```
1    var myArray: [String] = ["One", "Two", "Three"]
2    for myString in myArray {
3        print(myString)
4    }
```

The magic happens in line 2 of Listing 8-5. You tell Swift to assign each value of `myArray` to a new constant called `myString`. You can then do whatever you want to do with `myString`. In this case, you just print it. It will go through all of the objects in the array without you having to know the total number of objects. This is a fast and effective way to pull items out of an array.

Removing objects from an array is simple, too. You can use the `remove(at:)` method, as shown in Listing 8-6.

Listing 8-6. Removing an Object

```
var myArray: [String] = ["One", "Two", "Three"]
myArray.remove(at: 1)
for myString in myArray {
    print(myString)
}
```

The output from Listing 8-6 will be `One, Three`. This is because you removed the object with the index of 1. Remember, this is the second object in the array because array indexes always begin at 0.

You have seen how flexible Swift is in letting you interact with arrays. They are powerful collections that you will use on a regular basis as a programmer. This section covered the basics of arrays, but there are many more things arrays can do.

Using the Dictionary Class

The Swift Dictionary class is also a useful type of collection class. It allows the storage of objects, just like the Array class, but Dictionary is different in that it allows a *key* to be associated with the entry. For example, you could create a dictionary that stores a list of attributes about someone such as a firstName, lastName, and so on. Instead of accessing the attributes with an index like with an array, the dictionary could use a String like "firstName". However, all keys must be unique—that is, "firstName" cannot exist more than once. Depending on your program, finding unique names is normally not a problem.

Here's an example of how you create a dictionary:

```
var person: [String: String] = ["firstName": "John", "lastName": "Doe"]
```

This creates a simple dictionary called person. The next part of the declaration tells the dictionary what kinds of objects the keys and the values will be. In this case, the keys are Strings, and the values are Strings. You then add two keys to the dictionary. The first key is firstName, and that key has a value of John. The second key is lastName, and that has a value of Doe. You can access the values in the dictionary by using a similar notation to arrays:

```
print(person["firstName"])
```

This code will print the name Optional("John") since that is the value for the key firstName. The Optional appears in the previous example because the value of a key in a dictionary is an optional value. You can use the same style of code to change the values in a dictionary. Let's say, for this example, that John now likes to go by Joe instead. You can change the value in the dictionary with a simple line of code:

```
person["firstName"] = "Joe"
```

You can add a new key to a dictionary with the same notation:

```
person["gender"] = "Male"
```

If you decide you want to remove a key from a dictionary, such as the gender key you just added, you can do so by setting the value of that key to nil:

```
person["gender"] = nil
```

Now the dictionary will contain only firstName and lastName. Remember that dictionaries are not ordered. You cannot rely on the order, but there will be times when you need to iterate over a dictionary. This is done in a manner similar to arrays. The main difference is that in an array, you assign one variable, while in a dictionary, you need to assign the key and the value. See Listing 8-7.

Listing 8-7. Iterating over a Dictionary

```
var person: [String: String] = ["firstName": "John", "lastName": "Doe"]
for (myKey, myValue) in person {
      print(myKey + ": " + myValue)
}
```

This example will print the following:

```
firstName: John
lastName: Doe
```

Dictionaries are a great way to organize data that does not need to be ordered. It is also a great way to look up data based on a certain key. They are very flexible in Swift and should be used to organize and optimize your code.

Creating the BookStore Application

You are going to create an app that will demonstrate how to use arrays. You will create a `UITableView` and use an array to populate the `UITableView` with data. Let's start by creating the base application project. Open Xcode and select a new Master-Detail Application project, as shown in Figure 8-1. In this project, you will create a few simple objects for what is to become your bookstore application: a `Book` object and the `BookStore` object. You'll visit properties again and see how to get and set the value of one during this project. Lastly, you'll put the bookstore objects to use, and you'll learn how to make use of objects once you've created them.

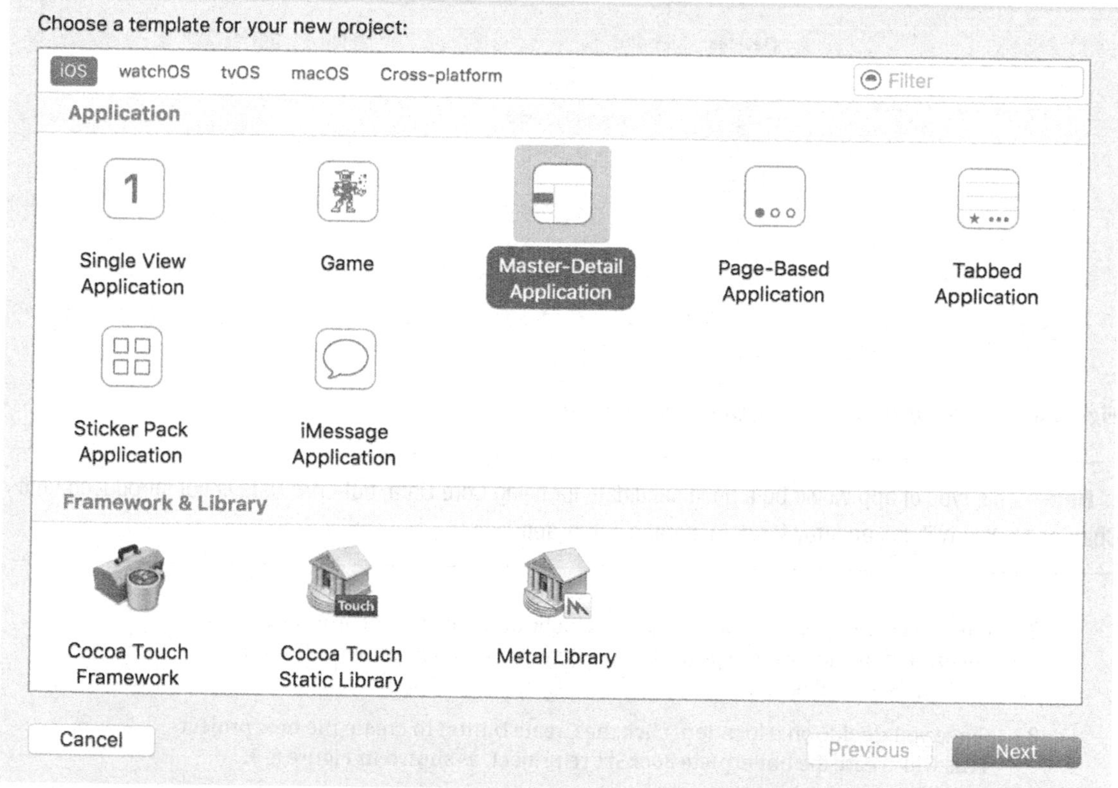

Figure 8-1. *Creating the initial project based on the Master-Detail Application template*

1. Click the Next button and name the project **BookStore**, as shown in Figure 8-2. The company name is required—you can use any company name, real or otherwise. The example uses `com.innovativeware`, which is perfectly fine. Make sure the device family is iPhone and that the Language is set to Swift. Do not check the Use Core Data checkbox.

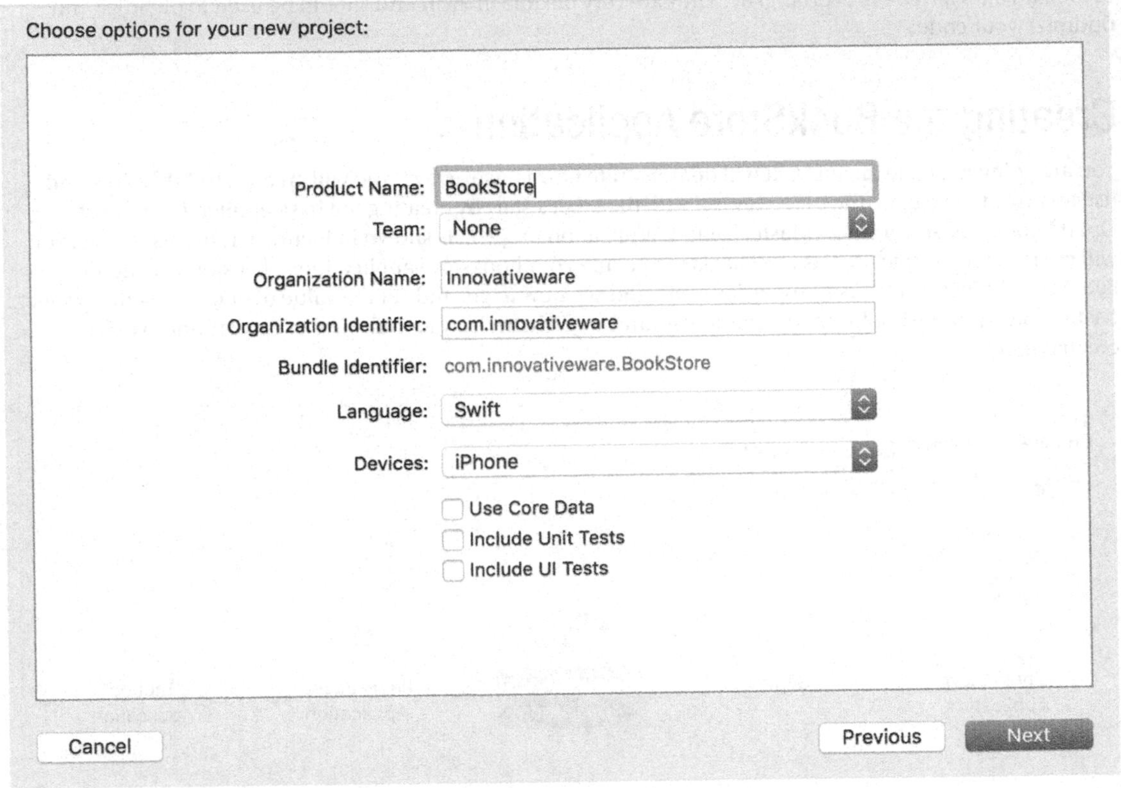

Figure 8-2. *Selecting the product (application) name and options*

■ **Note** This type of app would be a good candidate for using Core Data, but Core Data is not introduced until Chapter 11. You will use an array for data storage in this app.

---

2. Once everything is filled out, click the Next button. Xcode will prompt you to specify a place to save the project. Anywhere you can remember is fine—the desktop is a good place.

3. Once you decide on a location, click the Create button to create the new project. This will create the boilerplate `BookStore` project, as shown in Figure 8-3.

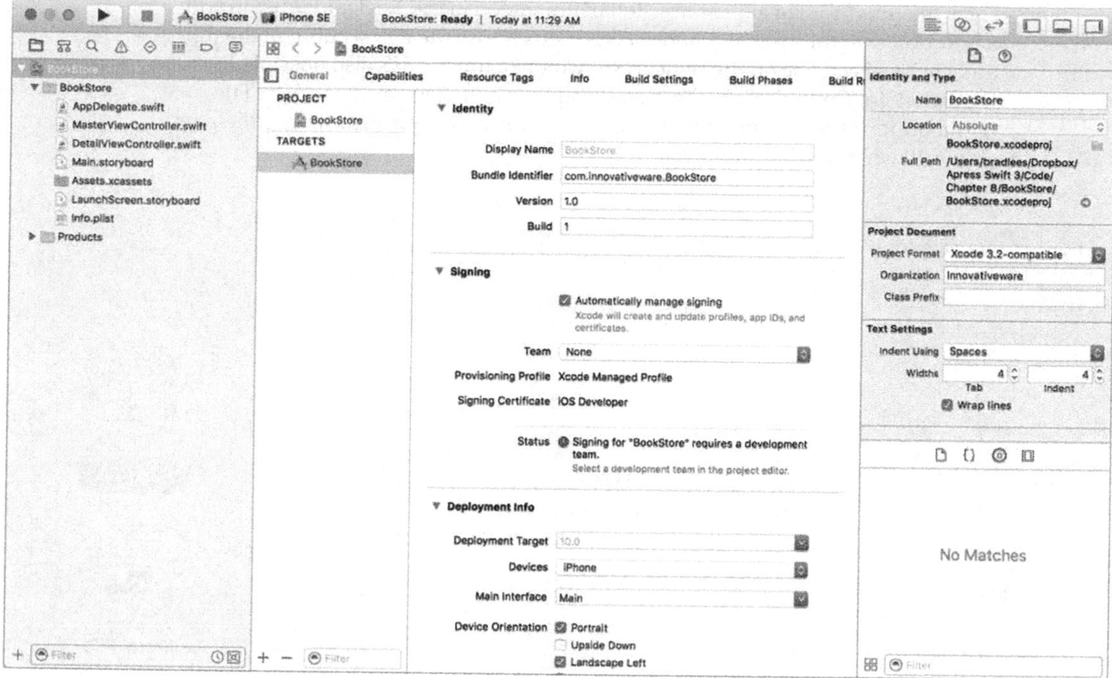

Figure 8-3. *The source listing of the boilerplate project*

4. Click the plus (+) sign at the lower-left of the screen in the Navigator area to add a new object to the project. Choose File. Then choose the iOS section on the top and choose Swift File on the right, as shown in Figure 8-4. It's also possible to right-click (or Control-click) the Navigation area and then select the New File menu option. There is no difference between this approach and clicking the plus sign—do whatever feels more natural.

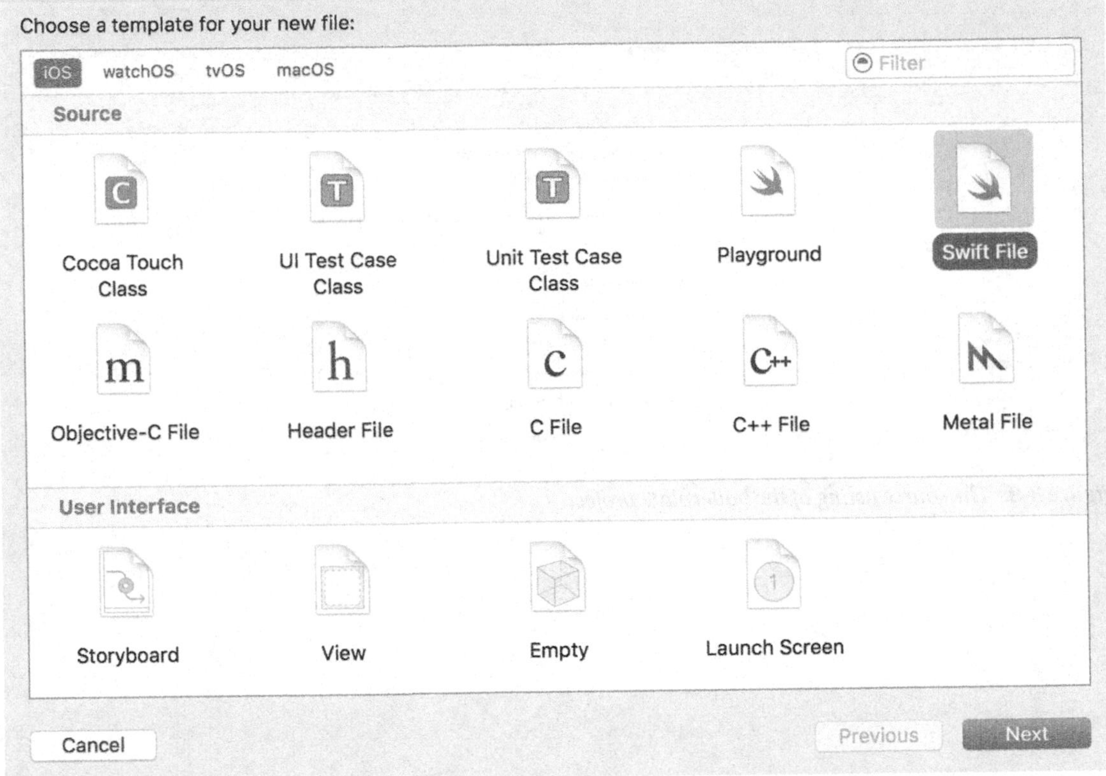

***Figure 8-4.** Creating a new Swift file*

5. You're choosing a plain Swift file, which will create a new empty Swift file that you're going to use for the Book class. After selecting this, click the Next button.

6. Xcode will ask you what to name your file. Use the name Book. Xcode will also ask to which folder it should save the new file. To keep things simple, choose the BookStore folder in your project. This is where all the other class files for the project are stored.

7. Double-click the `BookStore` folder and then click the Create button. You'll see the main edit window for Xcode and the new file, `Book.swift`, in the Navigator area, as shown in Figure 8-5.

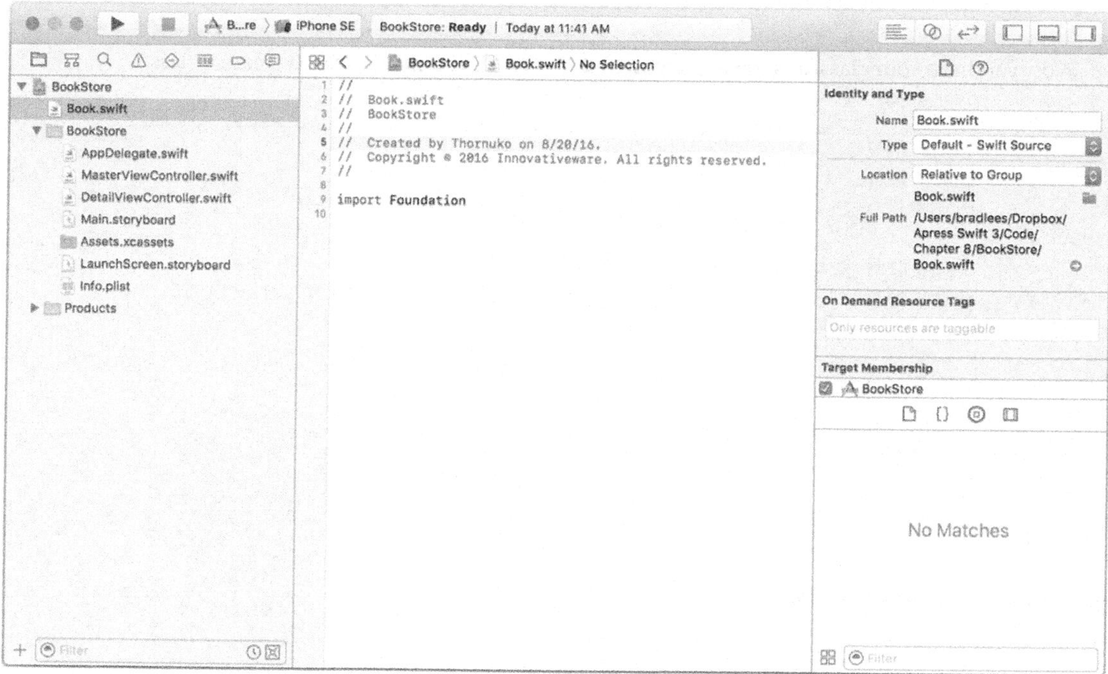

Figure 8-5. *The empty Swift file*

8. Repeat the previous steps and create a second object called `BookStore`. This will create a `BookStore.swift` file. You'll be using this class later in this chapter. For now, you'll concentrate on the Book class.

9. Click the `Book.swift` file and let's start defining your new class!

Creating Your Class

By adding a Swift rather than a Cocoa Touch class, Xcode creates an empty Swift file. You can add multiple classes to this file. Swift is more flexible, and it is not necessary to have only one class per file. Xcode allows you to add the classes as you want.

■ **Note** It is still a good idea to keep your Swift classes in separate files. This makes organizing and finding classes easier, especially when you're dealing with large projects. However, there will be cases where a smaller class is only used with another class and it makes sense to keep them in the same file.

Let's create the Book class. Type the following code into the `Book.swift` file:

```
class Book {

}
```

Now you have your class, as shown in Figure 8-6. That is all you need to do to create a class.

```
//
//  Book.swift
//  BookStore
//
//  Created by Thornuko on 8/20/16.
//  Copyright © 2016 Innovativeware. All rights reserved.
//

import Foundation

class Book {

}
```

Figure 8-6. *The empty Book class*

Introducing Properties

The class is simply called Book. True, you have a class, but it doesn't *store* anything at this point. For this class to be useful, it needs to be able to hold some information, which is done with properties. When an object is used, it has to be instantiated. Once the object is instantiated, it has access to its properties. These variables are available to the object as long as the object stays in scope. As you know from Chapter 7, scope defines the context in which an object exists. In some cases, an object's scope may be the life of the program. In other cases, the scope might be just a function or method. It all depends on where the object is declared and how it's used. Scope will be discussed later in more depth. For now, let's add some properties to the Book class to make it more useful.(See Listing 8-8.)

Listing 8-8. Adding Instance Variables to the Book.swift File

```
//
//  Book.swift
//  BookStore
//
//  Created by Thornuko on 8/20/16.
//  Copyright © 2016 Innovativeware. All rights reserved.
//

import Foundation
 class Book {
     var title: String = ""
     var author: String = ""
```

```
13        var description: String = ""
14
15    }
```

Listing 8-8 shows the same Book object from before, but now there are three new properties placed inside the braces, on lines 11 to 13. These are all `String` objects, which means they can hold text information for the Book object. So, the Book object now has a place to store title, author, and description information.

Accessing Properties

Now that you have some properties, how can you use them? How are they accessed? Unfortunately, simply declaring a property doesn't necessarily give you access to it. There are two ways to access these variables:

- One way, of course, is within the Book object.
- The second way is from outside the object—that is, another part of the program that uses the Book object.

If you are writing the code for a method within the Book object, accessing its property is quite simple. For example, you could simply write the following:

```
title = "Test Title"
```

From outside the object, you can still access the `title` variable. This is done through the use of dot notation:

```
myBookObject.title = "Test Title"
```

Finishing the BookStore Program

With the understanding of properties, you are going to now venture forth to create the actual bookstore program. The idea is simple enough—create a class called `BookStore` that will be stocked with a few Book objects.

Creating the View

Let's start by first getting the view ready. If you need a refresher on how to build an interface in Xcode, refer to Chapter 6.

1. Click the `Main.storyboard` file in the Navigator area. This will display Xcode's Interface Builder, as shown in Figure 8-7. You will see five scenes in the `Main.storyboard` file. Navigate to the right to find the Detail Scene.

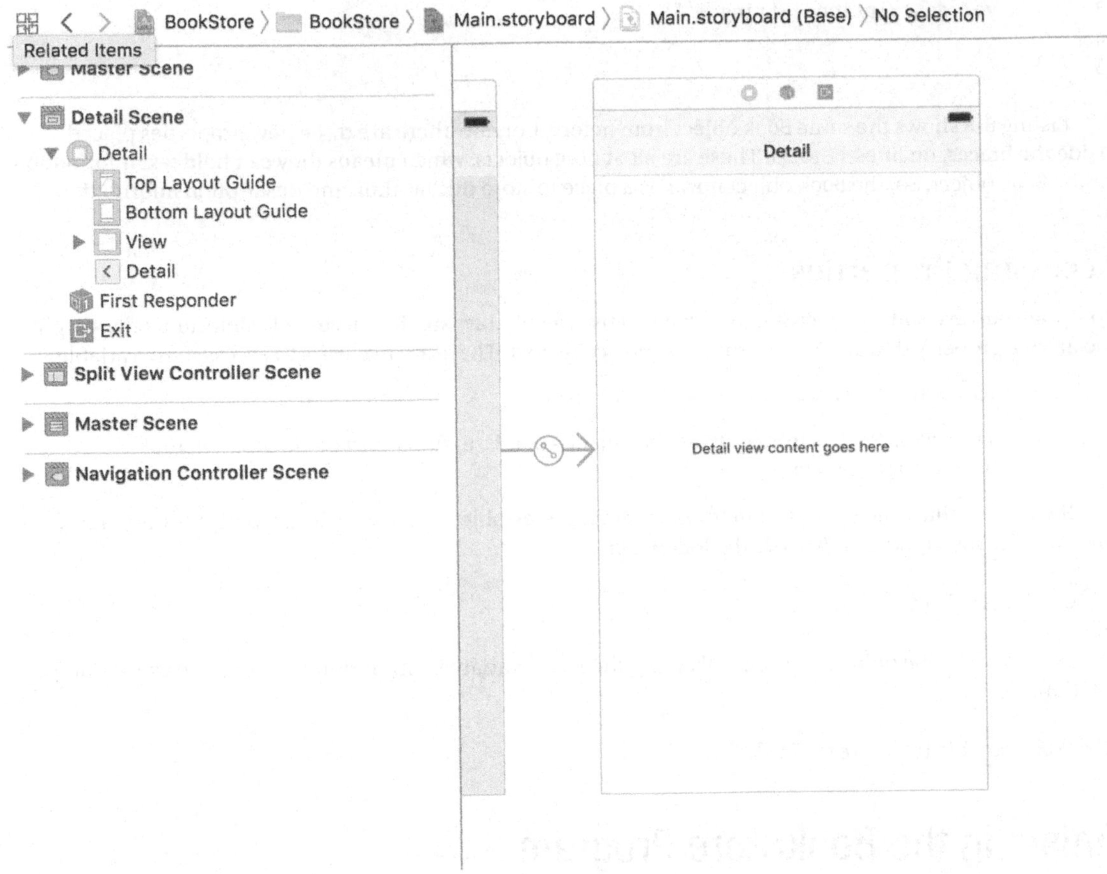

Figure 8-7. Preparing the Bookstore's Detail View

2. By default, when you create a blank Master-Detail application, Xcode adds a label with the text "Detail View content goes here." Select and delete this `Label` object because you are going to add your own. You're going to add some new fields to display some details about a selected book. Since you deleted this control, you also need to remove the code that references it.

   a. In the `DetailViewController.swift` file, remove the following line:

   ```
   @IBOutlet weak var detailDescriptionLabel: UILabel!
   ```

   b. In the `var detailItem: AnyObject?` property declaration, remove the following line:

   ```
   self.configureView()
   ```

c. In the method named configureView, remove the following lines:

```
// Update the user interface for the detail item.
if let detail: AnyObject = self.detailItem {
    if let label = self.detailDescriptionLabel {
    label.text = detail.description            }
}
```

Your DetailViewController.swift file should now look like Figure 8-8.

```
//
//  DetailViewController.swift
//  BookStore
//
//  Created by Thornuko on 8/20/16.
//  Copyright © 2016 Innovativeware. All rights reserved.
//

import UIKit

class DetailViewController: UIViewController {



    func configureView() {

    }

    override func viewDidLoad() {
        super.viewDidLoad()
        // Do any additional setup after loading the view,
            typically from a nib.

    }

    override func didReceiveMemoryWarning() {
        super.didReceiveMemoryWarning()
        // Dispose of any resources that can be recreated.
    }

    var detailItem: NSDate? {
        didSet {
            // Update the view.
            self.configureView()
        }
    }


}
```

Figure 8-8. *Modified DetailViewController*

3. Drag some `Label` objects from the Object Library onto the Detail View, as shown in Figure 8-9. Make sure that the lower Label controls are wider than the default. This is so that they can hold a fairly large amount of text. The two Label objects with the text "Label" in them are the ones you're going to hook up to hold two of the values from the `Book` object: `Title` and `Author`.

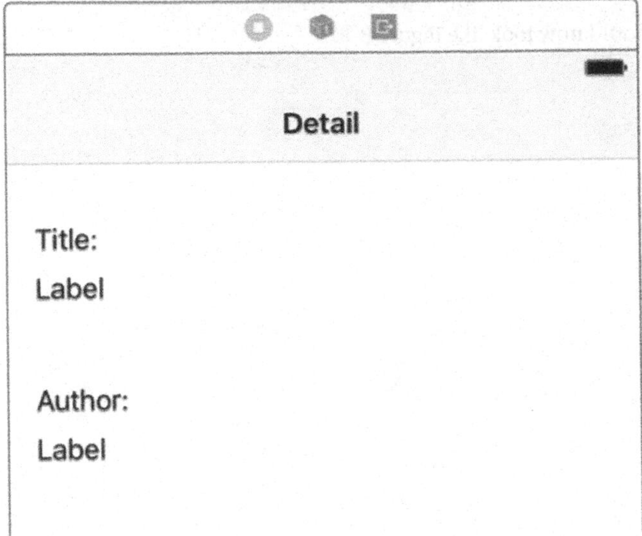

Figure 8-9. *Adding some Label objects*

Adding Properties

Next, you'll add some properties to the `DetailViewController` class. These properties will correspond to the Detail View's Label objects.

1. Click the Assistant Editor icon (it looks like two circles) in the top-right corner of Xcode to open the Assistant editor. Make sure the `DetailViewController.swift` file is showing in the editor.
2. Hold the Control key and drag the first blank Label control to the code on the right side, as shown in Figure 8-10. Name the first one `titleLabel` (see Figure 8-11) and click Connect. Repeat the process with the second one, naming it `authorLabel`. This will add two variables to your `DetailViewController` class, as seen in Listing 8-9, and hook them to the Label controls in the interface.

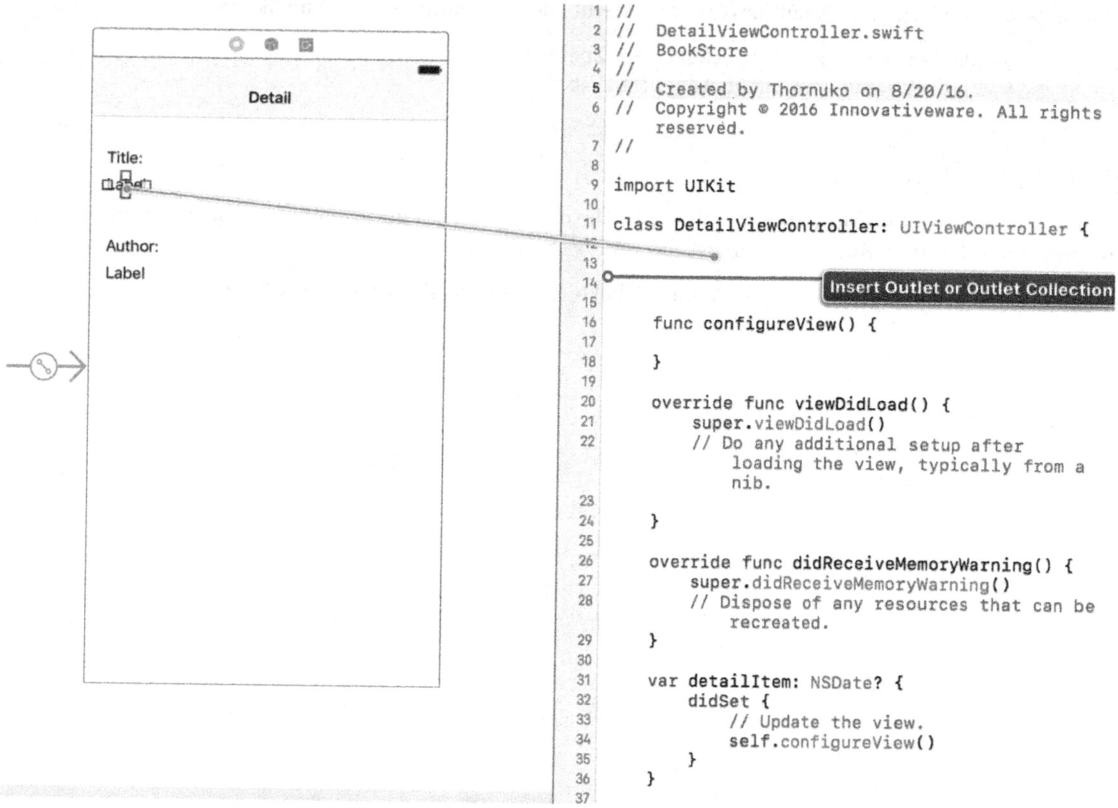

Detail

Title:

Label

Author:

Label

Insert Outlet or Outlet Collection

```
//
//  DetailViewController.swift
//  BookStore
//
//  Created by Thornuko on 8/20/16.
//  Copyright © 2016 Innovativeware. All rights
    reserved.
//

import UIKit

class DetailViewController: UIViewController {



    func configureView() {

    }

    override func viewDidLoad() {
        super.viewDidLoad()
        // Do any additional setup after
            loading the view, typically from a
            nib.

    }

    override func didReceiveMemoryWarning() {
        super.didReceiveMemoryWarning()
        // Dispose of any resources that can be
            recreated.
    }

    var detailItem: NSDate? {
        didSet {
            // Update the view.
            self.configureView()
        }
    }

```

Figure 8-10. *Creating variables*

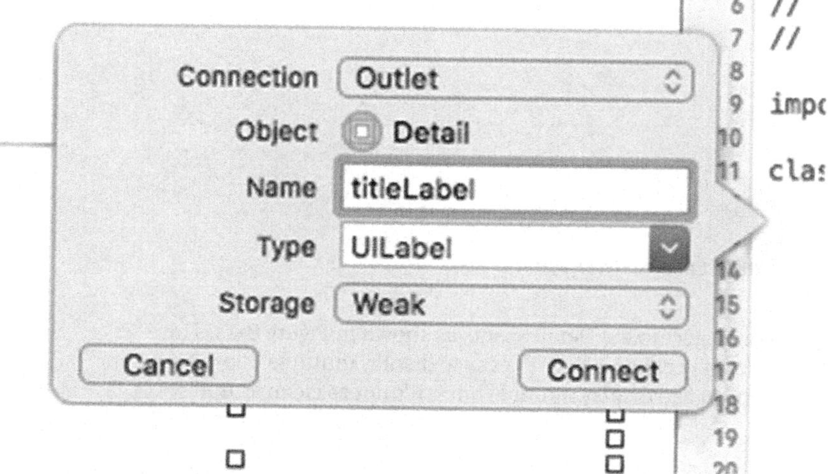

Figure 8-11. *Naming the new variable*

Listing 8-9. Modifying the DetailViewController.swift File to Include the New Labels

```
        @IBOutlet weak var titleLabel: UILabel!
        @IBOutlet weak var authorLabel: UILabel!
```

Adding a Description

Now you need to add the description to the view. The description is a little different in that it can span multiple lines. For this, you're going to use the `Text View` object.

1. Start by adding the "Description:" label to the view, as shown in Figure 8-12.

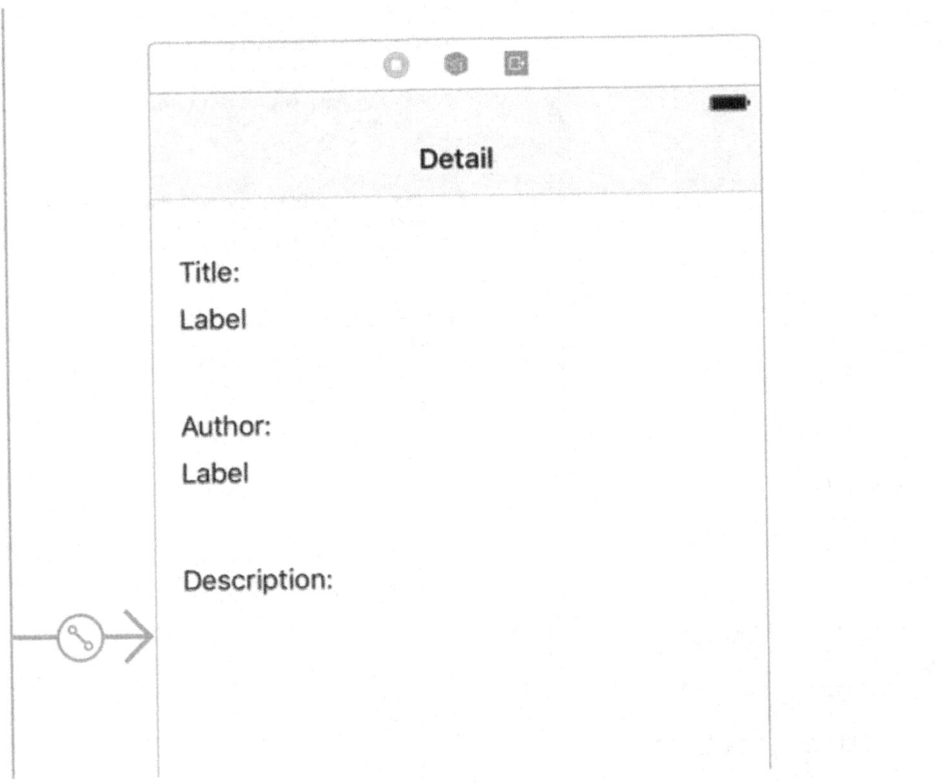

Figure 8-12. *Adding a new Label object for the description*

2. Next, add the `Text View` object to the Detail Scene, as shown in Figure 8-13. The advantage the `Text View` object has is that it's easy to display multiple lines of text. While the `Label` object can display multiple lines, it's not as clean as the `Text View` object.

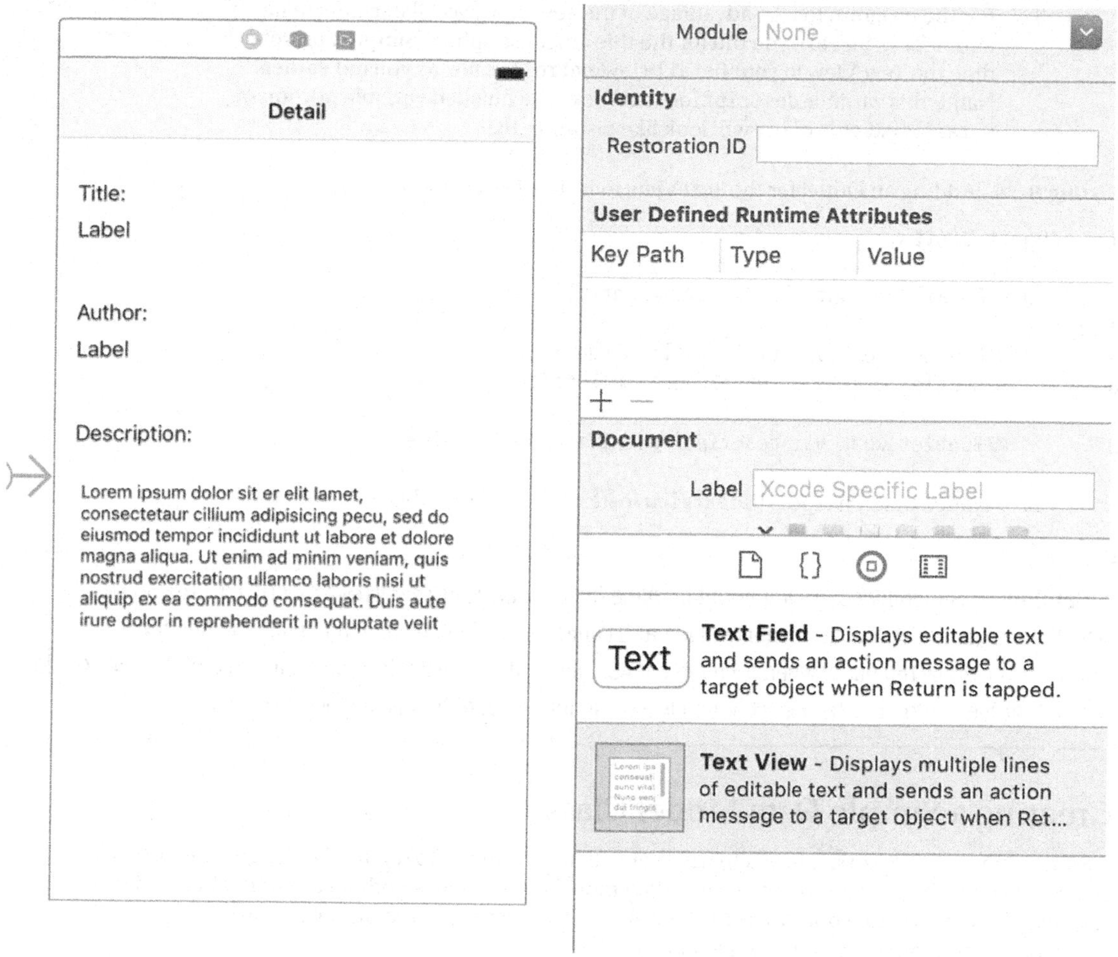

Detail

Title:
Label

Author:
Label

Description:

Lorem ipsum dolor sit er elit lamet, consectetaur cillium adipisicing pecu, sed do eiusmod tempor incididunt ut labore et dolore magna aliqua. Ut enim ad minim veniam, quis nostrud exercitation ullamco laboris nisi ut aliquip ex ea commodo consequat. Duis aute irure dolor in reprehenderit in voluptate velit

Module None
Identity
Restoration ID
User Defined Runtime Attributes
Key Path Type Value
Document
Label Xcode Specific Label
Text
Text Field - Displays editable text and sends an action message to a target object when Return is tapped.
Text View - Displays multiple lines of editable text and sends an action message to a target object when Ret...

***Figure 8-13.** Adding a Text View to the Detail View*

■ **Note** By default, the Text View control is filled with all kinds of seemingly random text. This text is called *Lorem Ipsum* text. If you ever need to fill up a page with text, you can find any number of Lorem Ipsum generators on the Web. As for the Text View control, the text can stay as it is since you'll remove it during runtime. Plus, if it's cleared, it becomes a little more difficult spotting exactly where the Text View control is on the screen—it's white on white!

---

3. For the program to take advantage of the Text View, you'll need to create an outlet for it, just like you did for the title and description. Simply Control-drag the Text View to your `DetailViewController` file, as you did earlier. Name this variable `descriptionTextView`. The finished variable portion of `DetailViewController` will look like Listing 8-10.

Listing 8-10. Adding an Outlet for the Text View to Hold a Description

```
import UIKit

class DetailViewController: UIViewController {

    @IBOutlet weak var titleLabel: UILabel!
    @IBOutlet weak var authorLabel: UILabel!

    @IBOutlet weak var descriptionTextView: UITextView!
```

4. Notice that the type is `UITextView` instead of `UILabel`—this is important.

■ **Caution** As mentioned, it's important to make the `descriptionTextView` property a `UITextView` type. If, for example, it was accidentally made a `UILabel` object, Xcode wouldn't be able to find the `descriptionTextView` outlet when trying to connect the Text View from the screen to the outlet. Why? Xcode knows that the control is a `UITextView` and is looking for an outlet that is of type `UITextView`.

Creating a Simple Data Model Class

For the application to work, it needs to have some data to display. To do this, you're going to use the `BookStore` object you created earlier as the data model class. There's nothing different about a data model class except that its whole purpose is to allow an application to access data via an object.

Modify the `BookStore.swift` file to look like Listing 8-11.

Listing 8-11. Modifying the BookStore.swift Class to Include an Array

```
//
//  BookStore.swift
//  BookStore
//
//  Created by Brad Lees on 8/20/16.
//  Copyright © 2016 Innovativeware. All rights reserved.
//

 import Foundation

 class BookStore {
     var theBookStore: [Book] = []
 }
```

On line 12, you add a variable that will hold the list of books; the property is simply named `theBookStore`. Note that `theBookStore` is an array, which will allow you to add a series of objects, in this case, a set of Book objects.

Next, let's continue adding the code to the Swift file, `BookStore.swift`, as shown in Listing 8-12.

Listing 8-12. Implementing the BookStore Data Object

```
1 //
2 //  BookStore.swift
3 //  BookStore
4 //
5 //  Created by Brad Lees on 8/20/16.
6 //  Copyright © 2016 Innovativeware. All rights reserved.
7 //
8
9    import Foundation
10
11    class BookStore {
12        var theBookStore: [Book] = []
13
14        init() {
15            var newBook = Book()
16            newBook.title = "Swift for Absolute Beginners"
17            newBook.author = "Bennett and Lees"
18            newBook.description = "iOS Programming made easy."
19            theBookStore.append(newBook)
20
21            newBook = Book()
22            newBook.title = "A Farewell To Arms"
23            newBook.author = "Ernest Hemingway"
24            newBook.description = "The story of an affair between an English nurse and an American soldier on the Italian front during World War I."
25
26            theBookStore.append(newBook)
27        }
28    }
```

In Listing 8-12, lines 14 to 27 define the `init` method of the object, which is called whenever the object is first initialized. In this method, you initialize the two books you plan to add to your bookstore. Line 15 is where the first Book object is allocated and initialized. Lines 16 to 18 add a title, author, and description to your first book. Finally, line 19 adds the new Book object to the `theBookStore` array. The important thing to note here is that once the object is added to the array, the code can forget about it; the array now owns that object. Because of this, line 21 is not a problem.

Line 21 allocates a new Book object overwriting the old value. This tells the compiler that you're no longer interested in using the old value.

Lines 22 to 26 simply initialize and add the second book to the array.

That's it! That's all you need to define a simple data model class. Next, you need to modify `MasterViewController` to access this class so that it can start displaying some data.

Modifying MasterViewController

The simple application has two view controllers: the main view controller, which is called `MasterViewController`, and a secondary one called `DetailViewController`. View controllers are objects that simply control the behavior of a view. For the application to start displaying data from the data model, you need to first modify `MasterViewController`—this is where the navigation of the application begins. The following code is already in place in the template that Xcode has provided. You're just going to modify it to add your data model.

First, you'll need to modify the `MasterViewController.swift` file. You need to add a variable to hold the `Bookstore` object. Listing 8-13 shows that the instance variable is added as a property on line 15.

Listing 8-13. Adding the BookStore Object

```
1 //
2 //  MasterViewController.swift
3 //  BookStore
4 //
5 //  Created by Thornuko on 8/20/16.
6 //  Copyright (c) 2016 Innovativeware. All rights reserved.
7 //
8
9 import UIKit
10
11
12 class MasterViewController: UITableViewController {
13
14    var detailViewController: DetailViewController? = nil
15     var objects = [AnyObject]()
16     var myBookStore: BookStore = BookStore()
```

Now that the `BookStore` object is initialized, you need to tell `MasterViewController` how to display the list of books—not the detail, just the book titles. To do this, you'll need to modify a few methods. Fortunately, Xcode has provided a nice template, so the modifications are small.

`MasterViewController` is a subclass of what's called a `UITableViewController` class, which displays rows of data to the screen. In this case, these are rows of book titles (well, just two for this simple program, but a list nonetheless).

There are three main methods that control what and how data is displayed in a `UITableViewController`.

- The first is `numberOfSections(in:)`: Since the application has only one list, or section, this method returns 1.
- The second is `tableView(_:numberOfRowsInSection:)`: In this program, you return the number of books in the bookstore array. Since this is the only section, the code is straightforward.
- The third method is `tableView(_:cellForRowAt:)`: This method is called for each row that is to be displayed on the screen, and it's called one row at a time.

Listing 8-14 details the changes you need to make to get the list of books displaying on the view. The changes start on line 63 in the source file.

Listing 8-14. Setting Up the View to Display the Books

```
63 override func numberOfSections(in tableView: UITableView) -> Int {
64         return 1
65     }
66
67     override func tableView(_ tableView: UITableView, numberOfRowsInSection section: Int)
-> Int {
68         return myBookStore.theBookStore.count
69     }
70
71     override func tableView(_ tableView: UITableView, cellForRowAt indexPath: IndexPath) ->
UITableViewCell {
72         let cell = tableView.dequeueReusableCellWithIdentifier("Cell", forIndexPath:
indexPath)
73         cell.textLabel!.text = myBookStore.theBookStore[indexPath.row].title
74         cell.accessoryType =.disclosureIndicator
75         return cell
76     }
```

Out of all of this code, you need to modify only a few lines. Everything else can stay the way it is. This is one of the advantages of using the Xcode templates. Line 68 simply returned 1; you needed to change it so that it now returns the count of items in the BookStore class.

Line 73 looks a little more complicated. Basically, each line of the `UITableView` is what is called a *cell* (a `UITableViewCell` to be specific). Line 73 sets the text of the cell to the title of a book. Let's look at that code a little more specifically:

```
cell.textLabel!.text = myBookStore.theBookStore[indexPath.row].title
```

First, `myBookStore` is the `BookStore` object, which is pretty clear. You're referencing the array in the `BookStore` object called `theBookStore`. Since `theBookStore` is an array, you can access the book you want in brackets in the `indexPath.row`. The value `indexPath.row` specifies which row you're interested in—`indexPath.row` will always be less than the total count minus 1. So, calling `myBookStore.theBookStore[indexPath.row]` returns a `Book` object. The last part, `.title`, accesses the `title` property from the returned `Book` object. The following code is equivalent to what you just did in one line:

```
var book: Book
book = myBookStore.theBookStore[indexPath.row]
cell.textLabel!.text = book.title
```

Now, you should be able to build and run the application and see the two books you created in the data model, as shown in Figure 8-14.

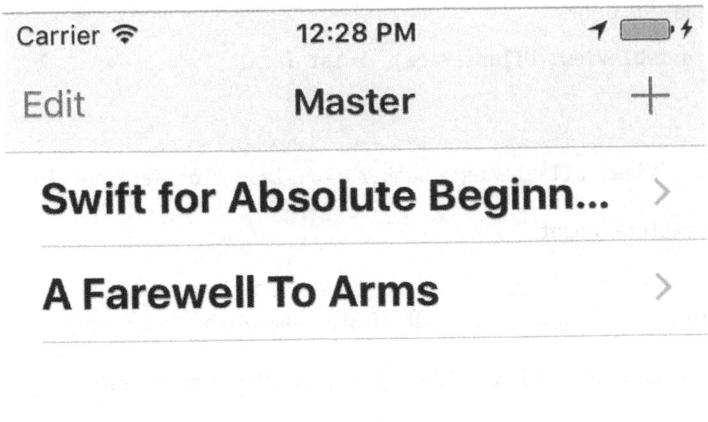

Figure 8-14. *Running the application for the first time*

But, you're not done yet. You need to make the application display the book when you click one of them. To make this happen, you need to make one last modification to `MasterViewController`.

The method `prepareForSegue` is called whenever a row is touched on the screen. This method is called each time your app transitions to a different view in the Storyboard. Listing 8-15 shows the small changes you need to make in order to hook the Detail View to the book data.

Listing 8-15. Selecting the Book When Touched

```
50 override func prepareForSegue(segue: UIStoryboardSegue, sender: AnyObject?) {
51         if segue.identifier == "showDetail" {
52             if let indexPath = self.tableView.indexPathForSelectedRow {
53                 let selectedBook:Book = myBookStore.theBookStore[indexPath.row]
54                 let controller = (segue.destination as! UINavigationController).
topViewController as! DetailViewController
55                 controller.detailItem = selectedBook
56                 controller.navigationItem.leftBarButtonItem = self.splitViewController?.
displayModeButtonItem()
57                 controller.navigationItem.leftItemsSupplementBackButton = true
58             }
59         }
60     }
```

If line 53 looks similar to line 73 in Listing 8-14, that's because it's basically the same thing. Based on `indexPath.row`, you select the specific book from the `BookStore` object and save it in a constant called `selectedBook`.

On line 55, you take `selectedBook` and store it in a property called `detailItem` that is already part of the existing `DetailViewController` class. That's all you need to do in `MasterViewController`. You've basically passed off the book to `DetailViewController`. You're almost done. Now you need to make a few small modifications to the `DetailViewController` so that it displays the `Book` object properly.

Modifying the DetailViewController

Earlier in this chapter, you modified the `DetailViewController` so that it would display some detail information about a book. In the code you just finished, you modified the `MasterViewController` so that it passes the selected book to the `DetailViewController`. Now all that remains is to simply move the information from the Book object in the `DetailViewController` to the appropriate fields on the screen. All of this is done in one method—`configureView`—as seen in Listing 8-16.

Listing 8-16. Moving the Book Object Data to the Detail View

```
19        func configureView() {
20            if let detail: AnyObject = self.detailItem {
21                let myBook = detail as! Book
22                titleLabel.text = myBook.title
23                authorLabel.text = myBook.author
24                descriptionTextView.text = myBook.description
25            }
26        }
```

The `configureView` method is one of many convenient methods included in the Xcode template and is called whenever the `DetailViewController` is being initialized. This is where you will move your selected Book object's information to the fields in the view.

Lines 20 to 26 in the `DetailViewController.swift` file is where you move the information from the Book object to the view. If you recall, line 51 in Listing 8-15 set the selected book into a property on the `DetailViewController` called `detailItem`. Lines 20 to 21 pull that item out into a Book object called `myBook`.

Lines 22 to 24 simply move each of the Book object's properties to the view controls you built earlier in the chapter.

There is one more line of code that needs to be changed. Line 40 declared `detailItem` as an NSDate. We need to change it to be a Book object. We also need to remove the call to configureView on line 43. The final declaration should look like Listing 8-17.

Listing 8-17. Changing the detailItem

```
40  var detailItem: Book? {
41          didSet {
42              // Update the view.
43          }
44      }
```

Now we need to tell your view to call the configureView method when it is loaded. Add the following line to the end of the viewDidLoad function:

```
self.configureView()
```

That's all you need to do in this class. If you build and run the project and click one of the books, you should see something like Figure 8-15.

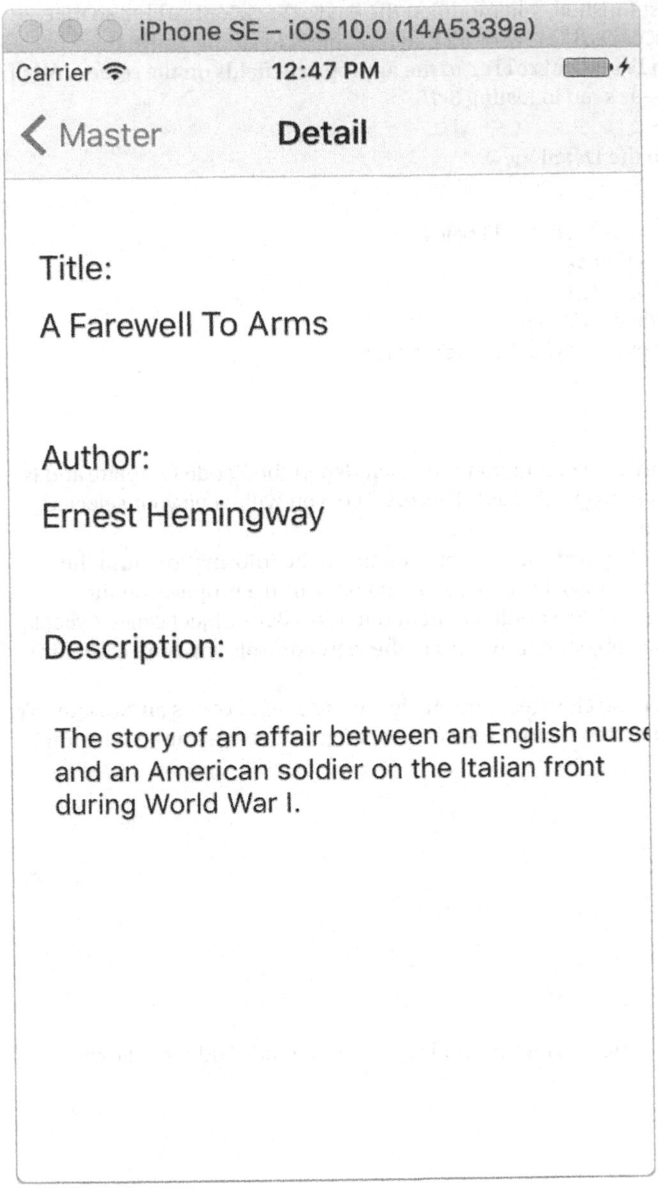

Figure 8-15. *Viewing the book details for the first time*

Summary

We've reached the end of this chapter! Here is a summary of the topics covered:

- *Understanding collection classes*: Collection classes are a powerful set of classes that come with Foundation and allow you to store and retrieve information efficiently.
- *Using properties*: Properties are variables that are accessible once the class has been instantiated.
- *Looping with for...in*: This feature offers a new way to iterate through an enumerated list of items.
- *Building a Master-Detail application*: You used Xcode and the Master-Detail Application template to build a simple bookstore program to display books and the details of an individual book.
- *Creating a simple data model*: Using the collection classes you learned about, you used an array to construct a `BookStore` object and used it as a data source in the bookstore program.
- *Connecting data to the view*: You connected the `Book` object's data to the interface fields using Xcode.

EXERCISES

- Add more books to the bookstore using the original program as a guide.
- On the Master Scene, remove the Edit button as we will not be using it in this app.
- Enhance the `Book` class so it can store another attribute—a price or genre, for example.
- Modify the `DetailViewController` so that the new fields are displayed. Remember to connect an interface control to a property.
- Change the `BookStore` object so that a separate method is called to initialize the list of `Book` objects (instead of putting it all in the `init` method).
- There is another attribute to a `UITableViewCell` called the `detailTextLabel`. Try to make use of it by setting its `text` property to something.
- Using Xcode to modify the interface, play with changing the background color of the `DetailViewController` in the storyboard file.

For a tougher challenge:

- Sort the books in the `BookStore` object so they appear in ascending order on the `MasterDetailView`.

CHAPTER 9

Comparing Data

In this chapter, we will discuss one of the most basic and frequent operations you will perform as you program: comparing data. In the bookstore example, you may need to compare book titles if your clients are looking for a specific book. You may also need to compare authors if your clients are interested in purchasing books by a specific author. Comparing data is a common task performed by developers. Many of the loops you learned about in Chapter 8 will require you to compare data so that you know when your code should stop looping.

Comparing data in programming is like using a scale. You have one value on one side and another value on the other side. In the middle, you have an operator. The operator determines what kind of comparison is being done. Examples of operators are "greater than," "less than," or "equal to."

The values on either side of the scale are usually variables. You learned about the different types of variables in Chapter 3. In general, the comparison functions for different variables will be slightly different. It is imperative that you become familiar with the functions and syntax to compare data because this will form the basis of your development.

For the purposes of this chapter, we will use an example of a bookstore application. This application will allow users to log in to the application, search for books, and purchase them. We will cover the different ways of comparing data to show how they would be used in this type of application.

Revisiting Boolean Logic

In Chapter 4, we introduced Boolean logic. Because of its prevalence in programming, we will revisit this subject in this chapter and go into more detail.

The most common comparisons that you will program your application to perform are comparisons using Boolean logic. Boolean logic usually comes in the form of *if/then* statements. Boolean logic can have only one of two answers: *yes* or *no*. The following are some good examples of Boolean questions that you will use in your applications:

- Is 5 larger than 3?
- Does *now* have more than five letters?
- Is 6/1/2010 later than today?

Notice that there are only two possible correct answers to these questions: *yes* and *no*. If you are asking a question that could have more than these two answers, that question will need to be worded differently for programming.

Each of these questions will be represented by an *if/then* statement. (For example, "If 5 is greater than 3, then print a message to the user.") Each *if* statement is required to have some sort of relational operator. A relational operator can be something like "is greater than" or "is equal to."

To start using these types of questions in your programs, you will first need to become familiar with the different relational operators available to you in the Swift language. We will cover them first. After that, you will learn how different variables can behave with these operators.

G. Bennett and B. Lees, *Swift 3 for Absolute Beginners*, DOI 10.1007/978-1-4842-2331-4_9

Using Relational Operators

Swift uses five standard comparison operators. These are the standard algebraic operators with only one real change: In the Swift language, as in most other programming languages, the "equal to" operator is made by two equals signs (==). Table 9-1 describes the operators available to you as a developer.

Table 9-1. *Comparison Operators*

Operator	Description
>	Greater than
<	Less than
>=	Greater than or equal to
<=	Less than or equal to
==	Equal to

■ **Note** A single equals sign (=) is used to assign a value to a variable. Two equals signs (==) are needed to compare two values. For example, `if(x=9)` will try to assign the value of 9 to the variable `x`, but now Xcode throws an error in this case. `if(x==9)` will do a comparison to see whether `x` equals 9.

Comparing Numbers

One of the difficulties developers have had in the past was dealing with different data types in comparisons. Earlier in this book, we discussed the different types of variables. You may remember that 1 is an integer. If you wanted to compare an integer with a float such as 1.2, this could cause some issues. Thankfully, Swift helps with this. In Swift, you can compare any two numeric data types without having to typecast. (Typecasting is still sometimes needed when dealing with other data types, which we cover later in the chapter.) This allows you to write code without worrying about the data types that need to be compared.

■ **Note** Typecasting is the conversion of an object or variable from one type to another.

In the bookstore application, you will need to compare numbers in many ways. For example, let's say the bookstore offers a discount for people who spend more than $30 in a single transaction. You will need to add the total amount the person is spending and then compare this to $30. If the amount spent is larger than $30, you will need to calculate the discount. See the following example:

```
var discountThreshold = 30
var discountPercent = 0
var totalSpent = calculateTotalSpent()

if totalSpent > discountThreshold {
    discountPercent = 10
}
```

Let's walk through the code. First, you declare the variables (`discountThreshhold`, `discountPercent`, and `totalSpent`) and assign a value to them. Notice you do not need to specify the type of number for the variables. The type will be assigned when you assign it a value. You know that `discountThreshold` and `discountPercent` will not contain decimals, so the compiler will create them as `Ints`. In this example, you can assume you have a function called `calculateTotalSpent`, which will calculate the total spent in this current order. You then simply check to see whether the total spent is larger than the discount threshold; if it is, you set the discount percent. If we wanted a customer who spent exactly $30 to get the same discount, we could use a `>=` instead of a `>`. Also notice that it was not necessary to tell the code to convert the data when comparing the different numeric data types. As mentioned earlier, Swift handles all this.

Another action that requires the comparison of numbers is looping. As discussed in Chapter 4, looping is a core action in development, and many loop types require some sort of comparison to determine when to stop. Let's take a look at a `for` loop:

```
var numberOfBooks: Int
numberOfBooks = 50

for y in 0..<numberOfBooks {
    doSomething()
}
```

In this example, you iterate, or *loop*, through the total number of books in the bookstore. The `for` statement is where the interesting stuff starts to happen. Let's break it down.

The for loop declares a variable with an initial value of 0 and will increment it while it is less than `numberOfBooks`. This is a much quicker way of doing for loops than was required in Objective-C.

Creating an Example Xcode App

Now let's create an Xcode application so you can start comparing numeric data.

1. Launch Xcode. From the Finder, go to the Applications folder. Drag Xcode to the Dock because you will be using it throughout the rest of this book. See Figure 9-1.

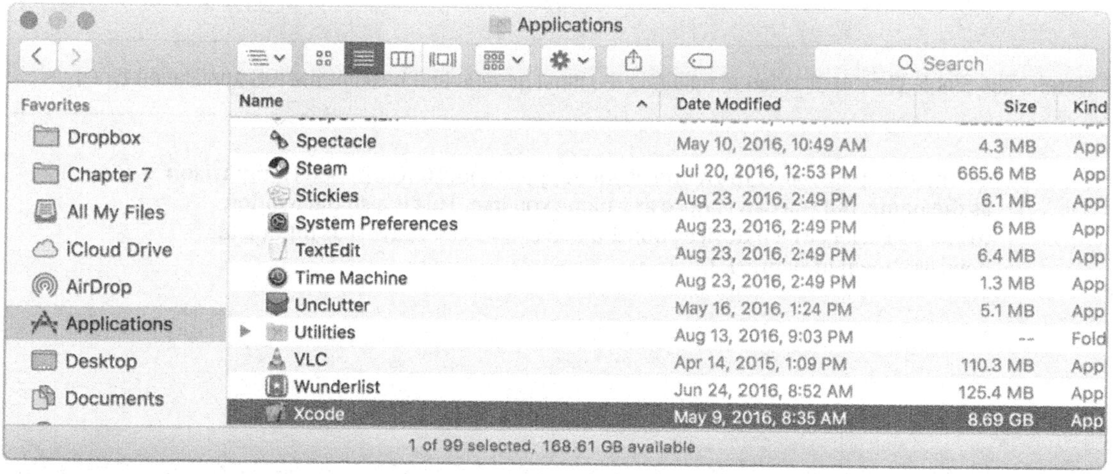

Figure 9-1. *Launching Xcode*

2. Click “Create a New Xcode Project” to open a new window. On the top under iOS, select Single View Application on the right side. Click Next, as shown in Figure 9-2.

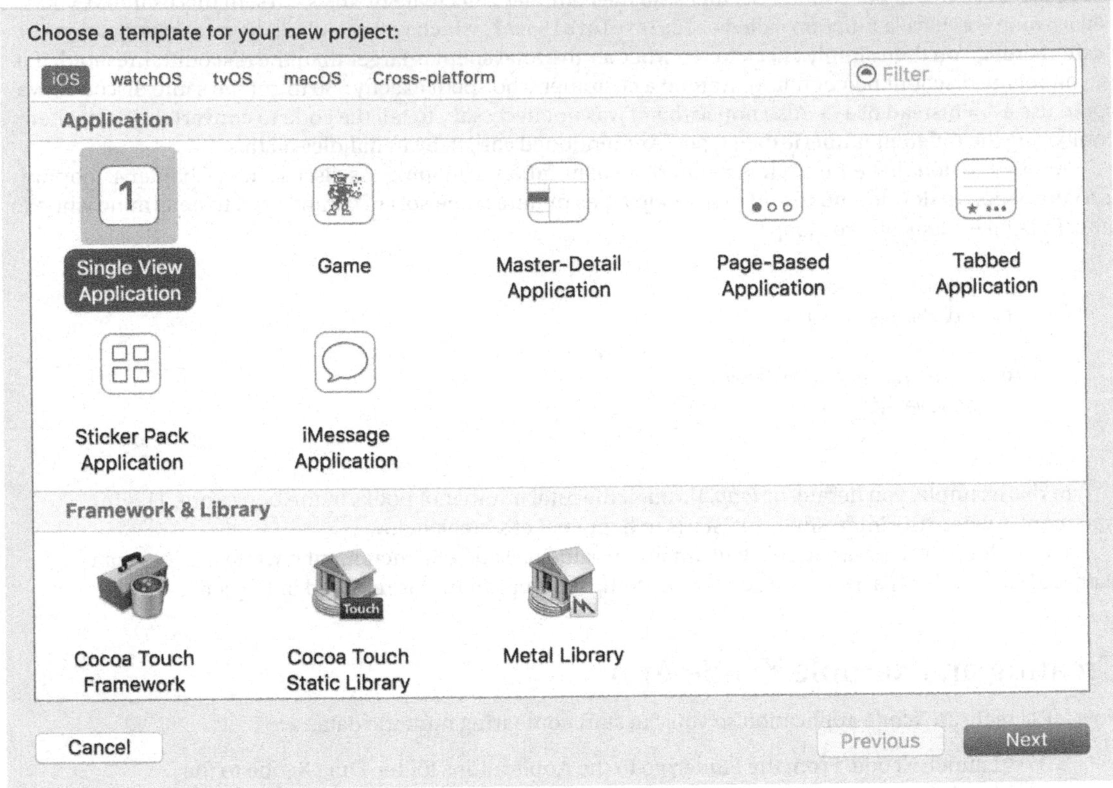

Figure 9-2. *Creating a new project*

■ **Note** The Single View Application template is the most generic and basic of the iOS application types.

---

3. On the next page, enter the name of your application. Here we used **Comparison** as the name, but you can choose any name you like. This is also the window where you select which device you would like to target. Leave it as iPhone for now, as shown in Figure 9-3.

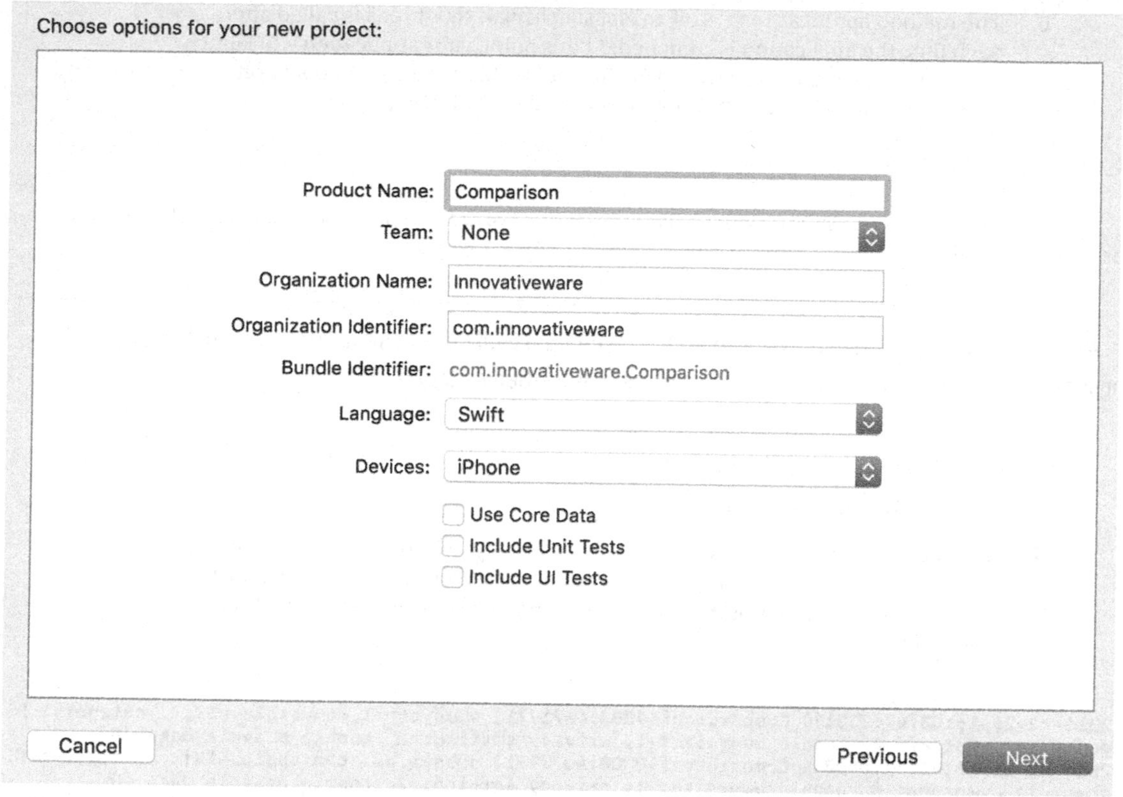

Figure 9-3. Selecting the project type and name

■ **Note** Xcode projects, by default, are saved in the `Documents` folder in your user home.

---

4. Once the new project is created, you will see the standard Xcode window. Select the arrow next to the `Comparison` folder to expand it if it is not already expanded. You will see several files. The main file for your project is called `AppDelegate.swift`. You will also see a `ViewController.swift` file. This file is the source that controls the single window that is created by default for you in this type of app. For the purposes of these examples, you will be focusing on the `AppDelegate.swift` file.

5. Click the `AppDelegate.swift` file. You will see the following code:

```
    func application(_ application: UIApplication,
didFinishLaunchingWithOptions launchOptions:
[UIApplicationLaunchOptionsKey: Any]?) -> Bool {

        // Override point for customization after application launch.
        return true
    }
```

6. The method `application: didFinishLaunchingWithOptions` is called after each time the application is launched. At this point, your application will launch and display a window. You will add a little `Hello World` to your application. Before the line `returns true`, you need to add the following code:

```
NSLog("Hello World")
```

This line creates a new `String` with the contents `Hello World` and passes it to the `NSLog` function that is used for debugging.

■ **Note** The `NSLog` method is available to Objective-C and Swift. It is commonly used for debugging an application because you can show information easily in the Debug area.

Let's run the application to see how it works:

1. Click the Run button in the default toolbar.
2. The iOS simulator will launch. This will just display a window. Back in Xcode, a Console window will appear at the bottom of the screen, as shown in Figure 9-4. You can always toggle this window by selecting View ➤ Debug Area ➤ Show/ Hide Debug Area.

```
2016-08-26 16:03:47.033138 Comparison[49300:4071971] subsystem: com.apple.UIKit, category: HI
generate_symptoms: 0, enable_oversize: 1, privacy_setting: 2, enable_private_data: 0
2016-08-26 16:03:47.039844 Comparison[49300:4071971] subsystem: com.apple.UIKit, category: HI
generate_symptoms: 0, enable_oversize: 1, privacy_setting: 2, enable_private_data: 0
2016-08-26 16:03:47.052828 Comparison[49300:4071968] subsystem: com.apple.BaseBoard, category
generate_symptoms: 0, enable_oversize: 0, privacy_setting: 0, enable_private_data: 0
2016-08-26 16:03:47.071965 Comparison[49300:4071248] subsystem: com.apple.UIKit, category: St
generate_symptoms: 0, enable_oversize: 1, privacy_setting: 2, enable_private_data: 0
2016-08-26 16:03:47.125 Comparison[49300:4071248] Hello World
2016-08-26 16:03:47.132424 Comparison[49300:4071248] subsystem: com.apple.BackBoardServices.f
0, generate_symptoms: 0, enable_oversize: 0, privacy_setting: 0, enable_private_data: 0
```

***Figure 9-4.** Debugger window*

You will now see several lines of text in your debugger. You will need to look down several lines to see the output of the NSLog call. The first part of the line shows the date, time, and name of the application. The `Hello World` part was generated by the `NSLog` line that you added.

1. Go back to Xcode and open the `AppDelegate.swift` file.
2. Go to the beginning of the line that begins with `NSLog`. This is the line that is responsible for printing the `Hello World` section. You are going to comment out this line by placing two forward slashes (//) in front of the line of code. Commenting out code tells Xcode to ignore it when it builds and runs the application. In other words, code that is commented out will not run.
3. Once you comment out the line of code, the code will no longer be run so Hello World will no longer show in the log.

4. We want to use the log to output the results of comparisons. Add one line, as shown here:

```
NSLog("The result is \(6 > 5 ? "True" : "False")")
```

■ **Note** The previous code, `(6>5 ? "True" : "False")`, is called a *ternary* operation. It is essentially just a simplified way of writing an `if/else` statement.

---

5. Place this line in your code. This line is telling your application to print `The result is`. Then it will print `True` if 6 is greater than 5, or it will print `False` if 5 is greater than 6.

Because 6 is greater than 5, it will print `True`.

You can change this line to test any comparisons we have already discussed in this chapter or any of the examples you will do later.

Let's try another example.

```
var i = 5
var y = 6
NSLog("The result is %@", (y > i ? "True" : "False"))
```

In this example, you create a variable and assign its value to 5. You then create another variable and assign the value to 6. You then change the `NSLog` example to compare the variables `i` and `y` instead of using actual numbers. When you run this example, you will get the result shown in Figure 9-5.

```
2016-08-26 16:07:30.343266 Comparison[49566:4082918] subsystem: com.apple.UIKit, category:
generate_symptoms: 0, enable_oversize: 1, privacy_setting: 2, enable_private_data: 0
2016-08-26 16:07:30.400 Comparison[49566:4082918] The result is True
2016-08-26 16:07:30.408737 Comparison[49566:4082918] subsystem: com.apple.BackBoardService
0, generate_symptoms: 0, enable_oversize: 0, privacy_setting: 0, enable_private_data: 0
```

Figure 9-5. *NSLog output*

■ **Note** You may get compiler warnings when using this code. The compiler will tell you that the false portion of the ternary operator will never be executed. The compiler can look at the values while you are typing the code and know that the comparison will be true.

You will now explore other kinds of comparisons, and then you will come back to the application and test some of them.

Using Boolean Expressions

A Boolean expression is the easiest of all comparisons. Boolean expressions are used to determine whether a value is true or false. Here's an example:

```
var j = 5
if  j > 0 {
    someCode()
}
```

The *if* statement will always evaluate to `true` because the variable `j` is greater than zero. Because of that, the program will run the `someCode()` method.

■ **Note** In Swift, if a variable is optional and therefore not assigned a value, you should use a question mark after the variable declaration. For example, `var j` becomes `var j:Int?`.

If you change the value of `j`, the statement will evaluate to `false` because `j` is now 0. This can be used with `Bool` and number variables.

```
var j = 0
if j > 0 {
    someCode()
}
```

Placing an exclamation point in front of a Boolean expression will change it to the opposite value (a `false` becomes a `true`, and a `true` becomes a `false`). This line now asks "If not `j>0`," which, in this case, is `true` because `j` is equal to 0. This is an example of using an integer to act as a Boolean variable. As discussed earlier, Swift also has variables called `Bool` that have only two possible values: `true` or `false`.

```
var j = 0
if !(j > 0) {
    someCode()
}
```

■ **Note** Swift, like many other programming languages, uses `true` or `false` when assigning a value to a Boolean variable.

Let's look at an example related to the bookstore. Say you have a frequent buyers' club that entitles all members to a 15 percent discount on all books they purchase. This is easy to check. You simply set the variable `clubMember` to `true` if the person is a member and `false` if he or she is not. The following code will apply the discount only to club members:

```
var discountPercent = 0
var clubMember: Bool = false

if clubMember {
    discountPercent = 15
}
```

Comparing Strings

Strings are a difficult data type for most C languages. In ANSI C (or standard C), a string is just an array of characters. Objective-C took the development of the string even further and made it an object called NSString. Swift has taken the String class even further and made it easier to work with. Many more properties and methods are available to you when working with an object. Fortunately for you, String has many methods for comparing data, which makes your job much easier.

Let's look at an example. Here, you are comparing passwords to see whether you should allow a user to log in:

```
var enteredPassword = "Duck"
var myPassword = "duck"

var continueLogin = false

if enteredPassword == myPassword {
    continueLogin = true
}
```

The first line just declares a String and sets it value to Duck. The next line declares another String and sets its value to duck. In your actual code, you will need to get the enteredPassword string from the user.

The next line is the part of the code that actually does the work. You simply ask the strings if they are equal to each other. The example code will always be false because of the capital "D" in the enteredPassword versus the lowercase "d" in the myPassword.

There are many other different comparisons you might have to perform on strings. For example, you may want to check the length of a certain string. This is easy to do.

```
var enteredPassword = "Duck"
var myPassword = "duck"
var continueLogin = false
if enteredPassword.characters.count > 5 {
    continueLogin = true
}
```

Note count is a property that can be used to count strings, arrays, and dictionaries.

This code checks to see whether the entered password is longer than five characters.

There will be other times when you will have to search within a string for some data. Fortunately, Swift makes this easy to do. String provides a function called contains, which allows you to search within a string for another string. The function contains takes only one argument, which is the string for which you are searching.

```
var searchTitle: String
var bookTitle: String
searchTitle = "Sea"
bookTitle = "2000 Leagues Under the Sea"

if bookTitle.contains(searchTitle) {
    addToResults()
}
```

This code is similar to other examples you have examined. This example takes a search term and checks to see whether the book title has that same search term in it. If it does, it adds the book to the results. This can be adapted to allow users to search for specific terms in book titles, authors, or even descriptions.

For a complete listing of the methods supported by `String`, see the Apple documentation at `https://swift.org/documentation/#the-swift-programming-language`.

Using the switch Statement

Up to this point, you've seen several examples of comparing data by simply using the *if* statement.

```
if someValue == SOME_CONSTANT {
    ...
} else if someValue == SOME_OTHER_CONSTANT {
    ...
} else if someValue == YET_SOME_OTHER_CONSTANT {
    ...
}
```

If you need to compare a variable to several constant values, you can use a different method that can simplify the comparison code: the `switch` statement.

■ **Note** In Objective-C, you could only use integers to compare in a `switch` statement. Swift allows developers more freedom in using the `switch` statement.

The `switch` statement allows you to compare one or more values against another variable.

```
var customerType = "Repeat"

switch  customerType {      // The switch statement followed by a begin brace
case "Repeat":          // Equivalent to if (customerType == "Repeat")
   ...                  // Call functions and put any other statements here after the case.
   ...
case "New":
   ...
   ...
case "Seasonal":                    ...
   ...
default:                // Default is required in Swift

} // End of the switch statement.
```

The `switch` statement is powerful, and it simplifies and streamlines comparisons to several different values. In Swift, the `switch` statement is a powerful statement that can be used to simplify repeated *if/else* statements.

Comparing Dates

Dates are a fairly complicated variable type in any language, and unfortunately, depending on the type of application you are writing, they are common. Swift 3 now has its own native `Date` type. This means developers no longer have to use the Cocoa date type `NSDate`. The new Swift 3 `Date` class has a lot of nice methods that make comparing dates easy. We will focus on the `compare` function. The `compare` function returns an `ComparisonResult`, which has three possible values: `orderedSame`, `orderedDescending`, and `orderedAscending`.

```
// Today's Date
        let today: Date = Date()

        // Sale Date = Tomorrow
        let timeToAdd: TimeInterval = 60*60*24
        let saleDate: Date = today.addingTimeInterval(timeToAdd)

        var saleStarted = false
        let result: ComparisonResult  = today.compare(saleDate)

        switch result {
        case ComparisonResult.orderedAscending:
            // Sale Date is in the future
            saleStarted = false
        case ComparisonResult.orderedDescending:
            // Sale Start Date is in the past so sale is on
            saleStarted = true
        default:
            // Sale Start Date is now
            saleStarted = true
        }
```

This may seem like a lot of work just to compare some dates. Let's walk through the code and see whether you can make sense of it.

```
let today: Date = Date()
let timeToAdd: TimeInterval = 60*60*24
let saleDate: Date = today.addingTimeInterval(timeToAdd)
```

Here, you declare two different `Date` objects. The first one, named `today`, is initialized with the system date or your device date. Before creating the second date, you need to add some time to the first date. You do this by creating a `TimeInterval`. This is a number in seconds. To add a day, you add `60*60*24`. The second date, named `saleDate`, is initialized with a date some time in the future. You will use this date to see whether this sale has begun. We will not go into detail about the initialization of `Date` objects.

■ **Note** In most programming languages, dates are dealt with in a specific pattern. They usually start with the four-digit year followed by a hyphen, then a two-digit month followed by a hyphen, and then a two-digit day. If you are using a data format with a time, this data is usually presented in a similar manner. Times are usually presented with the hour, minute, and second, each separated by a colon. Swift inherits time zone support from Cocoa.

The result of using the compare function of a Date object is a ComparisonResult. You have to declare a ComparisonResult to capture the output from the compare function.

```
let result: ComparisonResult = today.compare(saleDate)
```

This simple compares the two dates. It places the resulting ComparisonResult into the constant called result.

```
switch result {
        case ComparisonResult.orderedAscending:
            // Sale Date is in the future
            saleStarted = false
        case ComparisonResult.orderedDescending:
            // Sale Start Date is in the past so sale is on
            saleStarted = true
        default:
            // Sale Start Date is now
            saleStarted = true
        }
```

Now you need to find out what value is in the variable result. To accomplish this, you perform a switch statement that compares the result to the three different options for ComparisonResult. The first line finds out whether the sale date is greater than today's date. This means that the sale date is in the future, and thus the sale has not started. You then set the variable saleStarted to false. The next line finds out whether the sale date is less than today. If it is, the sale has started, and you set the saleStarted variable to true. The next line just says default. This captures all other options. You know, though, that the only other option is orderedSame. This means the two dates and times are the same, and thus the sale is just beginning.

There are other methods that you can use to compare Date objects. Each of these methods will be more efficient at certain tasks. We have chosen the compare method because it will handle most of your basic date comparison needs.

■ **Note** Remember that a Date holds both a date and a time. This can affect your comparisons with dates because it compares not only the date but also the time.

Combining Comparisons

As discussed in Chapter 4, you'll sometimes need something more complex than a single comparison. This is where logical operators come in. Logical operators enable you to check for more than one requirement. For example, if you have a special discount for people who are members of your book club *and* who spend more than $30, you can write one statement to check this.

```
var totalSpent = 31
var discountThreshhold = 30
var discountPercent = 0
var clubMember = true

 if totalSpent > discountThreshhold && clubMember {
     discountPercent = 15
}
```

We have combined two of the examples shown earlier. The new comparison line reads as follows: "If `totalSpent` is greater than `discountThreshold` AND `clubMember` is `true`, then set the `discountPercent` to 15." For this to return `true`, both items need to be true. You can use || instead of && to signify "or." You can change the previous line to this:

```
if totalSpent > discountThreshhold || clubMember  {
        discountPercent = 15
}
```

Now this reads as follows: "If `totalSpent` is greater than `discountThreshold` ***OR*** `clubMember` is `true`, then set the discount percent to 15." This will return `true` if either of the options is `true`.

You can continue to use the logical operations to string as many comparisons together as you need. In some cases, you may need to group comparisons using parentheses. This can be more complicated and is beyond the scope of this book.

Summary

You've reached the end of the chapter! Here is a summary of the topics that were covered:

- *Comparisons*: Comparing data is an integral part of any application.
- *Relational operators:* You learned about the five standard relational operators and how each is used.
- *Numbers*: Numbers are the easiest pieces of information to compare. You learned how to compare numbers in your programs.
- *Examples*: You created a sample application where you could test your comparisons and make sure that you are correct in your logic. Then you learned how to change the application to add different types of comparisons.
- *Boolean*: You learned how to check Boolean values.
- *Strings*: You learned how strings behave differently from other pieces of information you have tested.
- *Dates*: You learned how difficult it can be to compare dates and that you must be careful to make sure you are getting the response you desire.

EXERCISES

- Modify the example application to compare some string information.
- Write a Swift application that determines whether the following years are leap years: 1800, 1801, 1899, 1900, 2000, 2001, 2003, and 2010. Output should be written to the console in the following format: `The year 2000 is a leap year` or `The year 2001 is not a leap year`. See `http://en.wikipedia.org/wiki/Leap_year` for information on determining whether a year is a leap year.

CHAPTER 10

Creating User Interfaces

Interface Builder enables iOS developers to easily create their user interfaces using a powerful graphical user interface. It provides the ability to build user interfaces by simply dragging objects from Interface Builder's library to the editor.

Interface Builder stores your user interface design in one or more resource files, called storyboards. These resource files contain the interface objects, their properties, and their relationships.

To build a user interface, simply drag objects from Interface Builder's Object Library pane onto your view or scene. Actions and outlets are two key components of Interface Builder that help you streamline the development process.

Your objects trigger actions in your views, and the actions are connected to your methods in the app's code. Outlets are declared in your `.swift` file and are connected to specific controls as properties. See Figure 10-1.

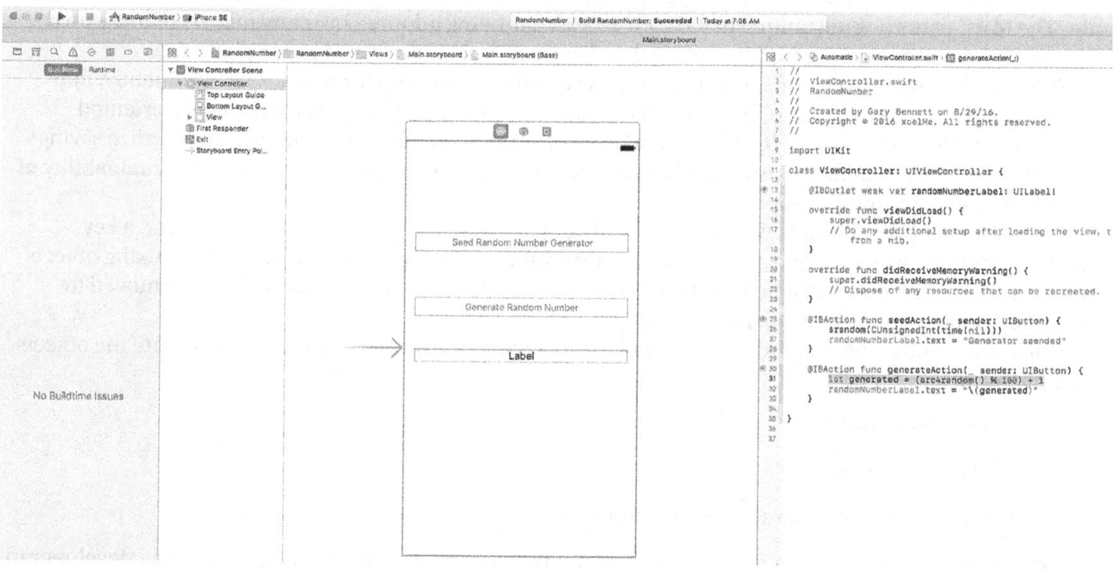

Figure 10-1. *Interface Builder*

G. Bennett and B. Lees, *Swift 3 for Absolute Beginners*, DOI 10.1007/978-1-4842-2331-4_10

■ **Note** Interface Builder was once a stand-alone application that developers used to design their user interfaces. Starting with Xcode 4.0, Interface Builder has been integrated into Xcode.

Understanding Interface Builder

Interface Builder saves the user interface file as a bundle that contains the interface objects and relationships used in the application. These bundles previously had the file extension `.nib`. Version 3.0 of Interface Builder used a new XML file format, and the file extension changed to `.xib`. However, developers still call these files *nib* files. Later Apple introduced storyboards. Storyboards enable you to have all of your views in one file with a `.storyboard` extension.

Unlike most other graphical user interface applications, XIBs and storyboards are often referred to as *freeze-dried* because they contain the archived objects themselves and are ready to run.

The XML file format is used to facilitate storage with source control systems such as Subversion and Git.

In the next section, we'll discuss an app design pattern called Model-View-Controller. This design pattern enables developers to more easily maintain code and reuse objects over the life of an app.

The Model-View-Controller Pattern

Model-View-Controller (MVC) is the most prevalent design pattern used in iOS development, and learning about it will make your life as a developer much easier. MVC is used in software development and is considered an architectural pattern.

Architectural patterns describe solutions to software design problems that developers can use in their code. The MVC pattern is not unique to iOS developers; it is being adopted by many makers of integrated development environments (IDEs), including those running on Windows and Linux platforms.

Software development is considered an expensive and risky venture for businesses. Frequently, apps take longer than expected to write, come in over budget, and don't work as promised. Object-oriented programming (OOP) produced a lot of hype and gave the impression that companies would realize savings if they adopted its methodology, primarily because of the reusability of objects and easier maintainability of the code. Initially, this didn't happen.

When engineers looked at why OOP wasn't living up to these expectations, they discovered a key shortcoming with how developers were designing their objects: Developers were frequently mixing objects in such a way that the code became difficult to maintain as the application matured, the code moved to different platforms, or hardware displays changed.

Objects were often designed so that if any of the following changed, it was difficult to isolate the objects that were impacted:

- Business rules
- User interfaces
- Client-server or Internet-based communication

Objects can be broken down into three task-related categories. It is the responsibility of the developer to ensure that each of these categories keeps their objects from drifting across other categories.

As objects are categorized in these groups, apps can be developed and maintained more easily over time. The following are examples of objects and their associated MVC category for an iPhone banking application:

Model

- Account balances
- User encryption
- Account transfers
- Account login

View

- Account balances table cell
- Account login spinner control

Controller

- Account balance view controller
- Account transfer view controller
- Logon view controller

The easiest way to remember and classify your objects in the MVC design pattern is the following:

- *Model*: Unique business or application rules or code that represent the real world. This is where the data resides.
- *View*: Unique user interface code
- *Controller*: Anything that controls or communicates with the model or view objects

Figure 10-2 represents the MVC paradigm.

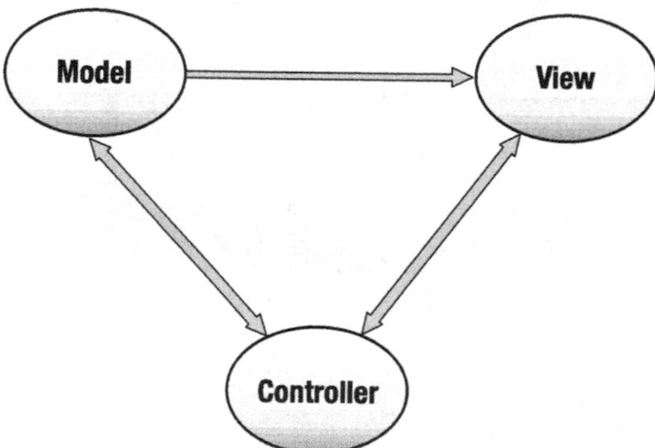

Figure 10-2. *MVC paradigm*

Neither Xcode nor Interface Builder forces developers to use the MVC design pattern. It is up to the developers to organize their objects in such a way to use this design pattern.

It is worth mentioning that Apple strongly embraces the MVC design pattern, and all of the frameworks are designed to work in an MVC world. This means that if you also embrace the MVC design pattern, working with Apple's classes will be much easier. If you don't, you'll be swimming upstream.

Human Interface Guidelines

Before you get too excited and begin designing dynamic user interfaces for your app, you need to learn some of the ground rules. Apple has developed one of the most advanced operating systems in the world with iOS 10. Additionally, Apple's products are known for being intuitive and user-friendly. Apple wants users to have the same experience from one app to the next.

To ensure a consistent user experience, Apple provides developers with guidelines on how their apps should look and feel. These guidelines, called the Human Interface Guidelines (HIG), are available for iOS, macOS, watchOS, and tvOS. You can download these documents at `http://developer.apple.com`, as shown in Figure 10-3.

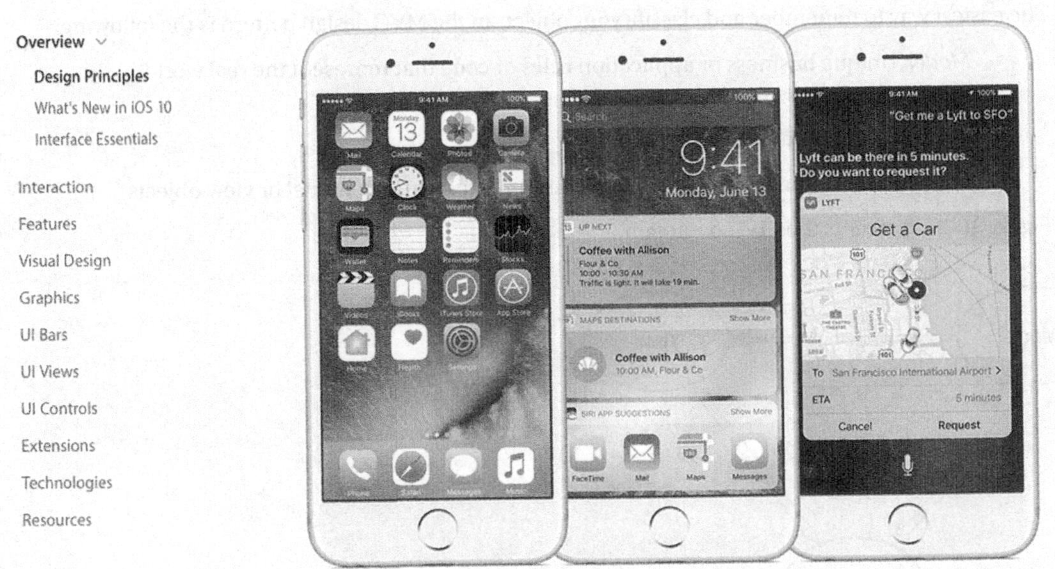

***Figure 10-3.** Apple's Human Interface Guidelines for iOS devices*

■ **Note** Apple's HIG is more than recommendations or suggestions. Apple takes it very seriously. While the HIG doesn't describe how to implement your user interface designs in code, it is great for understanding the proper way to implement your views and controls.

The following are some of the top reasons apps are rejected in Apple's iTunes App Store:

- The app crashes.
- The app violates the HIG.
- The app uses Apple's private APIs.
- The app doesn't function as advertised on the iTunes App Store.

■ **Note** You can read, learn, and follow the HIG before you develop your app, or you can read, learn, and follow the HIG after your app gets rejected by Apple and you have to rewrite part or all of it. Either way, all iOS developers will end up becoming familiar with the HIG.

Many new iOS developers find this out the hard way, but if you follow the HIG from day one, your iOS development will be a far more pleasurable experience.

Creating an Example iPhone App with Interface Builder

Let's get started by building an iPhone app that generates and displays a random number, as shown in Figure 10-4. This app will be similar to the app you created in Chapter 4, but you'll see how much more interesting the app becomes with an iOS user interface (UI).

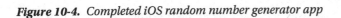

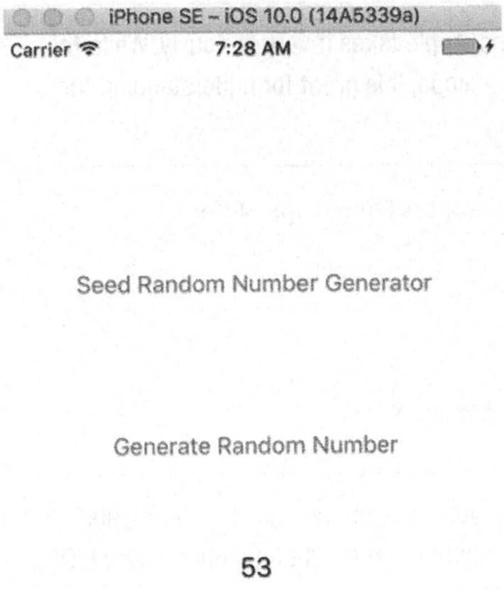

iPhone SE – iOS 10.0 (14A5339a)

Carrier 7:28 AM

Seed Random Number Generator

Generate Random Number

53

Figure 10-4. *Completed iOS random number generator app*

1. Open Xcode and select Create a new Xcode project. Make sure you select Single View Application for iOS and then click Next, as shown in Figure 10-5.

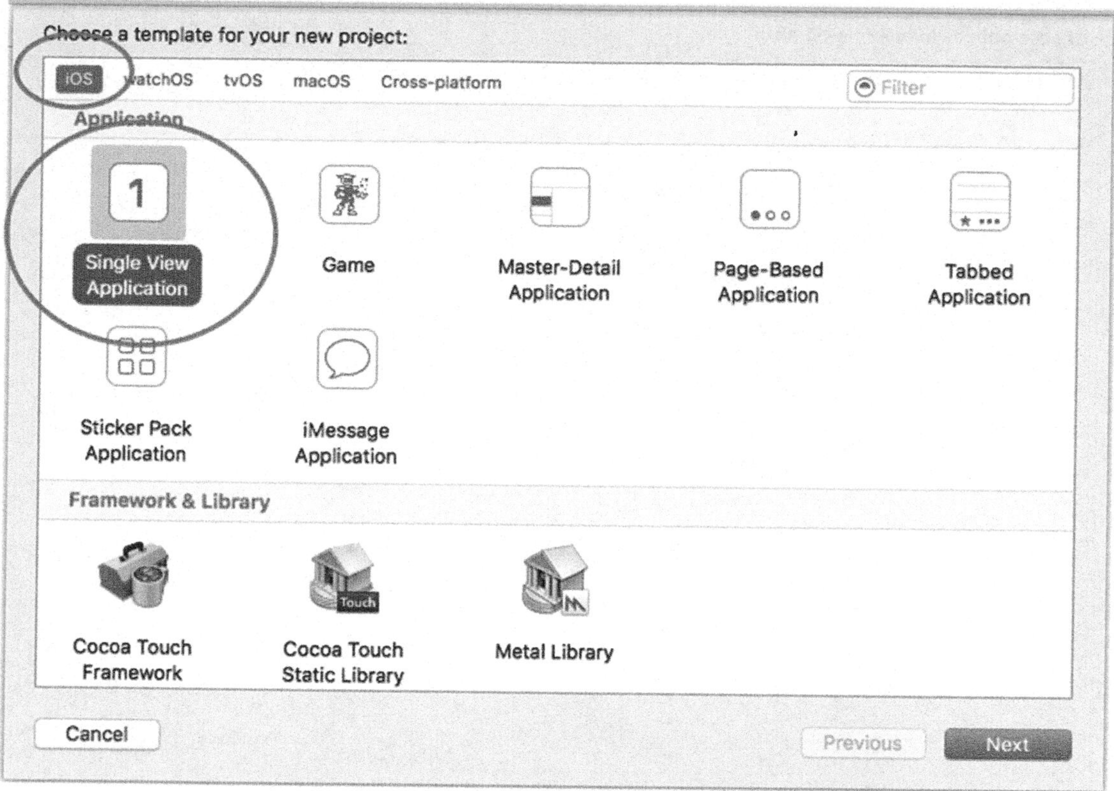

Figure 10-5. *Creating an iPhone app based on the Single View Application template*

2. Name your project `RandomNumber`, select Swift for the language and iPhone for the Device, click Next, and save your project, as shown in Figure 10-6.

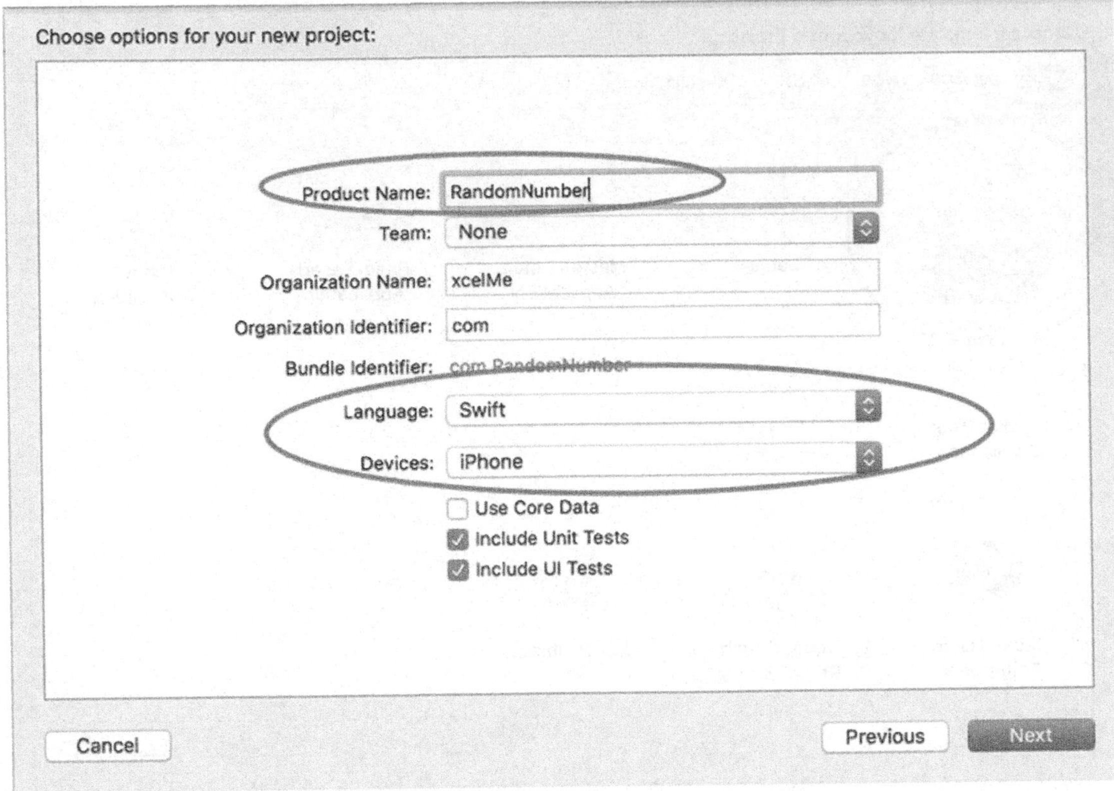

Figure 10-6. *Naming your iPhone project*

3. Your project files and settings are created and displayed, as shown in Figure 10-7.

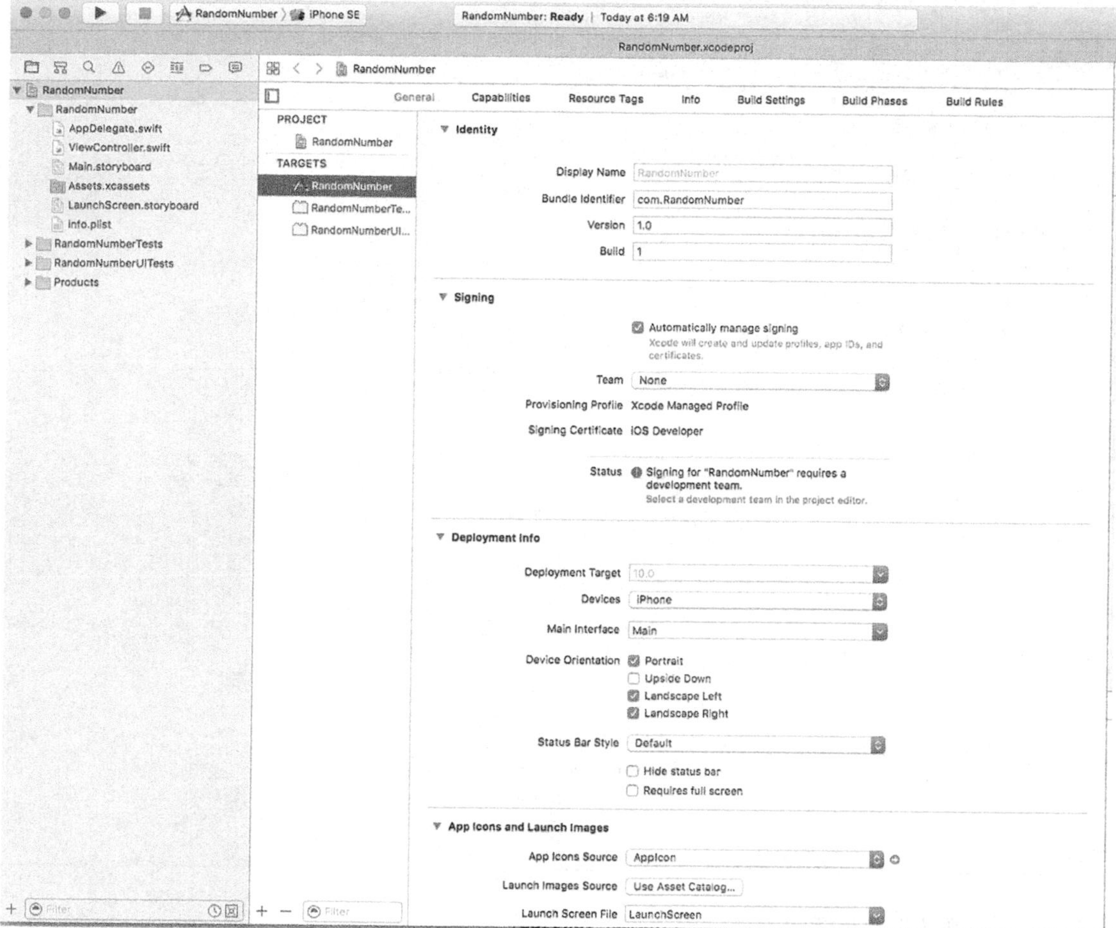

Figure 10-7. *Source files*

Although you have only one controller in this project, it's good programming practice to make your MVC groups at the beginning of your development. This helps remind you to keep the MVC paradigm and not put all of your code unnecessarily in your controller.

4. Right-click the `RandomNumber` folder and then select New Group, as shown in Figure 10-8.

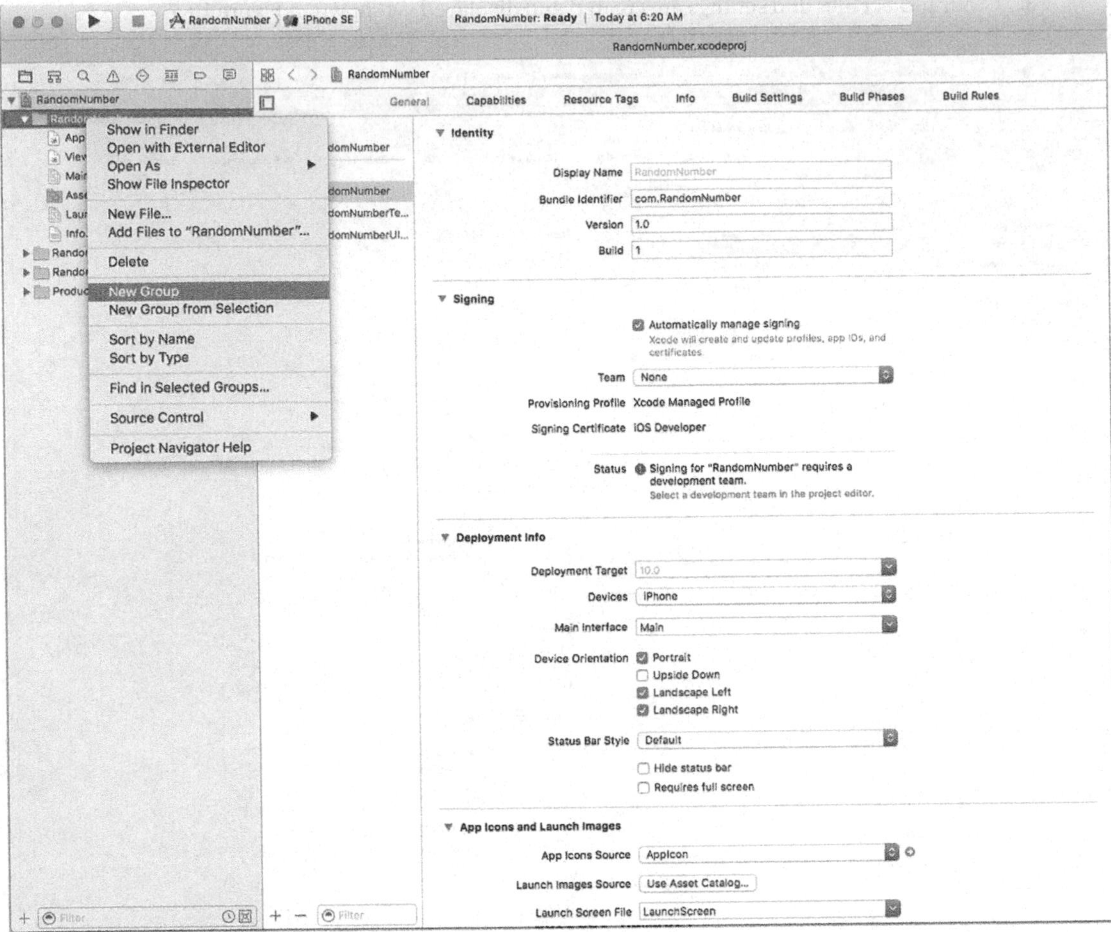

Figure 10-8. *Creating new groups*

5. Create a Models group, a Views group, and a Controllers group.
6. Drag the `ViewController.swift` file to the Controllers group. Drag the `Main.storyboard` and `LaunchScreen.storyboard` files to the Views group. Having these groups reminds you to follow the MVC design pattern as you develop your code and prevents you from placing all of your code in the controllers, as shown in Figure 10-9.

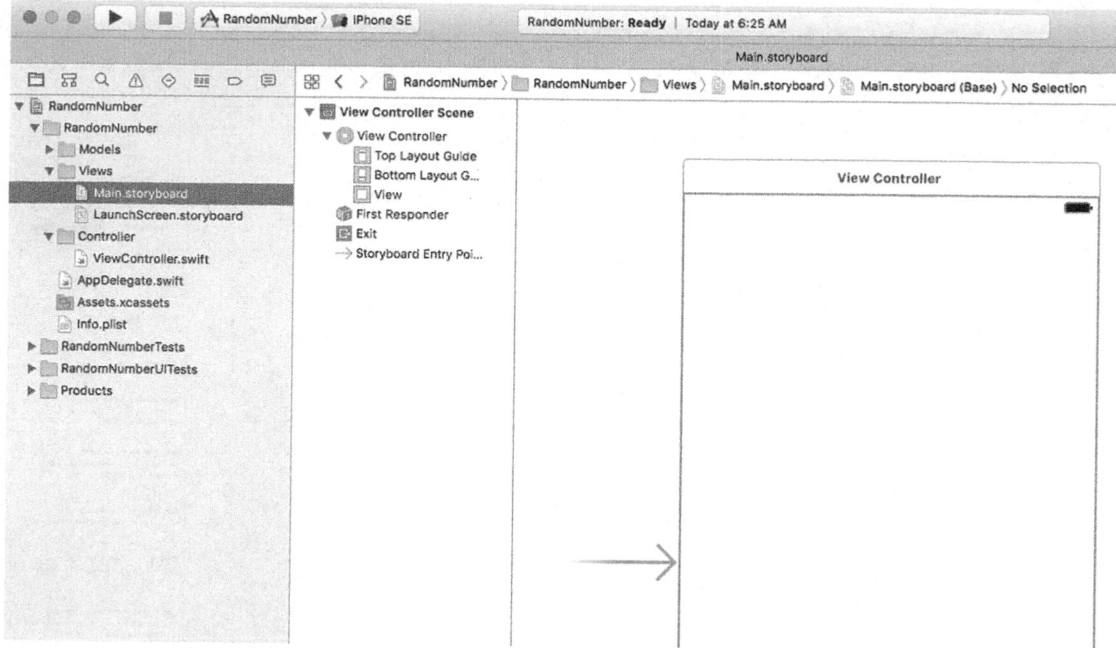

Figure 10-9. *MVC groups with controller and storyboard files organized*

Developers have found it helpful to keep their storyboard and XIB files with their controllers as their projects grow. It is not uncommon to have dozens of controllers and XIB files in your project. Keeping them together helps keep everything organized. Using storyboards resolves many of the issues of having lots of XIBs.

7. Click the `Main.storyboard` file to open Interface Builder.

Using Interface Builder

The most common way to launch Interface Builder and begin working on your view is to click the storyboard or XIB file related to the view, as shown in Figure 10-10.

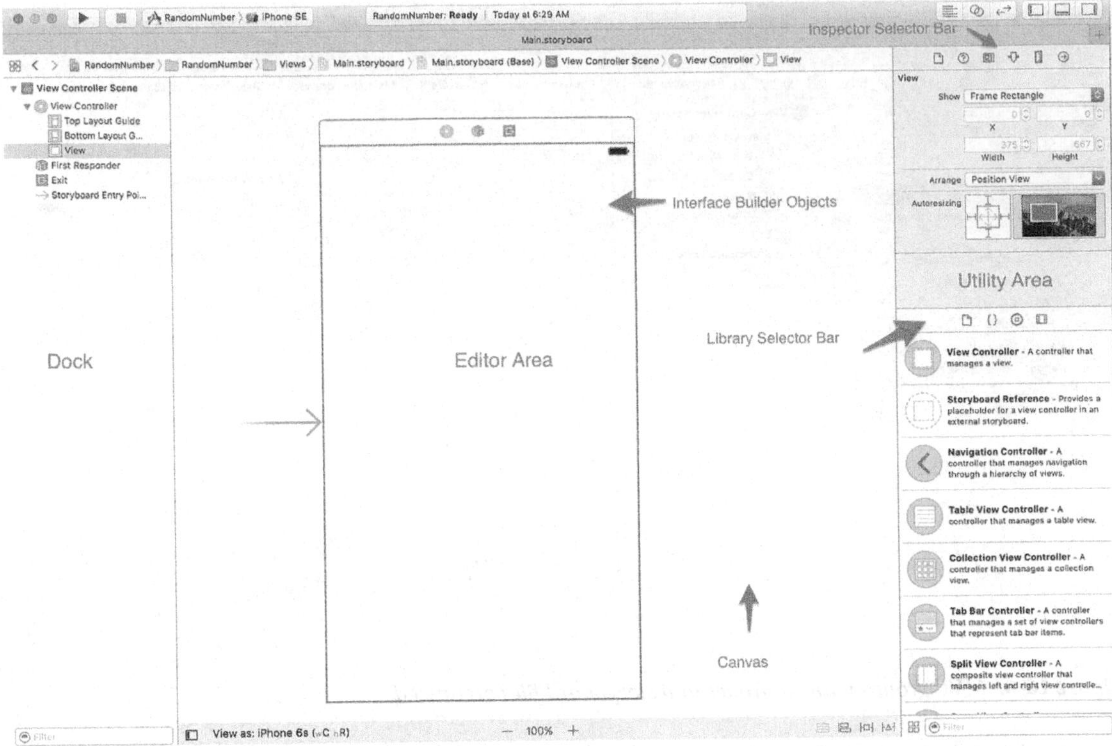

Figure 10-10. *Interface Builder in the workspace window*

When Interface Builder opens, you can see your scenes displayed on the canvas. You are now able to design your user interface. First, you need to understand some of the sub-windows within Interface Builder.

The Document Outline

The storyboard shows all the objects that your view contains. The following are some examples of these objects:

- Buttons
- Labels
- Text fields
- Web views
- Map views
- Picker views
- Table views

■ **Note** You can expand the width of the Document Outline to see a detailed list of all your objects, as shown in Figure 10-11. To get more real estate for the canvas, you can shrink or hide your file navigator.

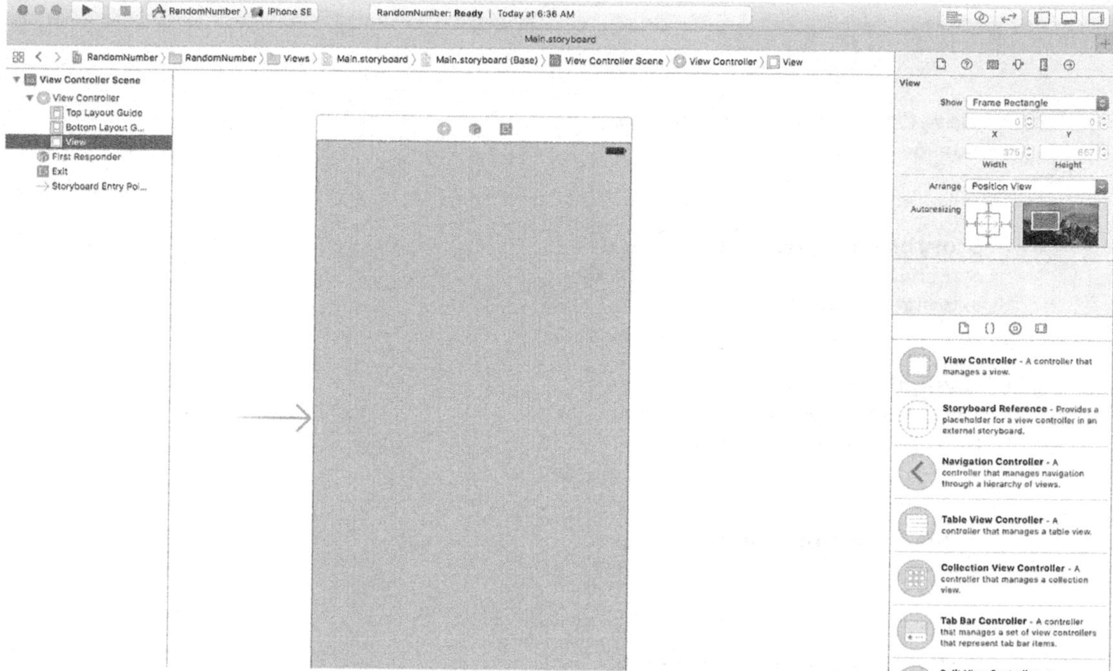

Figure 10-11. *The Document Outline's width is expanded to show a detailed view of all the objects in your storyboard.*

The Object Library

The Object Library is where you can exploit your creativity. It's a smorgasbord of objects that you can drag and drop into the View.

- The Library pane can grow and shrink by moving the window splitter in the middle of the view, as shown in Figure 10-12.

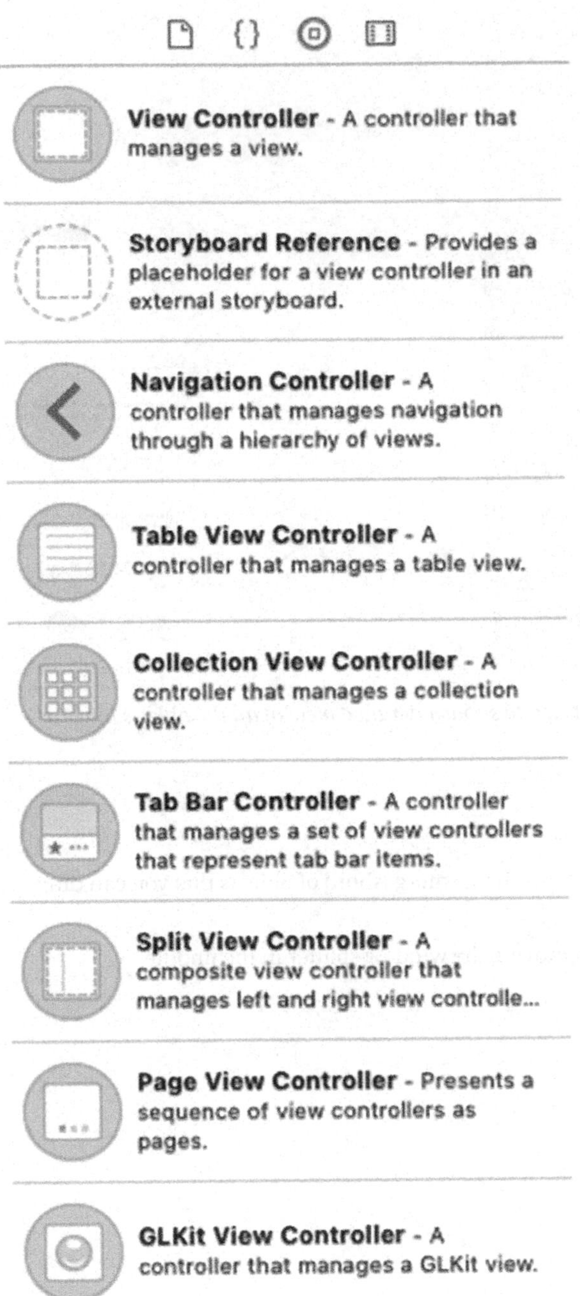

View Controller - A controller that manages a view.
Storyboard Reference - Provides a placeholder for a view controller in an external storyboard.
Navigation Controller - A controller that manages navigation through a hierarchy of views.
Table View Controller - A controller that manages a table view.
Collection View Controller - A controller that manages a collection view.
Tab Bar Controller - A controller that manages a set of view controllers that represent tab bar items.
Split View Controller - A composite view controller that manages left and right view controlle...
Page View Controller - Presents a sequence of view controllers as pages.
GLKit View Controller - A controller that manages a GLKit view.

Figure 10-12. *Expand the Library pane to see more controls and slide the splitter to resize the window with the mouse*

For Cocoa Touch objects, the Library contains the following (see Figure 10-13):

- Controls
- Data views
- Gesture recognizers
- Objects and controllers
- Window and bars

***Figure 10-13.** Various Cocoa Touch objects in the Library pane*

Inspector Pane and Selector Bar

The Inspector pane enables you to change the properties of the controls to make your objects follow your command. The Inspector pane has six tabs across the top, as shown in Figure 10-14.

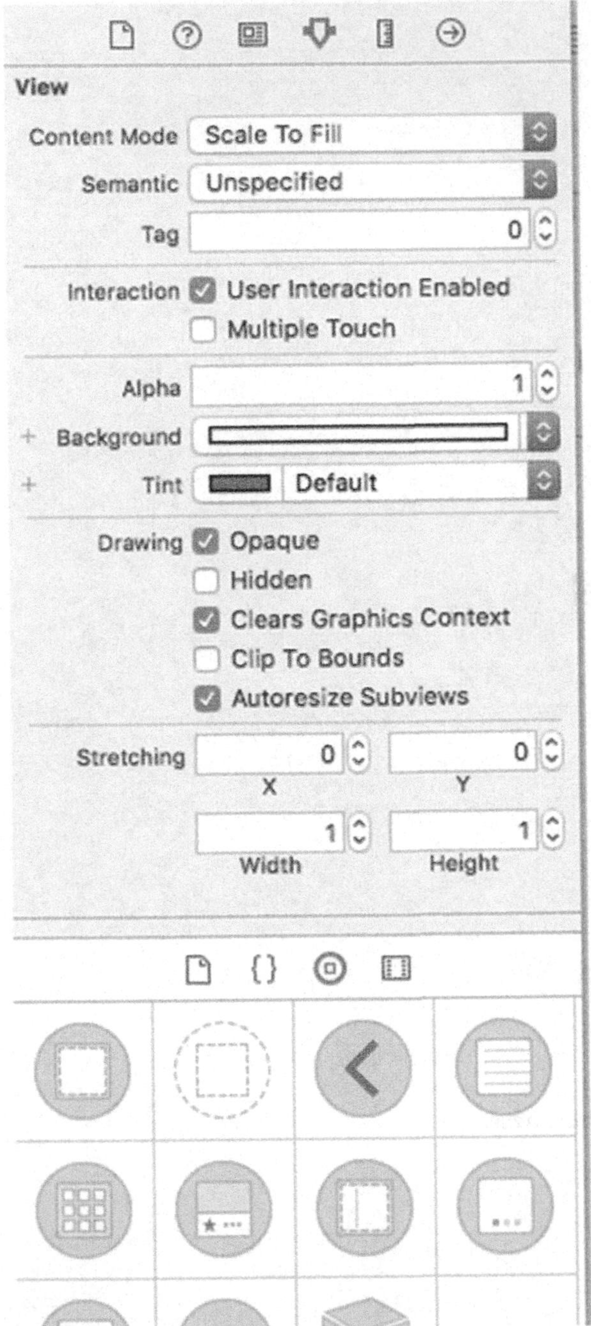

Figure 10-14. *The Attributes inspector and Selector Bar*

- File inspector
- Quick Help inspector
- Identity inspector
- Attributes inspector
- Size inspector
- Connections inspector

Creating the View

The random number generator will have three objects in the view: one label and two buttons. One button will generate the seed, another button will generate the random number, and the label shows the random number generated by the app.

1. Drag a Label control from the Library Pane Controls section to the View window, as shown in Figure 10-15.

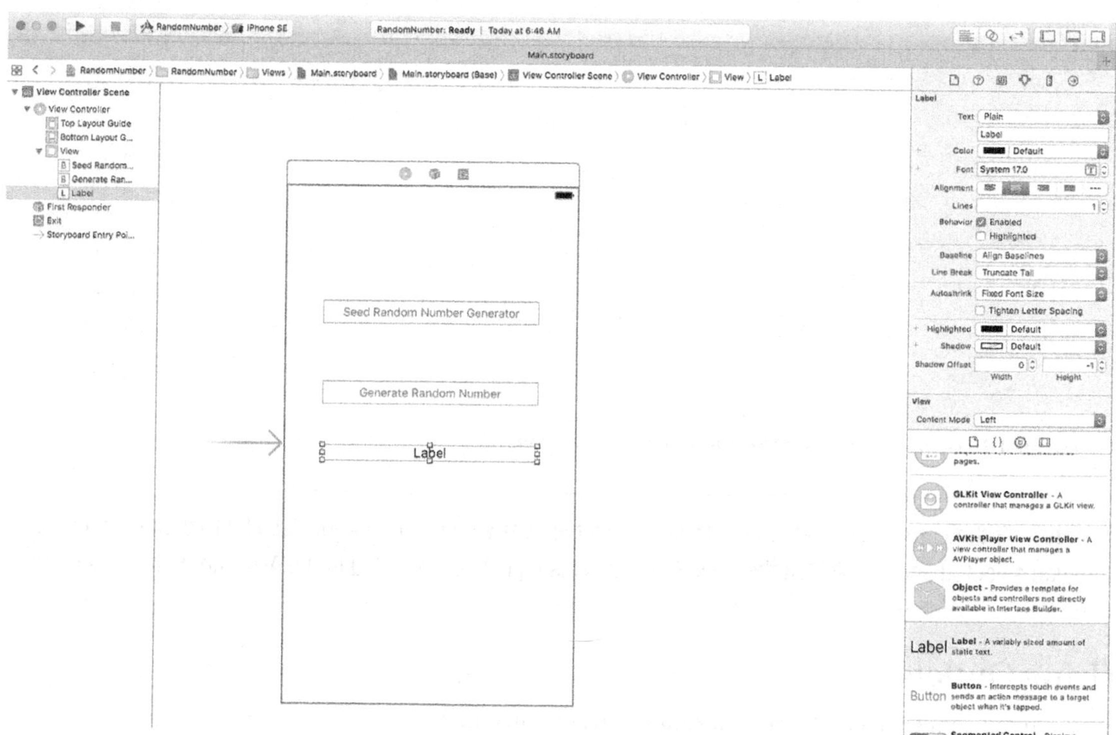

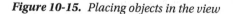

Figure 10-15. *Placing objects in the view*

2. Drag two buttons from the Library window to the View window.
3. Click the top button and change its title to Seed Random Number Generator.
4. Click the bottom button and change its title to Generate Random Number, as shown in Figure 10-15.

Now you get to use a great feature of Xcode. You can quickly and easily connect your outlets and actions to your code. Xcode actually goes one step further; it will create some of the code for you. All you have to do is drag and drop.

5. Click the Assistant Editor icon at the top right of the screen. This will display the associated `.swift` file for the view selected in the storyboard, as shown in Figure 10-16.

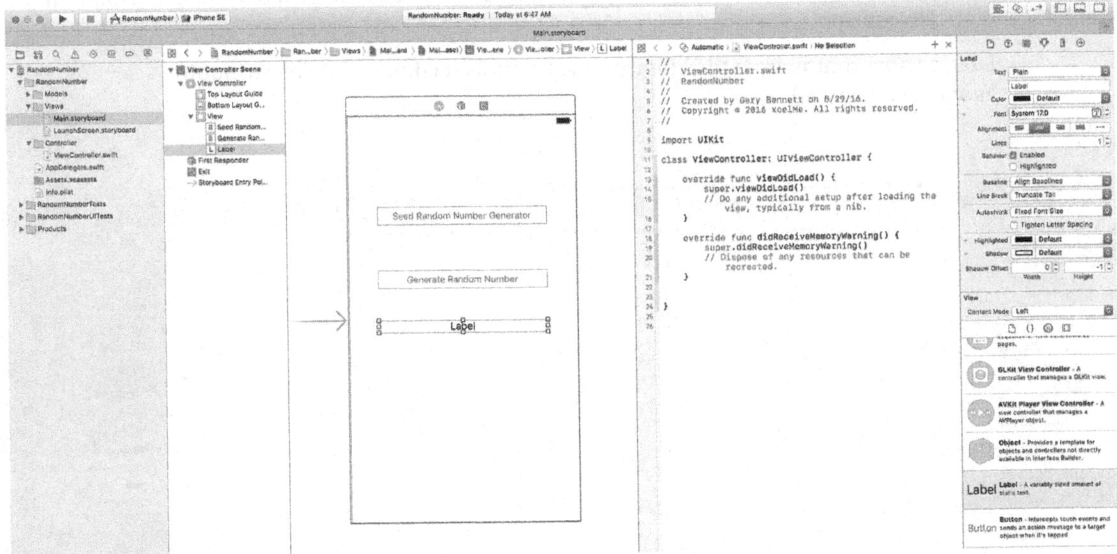
Automatic
ViewController.swift
No Selection
Seed Random Number Generator
Generate Random Number
Label
//
// ViewController.swift
// RandomNumber
//
// Created by Gary Bennett on 8/29/16.
// Copyright © 2016 xcelMe. All rights reserved.
//
import UIKit
class ViewController: UIViewController {
override func viewDidLoad() {
super.viewDidLoad()
// Do any additional setup after loading the view, typically from a nib.
}
override func didReceiveMemoryWarning() {
super.didReceiveMemoryWarning()
// Dispose of any resources that can be recreated.
}
}

Figure 10-16. *Using the Assistant Editor to display the .swift file*

■ **Note** If the correct associated `.swift` file doesn't appear when you click the Assistant Editor icon, make sure you selected and highlighted the view. Automatic also has to be selected in the Assistant Editor's jump bar.

Using Outlets

Now you can connect your label to your code by creating an outlet.

1. Control-drag from the label in the view to the top of your class file, as shown in Figure 10-17. This is holding down the Control key on the keyboard while clicking and dragging with the mouse. You can also right-click and drag.

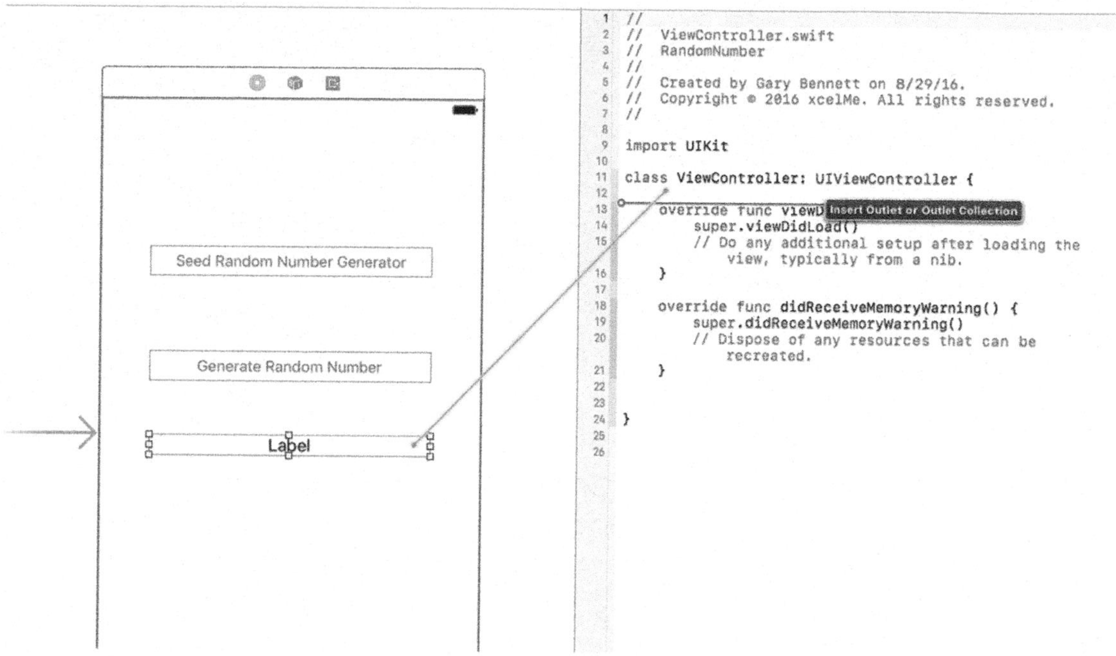
Seed Random Number Generator
Generate Random Number
Label
//
// ViewController.swift
// RandomNumber
//
// Created by Gary Bennett on 8/29/16.
// Copyright © 2016 xcelMe. All rights reserved.
//
import UIKit
class ViewController: UIViewController {
override func viewD
Insert Outlet or Outlet Collection
super.viewDidLoad()
// Do any additional setup after loading the view, typically from a nib.
}
override func didReceiveMemoryWarning() {
super.didReceiveMemoryWarning()
// Dispose of any resources that can be recreated.
}
}

Figure 10-17. *Control-dragging to create the code for the randomNumberLabel outlet*

2. A pop-up window will appear. This enables you to name and specify the type of outlet.

3. Complete the pop-up as shown in Figure 10-18 and click the Connect button.

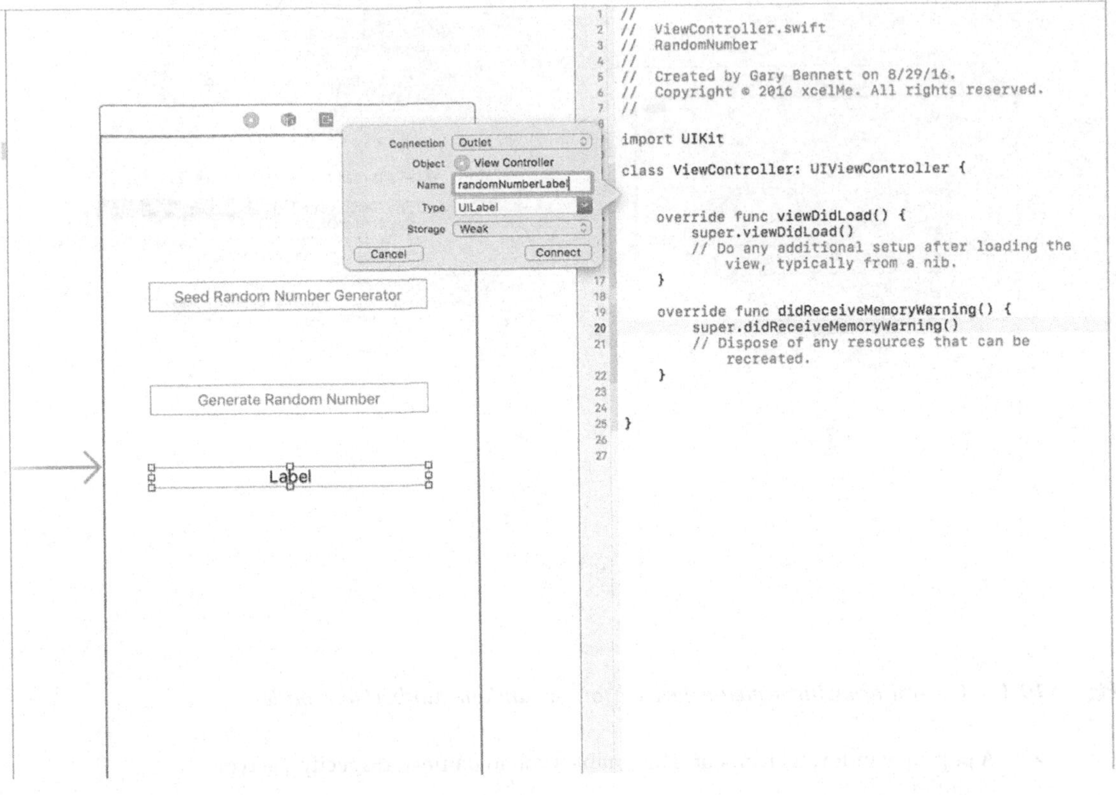
Connection
Outlet
Object
View Controller
Name
randomNumberLabel
Type
UILabel
Storage
Weak
Cancel
Connect
Seed Random Number Generator
Generate Random Number
Label
//
// ViewController.swift
// RandomNumber
//
// Created by Gary Bennett on 8/29/16.
// Copyright © 2016 xcelMe. All rights reserved.
//
import UIKit
class ViewController: UIViewController {
override func viewDidLoad() {
super.viewDidLoad()
// Do any additional setup after loading the
view, typically from a nib.
}
override func didReceiveMemoryWarning() {
super.didReceiveMemoryWarning()
// Dispose of any resources that can be
recreated.
}
}

Figure 10-18. *Pop-up for randomNumberLabel outlet*

The code is created for the outlet, and the outlet is now connected to the Label object in your `Main.storyboard` file. The shaded circle next to line 13 indicates the outlet is connected to an object in the `Main.storyboard` file, as shown in Figure 10-19.

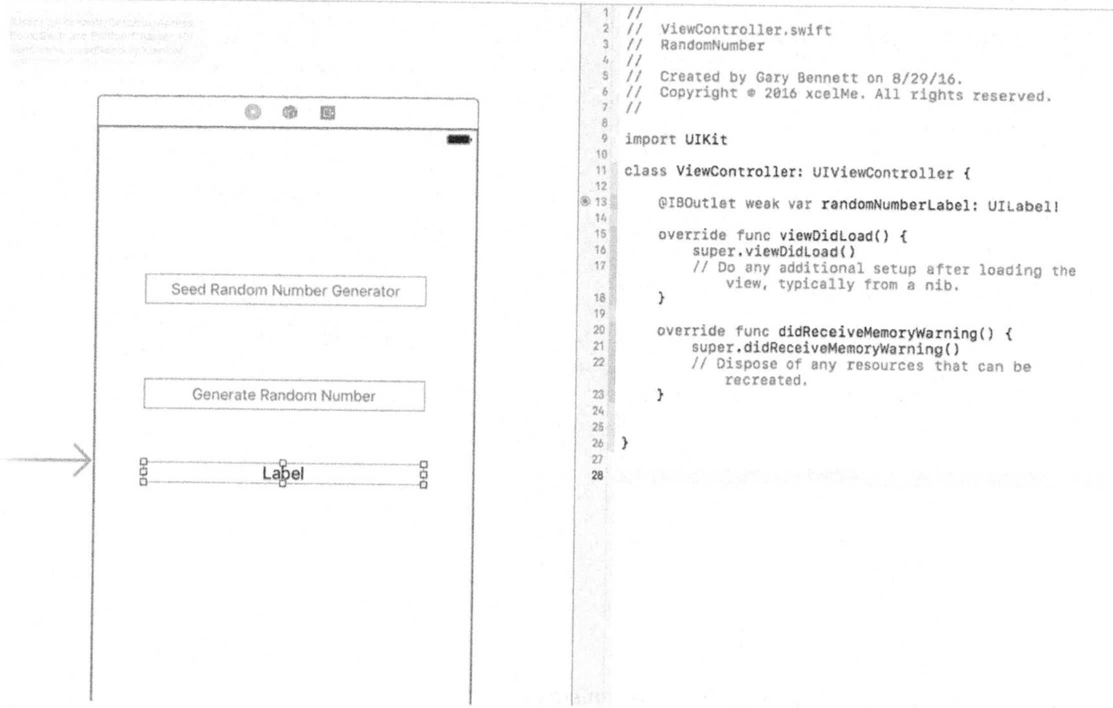
Seed Random Number Generator
Generate Random Number
Label
//
// ViewController.swift
// RandomNumber
//
// Created by Gary Bennett on 8/29/16.
// Copyright © 2016 xcelMe. All rights reserved.
//
import UIKit
class ViewController: UIViewController {
@IBOutlet weak var randomNumberLabel: UILabel!
override func viewDidLoad() {
super.viewDidLoad()
// Do any additional setup after loading the view, typically from a nib.
}
override func didReceiveMemoryWarning() {
super.didReceiveMemoryWarning()
// Dispose of any resources that can be recreated.
}
}

Figure 10-19. *Outlet property code generated and connected to the Label object*

There is a declaration that may be new to you called `IBOutlet`, commonly referred to simply as an *outlet.* Outlets signal to your controller that this property is connected to an object in Interface Builder. `IBOutlet` will enable Interface Builder to see the outlet and enable you to connect the property to the object in Interface Builder.

Using the analogy of an electrical wall outlet, these property outlets are connected to objects. Using Interface Builder, you can connect these properties to the appropriate object. When you change the properties of a connected outlet, the object that it is connected to will automatically change.

Using Actions

User interface object events, also known as *actions*, trigger methods.

Now you need to connect the object actions to the buttons.

1. Control-drag from the Seed Random Number Generator button to the bottom of your class. Complete the pop-up as indicated in Figure 10-20 and click the Connect button. Make sure you change the connection to an Action and not an Outlet.

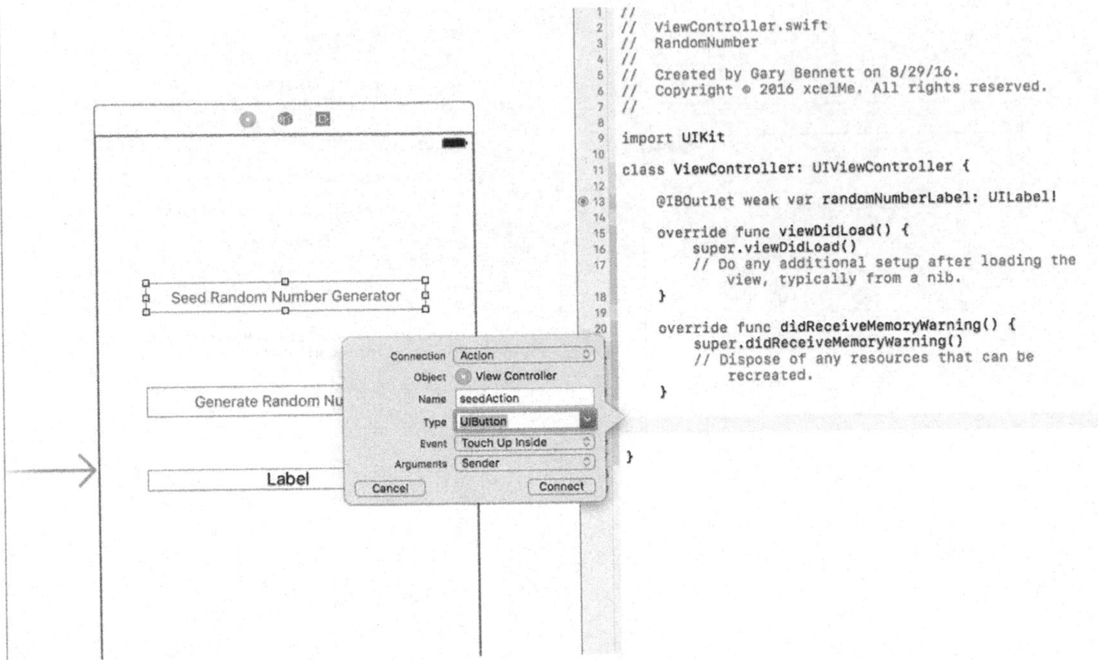
Seed Random Number Generator
Generate Random Nu
Label
Connection
Action
Object
View Controller
Name
seedAction
Type
UIButton
Event
Touch Up Inside
Arguments
Sender
Cancel
Connect
//
// ViewController.swift
// RandomNumber
//
// Created by Gary Bennett on 8/29/16.
// Copyright © 2016 xcelMe. All rights reserved.
//
import UIKit
class ViewController: UIViewController {
@IBOutlet weak var randomNumberLabel: UILabel!
override func viewDidLoad() {
super.viewDidLoad()
// Do any additional setup after loading the view, typically from a nib.
}
override func didReceiveMemoryWarning() {
super.didReceiveMemoryWarning()
// Dispose of any resources that can be recreated.
}
}

Figure 10-20. *Completing the pop-up for the Seed method*

2. Repeat the previous steps for the Generate Random Number button (see Figure 10-21).

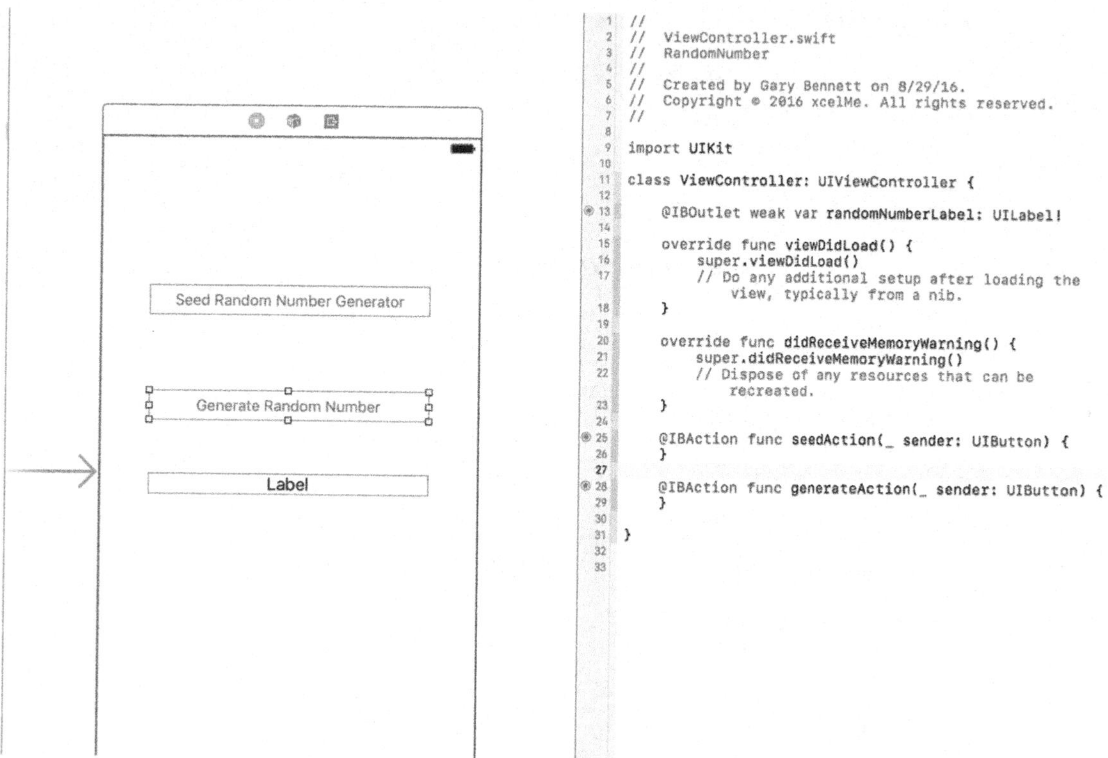
Seed Random Number Generator
Generate Random Number
Label
//
// ViewController.swift
// RandomNumber
//
// Created by Gary Bennett on 8/29/16.
// Copyright © 2016 xcelMe. All rights reserved.
//
import UIKit
class ViewController: UIViewController {
@IBOutlet weak var randomNumberLabel: UILabel!
override func viewDidLoad() {
super.viewDidLoad()
// Do any additional setup after loading the view, typically from a nib.
}
override func didReceiveMemoryWarning() {
super.didReceiveMemoryWarning()
// Dispose of any resources that can be recreated.
}
@IBAction func seedAction(_ sender: UIButton) {
}
@IBAction func generateAction(_ sender: UIButton) {
}
}

Figure 10-21. *Generate and Seed actions connected to their Button objects*

The Class

All that is left is to complete the code for your outlet and actions in the `.swift` file for the controller.

Open the `ViewController.swift` file and complete the `seedAction` and `generateAction` methods, as shown in Figure 10-22.

```
//

import UIKit

class ViewController: UIViewController {

    @IBOutlet weak var randomNumberLabel: UILabel!

    override func viewDidLoad() {
        super.viewDidLoad()
        // Do any additional setup after loading the view, typically
            from a nib.
    }

    override func didReceiveMemoryWarning() {
        super.didReceiveMemoryWarning()
        // Dispose of any resources that can be recreated.
    }

    @IBAction func seedAction(_ sender: UIButton) {
        srandom(CUnsignedInt(time(nil)))
        randomNumberLabel.text = "Generator seended"
    }

    @IBAction func generateAction(_ sender: UIButton) {
        let generated = (arc4random() % 100) + 1
        randomNumberLabel.text = "\(generated)"
    }

}
```

Figure 10-22. *The seedAction and generateAction methods completed*

There is some code you should examine a bit further. The following line seeds the random generator so that you get a random number each time you run the app. There are easier ways of to do this, but for the purposes of this section, you just want to see how actions and outlets work.

```
srandom(CUnsignedInt(time(nil)))
```

In the following code, the property `text` sets the `UILabel` value in your view. The connection you established in Interface Builder from your outlet to the `Label` object does all the work for you.

```
randomNumber.text
```

There is just one more thing you need to do now. Select the `Main.storyboard` file and then select your view controller scene. Then click Resolve Auto Layout Issues. Then click Add Missing Constraints. This will enable your controls to center correctly in your view, as shown in Figure 10-23.

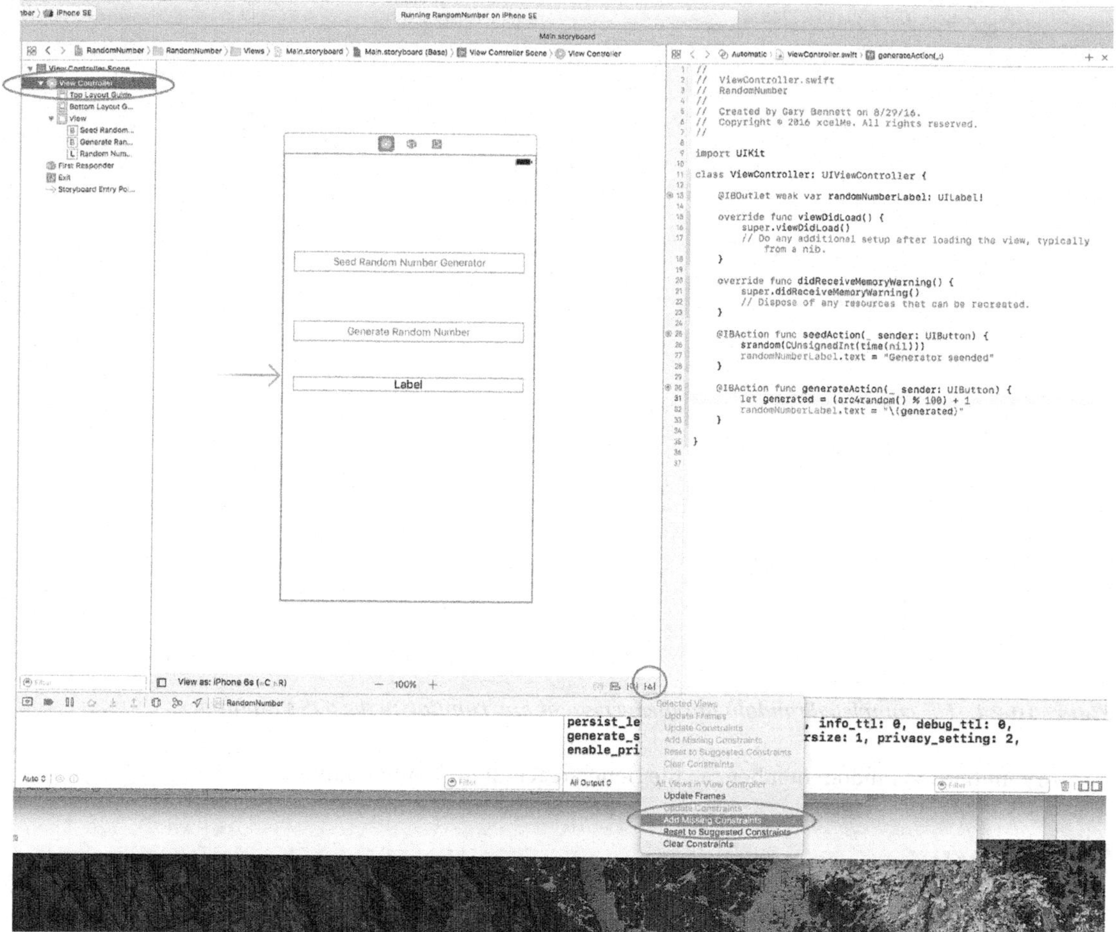

Figure 10-23. *Auto Layout*

That's it!

To run your iPhone app in the iPhone simulator, click the Play button. Your app should launch in the simulator, as shown in Figure 10-24.

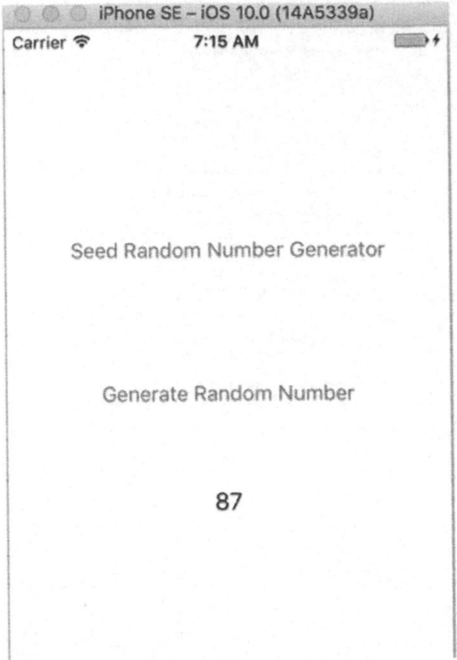

***Figure 10-24.** The completed random number generator app running in the iOS simulator*

To generate the random number, tap the Generate Random Number button.

Summary

Great job! Interface Builder saves you a lot of time when creating user interfaces. You have a powerful set of objects to use in your application and are responsible for a minimal amount of coding.

Interface Builder handles many of the details you would normally have to deal with.

You should be familiar with the following terms:

- Storyboard and XIB files
- Model-View-Controller
- Architectural patterns
- Human Interface Guidelines (HIG)
- Outlets
- Actions

EXERCISES

- Extend the random number generator app to show a date and time in a `Label` object when the app starts.
- After showing a date and time label, add a button to update the data and time label with the new time.

CHAPTER 11

Storing Information

As a developer, there will be many different situations when you will need to store data. Users will expect your application (*app*) to remember preferences and other information each time they launch it. Previous chapters discussed the BookStore app. With this app, users will expect your application to remember all of the books in the bookstore. Your application will need a way to store this information, retrieve it, and possibly search and sort this data. Working with data can sometimes be difficult. Fortunately, Apple has provided methods and frameworks to make this process easier.

This chapter discusses two different formats in which data will need to be stored. It discusses how to save a preference file for an iOS device and then how to use an SQLite database in your application to store and retrieve data.

Storage Considerations

There are some major storage differences between the Mac and the iPhone, and these differences will affect how you work with data. Let's start by discussing the Mac and how you will need to develop for it.

On the Mac, by default, applications are stored in the `Applications` folder. Each user has their own home folder where preferences and information related to that user are stored. Not all of the users will have access to write to the `Applications` folder or to the application bundle itself.

On the iPhone and iPad, developers do not need to deal with different users. Every person who uses the iPhone has the same permissions and the same folders. There are some other factors to consider with the iPhone, though. Every application on an iOS device is in its own *sandbox*. This means that files written by an application can be seen and used only by that individual application. This makes for a more secure environment for the iPhone, but it also presents some changes in the way you work with data storage.

Preferences

There are some things to consider when deciding where to store certain kinds of information. The easiest way to store information is within the preferences file, but this method has some downsides.

- All of the data is both read and written at the same time. If you are going to be writing often or writing and reading large amounts of data, this could take time and slow down your application. As a general rule, your preferences file should never be larger than 100KB. If your preferences file starts to become larger than 100KB, consider using Core Data as a way to store your information.
- The preferences file does not provide many options when it comes to searching and ordering information.

G. Bennett and B. Lees, *Swift 3 for Absolute Beginners*, DOI 10.1007/978-1-4842-2331-4_11

The preferences file is really nothing more than a standardized XML file with accompanying classes and methods to store application-specific information. A preference would be, for example, the sorting column and direction (ascending/descending) of a list. Anything that is generally customizable within an app should be stored in a preferences file.

■ **Caution** Sensitive data should not be stored in the preferences file or in a database without additional encryption. Luckily, Apple provides a way to store sensitive information. It is called the *keychain*. Securing data in the keychain is beyond the scope of this book.

Writing Preferences

Apple has provided developers with the `UserDefaults` class; this class makes it easy to read and write preferences for iOS, Mac OS XmacOS, tvOS, and watchOS. The great thing is that, in this case, you can use the same code for iOS, macOS, and tvOS. The only difference between the two implementations is the location of the preferences file.

■ **Note** For macOS, the preferences file is named `com.yourcompany.applicationname.plist` and is located in the `/Users/username/Library/Preferences` folder. On iOS, the preferences file is located in your application's container in the `/Library/Preferences` folder.

All you need to do to write preferences is to create a `UserDefaults` object. This is done with the following line:

```
var prefs: UserDefaults = UserDefaults.standard
```

This instantiates the `prefs` object so you can use it to set preference values. Next, you need to set the preference keys for the values that you want to save. The `BookStore` app example will be used to demonstrate specific instructions throughout this chapter. When running a bookstore, you might want to save a username or encrypted password in the preferences. You also might want to save things such as a default book category or recent searches. The preferences file is a great place to store this type of information because this is the kind of information that needs to be read only when the application is launched.

Also, on iOS, it is often necessary to save your current state. If a person is using your application and then gets a phone call, you want to be able to bring them back to the exact place they were in your application when they are done with their phone call. This is less necessary now with the implementation of multitasking, but your users will still appreciate it if your application remembers what they were doing the next time they launch it.

Once you have instantiated the object, you can just call `setForKey` to set an object. If you wanted to save the username of `sherlock.holmes`, you would call the following line of code:

```
prefs.set ("sherlock.holmes", forKey: "username")
```

After a certain period of time, your app will automatically write changes to the preferences file. You can force your app to save the preferences by calling the `synchronize` function, but this should only be used if you cannot wait for the next synchronization interval such as if you app is immediately going to exit. To call the `synchronize` function, you would write the following line:

```
prefs.synchronize()
```

With just three lines of code, you are able to create a preference object, set a preference value, and write the preferences file. It is an easy and clean process. Here is all of the code:

```
var prefs: UserDefaults = UserDefaults.standard
prefs.set("sherlock.holmes", forKey: "username")
prefs.synchronize()
```

Reading Preferences

Reading preferences is similar to writing preferences. Just like with writing, the first step is to obtain the `UserDefaults` object. This is done in the same way as it was done in the writing process:

```
var prefs: UserDefaults = UserDefaults.standard
```

Now that you have the object, you are able to access the preference values that are set. For writing, you use the `set` syntax; for reading, you use the `string(forKey:)` method. You use the `string(forKey:)` method because the value you put in the preference was a `String`. In the writing example, you set preferences for the username and for the number of books in the list to display. You can read those preferences by using the following simple lines of code:

```
var username = prefs.string(forKey: "username")
var booksInList = prefs.integer(forKey: "booksInList")
```

Pay close attention to what is happening in each of these lines. You start by declaring the variable `username`, which is a `String`. This variable will be used to store the preference value of the username you stored in the preferences. Then, you just assign it to the value of the preference `username`. You will notice that in the read example you do not use the `synchronize` method. This is because you have not changed the values of the preferences; therefore, you do not need to make sure they are written to a disk.

Databases

You have learned how to store some small pieces of information and retrieve them at a later point. What if you have more information that needs to be stored? What if you need to conduct a search within this information or put it in some sort of order? These kinds of situations call for a database.

A database is a tool for storing a significant amount of information in a way that it can be easily searched or retrieved. When reading data from a database, pieces of data are returned rather than the entire file. Many applications you use in your daily life are based on databases of some sort. Your online banking application retrieves your account activity from a database. Your supermarket uses a database to retrieve prices for different items. A simple example of a database is a spreadsheet. You may have many columns and many rows in your spreadsheet. The columns in your spreadsheet represent different types of information you want to store. In a database, these are considered *attributes*. The rows in your spreadsheet would be considered different *records* in your database.

Storing Information in a Database

Databases are usually an intimidating subject for a developer; most developers associate databases with enterprise database servers such as Microsoft SQL Server or Oracle. These applications can take time to set up and require constant management. For most developers, a database system like Oracle would be too much to handle. Luckily, Apple has included a small and efficient database engine called SQLite in iOS, macOS, and tvOS. This allows you to gain many of the features of complex database servers without the overhead.

SQLite will provide you with a lot of flexibility in storing information for your application. It stores the entire database in a single file. It is fast, reliable, and easy to implement in your application. The best thing about the SQLite database is that there is no need to install any software; Apple has taken care of that for you.

However, SQLite does have some limitations that, as a developer, you should be aware of.

- SQLite was designed as a single-user database. You will not want to use SQLite in an environment where more than one person will be accessing the same database. This could lead to data loss or corruption.
- In the business world, databases can grow to become very large. It is not surprising for a database manager to handle databases as large as half a terabyte, and in some cases databases can become much larger than that. SQLite should be able to handle smaller databases without any issues, but you will begin to see performance issues if your database starts to get too large.
- SQLite lacks some of the backup and data restore features of the enterprise database solutions.

For the purposes of this chapter, you will focus on using SQLite as your database engine. If any of the mentioned limitations are present in the application you are developing, you may need to look into an enterprise database solution, which is beyond the scope of this book.

■ **Note** SQLite (pronounced "sequel-lite") gets its name from Structured Query Language (SQL, pronounced "sequel"). SQL is the language used to enter, search, and retrieve data from a database.

Apple has worked hard to iron out a lot of the challenges of database development. As a developer, you will not need to become familiar with SQL because Apple has taken care of the direct database interaction for you through a framework called Core Data, which makes interacting with the database much easier. Core Data has been adapted by Apple from a NeXT product called Enterprise Object Framework, and working with Core Data is a lot easier than interfacing directly with the SQLite database. Directly accessing a database via SQL is beyond the scope of this book.

Getting Started with Core Data

Let's start by creating a new Core Data project.

1. Open Xcode and select File ➤ New ➤ Project. To create an iOS Core Data project, select iOS from the menu on the top. Then select Single View Application, as shown in Figure 11-1.

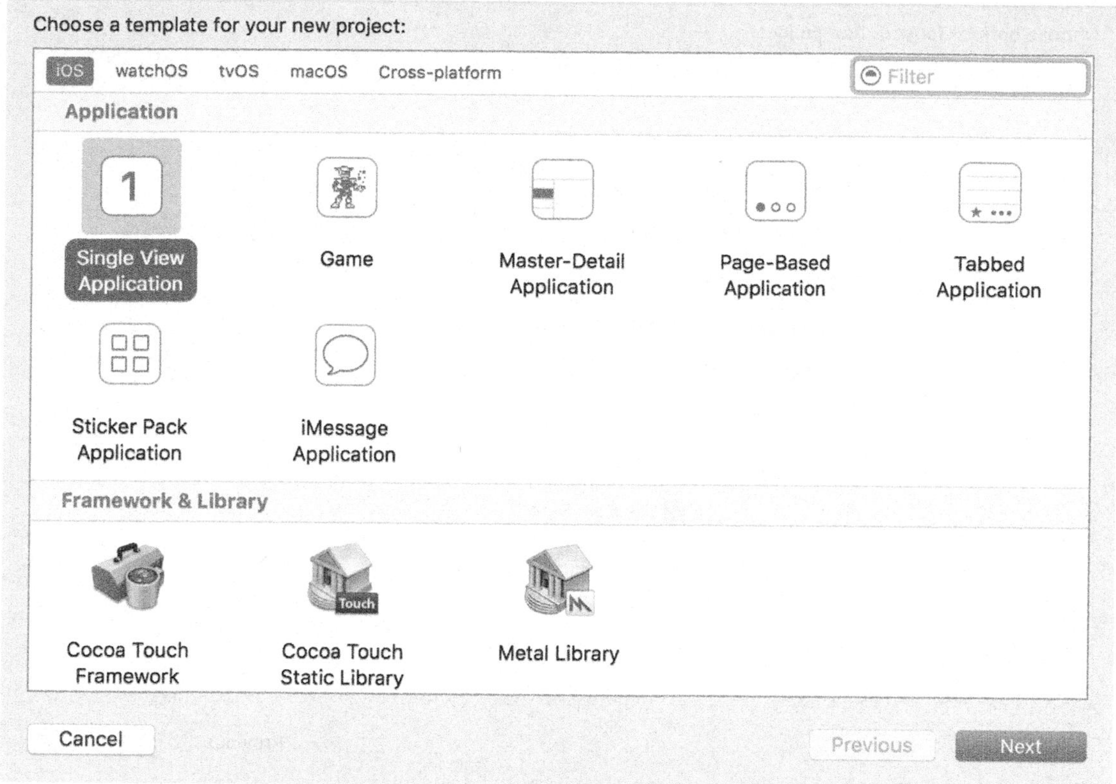

Figure 11-1. *Creating a new project*

2. Click the Next button when you're done. The next screen will allow you to enter the name you want to use. For the purposes of this chapter, you will use the name `BookStore`.
3. Near the bottom, you will see the checkbox called Use Core Data. Make sure this is checked and then click Next, as shown in Figure 11-2.

■ **Note** Core Data can be added to any project at any point. Checking that box when creating a project will add the Core Data frameworks and a default data model to your application. If you know you are going to use Core Data, checking this box will save you time.

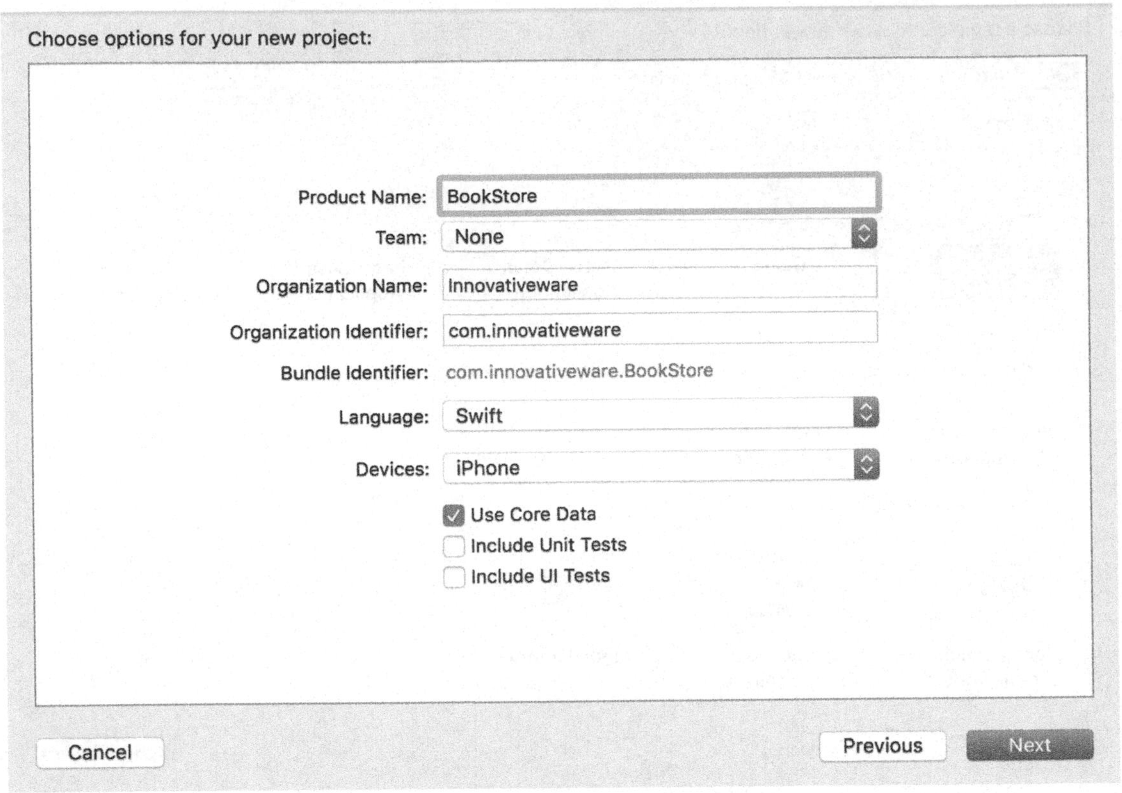

Figure 11-2. *Adding Core Data to your project*

4. Select a location to save the project and click Create.

Once you are done with that, your new project will open. It will look similar to a standard application, except now you will have a `BookStore.xcdatamodeld` file. This file is called a *data model* and will contain the information about the data that you will be storing in Core Data.

The Model

In your BookStore folder on the right, you will see a file called `BookStoreCoreData.xcdatamodeld`. This file will contain information about the data you want stored in the database. Click the model file (`.xcdatamodeld`) to open it. You will see a window similar to the one shown in Figure 11-3.

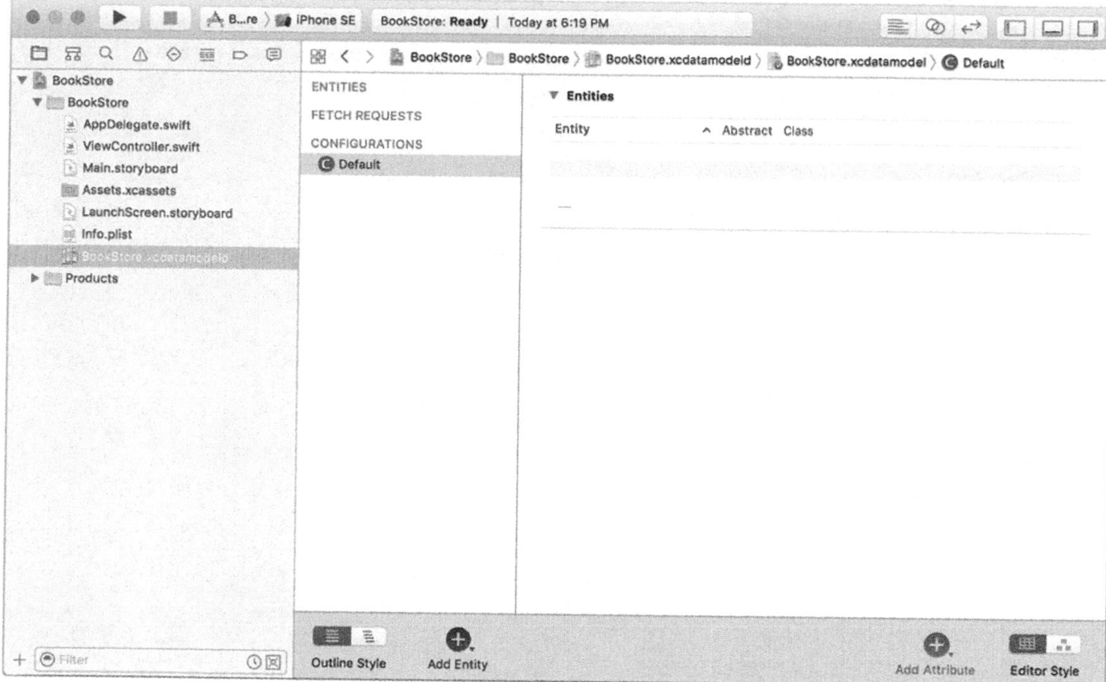

Figure 11-3. *The blank model*

The window is divided into four sections. On the left, you have your entities. In more common terms, these are the objects or items that you want to store in the database.

The top-right section contains the entity's attributes. Attributes are pieces of information about the entities. For example, a book would be an entity, and the title of the book would be an attribute of that entity.

■ **Note** In database terms, entities are your *tables*, and the attributes of the entities are called *columns*. The objects created from those entities are referred to as *rows*.

The middle window on the right will show you all the relationships of an entity. A relationship connects one entity to another. For example, you will create a `Book` entity and an `Author` entity. You will then relate them so that every book can have an author. The bottom-right portion of the screen will deal with fetched properties. Fetched properties are beyond the scope of this book, but they allow you to create filters for your data.

Let's create an entity.

1. Click the plus sign in the bottom-left corner of the window, or select Editor ➤ Add Entity from the menu, as shown in Figure 11-4.

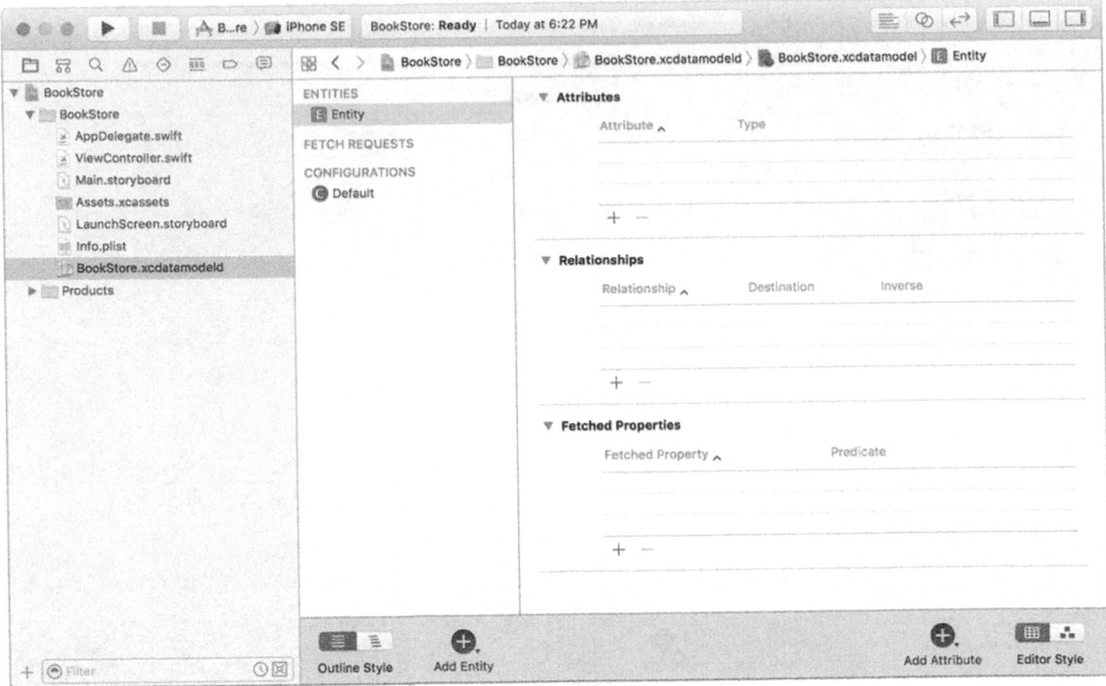

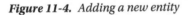

Figure 11-4. Adding a new entity

2. On the left side, double click the Entity name and change the name to **Book**.

■ **Note** You must capitalize your entities' names.

---

3. Now let's add some attributes. Attributes would be considered the details of a book, so you will store the title, author, price, and year the book was published. Obviously, in your own applications, you may want to store more information, such as the publisher, page count, and genre, but you want to start simple. Click the plus sign at the bottom right of the window, or select Editor ➤ Add Attribute, as shown in Figure 11-5. If you do not see the option to add an attribute, make sure you have selected the Book entity on the left side.

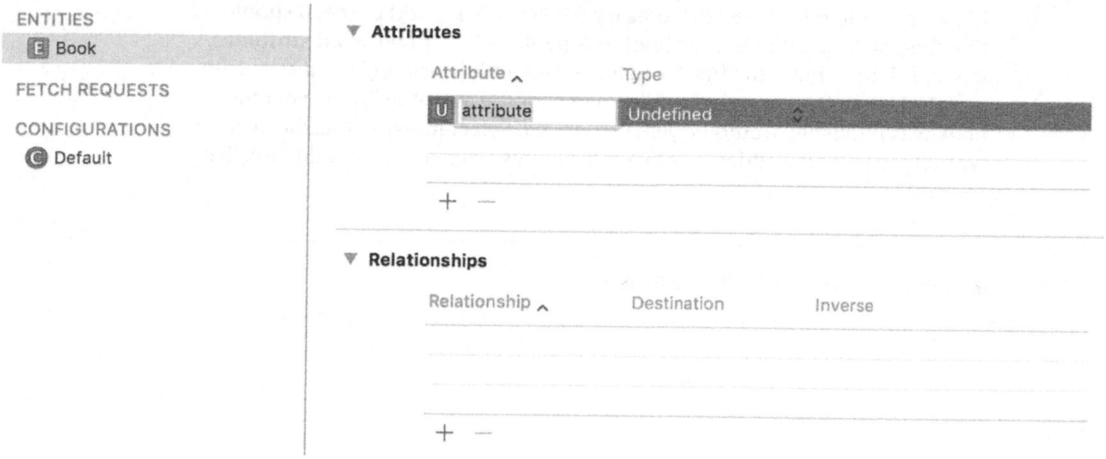

Figure 11-5. Adding a new attribute

4. You will be given only two options for your attribute, the name and the data type. Let's call this attribute **title**. Unlike entities, attribute names must be lowercase.

5. Now, you will need to select a data type. Selecting the correct data type is important. It will affect how your data is stored and retrieved from the database. The list has 12 items in it and can be daunting. We will discuss the most common options and, as you become more familiar with Core Data, you can experiment with the other options. The most common options are String, Integer 32, Decimal, and Date. For the title of the book, select String.

   String: This is the type of attribute used to store text. This should be used to store any kind of information that is not a number or a date. In this example, the book title and author will be strings.

   Integer 32: There are three different integer values possible for an attribute. Each of the integer types differs only in the minimum and maximum values possible. Integer 32 should cover most of your needs when storing an integer. An integer is a number without a decimal. If you try to save a decimal in an integer attribute, the decimal portion will be truncated. In this example, the year published will be an integer.

   Decimal: A decimal is a type of attribute that can store numbers with decimals. A decimal is similar to a double attribute, but they differ in their minimum and maximum values and precision. A decimal should be able to handle any currency values. In this example, you will use a decimal to store the price of the book.

   Date: A date attribute is exactly what it sounds like. It allows you to store a date and time and then performs searches and lookups based on these values. You will not use this type in this example.

6. Let's create the rest of the attributes for the book. Now, add `price`. It should be a Decimal. Add the year the book was published. For two-word attributes, it is standard to make the first word lowercase and the second word start with a capital letter. For example, an ideal name for the attribute for the year the book was published would be `yearPublished`. Select Integer 32 as the attribute type. Once you have added all of your attributes, your screen should look like Figure 11-6.

■ **Note** Attribute names cannot contain spaces.

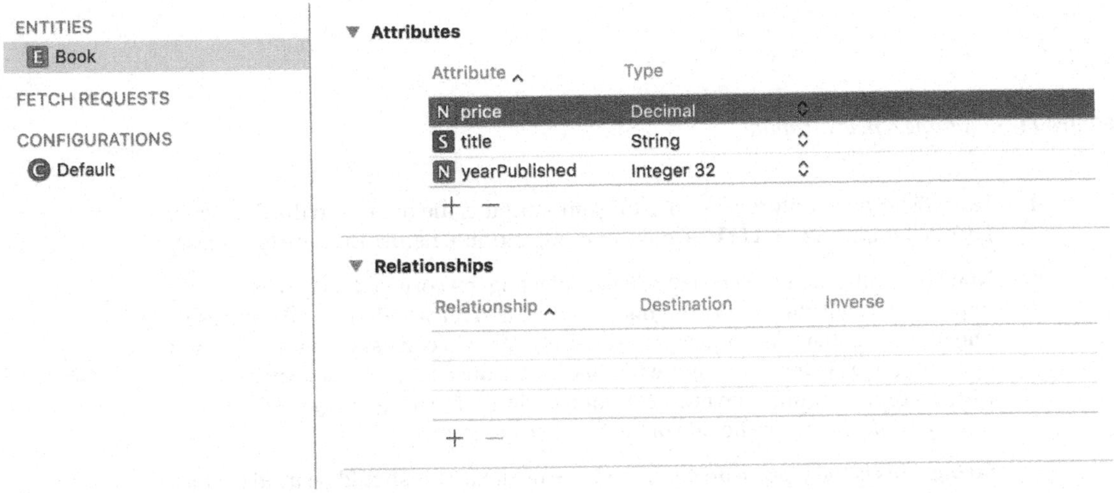

Figure 11-6. *The finished Book entity*

■ **Note** If you are used to working with databases, you will notice that you did not add a primary key. A primary key is a field (usually a number) that is used to uniquely identify each record in a database. In Core Data databases, there is no need to create primary keys. The Framework will manage all of that for you.

Now that you have finished the Book entity, let's add an `Author` entity.

1. Add a new entity and call it **`Author`**.
2. To this entity, add `lastName` and `firstName`, both of which are strings.

Once this is done, you should have two entities in your entity list. Now you need to add the relationships.

1. Click the Book entity, and then click and hold on the plus sign that is located on the bottom right of the screen. Select Add Relationship, as shown in Figure 11-7. (You can also click the plus under the Relationships section of the Core Data model.)

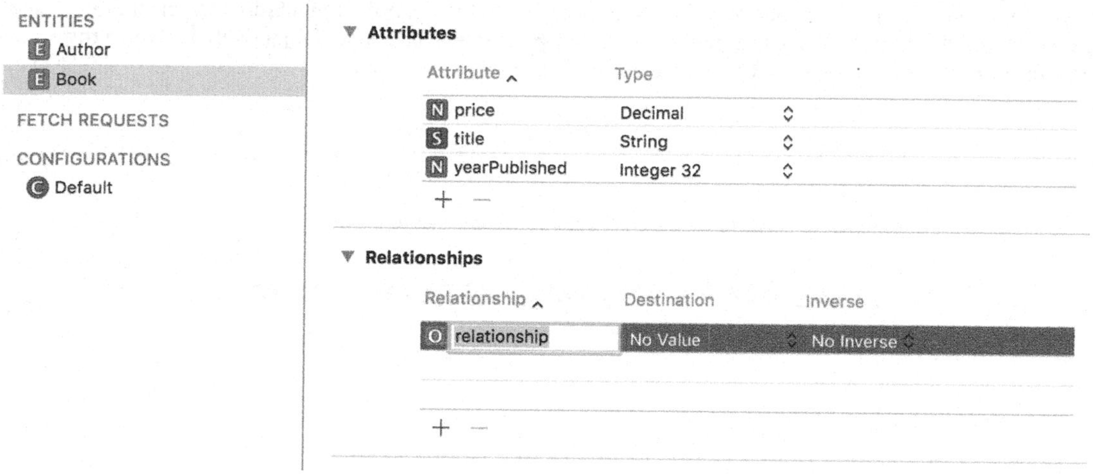

Figure 11-7. Adding a new relationship

2. You will be given the opportunity to name your relationship. You usually give a relationship the same name as the entity to which it derived from. Type in `author` as the name and select Author from the Destination drop-down menu.

3. You have created one- half of your relationship. To create the other half, click the `Author` entity. Click the plus sign located at the bottom right of the screen and select Add Relationship. You will use the entity name that you are connecting to as the name of this relationship, so you will call it `books`. (You are adding an *s* to the relationship name because an author can have many books.) Under Destination, select Book, and under Inverse, select the author relationship you made in the previous step. In the Utilities window on the right side of the screen, select the Data Model Inspector. Select To Many for the type of the relationship. Your model should now look like Figure 11-8.

■ **Note** Sometimes in Xcode, when working with models, it is necessary to press the Tab key for the names of entities, attributes, and relationships to update. This little quirk can be traced all the way back to WebObjects tools.

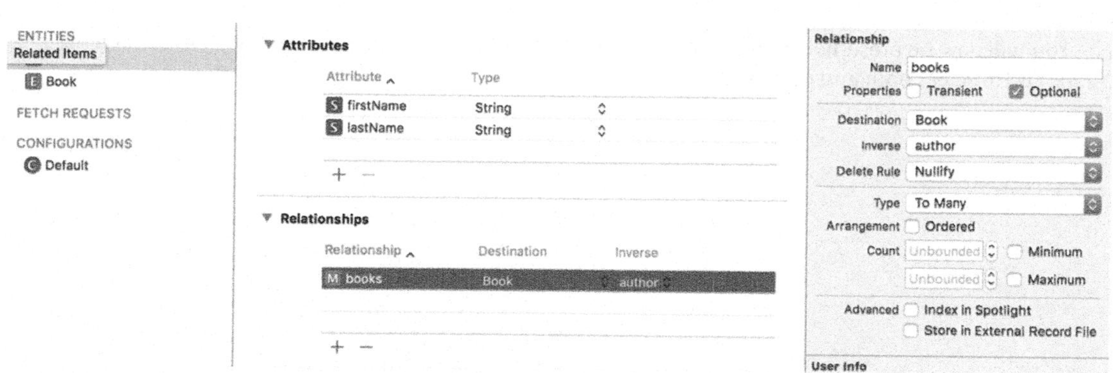

Figure 11-8. The final relationship

Now you need to tell your code about your new entity. To do this, hold down Shift and select the `Book` entity and the `Author` entity and then select Editor ➤ Create NSManagedObject Subclass from the Application menu. Your screen should look like Figure 11-9.

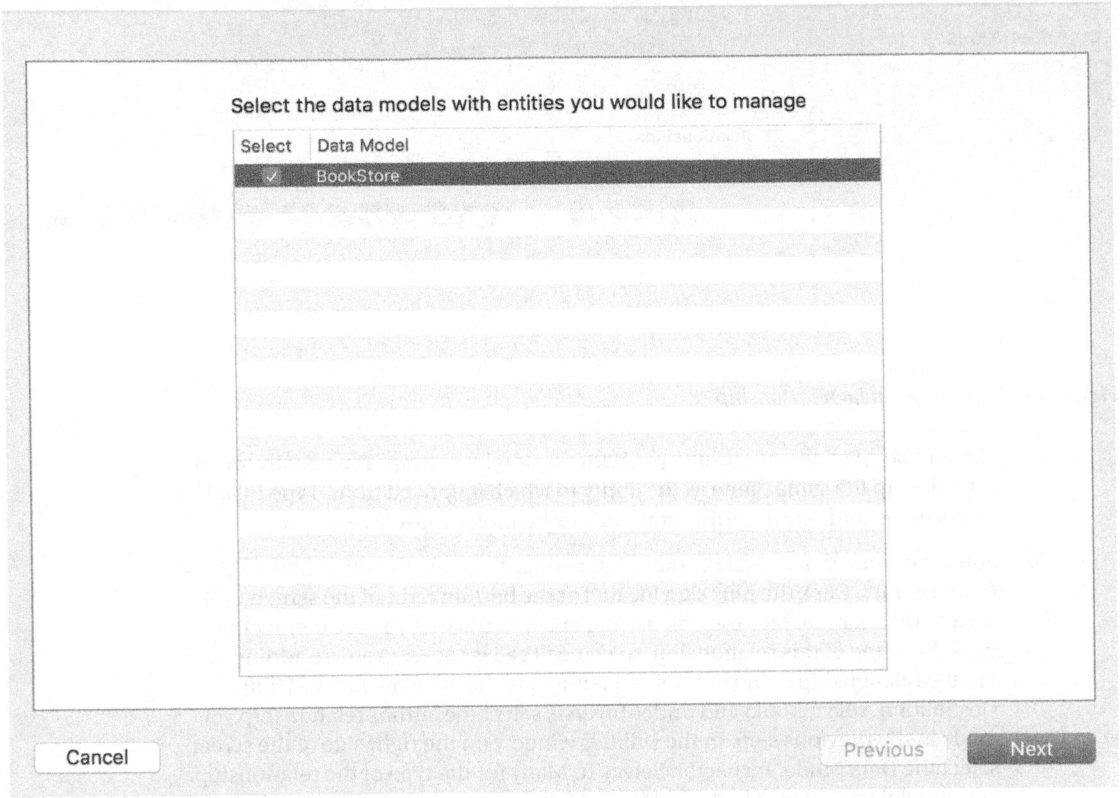

Figure 11-9. *Adding the managed objects to your project*

This screen allows you to select the data model you would like to create managed objects for. In this case, you have only a single data model. In some complicated applications, you may have more than one. Managed objects represent instances of an entity from your data model. Select the BookStore data model and click Next.

You will now be presented with a screen to select the entities to create managed objects, as seen in Figure 11-10. Select both and click Next.

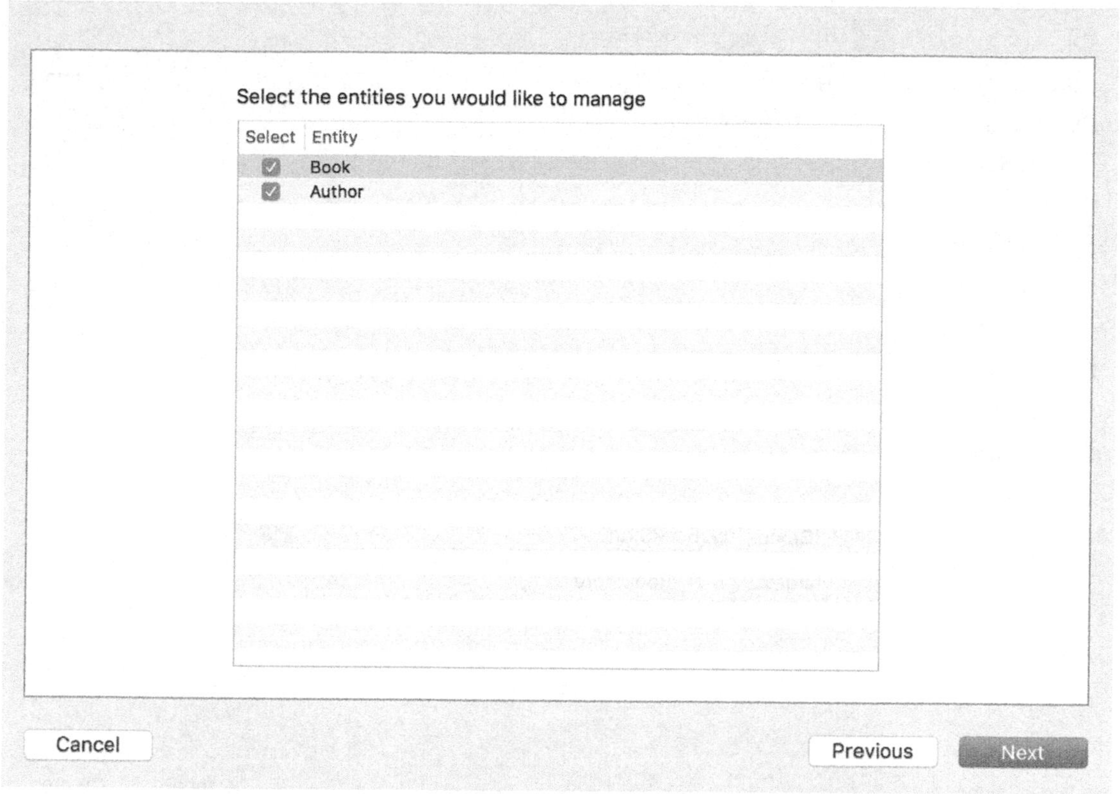

Figure 11-10. *Select the entities to create managed objects*

Select the storage location and add it to your project, as seen in Figure 11-11. Then click Create. You will notice that four files have been added to your project. `Book+CoreDataProperties.swift` and `Author+CoreDataProperties.swift` contain the information about the book and author entities you just created. `Book+CoreDataClass.swift` and `Author+CoreDataClass.swift` will be used for logic relating to your new entities. These files will need to be used to access the entities and attributes you added to your data model. These files are fairly simple because Core Data will do most of the work with them. You should also notice that if you go back to your model and click Book, it will have a new class in the Data Model Inspector. Instead of an `NSManagedObject`, it will have a `Book` class.

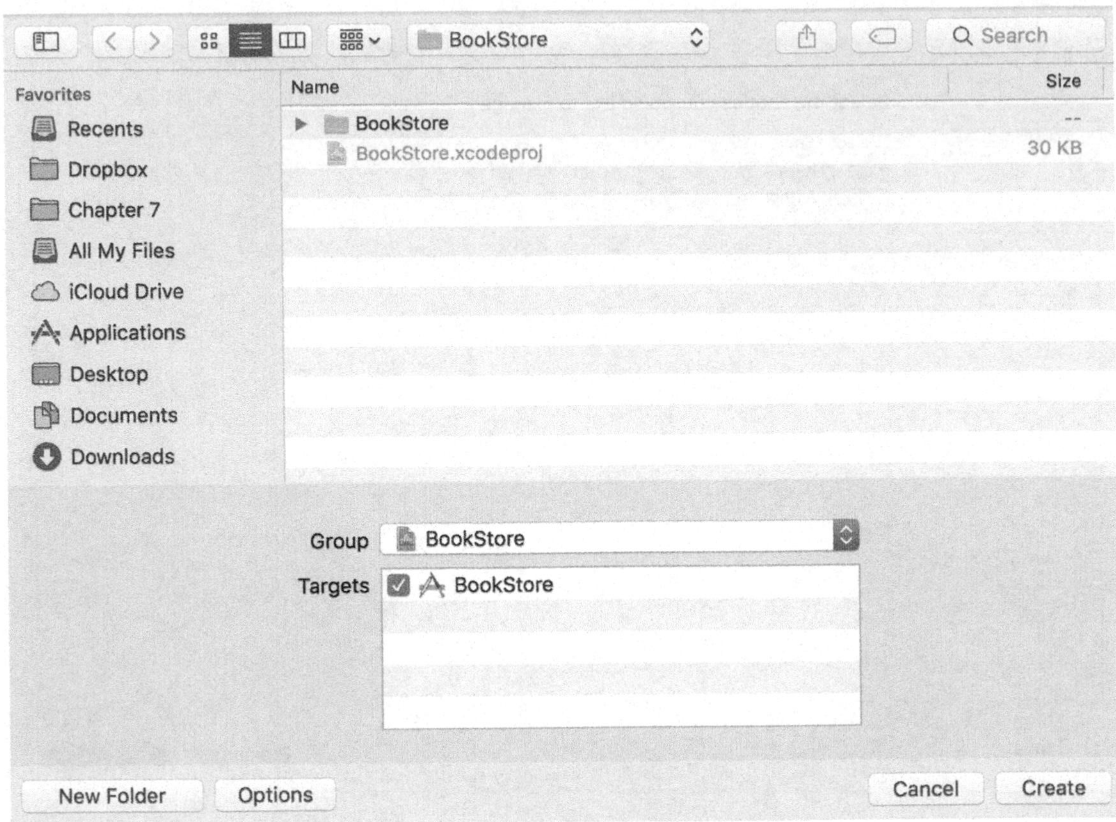

Figure 11-11. *Select the save location for your new managed objects*

Let's look at some of the contents of Book+CoreDataProperties.swift:

```
import Foundation
import CoreData

extension Book {

    @nonobjc public class func fetchRequest() -> NSFetchRequest<Book> {
        return NSFetchRequest<Book>(entityName: "Book");
    }

    @NSManaged public var title: String?
    @NSManaged public var yearPublished: Int32
    @NSManaged public var price: NSDecimalNumber?
    @NSManaged public var author: Author?

}
```

You will see that the file starts by including the Foundation and Core Data frameworks. This allows Core Data to manage your information. This file contains an extension to the Book class. An extension allows you to add new computed properties and functionality to an existing class. By creating the Book+CoreDataClass.swift and the Book+CoreDataProperties.swift files, Xcode allows the developer to separate the attributes from the basic logic. The superclass for the new Book object is NSManagedObject. NSManagedObject is an object that handles all of the Core Data database interaction. It provides the methods and properties you will be using in this example. Later in the file, you will see the three attributes and the one relationship you created.

Managed Object Context

You have created a managed object class called Book. The nice thing with Xcode is that it will generate the necessary code to manage these new data objects. In Core Data, every managed object should exist within a managed object context. The context is responsible for tracking changes to objects, carrying out undo operations, and writing the data to the database. This is helpful because you can now save a bunch of changes at once rather than saving each individual change. This speeds up the process of saving the records. As a developer, you do not need to track when an object has been changed. The managed object context will handle all of that for you.

Setting Up the Interface

The following steps will assist you in setting up your interface:

1. In the BookStore folder in your project, you should have a Main.storyboard file. Click this file and Xcode will open it in the editing window, as shown in Figure 11-12.

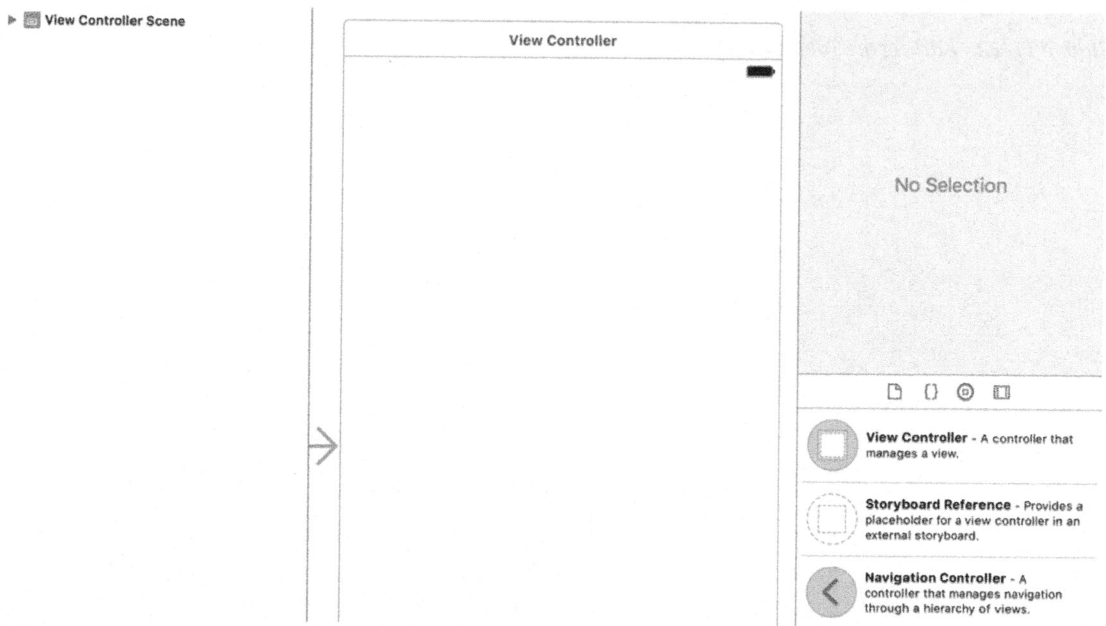
View Controller Scene
View Controller
No Selection
View Controller - A controller that manages a view.
Storyboard Reference - Provides a placeholder for a view controller in an external storyboard.
Navigation Controller - A controller that manages navigation through a hierarchy of views.

Figure 11-12. *Creating the interface*

2. There should be a blank window. To add some functionality to your window, you need to add some objects from the Object Library. Type `table` into the search field on the bottom right of the screen. This should narrow the objects, and you should see Table View Controller and Table View. Drag the Table view to the view, as shown in Figure 11-13.

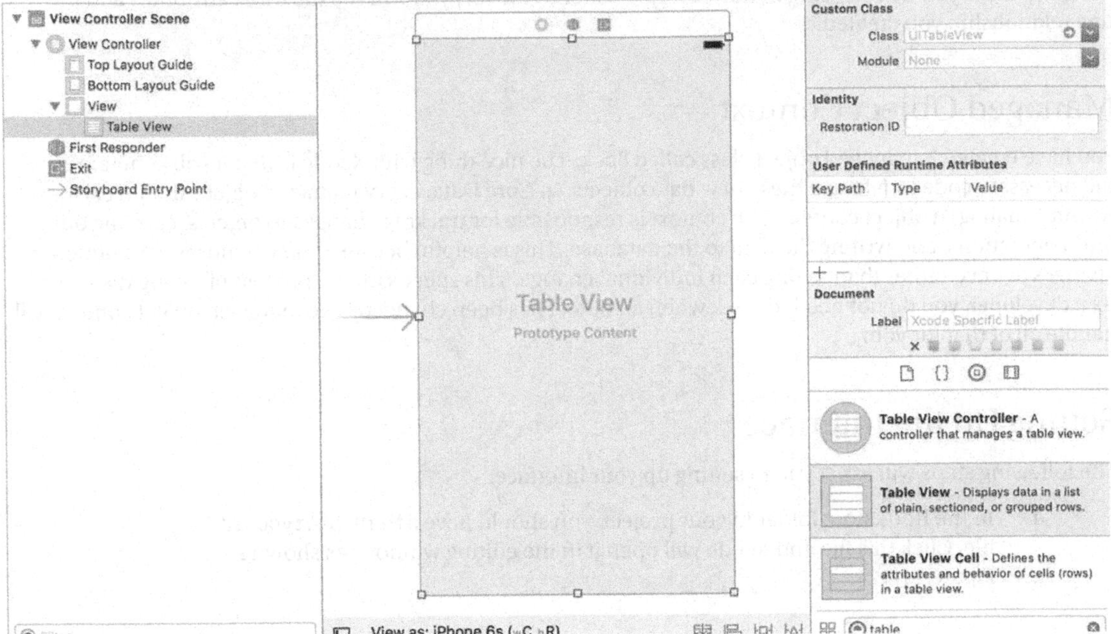

Figure 11-13. *Adding the Table view*

3. You now have a Table View. You will need to stretch the Table View to fill your view. To create cells in your Table View, you need to add a `UITableViewCell`. Search for *table* in your Object Library, and drag a Table View Cell to your table. You now have a table and a cell on your view, as shown in Figure 11-14.

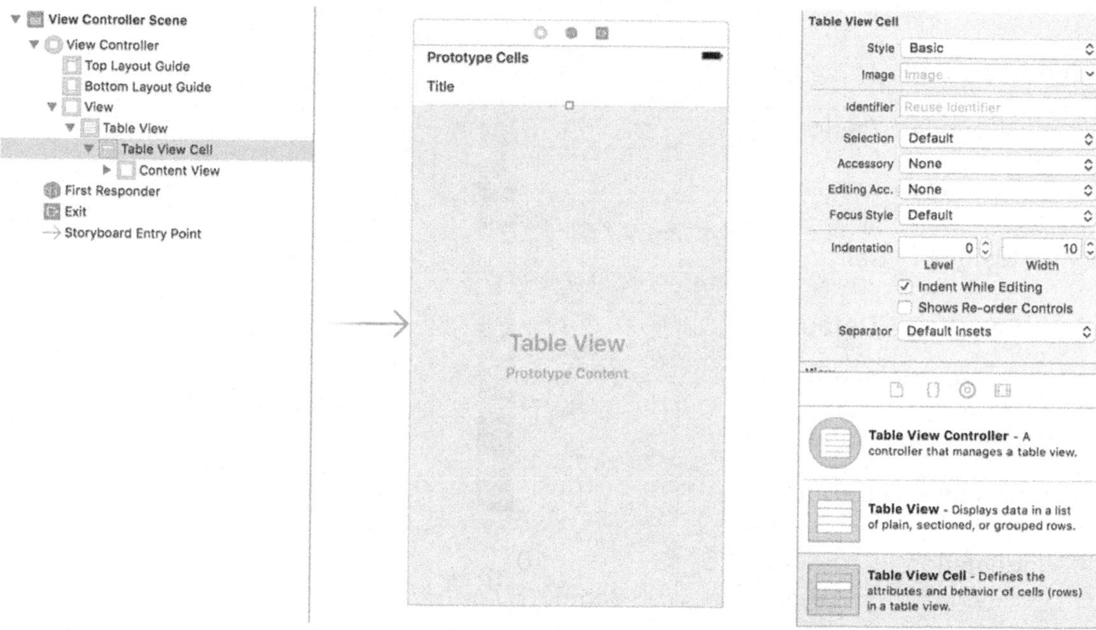

Figure 11-14. *Adding the Table View Cell*

4. Select the cell, and in the Attributes Inspector in the utilities section set Style to Basic. Also, set the Identifier to Cell. The identifier is used for when your Table View contains multiple styles of cells. You will need to differentiate them with unique identifiers. For most of your projects, you can set this to Cell and not worry about it, as shown in Figure 11-15.

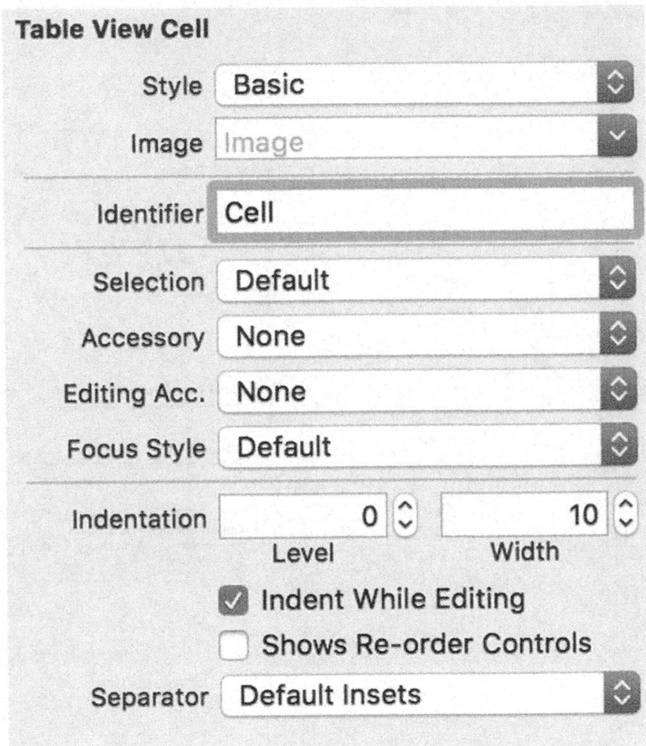

Figure 11-15. *Changing the style and identifier of the cell*

5. When using a Table View, it is usually a good idea to put it in a Navigation Controller. You will be using the Navigation Controller to give you space to put an Add button on your Table View. To add a Navigation Controller, select your View Controller in the Scene list, which is the window to the left of your storyboard that shows your View Controllers (your View Controller will have a yellow icon next to it). From the Application menu, select Editor ➤ Embed In ➤ Navigation Controller, as shown in Figure 11-16.

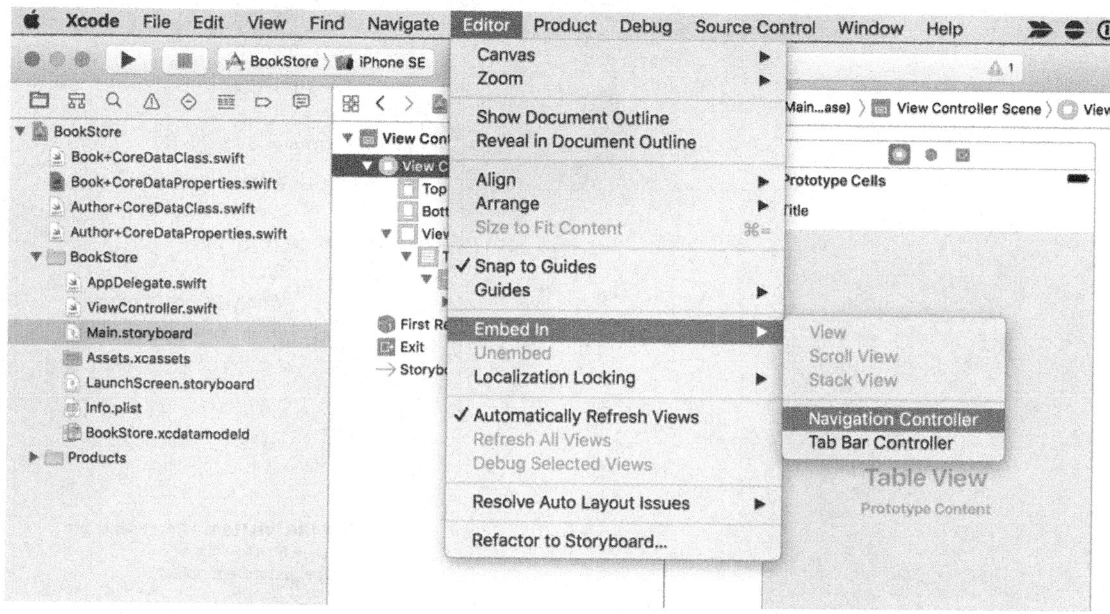

Figure 11-16. *Embedding in a Navigation Controller*

6. You will now have a navigation bar at the top of your view. You will now add a button to the bar. This type of button is called a `UIBarButtonItem`. Search for *bar button* in your Object Library and drag a Bar Button item to the top right of your view on the navigation bar, as shown in Figure 11-17.

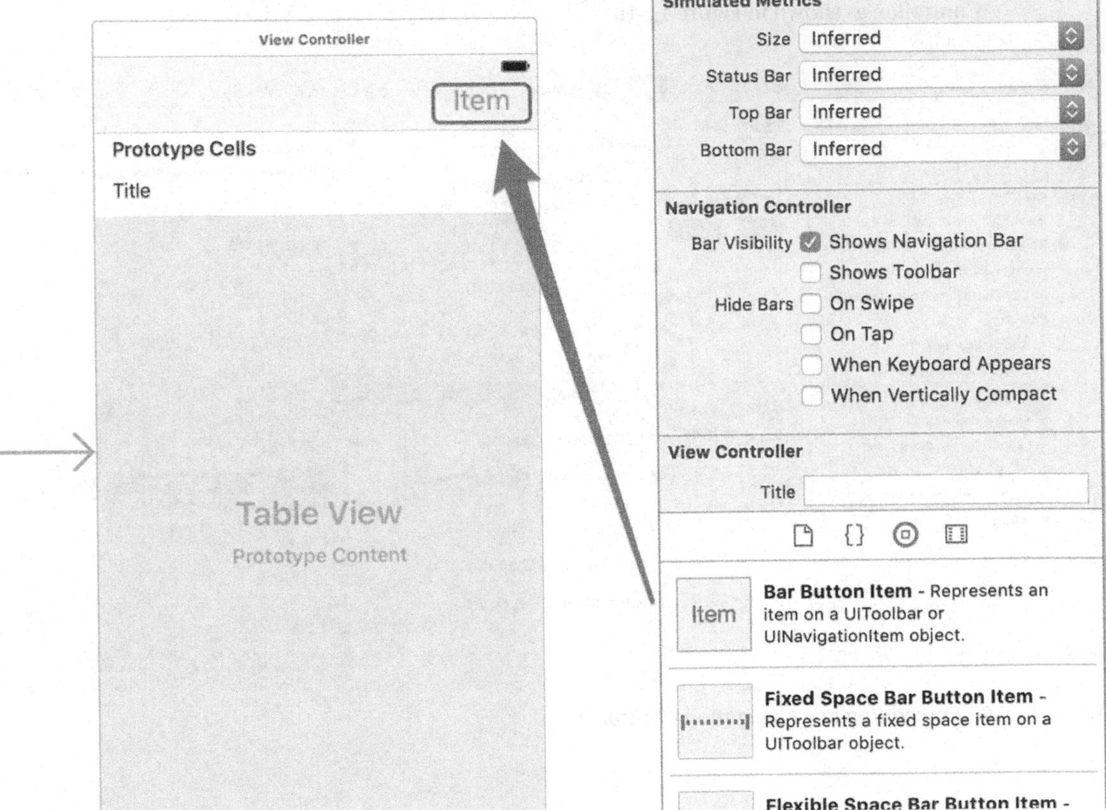

Figure 11-17. *Adding a Bar Button Item to the navigation bar*

7. Select the Bar Button Item and change the System Item from Custom to Add. This will change the look of your Bar Button Item from the word *Item* to a plus icon, as shown in Figure 11-18.

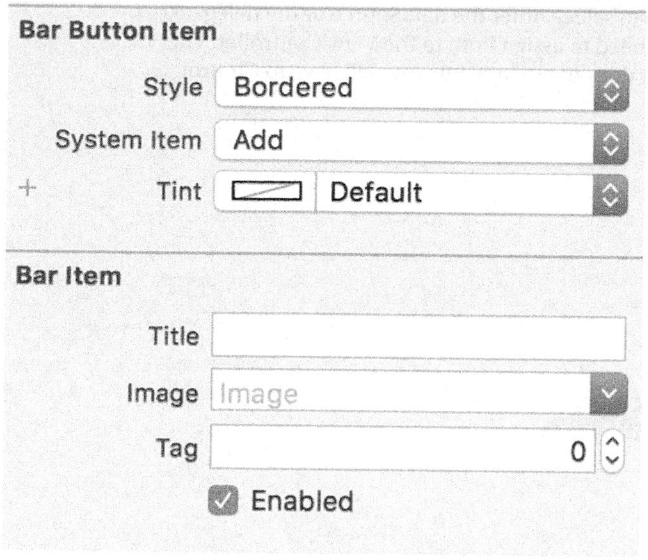

Figure 11-18. Changing the Bar Button Item

8. Now you have created the interface, you need to hook it up to your code. Hold down the Control key and drag your Table view to the View Controller in the Document Outline, as shown in Figure 11-19.

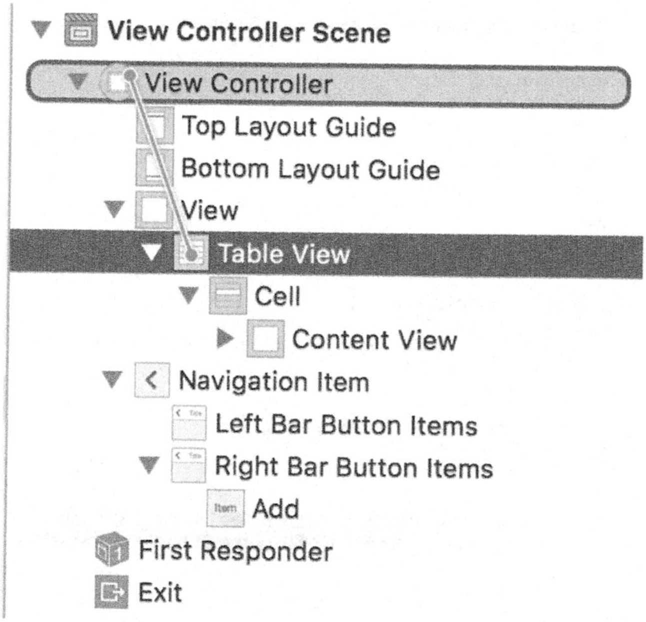

Figure 11-19. Connecting the Table view

9. A pop-up will appear allowing you to select either the dataSource or the delegate, as shown in Figure 11-20. You will need to assign both to the View Controller. The order in which you select the items does not matter, but you will have to Control-drag the Table View twice.

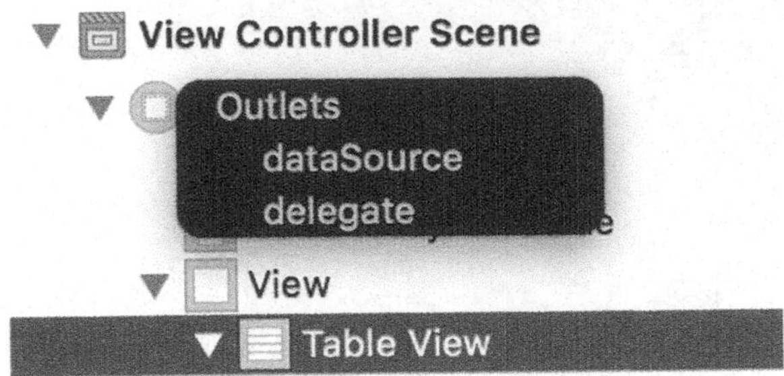
View Controller Scene
Outlets
dataSource
delegate
View
Table View

Figure 11-20. *Hooking up the Table View*

10. Now your Table View should be ready to go. You need to hook up your button to make it do something. In the top right of your Xcode window, click the Assistant Editor button (it looks like two circles). This will open your code on the right side and your storyboard on the left side. Now Control-drag your Add button to the View Controller code on the right, as shown in Figure 11-21.

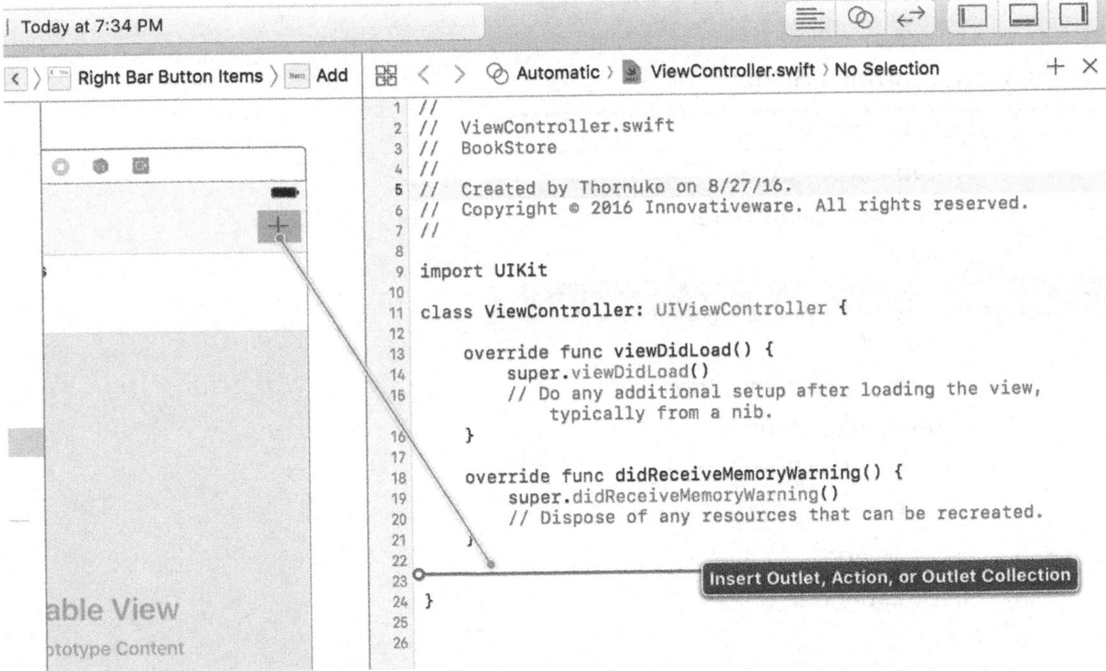
Today at 7:34 PM
Right Bar Button Items
Add
Automatic
ViewController.swift
No Selection
//
// ViewController.swift
// BookStore
//
// Created by Thornuko on 8/27/16.
// Copyright © 2016 Innovativeware. All rights reserved.
//
import UIKit
class ViewController: UIViewController {
override func viewDidLoad() {
super.viewDidLoad()
// Do any additional setup after loading the view, typically from a nib.
}
override func didReceiveMemoryWarning() {
super.didReceiveMemoryWarning()
// Dispose of any resources that can be recreated.
}
}
Insert Outlet, Action, or Outlet Collection
able View
ototype Content

Figure 11-21. *Adding an action for your Button object*

11. It does not matter where you place the Add button in your code as long as it is in your class and outside of any methods. It should be after your class properties just for organization. When you let go, you will be prompted for the type of connection you are creating. Set Connection to Action. Then add a name for your new method, such as `addNew`, as shown in Figure 11-22. Click Connect to finish the connection.

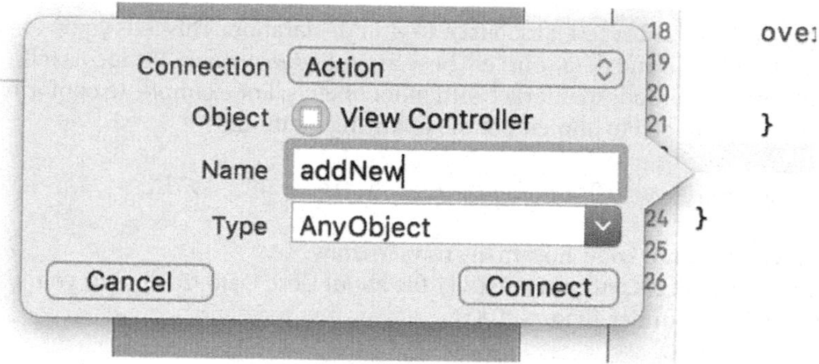

***Figure 11-22.** Changing the type and name of the connection*

12. You also need to create an outlet for your Table View. Drag your Table View from the View Controller scene to the top of the code (just under the class definition, as seen in Figure 11-23). Make sure the connection is set to Outlet and name the Table View **`myTableView`**. You will need this outlet later to tell your Table View to refresh. Click Connect to finish the connection.

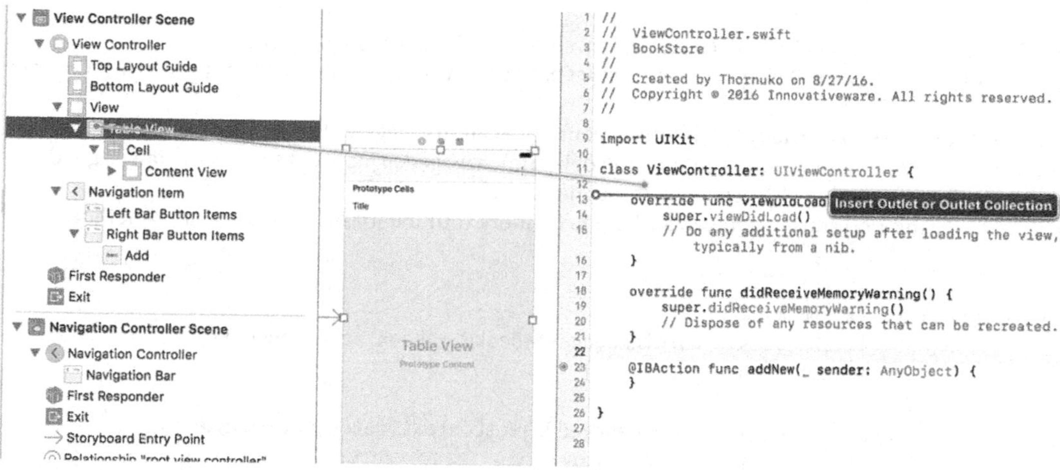

***Figure 11-23.** Creating an outlet for the Table view*

The interface is complete now, but you still need to add the code to make the interface do something. Go back to the Standard editor (click the list icon to the left of the two circles icon in the top right of the Xcode toolbar) and select the `ViewController.swift` file from the file list on the left side. Because you now have a Table View you have to worry about, you need to tell your class that it can handle a Table View. Change your class declaration at the top of your file to the following:

```
class ViewController: UIViewController, UITableViewDelegate, UITableViewDataSource {
```

You added `UITableViewDelegate` and `UITableViewDataSource` to your declaration. This tells your controller that it can act as a table view delegate and data source. These are called ***protocols.*** Protocols tell an object that they must implement certain methods to interact with other objects. For example, to conform to the `UITableViewDataSource` protocol, you need to implement the following method:

```
func tableView(tableView: UITableView, numberOfRowsInSection section: Int) -> Int
```

Without this method, the Table View will not know how many rows to draw.

Before continuing, you need to tell your `ViewController.swift` file about Core Data. To do this, you add the following line to the top of the file just under `import UIKit`:

```
import CoreData
```

You also need to add a managed object context to your `ViewController` class. Add the following line right after the `class ViewController` line:

```
var managedObjectContext: NSManagedObjectContext!
```

Now that you have a variable to hold your `NSManagedObjectContext`, you need to instantiate it so you can add objects to it. To do this, you need to add the following lines to your `override func viewDidLoad()` method:

```
let appDelegate: AppDelegate = UIApplication.shared.delegate as! AppDelegate
managedObjectContext = appDelegate.persistentContainer.viewContext as NSManagedObjectContext
```

The first line creates a constant that points to your application delegate. The second line points your `managedObjectContext` variable to the application delegate's `managedObjectContext`. It is usually a good idea to use the same managed object context throughout your app.

The first new method you are going to add is one to query your database records. Call this method `loadBooks`.

```
func loadBooks() -> [Book] {
            let fetchRequest: NSFetchRequest<Book> = Book.fetchRequest()
            var result: [AnyObject] = []
            do {
                     result = try managedObjectContext.fetch(fetchRequest)
             } catch let error as NSError {
                     NSLog("My Error: %@", error)
             }
             return result as! [Book]
}
```

This code is a little more complex than what you have seen before, so let's walk through it. Line 1 declares a new function called loadBooks, which returns an array of AnyObject. This means you will receive an array that can contain any type of objects you want. In this case, the objects will be Book. You then return the array once you have it loaded.

You will now need to add the data source methods for your Table View. These methods tell your Table View how many sections there are, how many rows are in each section, and what each cell should look like. Add the following code to your ViewController.swift file:

```
1 func tableView(_ tableView: UITableView, numberOfRowsInSection section: Int) -> Int {
2         return loadBooks().count
3     }
4
5     public func tableView(_ tableView: UITableView, cellForRowAt indexPath: IndexPath) -> UITableViewCell {
6         let cell = tableView.dequeueReusableCell(withIdentifier: "Cell") as UITableViewCell?
7         let book: Book = loadBooks()[indexPath.row]
8         cell?.textLabel?.text = book.title
9         return cell!
10    }
```

In line 2, you call a count on your array of Book for the number of rows in your Table view. In lines 5 to 9, you create your cell and return it. Line 6 creates a cell for you to use. This is standard code for creating a cell. The identifier allows you to have more than one type of cell in a Table View, but that is more complex. Line 7 grabs your Book object from your loadBooks() array. Line 8 assigns the book title to your textLabel in the cell. The textLabel is the default label in the cell. This is all you need to do to display the results of your loadBooks method in the Table view. You still have one problem. You do not have any books in your database yet.

To fix this issue, you will add code to the addNew method you created earlier. Add the following code inside the addNew method you created:

```
1     @IBAction func addNew(_ sender: AnyObject) {
2         let book: Book = NSEntityDescription.insertNewObject(forEntityName: "Book", into: managedObjectContext) as! Book
3         book.title = "My Book" + String(loadBooks().count)
4         do {
5             try managedObjectContext.save()
6         } catch let error as NSError {
7             NSLog("My Error: %@", error)
8         }
9         myTableView.reloadData()
10    }
11 }
```

Line 2 creates a new Book object for your book in the database from the Entity name and inserts that object into the managedObjectContext you created before. Remember that once the object is inserted into the managed object context, its changes are tracked, and it can be saved. Line 3 sets the book title to My Book and adds the number of items in the array. Obviously, in real life, you would want to set this to a name either given by the user or from some other list. Lines 4-8 save the managed object context.

In Swift 3.0, error handling has been changed. Now you try and then throw an error when you perform an operation that might cause an error. Line 9 tells the UITableView to reload itself to display the newly added Book. Now build and run the application. Click the + button several times. You will add new Book objects to your object store, as shown in Figure 11-24. If you quit the app and relaunch it, you will notice that the data is still there.

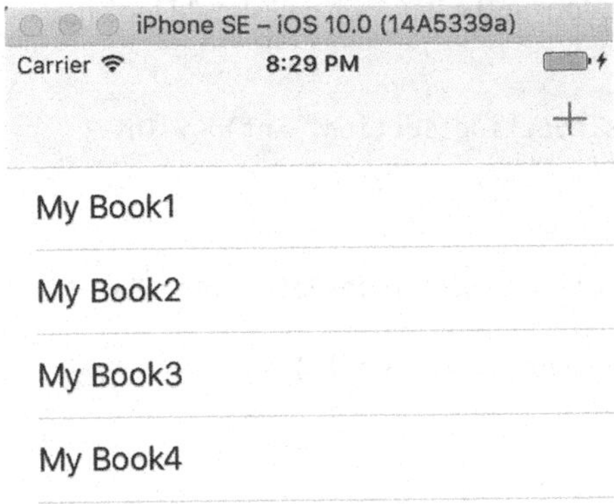

Figure 11-24. *The final app*

This was a cursory introduction to Core Data for iOS. Core Data is a powerful API, but it can also take a lot of time to master.

Summary

Here is a summary of the topics this chapter covered:

- *Preferences*: You learned to use UserDefaults to save and read preferences from a file, on iOS, macOS, tvOS, and watchOS.
- *Databases*: You learned what a database is and why using one can be preferable to saving information in a preferences file.
- *Database engine:* You learned about the database engine that Apple has integrated into macOS, tvOS, and iOS and its advantages and limitations.
- *Core Data:* Apple provides a framework for interfacing with the SQLite database. This framework makes the interface much easier to use.
- *Bookstore application:* You created a simple Core Data application and used Xcode to create a data model for your bookstore. You also learned how to create a relationship between two entities. Finally, you used Xcode to create a simple interface for your Core Data model.

EXERCISES

- Add a new view to the app for allowing the user to enter the name of a book.
- Provide a way to remove a book from the list.
- Create an Author object and add it to a Book object.

CHAPTER 12

Protocols and Delegates

Congratulations! You are acquiring the skills to become an iOS developer! However, iOS developers need to understand two additional topics in order to be successful: ***protocols*** and ***delegates***. It is not uncommon for new developers to get overwhelmed by these topics, which is why we introduced the foundational topics of the Swift language first. After reading this chapter, you will see that protocols and delegates are really useful and not hard to understand and implement.

Multiple Inheritance

We discussed object inheritance in Chapter 2. In a nutshell, object inheritance means that a child can inherit all the characteristics of its parent, as shown in Figure 12-1.

G. Bennett and B. Lees, *Swift 3 for Absolute Beginners*, DOI 10.1007/978-1-4842-2331-4_12

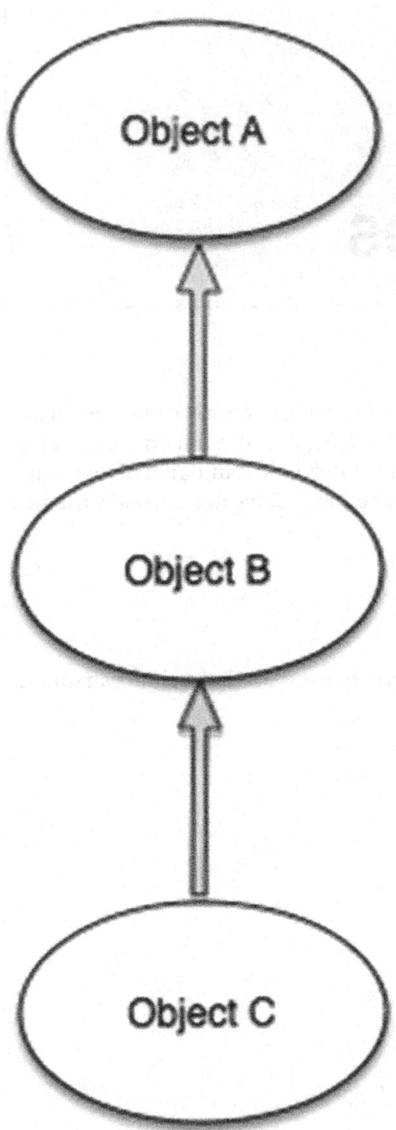

Figure 12-1. *Typical Swift inheritance*

C++, Perl, and Python all have a feature called *multiple inheritance*, which enables a class to inherit behaviors and features from more than one parent, as shown in Figure 12-2.

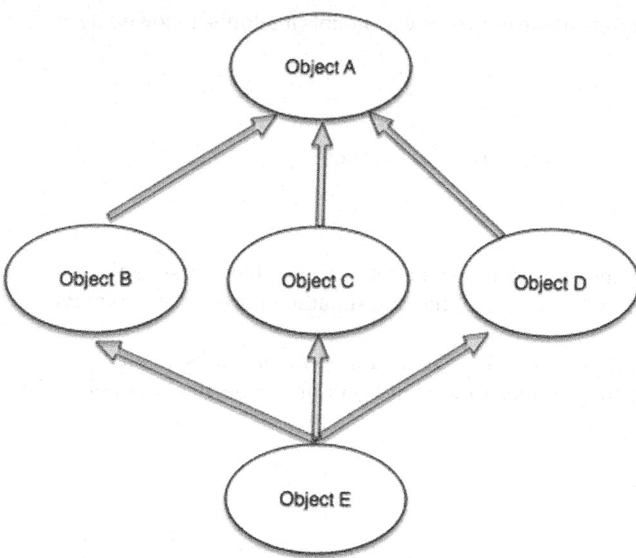

Figure 12-2. *Multiple inheritance*

Problems can arise with multiple inheritance because it allows for ambiguities to occur. Therefore, Swift does not implement multiple inheritances. Instead, it implements something called a ***protocol***.

Understanding Protocols

Apple defines a *protocol* as a list of function declarations, unattached to a class definition. A protocol is similar to a class with the exception that a protocol doesn't provide an implementation for any of the requirements; it describes only what an implementation should look like.

The protocol can be adopted by a class to provide an actual implementation of those requirements. Any type that satisfies the requirements of a protocol is said to *conform* to that protocol.

Protocol Syntax

Protocols are defined like classes are, as shown in Listing 12-1.

Listing 12-1. Protocol Definition

```
protocol RandomNumberGenerator {

    var mustBeSettable: Int { get set }
    var doesNotNeedToBeSettable: Int { get }

    func random() -> Double
}
```

If a class has a superclass, you list the superclass name before any protocols it adopts, followed by a comma, as shown in Listing 12-2.

Listing 12-2. Protocol Listed after Superclass

```
class MyClass: MySuperclass, RandomNumberGenerator, AnotherProtocol {
    // class definition goes here
}
```

The protocol also specifies whether each property must have a gettable or gettable *and* settable implementation. A gettable property is read-only, whereas a gettable and settable property is not (shown earlier in Listing 12-1).

Properties are always declared as variable properties, prefixed with `var`. Gettable and settable properties are indicated by `{ get set }` after their type declaration, and gettable properties are indicated by `{ get }`.

Delegation

Delegation is a design pattern that enables a class or structure to hand off (or *delegate*) some of its responsibilities to an instance of another type. This design pattern is implemented by defining a protocol that encapsulates the delegated responsibilities. Delegation can be used to respond to a particular action or to retrieve data from an external source without needing to know the underlying type of that source.

Listing 12-3 defines two protocols for use with a random number guessing game.

Listing 12-3. Protocol Definitions

```
protocol RandomNumberGame {
    var machine: Machine { get }
    func play()
}
protocol RandomNumberGameDelegate {
    func gameDidStart(game: RandomNumberGame)
    func game(game: RandomNumberGame, didStartNewTurnWithGuess randomGuess: Int)
    func gameDidEnd(game: RandomNumberGame)
}
```

The `RandomNumberGame` protocol can be adopted by any game that involves random number generating and guessing. The `RandomNumberGameDelegate` protocol can be adopted by any type of class to track the progress of a `RandomNumberGame` protocol.

Protocol and Delegation Example

This section shows you how to create a more sophisticated random number guessing app to illustrate how to use protocols and delegation. The app's home view displays the user's guess and whether the guess was high, low, or correct, as shown in Figure 12-3.

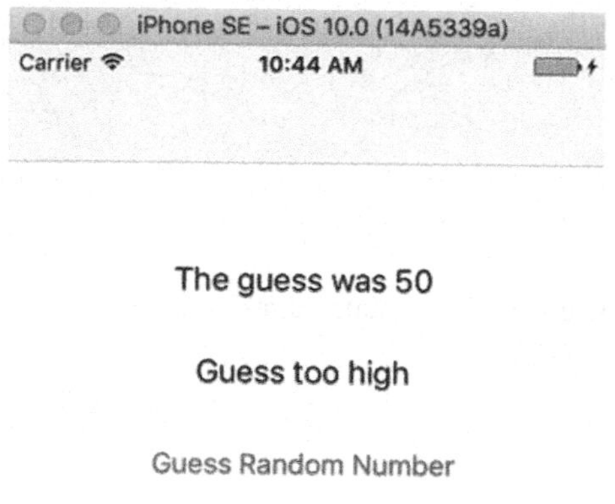

Figure 12-3. *Guessing game app home view*

When the users tap the Guess Random Number button, they are taken to an input screen to enter their guess, as shown in Figure 12-4.

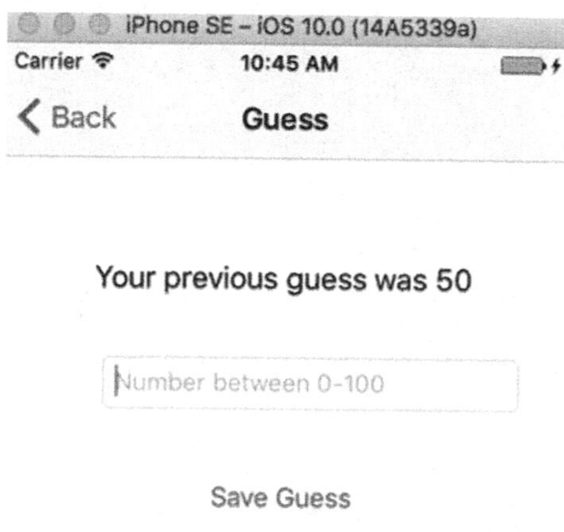

Figure 12-4. *Guessing game app user input view*

When the users enter their guess, the delegate method passes the guess back to the home view, and the home view displays the result.

Getting Started

Follow these steps to create the app:

1. Create a new Swift project based on the Single View Application template, name it `RandomNumberDelegate`, and save it, as shown in Figure 12-5.

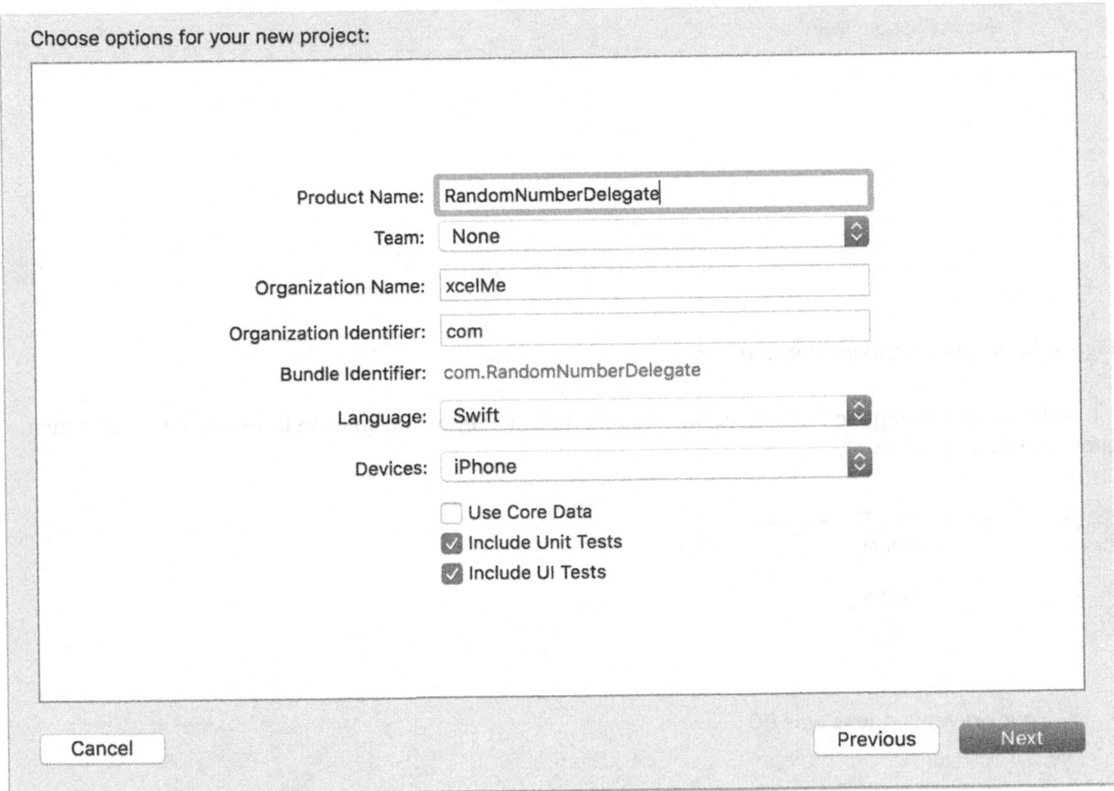

***Figure 12-5.** Creating the project*

2. From the Document Outline, select View Controller. Then select Editor ➤ Embed In ➤ Navigation Controller. This embeds your View Controller in a Navigation Controller and enables you to easily transition back and forth between other View Controllers, as shown in Figure 12-6.

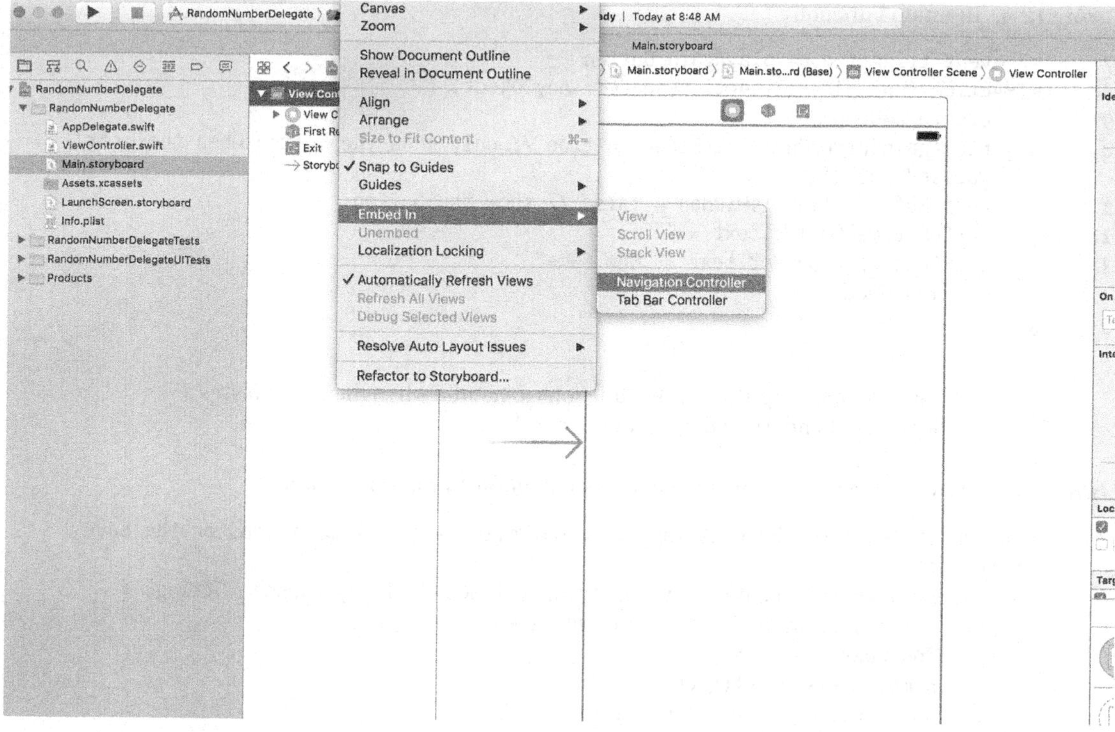

Figure 12-6. Embedding the View Controller in a Navigation Controller

3. In the View Controller, add two Label objects and two Button objects along with four controls, which will control the view, as shown in Figure 12-7 and Listing 12-4.

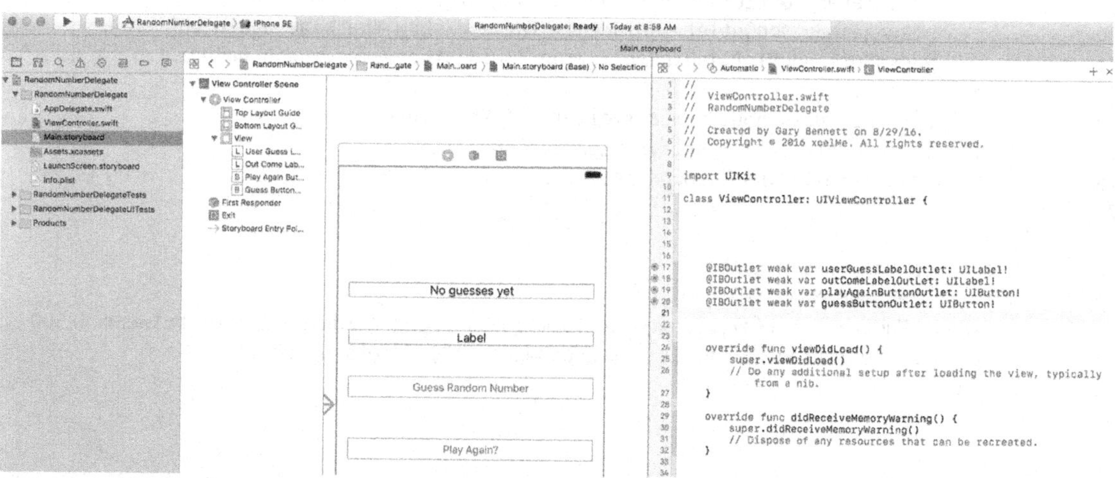

Figure 12-7. Outlets necessary to control the view

Listing 12-4. IBAction Function

```
    // event triggered by playAgain Button
    @IBAction func playAgainAction(sender: AnyObject) {
        createRandomNumber()
        playAgainButtonOutlet.isHidden = true // only show the button when the user guessed the right #
        guessButtonOutlet.isHidden = false // show the button
        outComeLabelOutlet.text = ""
        userGuessLabelOutlet.text = "New Game"
        previousGuess = ""
    }
```

4. Add the code in Listing 12-5 for the functions to handle when the user guesses a number and to handle creating a random number.

Listing 12-5. User Guess Delegate Function and createRandomNumber Function

```
// function called from the GuessInputViewController when the user taps on the Save Button button
    func userDidFinish(_ controller: GuessInputViewController, guess:  String) {
        userGuessLabelOutlet.text = "The guess was " +  guess
        previousGuess = guess
        let numberGuess = Int(guess)
        if (numberGuess! > randomNumber){
            outComeLabelOutlet.text = "Guess too high"
        }
        else if (numberGuess! < randomNumber) {
            outComeLabelOutlet.text = "Guess too low"
        }
        else {
            outComeLabelOutlet.text = "Guess is correct"
            playAgainButtonOutlet.isHidden = false //show the play again button
            guessButtonOutlet.isHidden = true //hide the guess again number
        }
        // pops the GuessInputViewController off the stack
        if let navController = self.navigationController {
            navController.popViewController(animated: true)
        }
    }
    // creates the random number
    func createRandomNumber() {
        randomNumber = Int(arc4random_uniform(100)) //get a random number between 0-100
        print("The random number is: \(randomNumber)") //lets us cheat
        return
    }
```

5. Declare and initialize the two variables on lines 13 and 14 in Listing 12-6.

Listing 12-6. Variable Declarations and Initializations

```
11 class ViewController: UIViewController, GuessDelegate {
12
13     var previousGuess = ""
14     var randomNumber = 0
15
16
17     @IBOutlet weak var userGuessLabelOutlet: UILabel!
18     @IBOutlet weak var outComeLabelOutlet: UILabel!
19     @IBOutlet weak var playAgainButtonOutlet: UIButton!
20     @IBOutlet weak var guessButtonOutlet: UIButton!!
```

6. Modify the function `viewDidLoad()` to handle how the view should look when it first appears and create the random number to guess, as shown in Listing 12-7.

Listing 12-7. viewDidLoad Function

```
override func viewDidLoad() {
        super.viewDidLoad()
        // Do any additional setup after loading the view, typically from a nib.
        self.createRandomNumber()
        playAgainButtonOutlet.isHidden = true
        outComeLabelOutlet.text = ""

    }
```

7. Now you need to create a view to enable the users to enter their guesses. In the `Main.storyboard` file, drag a new View Controller next to the home View Controller and add a label, a text field, and a button. For the Text Field object, in the Placeholder property, type `Number between 0-100`, as shown in Figure 12-8.

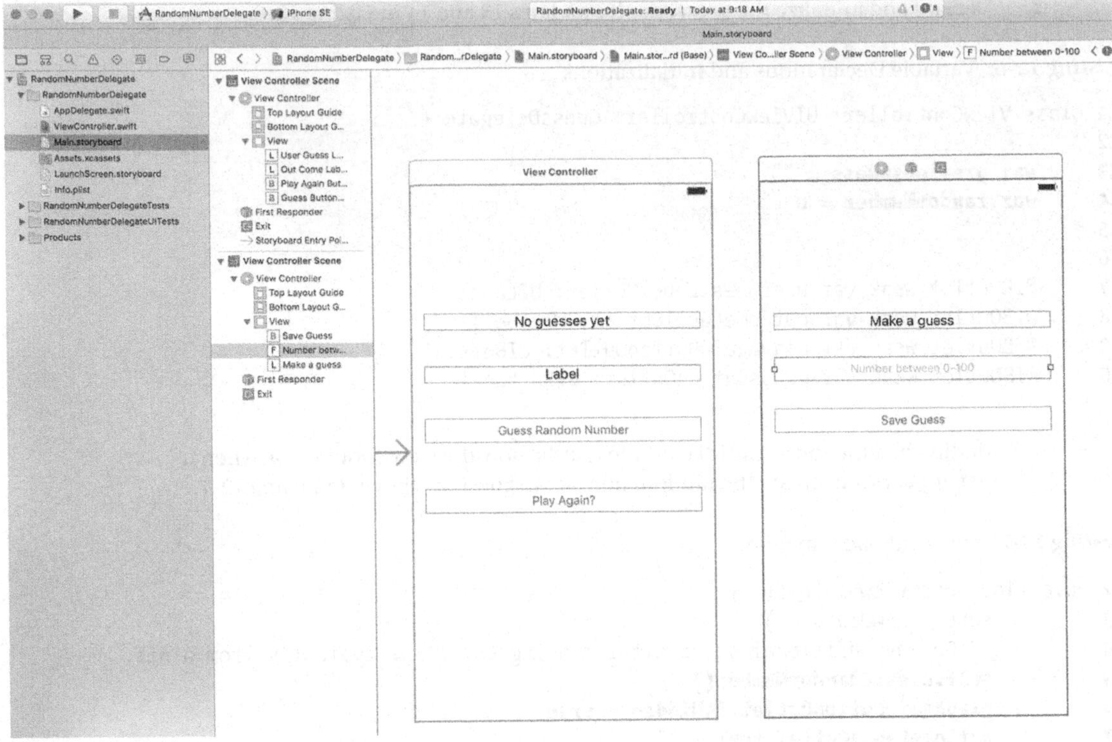

Figure 12-8. Create the Guess View Controller and objects

8. You need to create a class for the Guess Input View Controller. Create a Swift file and save it as `GuessInputViewController.swift`. Select File ➤ New ➤ File. Then choose iOS ➤ Source ➤ Cocoa Touch Class and name the class `GuessInputViewController`. It's subclassed from `UIViewController`, as shown in Figure 12-9.

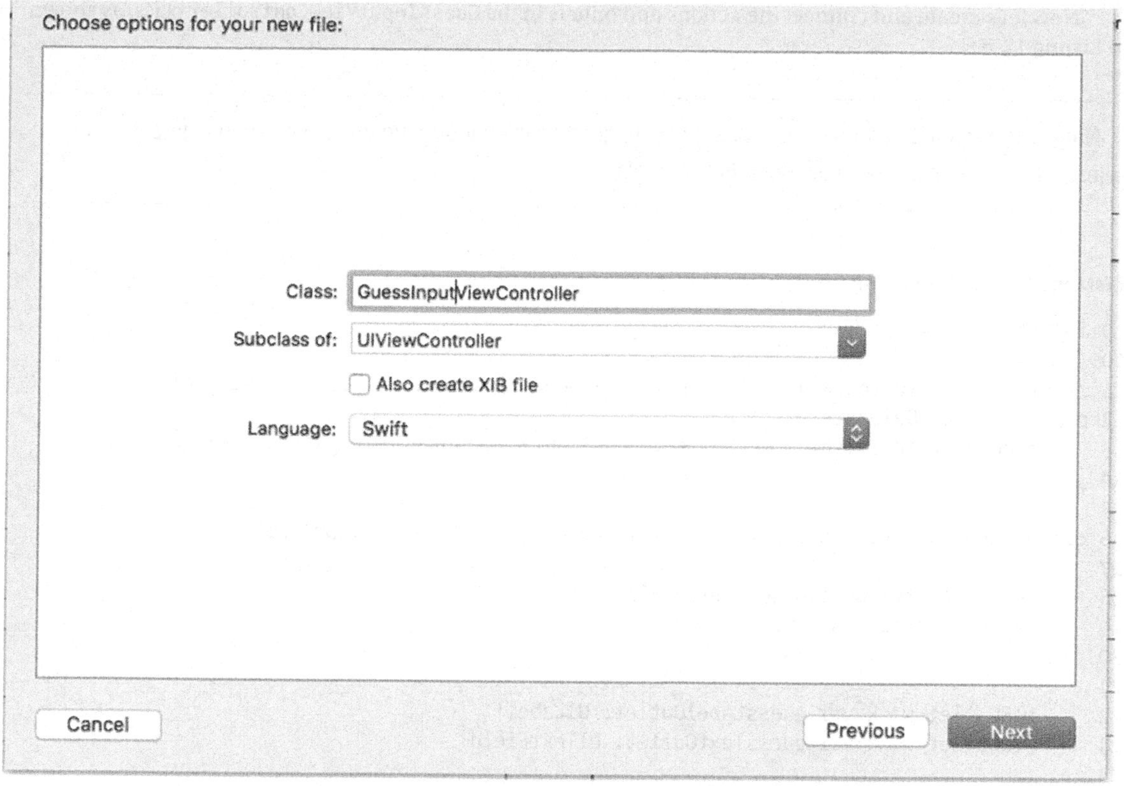

Choose options for your new file:

Class: GuessInputViewController

Subclass of: UIViewController

Also create XIB file

Language: Swift

Cancel

Previous

Next

Figure 12-9. Create the GuessInputViewController.swift file

9. Let's associate the `GuessInputViewController` class with the Guess View Controller created in Step 8. From the `Main.storyboard` file, select the Guess Input View Controller, select the Identity Inspector, and select or type `GuessInputViewController` in the Class field, as shown in Figure 12-10.

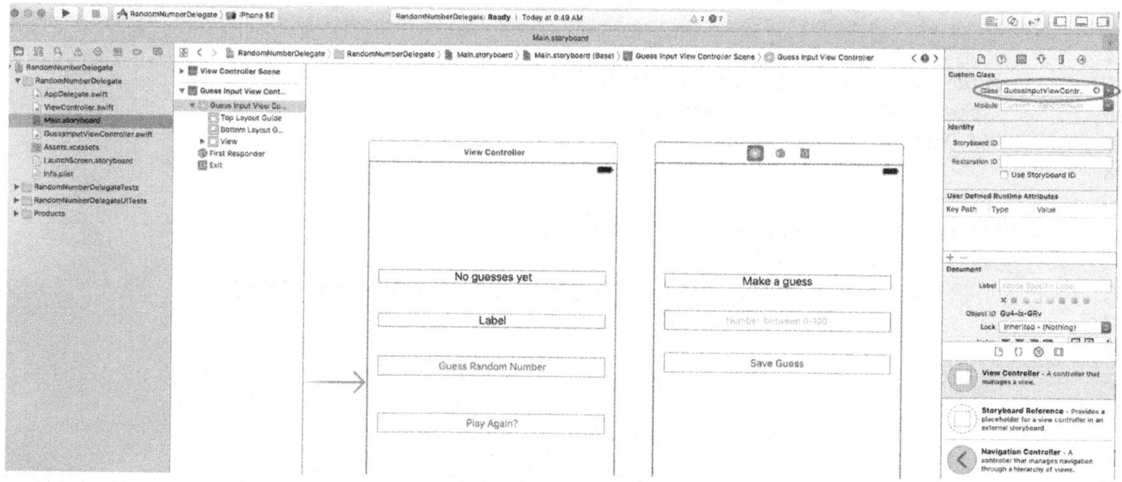

Figure 12-10. Creating the GuessInputViewController.swift file

Now let's create and connect the actions and outlets in the GuessInputViewController class, as shown in Listing 12-8.

■ **Note** To see the bound rectangles around your controls in your storyboard, as shown in Figure 12-11, select Editor ➤ Canvas ➤ Show Bounds Rectangle.

Listing 12-8. Class Listing

```
import UIKit

// protocol used to send data back to the home view controller's userDidFinish
protocol GuessDelegate {
    func userDidFinish(_ controller:GuessInputViewController, guess: String)
}

class GuessInputViewController: UIViewController,  UITextFieldDelegate {

    var delegate: GuessDelegate? = nil
    var previousGuess: String = ""


    @IBOutlet weak var guessLabelOutlet: UILabel!
    @IBOutlet weak var guessTextOutlet: UITextField!

    override func viewDidLoad() {
        super.viewDidLoad()

        // Do any additional setup after loading the view.
        if(!previousGuess.isEmpty) {
            guessLabelOutlet.text = "Your previous guess was \(previousGuess)"
        }
        guessTextOutlet.becomeFirstResponder()
    }

    override func didReceiveMemoryWarning() {
        super.didReceiveMemoryWarning()
        // Dispose of any resources that can be recreated.
    }

    @IBAction func saveGuessAction(_ sender: AnyObject) {
        if (delegate != nil) {
            delegate!.userDidFinish(self, guess: guessTextOutlet.text!)
        }
    }

}
```

10. You are almost done. You need to connect the scene with a segue. A *segue* enables you to transition from one scene to another. Control-drag from the Guess Random Number button to the Guess Input View Controller and select Show as the type of Action Segue, as shown in Figure 12-11.

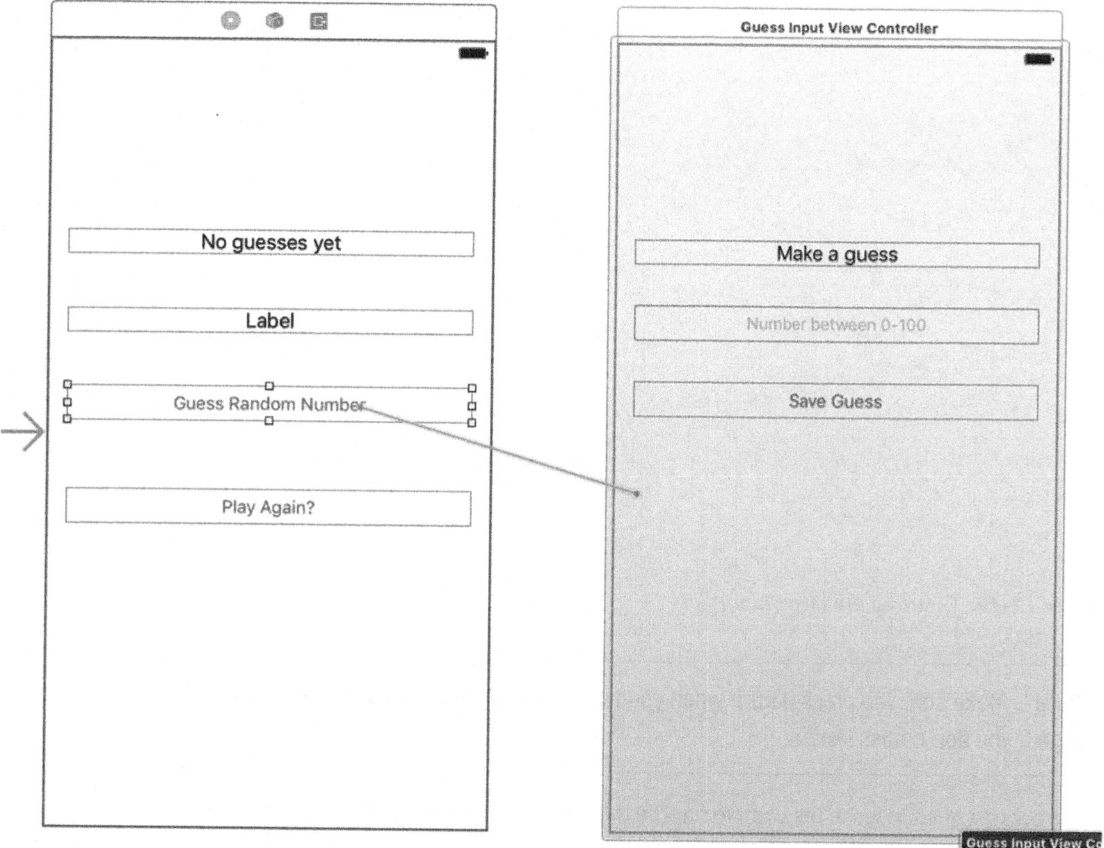

Figure 12-11. *Creating the segue that transitions scenes when the Guess Random Number button is tapped*

11. Now you need to give the segue an identifier. Click the segue arrow, select the Attributes Inspector, and name the segue `MyGuessSegue`, as shown in Figure 12-12.

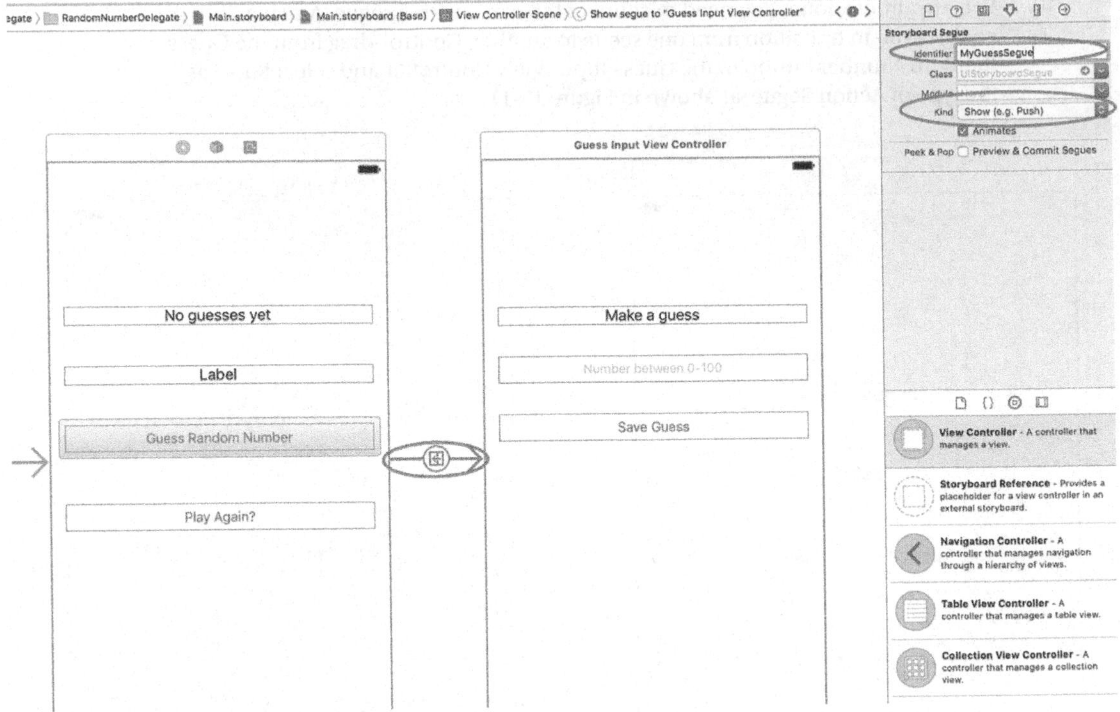

Figure 12-12. *Creating the segue identifier*

■ **Note** Make sure you press Return when you type the segue identifier. Xcode may not pick up the property change if you don't press Return.

Now you need to write the code to handle the segue. In the `ViewController` class, add the code in Listing 12-9.

Listing 12-9. prepareForSegue Function

```
override func prepare(for segue: UIStoryboardSegue, sender: Any!) {
        if segue.identifier == "MyGuessSegue" {
            let vc = segue.destination as! GuessInputViewController
            vc.previousGuess = previousGuess // passes the previousGuess property to the
            GuessInputViewController
            vc.delegate = self
        }
    }
```

When the user taps the Guess Random Number button, the segue gets called, and the function `prepareForSegue` gets called. You first check to see whether it was the `MyGuessSegue` segue. You then populate the `vc` variable with the `GuessInputViewController`.

Lines 27 and 28 pass the `previousGuess` number and delegate to the `GuessInputViewController`.

12. If you haven't added the `GuessDelegate` delegate to the `ViewController` class, do it now, as shown in Listing 12-10.

Listing 12-10. ViewController Class with GuessDelegate Listed

```
class ViewController: UIViewController, GuessDelegate {

    var previousGuess = ""
    var randomNumber = 0
```

13. Lastly, we need to add our constraints to our two views. Add missing constraints as shown in Figures 12-13 and 12-14.

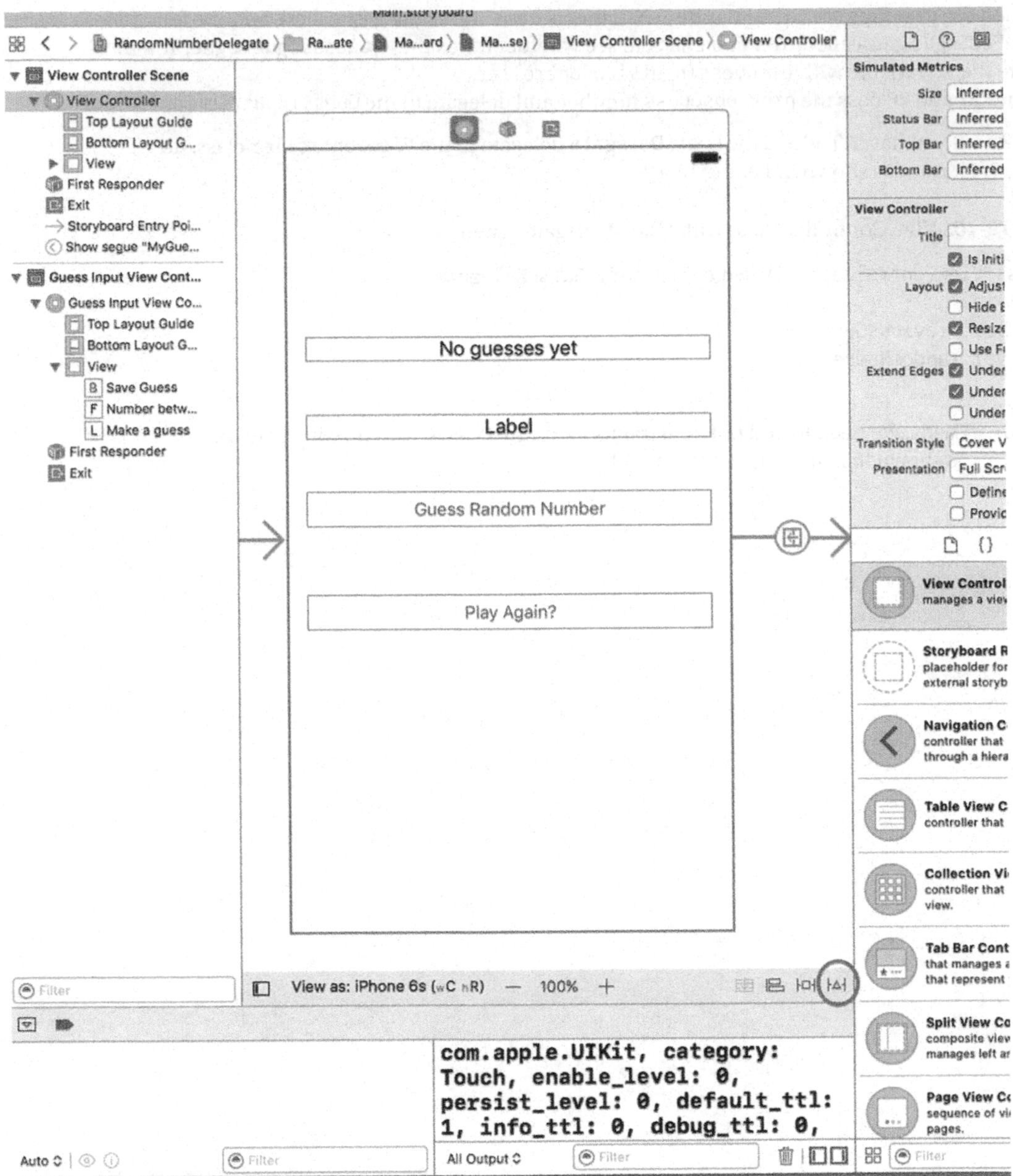

Figure 12-13. Add missing constraints to both views

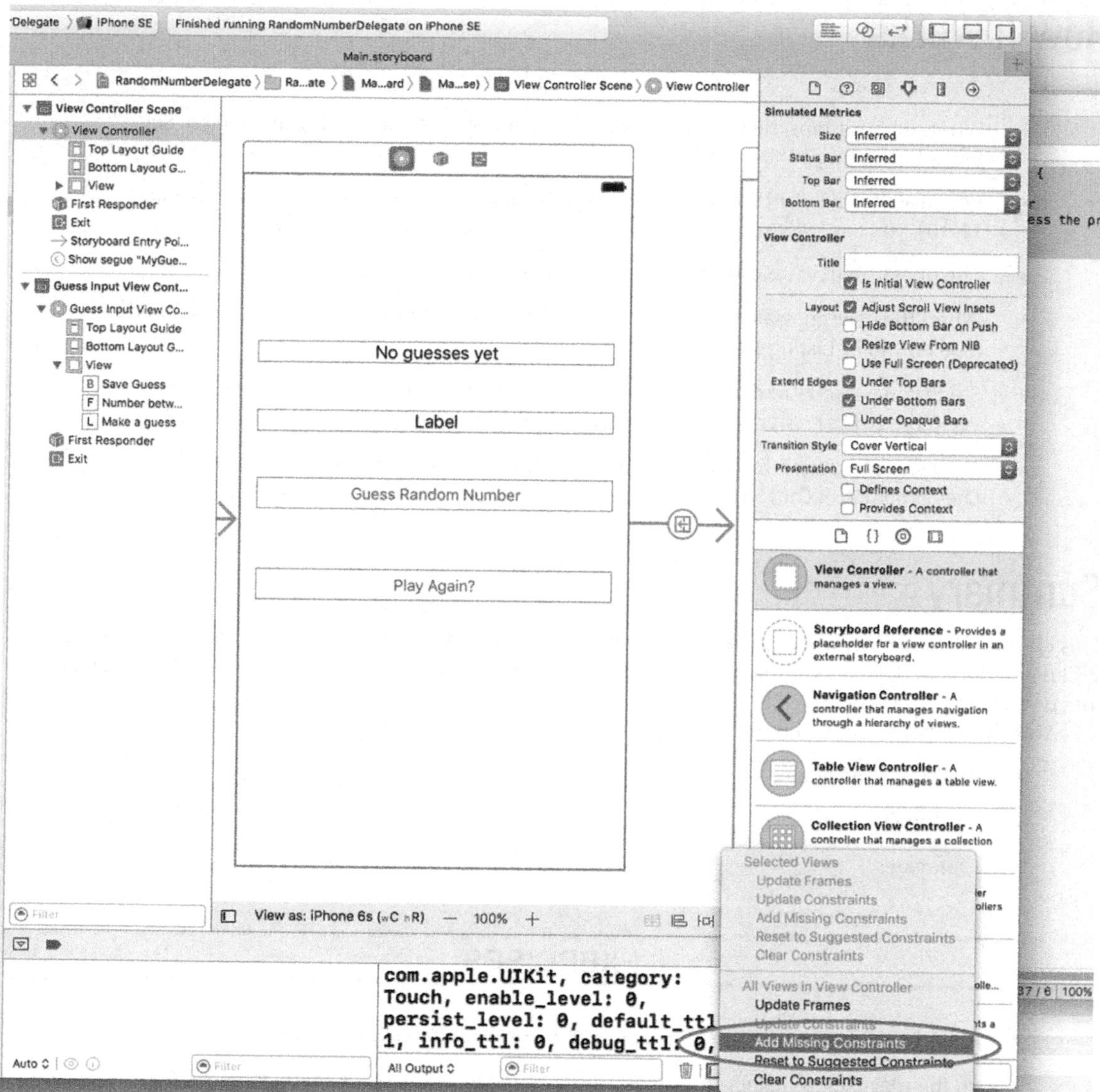

***Figure 12-14.** Add missing constraints to both views*

How It Works

Here is how the code works:

- When the user taps the Guess Random Number link, `prepareForSegue` is called. See line 24 in Listing 12-9.
- Because the `ViewController` conforms to the `GuessDelegate` (see line 11 in Listing 12-10), you can pass `self` to the delegate in `GuessInputViewController`.
- The `GuessInputViewController` scene is displayed.
- When the user guesses a number and taps Save Guess, the `saveGuessAction` is called (see line 40 in Listing 12-8).
- Since you passed `ViewController` as the delegate, it can pass the `guess` back to the `ViewController.swift` file via the userDidFinish method (see line 42 in Listing 12-8).
- Now you can determine whether the user guessed the correct answer and pop the `GuessInputViewController` view from the stack (see line 62 in Listing 12-5).

Summary

This chapter covered why multiple inheritance is not used in Swift and how protocols and delegates work. When you think of delegates, think of helper classes. When your class conforms to a protocol, the delegate's functions help your class.

You should be familiar with the following terms:

- Multiple inheritance
- Protocols
- Delegates

EXERCISES

- Change the random number the computer guesses from 0-100 to 0-50.
- In the main scene, display how many guesses the user has made trying to guess the random number.
- In the main scene, display how many games the user has played.

CHAPTER 13

Introducing the Xcode Debugger

Not only is Xcode provided free of charge on Apple's developer site and the Mac App Store, but it is also a great tool. Aside from being able to use it to create the next great Mac, iPhone, iPad, AppleTV, and Apple Watch apps, Xcode has a debugger built right into the tool.

What exactly is a debugger? Well, let's get something straight—programs do *exactly* what they are written to do, but sometimes what is written isn't exactly what the program is really meant to do. This can mean the program crashes or just doesn't do something that is expected. Whatever the case, when a program doesn't work as planned, the program is said to have ***bugs***. The process of going through the code and fixing these problems is called ***debugging***.

There is still some debate as to the real origin of the term *bug*, but one well-documented case from 1947 involved the late Rear Admiral Grace Hopper, a Naval reservist and programmer at the time. Hopper and her team were trying to solve a problem with the Harvard Mark II computer. One team member found a moth in the circuitry that was causing the problem with one of the relays. Hopper was later quoted as saying, "From then on, when anything went wrong with a computer, we said it had bugs in it."[1]

Regardless of the origin, the term stuck and programmers all over the world use debuggers, such as the one built into Xcode, to help find bugs in programs. But people are the real debuggers; debugging tools merely help programmers locate problems. No debugger, whatever the name might imply, fixes problems on its own.

This chapter highlights some of the more important features of the Xcode debugger and explains how to use them. Once you are finished with this chapter, you should have a good enough understanding of the Xcode debugger and of the debugging process in general to allow you to search for and fix the majority of programming issues.

Getting Started with Debugging

If you've ever watched a movie in slow motion just so you can catch a detail you can't see when the movie is played at full speed, you've used a tool to do something a little like debugging. The idea that playing the movie frame by frame will reveal the detail you are looking for is the same sort of idea you apply when debugging a program. With a program, sometimes it becomes necessary to slow things down a bit to see what's happening. The debugger allows you to do this using two main features: setting a breakpoint and stepping through the program line by line—more on these two features in a bit. Let's first look at how to get to the debugger and what it looks like.

First, you need to load an application. The examples in this chapter use the `BookStore` project from Chapter 8, so open Xcode and load the `BookStore` project.

[1]Michael Moritz, Alexander L. Taylor III, and Peter Stoler, "The Wizard Inside the Machine," *Time*, Vol.123, no. 16: pp. 56–63.

G. Bennett and B. Lees, *Swift 3 for Absolute Beginners*, DOI 10.1007/978-1-4842-2331-4_13

Second, make sure the Debug build configuration is chosen for the Run scheme, as shown in Figure 13-1. To edit the current scheme, choose Product ➤ Scheme ➤ Edit Scheme from the main menu. Debug is the default selection, so you probably won't have to change this. This step is important because if the configuration is set to Release, debugging will not work at all.

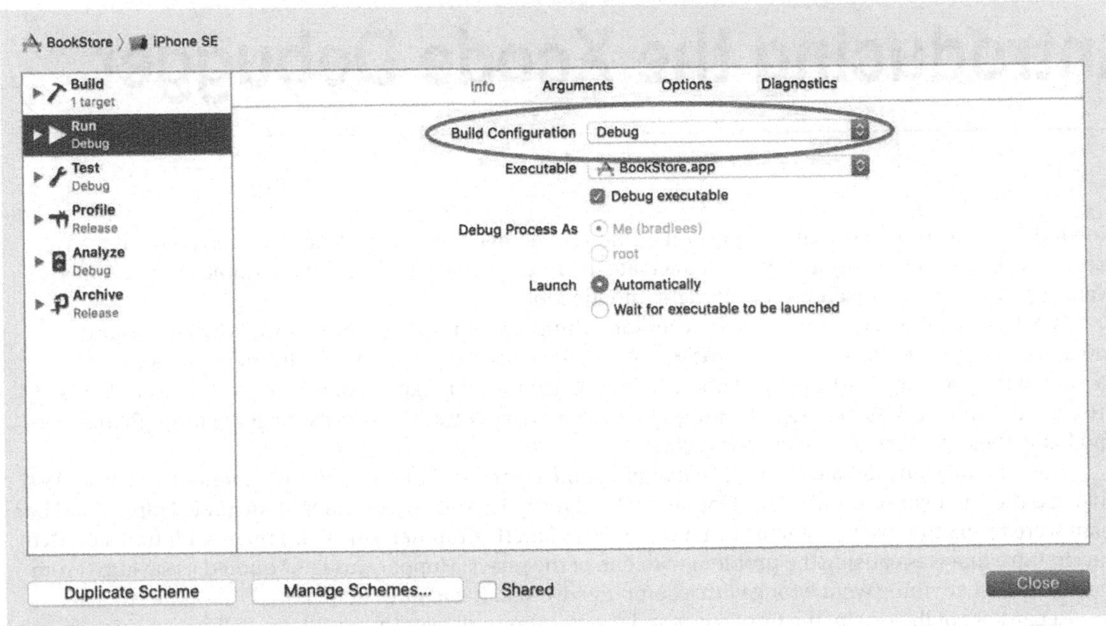

Figure 13-1. *Selecting the Debug configuration*

While this book won't discuss Xcode schemes, just know that by default Xcode provides both a Release configuration and a Debug configuration for any macOS, iOS, watchOS, or tvOS project you create. The main difference as it pertains to this chapter is that a Release configuration doesn't add any program information that is necessary for debugging an application, whereas the Debug configuration does.

Setting Breakpoints

To see what's going on in a program, you need to make the program pause at certain points that you as a programmer are interested in. A *breakpoint* allows you to do this. In Figure 13-2, there is a breakpoint on line 24 of the program. To set this, simply place the cursor over the line number (not the program text, but the number 24 to the left of the program text) and click once. You will see a small blue arrow behind the line number. This lets you know that a breakpoint is set.

If line numbers are not being displayed, simply choose Xcode ➤ Preferences from the main menu, click the Text Editing tab, and select the Line Numbers checkbox.

Main.storyboard
Assets.xcassets
LaunchScreen.storyboard
Info.plist
Products

```
class MasterViewController: UITableViewController {

    var detailViewController: DetailViewController? = nil
    var objects = [Any]()
    var myBookStore: BookStore = BookStore()


    override func viewDidLoad() {
        super.viewDidLoad()
        // Do any additional setup after loading the view, typically from a nib.
        self.navigationItem.leftBarButtonItem = self.editButtonItem

        let addButton = UIBarButtonItem(barButtonSystemItem: .add, target: self, action: #selector
            (insertNewObject(_:)))
        self.navigationItem.rightBarButtonItem = addButton
        if let split = self.splitViewController {
            let controllers = split.viewControllers
            self.detailViewController = (controllers[controllers.count-1] as!
                UINavigationController).topViewController as? DetailViewController
        }
    }

    override func viewWillAppear(_ animated: Bool) {
        self.clearsSelectionOnViewWillAppear = self.splitViewController!.isCollapsed
        super.viewWillAppear(animated)
    }
```

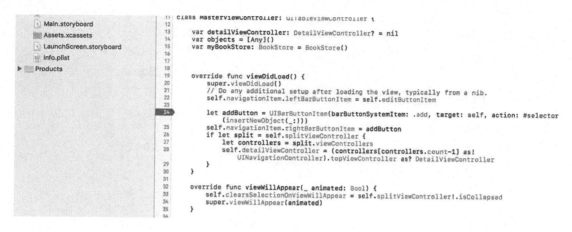

Figure 13-2. *Your first breakpoint*

The breakpoint can be removed by dragging the breakpoint to the left or right of the line number column and then dropping it. You can also right-click (or Control-click) the breakpoint, and you will be given the option to delete or disable a breakpoint. Figure 13-3 shows the right-click menu for a breakpoint. Disabling a breakpoint is convenient if you think you might need it again in the future.

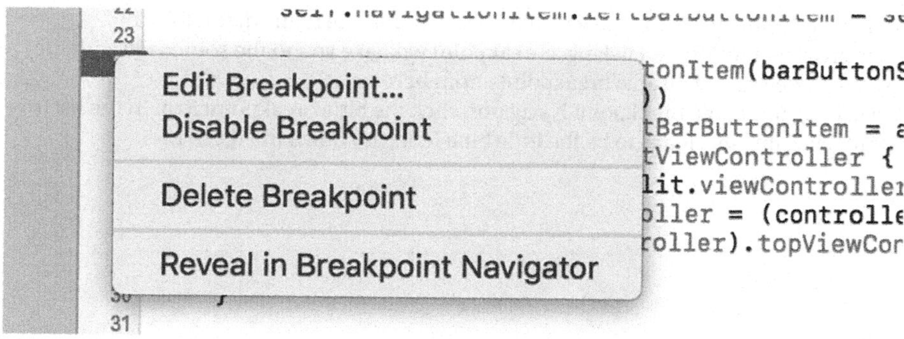

Figure 13-3. *Right-clicking a breakpoint*

Setting and deleting breakpoints are pretty straightforward tasks.

Using the Breakpoint Navigator

With small projects, knowing the locations of all the breakpoints isn't necessarily difficult. However, once a project gets larger than, say, your small BookStore application, managing all the breakpoints could be a little more difficult. Fortunately, Xcode provides a simple method to list all the breakpoints in an application; it's called the Breakpoint Navigator. Just click the Breakpoint Navigator icon in the navigation selector bar, as shown in Figure 13-4.

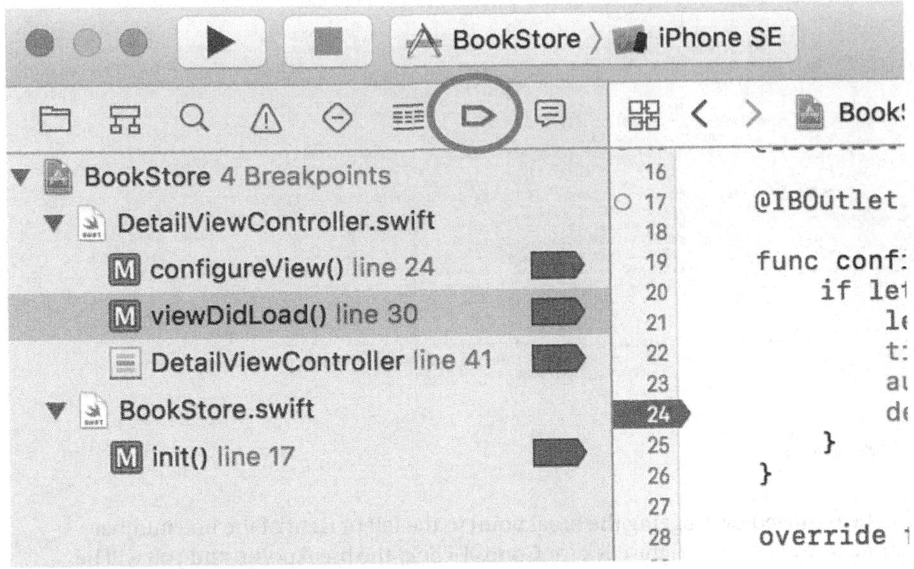

Figure 13-4. Accessing the Breakpoint Navigator in Xcode

Once you've clicked the icon, the navigator will list all the breakpoints currently defined in the application grouped by source file. From here, clicking a breakpoint will take you to the source file with the breakpoint. You can also easily delete and disable breakpoints from here.

To disable/enable a breakpoint in the Breakpoint Navigator, click the blue breakpoint icon in the list (or wherever it appears). Don't click the line; it has to be the little blue icon, as shown in Figure 13-5.

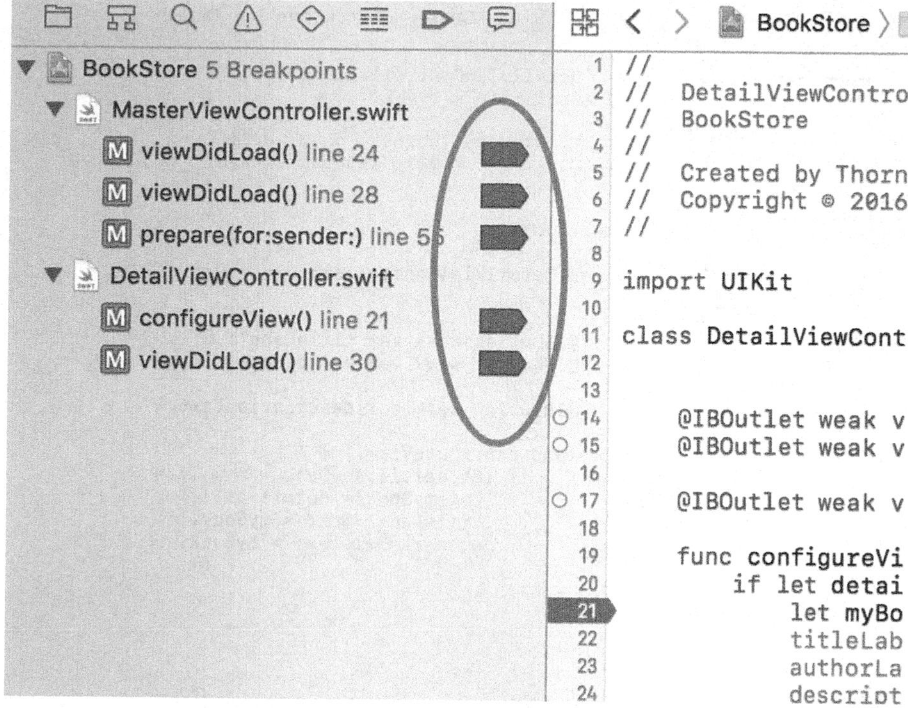

Figure 13-5. *Using the Breakpoint Navigator to enable/disable a breakpoint*

It is sometimes handy to disable a breakpoint instead of deleting it, especially if you plan to put the breakpoint back in the same place again. The debugger will not stop on these faded breakpoints, but they remain in place so they can be conveniently enabled and act as a marker to an important area in the code.

It's also possible to delete breakpoints from the Breakpoint Navigator. Simply select one or more breakpoints and press the Delete key. Make sure you select the correct breakpoints to delete since there is no undo feature.

It's also possible to select the file associated with the breakpoints. In this case, if you delete the file listed in the Breakpoint Navigator and press Delete, all breakpoints in that file will be deleted.

Note that breakpoints are categorized by the file that they appear in. In Figure 13-5, the files are `DetailViewController.swift` and `MasterViewController.swift`, with the breakpoints listed below those file names. Figure 13-6 shows an example of what a file looks like with more than a single breakpoint.

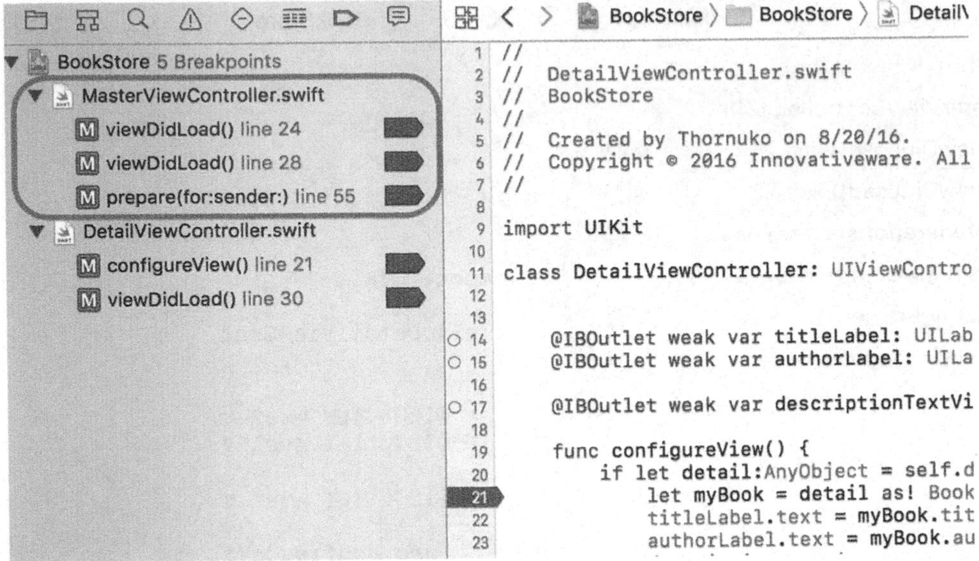

Figure 13-6. A file with several breakpoints

Debugging Basics

Set a breakpoint on the statement shown in Figure 13-2. Next, as shown in Figure 13-7, click the Run button to compile the project and start running it in the Xcode debugger.

Figure 13-7. The Build and Debug buttons in the Xcode toolbar

Once the project builds, the debugger will start. The screen will show the debugging windows, and the program will stop execution on the line statement, as shown in Figure 13-8.

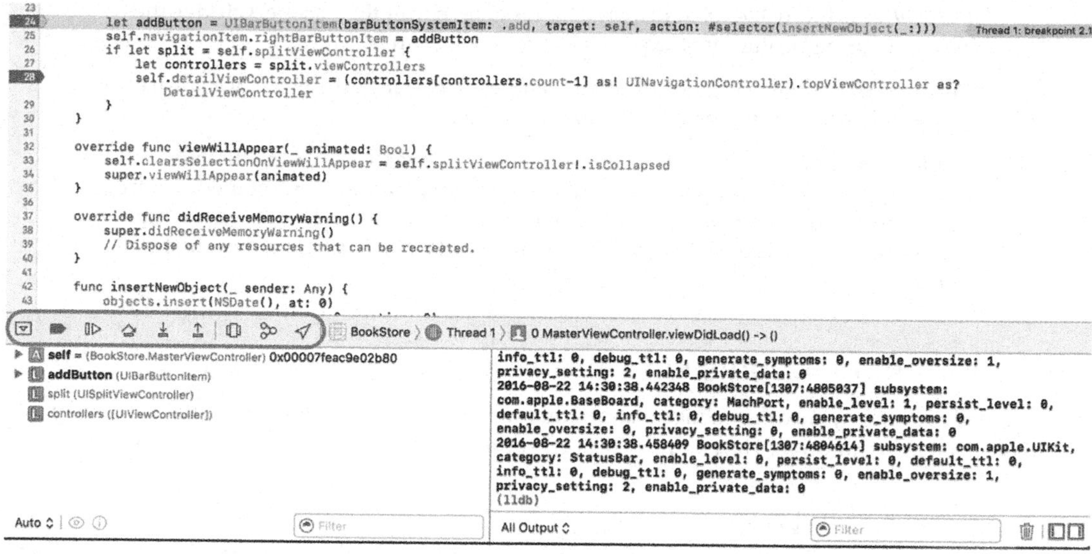

Figure 13-8. *The Debugger view with execution stopped on line 24*

The Debugger view adds some additional windows. The following are the different parts of the Debugger view shown in Figure 13-8:

- ***Debugger controls*** *(circled in Figure* 13-8*)*: The debugging controls can pause, continue, step over, step into, and step out of statements in the program. The stepping controls are used most often. The first button on the left is used to show or hide the debugger view. In Figure 13-8, the debugger view is shown. Figure 13-9 labels the different pieces of the debugger view.

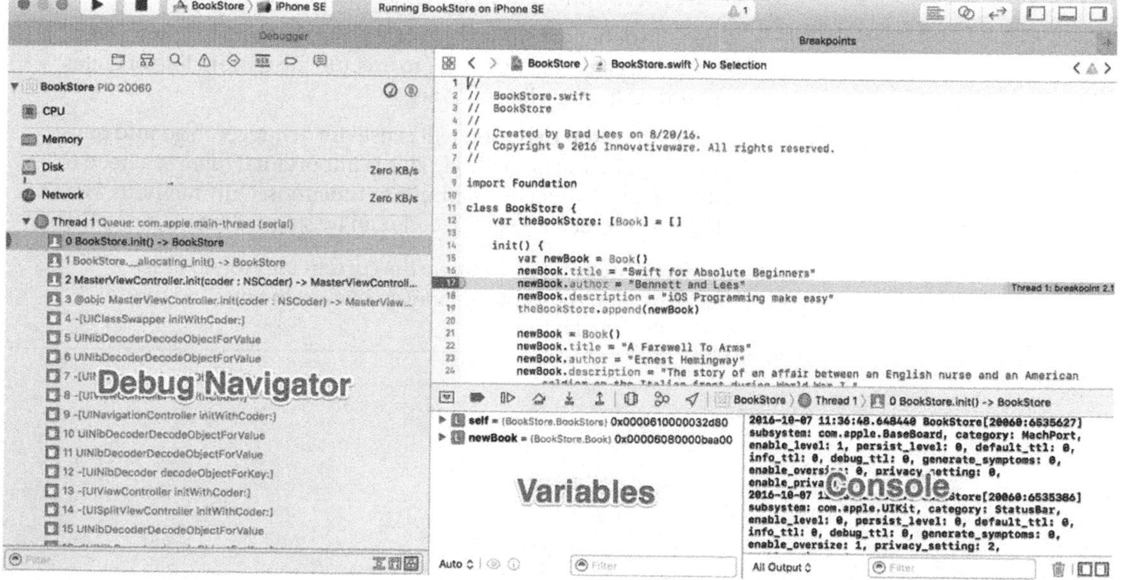

Figure 13-9. *The debugger locations*

- ***Variables*:** The Variables view displays the variables currently in scope. Clicking the little triangle just to the left of a variable name will expand it.
- ***Console*:** The output window will show useful information in the event of a crash or exception. Also, any `NSLog` or `print` output goes here.
- ***Debug navigator*:** The stack trace shows the call stack as well as all the threads currently active in the program. The stack is a hierarchical view of what methods are being called. For example, `main` calls `UIApplicationMain`, and `UIApplicationMain` calls the `UIViewController` class. These method calls "stack" up until they finally return.

Working with the Debugger Controls

As mentioned previously, once the debugger starts, the view changes. What appears are the debugging controls (circled in Figure 13-8). The controls are fairly straightforward and are explained in Table 13-1.

Table 13-1. *Xcode Debugging Controls*

Control	Description
	Clicking the **Stop** button will stop the execution of the program. If the iPhone or iPad emulator is running the application, it will also stop as if the user force quit the app. Clicking the **Run** button (looks like a Play button) starts debugging. If the application is currently in debug mode, clicking the **Run** button again will restart debugging the application from the beginning; it's like stopping and then starting again.
	Clicking this button causes the program to **continue** execution. The program will continue running until it ends, the **Stop** button is clicked, or the program runs into another breakpoint.
	When the debugger stops on a breakpoint, clicking the **Step Over** button will cause the debugger to execute the current line of code and stop at the next line of code.
	Clicking the **Step In** button will cause the debugger to go into the specified function or method. This is important if there is a need to follow code into specific methods or functions. Only methods for which the project has source code can be stepped into.
	The **Step Out** button will cause the current method to finish executing, and the debugger will go back to the method that originally called it.

Using the Step Controls

To practice using the step controls, let's step into a method. As the name implies, the Step In button follows program execution into the method or function that is highlighted. Select the `DetailViewController.swift` file on the left side. Then set a breakpoint on line 30, which is the call to `self.configureView()`. Click the Run button and select a book from the list. Your screen should look similar to Figure 13-10.

```
11 class DetailViewController: UIViewController {
12
13
14     @IBOutlet weak var titleLabel: UILabel!
15     @IBOutlet weak var authorLabel: UILabel!
16
17     @IBOutlet weak var descriptionTextView: UITextView!
18
19     func configureView() {
20         if let detail:AnyObject = self.detailItem {
21             let myBook = detail as! Book
22             titleLabel.text = myBook.title
23             authorLabel.text = myBook.author
24             descriptionTextView.text = myBook.description
25         }
26     }
27
28     override func viewDidLoad() {
29         super.viewDidLoad()
30         self.configureView()                                   Thread 1: breakpoint 2.1
31         // Do any additional setup after loading the view, typically from a nib.
32
33     }
34
```

Figure 13-10. The debugger stopped on line 38

Click the Step Into button, , which will cause the debugger to go into the `configureView()` method of the `DetailViewController` object. The screen should look like Figure 13-11.

```
9  import UIKit
10
11 class DetailViewController: UIViewController {
12
13
14     @IBOutlet weak var titleLabel: UILabel!
15     @IBOutlet weak var authorLabel: UILabel!
16
17     @IBOutlet weak var descriptionTextView: UITextView!
18
19     func configureView() {
20         if let detail:AnyObject = self.detailItem {            Thread 1: step in
21             let myBook = detail as! Book
22             titleLabel.text = myBook.title
23             authorLabel.text = myBook.author
24             descriptionTextView.text = myBook.description
25         }
26     }
27
28     override func viewDidLoad() {
29         super.viewDidLoad()
30         self.configureView()
31         // Do any additional setup after loading the view, typically from a nib.
32
33     }
34
```

Figure 13-11. Stepping into the configureView method of the DetailViewController object

The control Step Over, , continues execution of the program but doesn't go into a method. It simply executes the method and continues to the next line. Step Out, , is a little like the opposite of Step In. If the Step Out button is clicked, the current method continues execution until it finishes. The debugger then returns to the line after Step In was clicked. For example, if the Step In button is clicked on the line shown in Figure 13-9 and then the Step Out button is clicked, the debugger will return to the `viewDidLoad()` method of the `DetailViewController.swift` file on the statement shown in Figure 13-9 (line 30 in the example), which was the line where Step In was clicked.

Looking at the Thread Window and Call Stack

As mentioned earlier, the Debug navigator displays the current thread. However, it also displays the call stack. If you look at the difference between Figures 13-9 and 13-10 as far as the thread window goes, you can see that Figure 13-10 has the `configureView` method listed because `DetailViewController` calls the `configureView` method.

Now, the call stack is not simply a list of functions that *have* been called; rather, it's a list of functions that are currently *being* called. That's an important distinction. Once the `configureView` method is finished and returns (line 26), `configureView` will no longer appear in the call stack. You can think of a call stack almost like a breadcrumb trail. The trail shows you how to get back to where you started.

Debugging Variables

It is possible to view some information about a variable (other than its memory address) by hovering your mouse cursor over the variable in the code. When you get to where the value of a variable has been assigned in the local scope, you will most likely see the variable in the bottom Variables view. In Figure 13-12, you can see the `newBook` variable, and it has a title of Swift for Absolute Beginners. You can also see that there is no author or description assigned. In debugging, when you are stopped on a line, it is before the line is executed. This means that even though you are paused on the line to assign the `author` property, it has not been assigned yet.

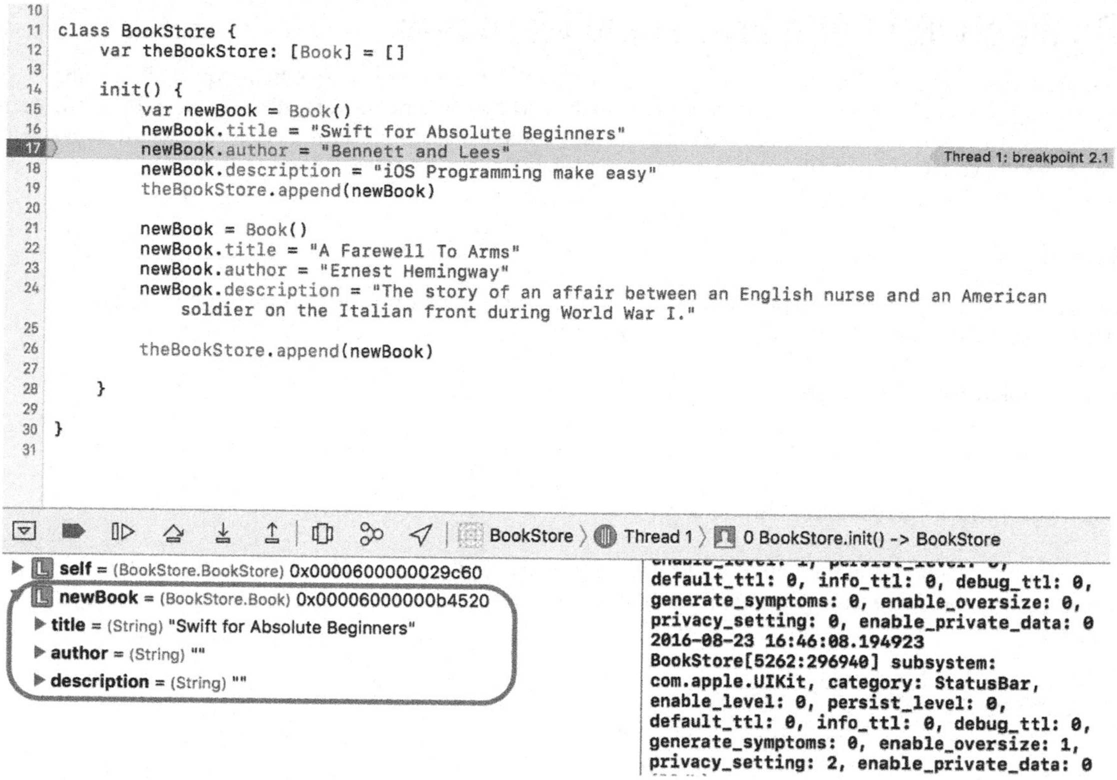

```
class BookStore {
    var theBookStore: [Book] = []

    init() {
        var newBook = Book()
        newBook.title = "Swift for Absolute Beginners"
        newBook.author = "Bennett and Lees"                    Thread 1: breakpoint 2.1
        newBook.description = "iOS Programming make easy"
        theBookStore.append(newBook)

        newBook = Book()
        newBook.title = "A Farewell To Arms"
        newBook.author = "Ernest Hemingway"
        newBook.description = "The story of an affair between an English nurse and an American
            soldier on the Italian front during World War I."

        theBookStore.append(newBook)

    }

}
```

```
BookStore 〉 Thread 1 〉 0 BookStore.init() -> BookStore

▶ self = (BookStore.BookStore) 0x0000600000029c60
▼ newBook = (BookStore.Book) 0x00006000000b4520
  ▶ title = (String) "Swift for Absolute Beginners"
  ▶ author = (String) ""
  ▶ description = (String) ""
```

```
default_ttl: 0, info_ttl: 0, debug_ttl: 0,
generate_symptoms: 0, enable_oversize: 0,
privacy_setting: 0, enable_private_data: 0
2016-08-23 16:46:08.194923
BookStore[5262:296940] subsystem:
com.apple.UIKit, category: StatusBar,
enable_level: 0, persist_level: 0,
default_ttl: 0, info_ttl: 0, debug_ttl: 0,
generate_symptoms: 0, enable_oversize: 1,
privacy_setting: 2, enable_private_data: 0
```

Figure 13-12. *Viewing a variable value*

Position the mouse cursor over any place the newBook variable appears and click the disclosure triangle to display the Book object. You should see what is displayed in Figure 13-13.

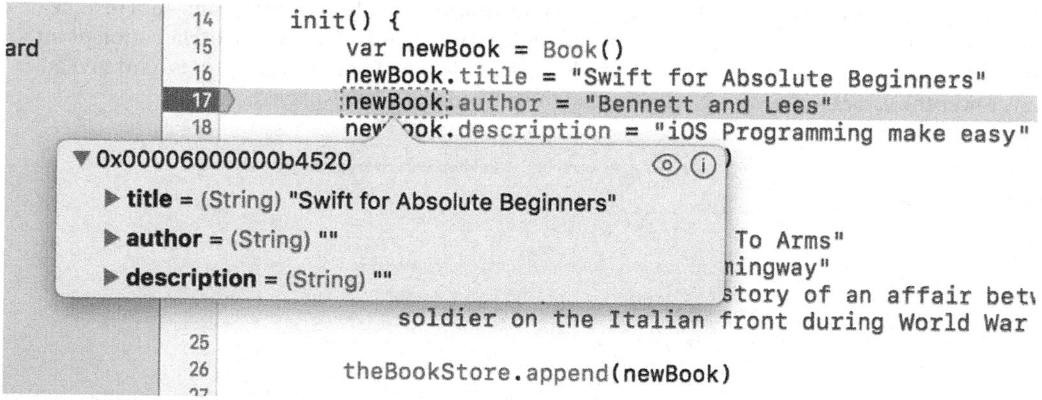

```
    init() {
        var newBook = Book()
        newBook.title = "Swift for Absolute Beginners"
        newBook.author = "Bennett and Lees"
        newBook.description = "iOS Programming make easy"

▼ 0x00006000000b4520
    ▶ title = (String) "Swift for Absolute Beginners"
    ▶ author = (String) ""
    ▶ description = (String) ""

            soldier on the Italian front during World War

        theBookStore.append(newBook)
```

Figure 13-13. *Hovering over the newBook variable reveals some information*

Hovering over the newBook variable reveals its information. In Figure 13-13, you can see the newBook variable expanded.

Dealing with Code Errors and Warnings

While coding errors and warnings aren't really part of the Xcode debugger, fixing them is part of the entire debugging process. Before a program can be run (with or without the debugger), all errors must be fixed. Warnings won't stop a program from building, but they could cause issues during program execution. It's best not to have warnings at all.

Errors

Let's take a look at a couple of types of errors. To start, let's add an error to the code. On line 15 of the `MasterViewController.swift` file, change the following:

```
var myBookStore: BookStore = BookStore()
```

to the following:

```
var myBookStore: BookStore = BookStore[]
```

Save the changes and then build the project by pressing ⌘+B. There will be an error, as shown in Figure 13-14, that may show up immediately or after the build.

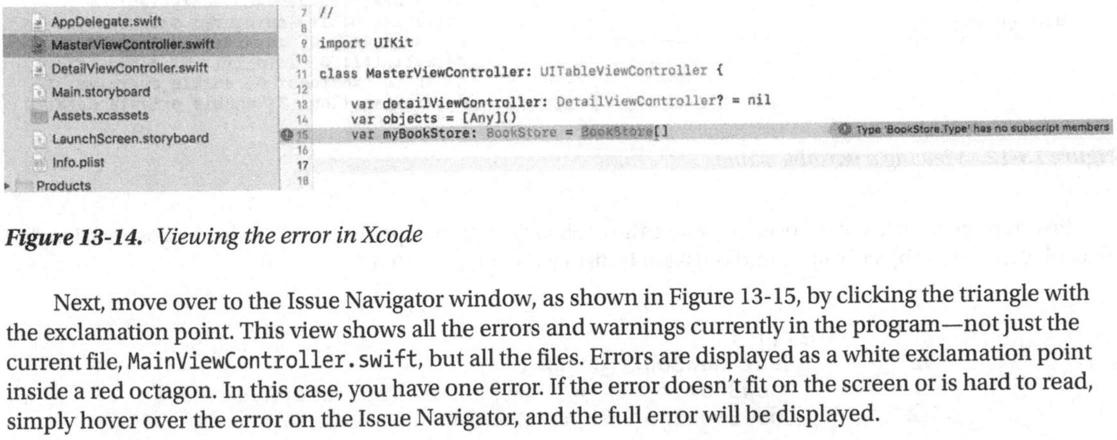

Figure 13-14. Viewing the error in Xcode

Next, move over to the Issue Navigator window, as shown in Figure 13-15, by clicking the triangle with the exclamation point. This view shows all the errors and warnings currently in the program—not just the current file, `MainViewController.swift`, but all the files. Errors are displayed as a white exclamation point inside a red octagon. In this case, you have one error. If the error doesn't fit on the screen or is hard to read, simply hover over the error on the Issue Navigator, and the full error will be displayed.

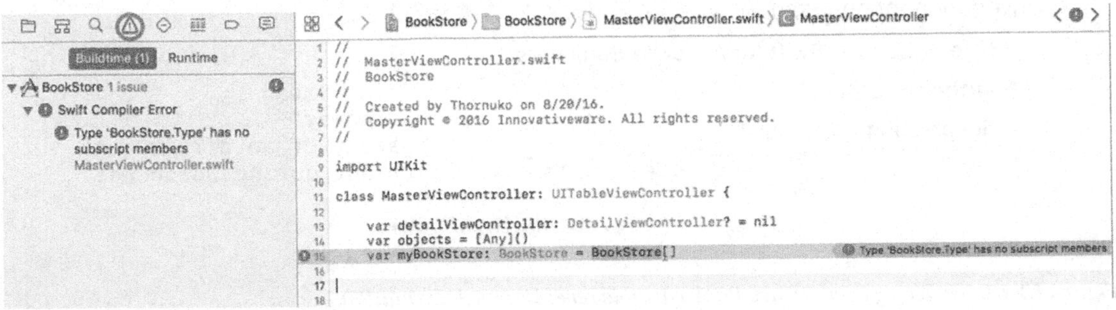

Figure 13-15. Viewing the Issue Navigator

Generally, the error points to the problem. In the previous case, the BookStore object was initialized as an array rather than as an object.

Go ahead and fix the error by changing [] to ().

Warnings

Warnings indicate potential problems with the program. As mentioned, warnings won't stop a program from building but may cause issues during program execution. It's outside the scope of this book to cover those warnings that may or may not cause problems during program execution; however, it's good practice to eliminate all warnings from a program.

Add the following code to the MasterViewController.swift viewDidLoad method:

```
if false {
   print("False")
}
```

The print command will never be executed because false will never be equal to true. Build the project by pressing ⌘+B. A warning will be displayed, as shown in Figure 13-16.

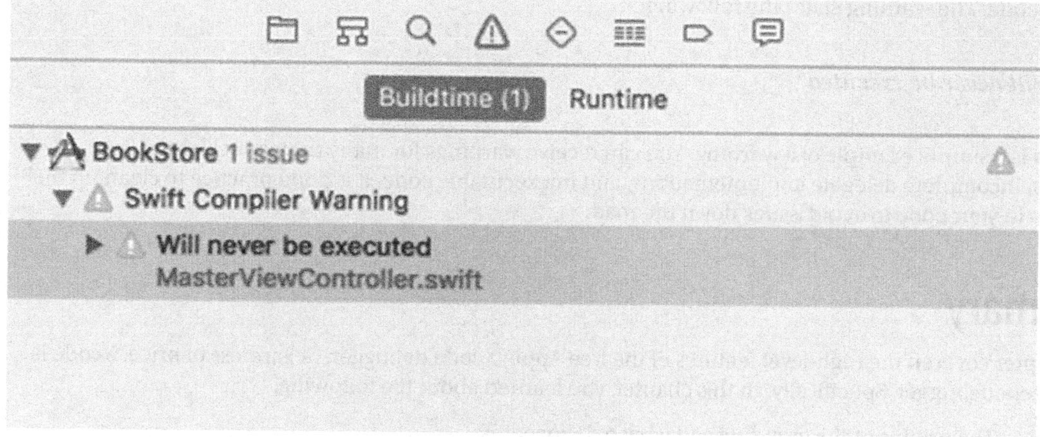

Figure 13-16. *Viewing the warnings in the Issue Navigator*

Clicking the first warning in the Issue Navigator will show you the code that is causing the first problem, as shown in Figure 13-17.

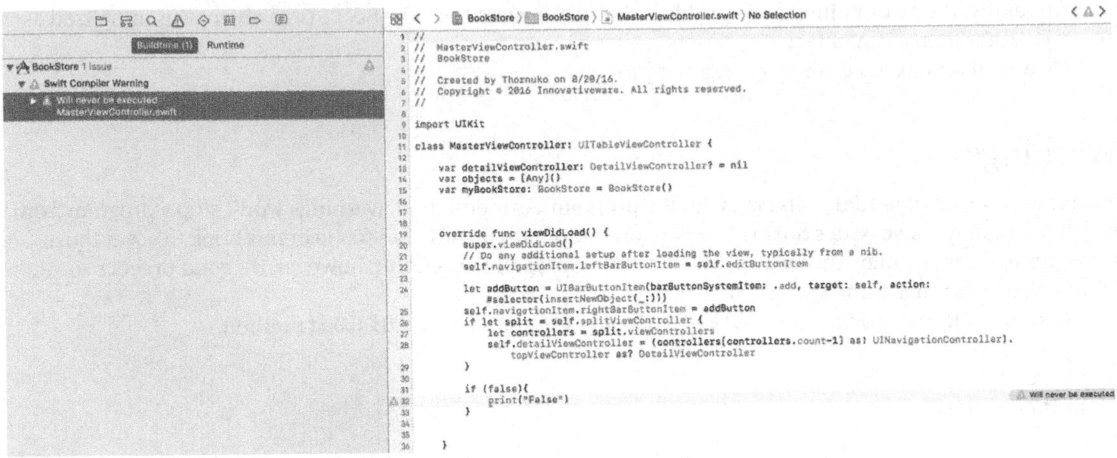

Figure 13-17. Viewing your first warning

In the main window, you can see the warning. In fact, this warning gives you a clue as to the problem with the code. The warning states the following:

"Will never be executed"

This is a simple example of a warning. You can receive warnings for many things such as unused variables, incomplete delegate implementations, and unexecutable code. It is good practice to clean up the warnings in your code to avoid issues down the road.

Summary

This chapter covered the high-level features of the free Apple Xcode debugger. Regardless of price, Xcode is an excellent debugger. Specifically, in this chapter, you learned about the following:

- The origins of the term *bug* and what a debugger is
- The high-level features of the Xcode debugger, including breakpoints and stepping through a program
- Using the debugging controls called Continue, Step Over, Step In, and Step Out
- Working with the various debugger views, including threads (call stack), Variables view, Text editor, and Console Output
- Looking at program variables
- Dealing with errors and warnings

CHAPTER 14

A Swift iPhone App

In Chapter 8, you created a basic bookstore iPhone app with Swift. In this chapter, you will add some features to the app to make it a bit more functional and use many of the technologies you have learned in this book, such as creating a class, using delegates and protocols, and using actions and outlets. You'll also learn about some new techniques such as switches, `UIAlertController`, and landmarks.

Let's Get Started

The bookstore example in Chapter 8 enabled you to view books in your bookstore in a TableView and then tap the book to see its details. In this chapter, you will add the following capabilities to the Chapter 8 bookstore app:

- Adding a book
- Deleting a book
- Modifying a book

See Figures 14-1 and 14-2.

G. Bennett and B. Lees, *Swift 3 for Absolute Beginners*, DOI 10.1007/978-1-4842-2331-4_14

Figure 14-1. *Add book functionality*

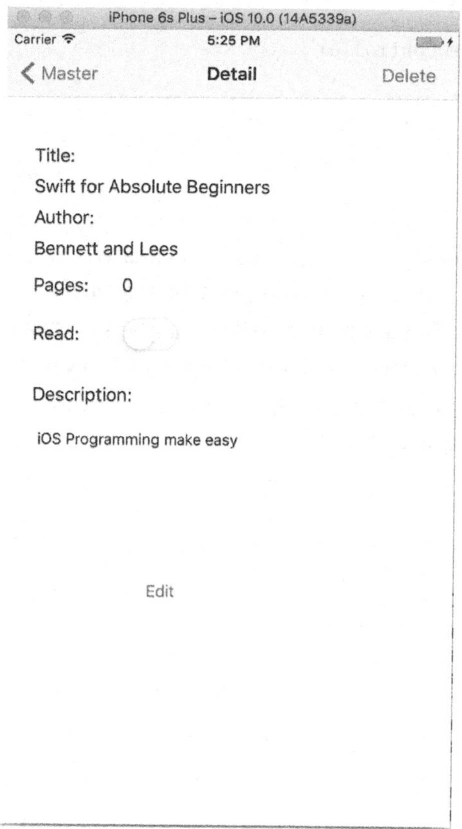

Figure 14-2. *Adding edit and delete functionality along with using a UISwitch*

The first step is to define the AddBookViewController, as shown in Listing 14-1.

Listing 14-1. The prepareForSegue Function

```
// MARK: - Segues

    override func prepare(for segue: UIStoryboardSegue, sender: Any?) {
        if segue.identifier == "showDetail" {
            if let indexPath = self.tableView.indexPathForSelectedRow {
                let selectedBook:Book = myBookStore.theBookStore[(indexPath as
                NSIndexPath).row]

                let nav = segue.destination as! UINavigationController
                let vc = nav.topViewController as! DetailViewController

                vc.detailItem = selectedBook
                vc.delegate = self
            }
        }
```

```
62          else if segue.identifier == "addBookSegue" {
63              let vc = segue.destination as! AddBookViewController
64              vc.delegate = self
65          }
66
67      }
```

■ **Note** Something new in Swift is on line 48: "`// MARK: - Segues`". `// MARK:` is called a ***landmark***. It is replacement of the #pragma mark, which is used in Objective-C. Landmarks help break up the code in the jump bar and enable you to quickly get to sections of code indicated by the landmark. When you type something following `// MARK:`, Xcode places the landmark in the jump bar's drop-down, as shown in Figure 14-3. If you just type `// MARK: -`, Xcode adds a line separator in the jump bar's drop-down. Swift also supports `// TODO:` and `// FIXME:` landmarks to annotate your code and list them in the jump bar.

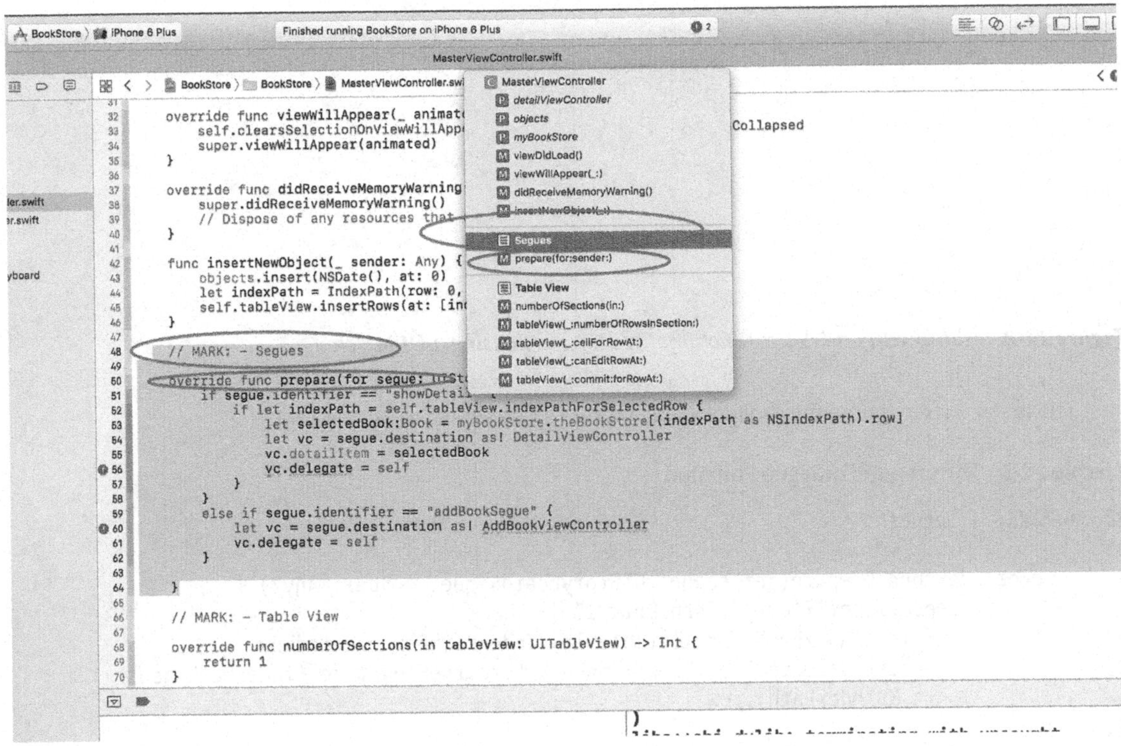

Figure 14-3. Swift's new landmarks

Now add the new view controller `AddBookViewController` mentioned in line 63 in Listing 14-1. Add a `View Controller` object to the storyboard by dragging a View Controller to the `Main.storyboard` file. Then add the objects in Figure 14-4 to enable the user to add a new book. Feel free to move the scene around to make it clear how they relate to each other, as shown in Figure 14-4.

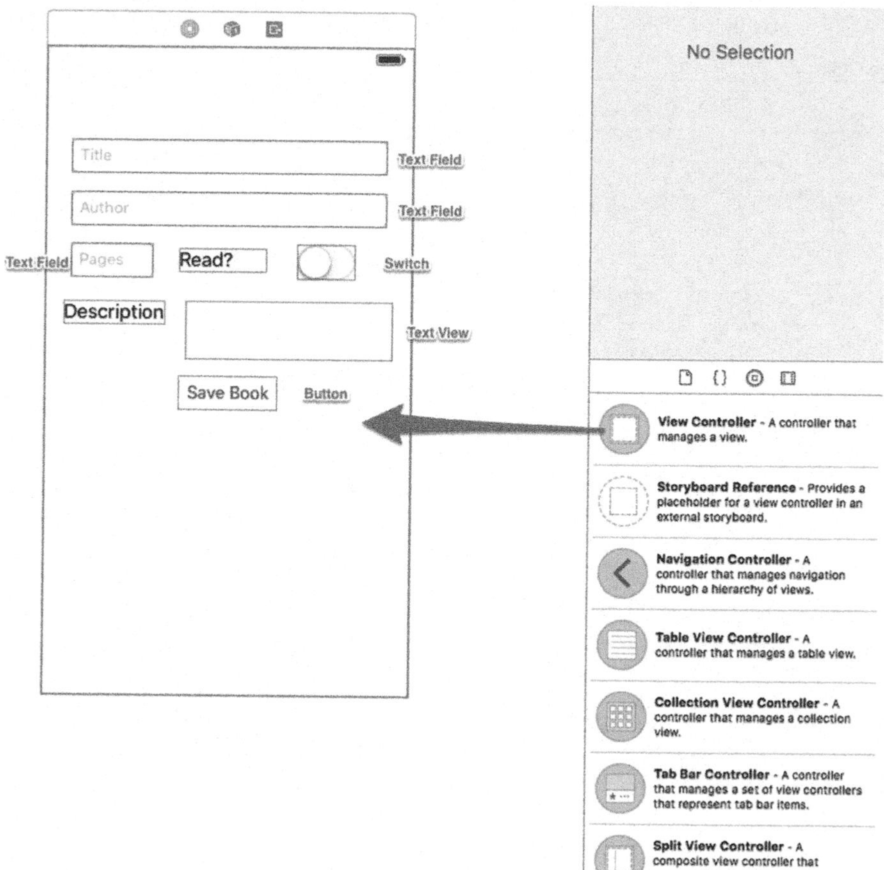
Title
Text Field
Author
Text Field
Text Field
Pages
Read?
Switch
Description
Text View
Save Book
Button
No Selection
View Controller - A controller that manages a view.
Storyboard Reference - Provides a placeholder for a view controller in an external storyboard.
Navigation Controller - A controller that manages navigation through a hierarchy of views.
Table View Controller - A controller that manages a table view.
Collection View Controller - A controller that manages a collection view.
Tab Bar Controller - A controller that manages a set of view controllers that represent tab bar items.
Split View Controller - A composite view controller that

Figure 14-4. *Adding the AddBookViewController and objects*

Add a `Show` Segue object from the Add Button Bar Item to the new View Controller by Control-dragging or right-clicking and dragging from the Add Button Bar Item to the new View Controller, as shown Figure 14-5.

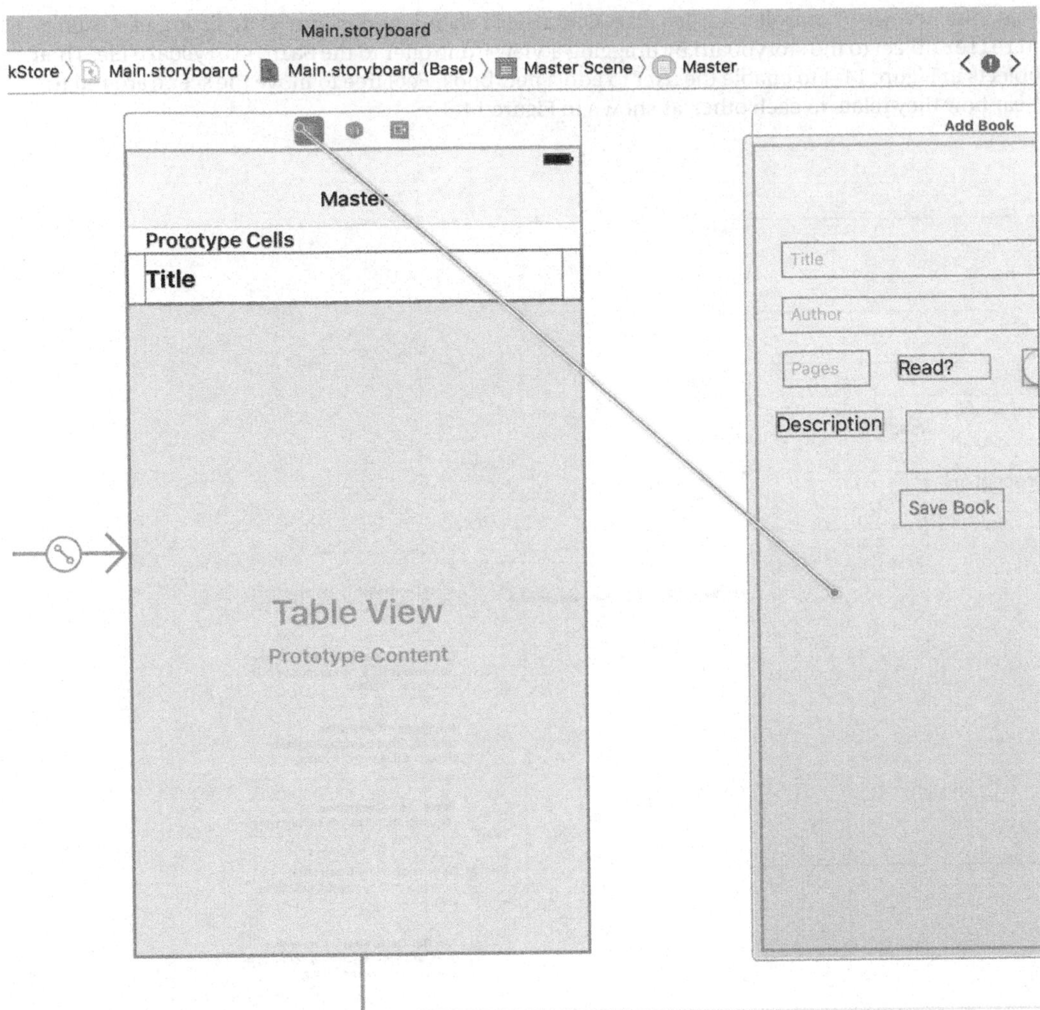

Figure 14-5. Add a Show Segue object to the new View Controller

Modify the `insertNewObject` function in the `MasterViewController.swift`, as shown in Listing 14-2.

Listing 14-2. insertNewObject Function

```
func insertNewObject(_ sender: Any) {
        self.performSegue(withIdentifier: "addBookSegue", sender: nil)
    }
```

Identify the Segue object by clicking the segue arrow and setting the identifier to addBookSegue, as shown in Figure 14-6.

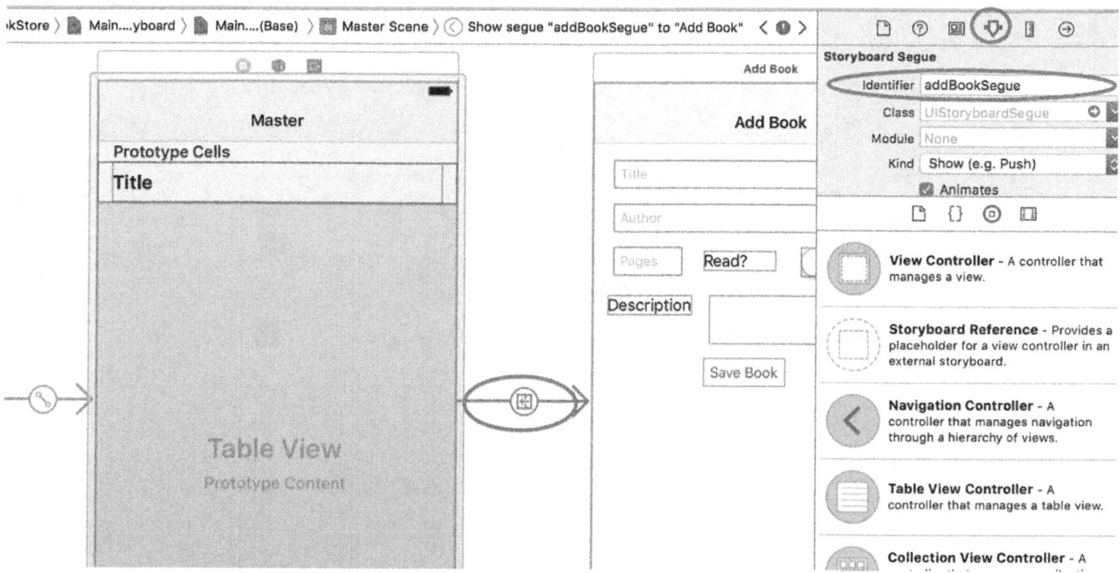

Figure 14-6. *Naming the Segue object addBookSegue*

Now you need to create a Swift class to go with the new View Controller. Create a new iOS Cocoa Touch class file and name it `AddBookViewController`, as shown in Figure 14-7. Make sure you select a subclass of `UIViewController`.

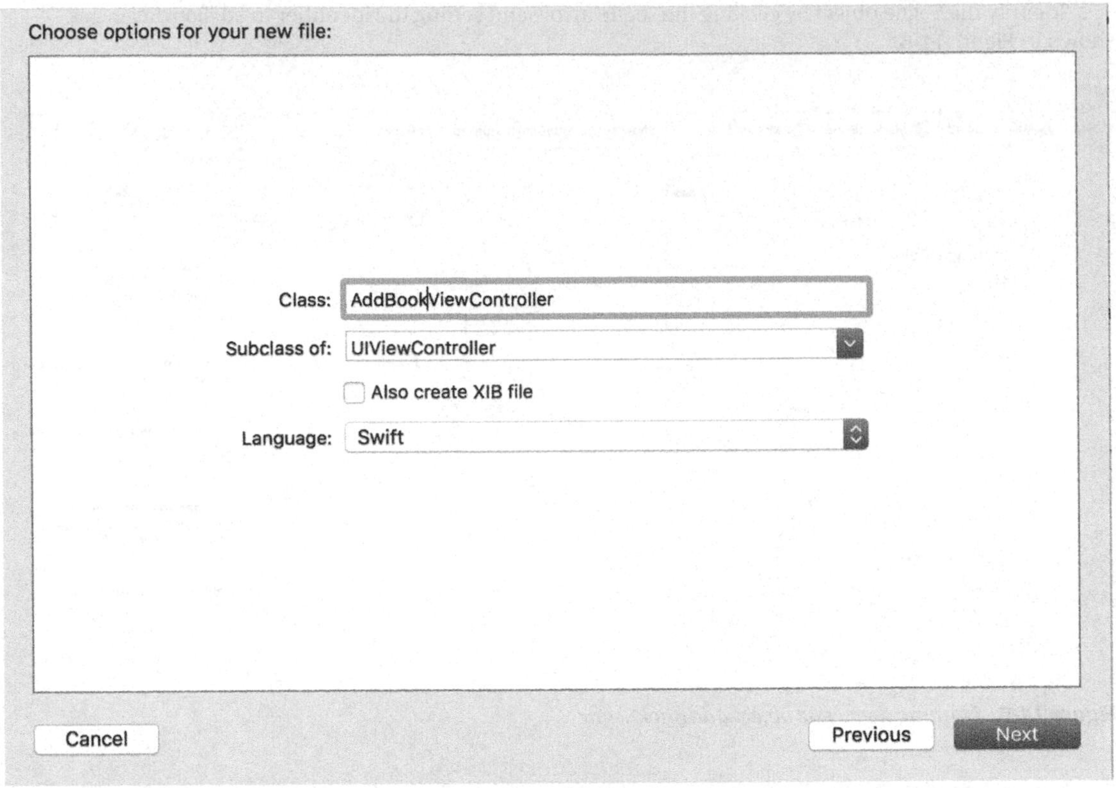

Choose options for your new file:

Class: AddBookViewController

Subclass of: UIViewController

Also create XIB file

Language: Swift

Cancel Previous Next

Figure 14-7. *Adding the AddBookViewController class*

Now you have to associate the new `AddBookViewController` class to the new View Controller. Select the View Controller, and in the Identity Inspector, type `AddBookViewController` for the class, as shown in Figure 14-8.

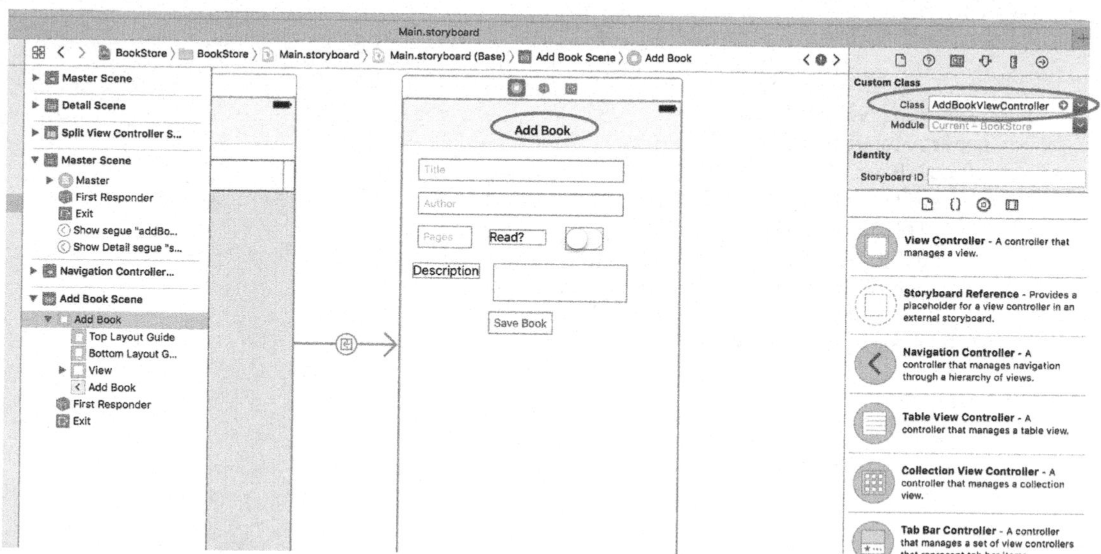

Figure 14-8. *Associating the AddBookViewController class to the new View Controller*

Set the title of the view to Add Book by adding a Navigation Item to the View Controller scene and double-clicking the Navigation Bar. Open the `AddBookViewController.swift` file and add the code shown in Listing 14-3.

Listing 14-3. The AddBookViewController.swift File

```
import UIKit

protocol BookStoreDelegate {
    func newBook(_ controller: AnyObject, newBook: Book)
    func editBook(_ controller: AnyObject, editBook: Book)
    func deleteBook(_ controller: AnyObject)
}



class AddBookViewController: UIViewController {
    var book = Book()
    var delegate: BookStoreDelegate?
    var read = false
    var editBook = false

    @IBOutlet weak var titleText: UITextField!
    @IBOutlet weak var authorText: UITextField!
    @IBOutlet weak var pagesText: UITextField!
    @IBOutlet weak var switchOutlet: UISwitch!

```

```
    @IBOutlet weak var descriptionText: UITextView!


    override func viewDidLoad() {
        super.viewDidLoad()
        if editBook == true {
            self.title = "Edit Book"
            titleText.text = book.title
            authorText.text = book.author
            pagesText.text = String(book.pages)
            descriptionText.text = book.description
            if book.readThisBook {
                switchOutlet.isOn = true
            }
            else {
               switchOutlet.isOn = false
            }
        }

        // Do any additional setup after loading the view.
    }

    override func didReceiveMemoryWarning() {
        super.didReceiveMemoryWarning()
        // Dispose of any resources that can be recreated.
    }


    @IBAction func saveBookAction(_ sender: UIButton) {
        book.title = titleText.text!
        book.author = authorText.text!
        book.description = descriptionText.text
        book.pages = Int(pagesText.text!)!
        if switchOutlet.isOn {
          book.readThisBook = true
        }
        else {
          book.readThisBook = false
        }
        if (editBook) {
            delegate!.editBook(self, editBook:book)
        }
        else {
            delegate!.newBook(self, newBook:book)
        }


    }

}
```

To the Book class, add two properties: pages and readThisBook. These are shown in lines 15 and 16 in Listing 14-4.

Listing 14-4. Book Class Changes

```
11 class Book {
12     var title: String = ""
13     var author: String = ""
14     var description: String = ""
15     var pages: Int = 0
16     var readThisBook: Bool = false
17 }
```

Switches

Connect the outlets in the AddBookViewController class by dragging them from their open circles to the controls, as shown in Figure 14-9.

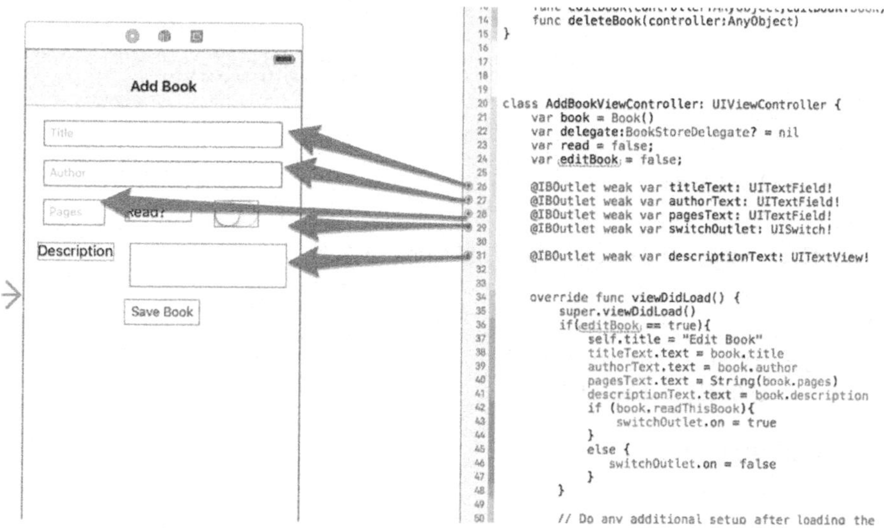

Figure 14-9. *Connecting the outlets*

Connect the saveBookAction action by dragging the outlet circle to the Save Book button, as shown in Figure 14-10.

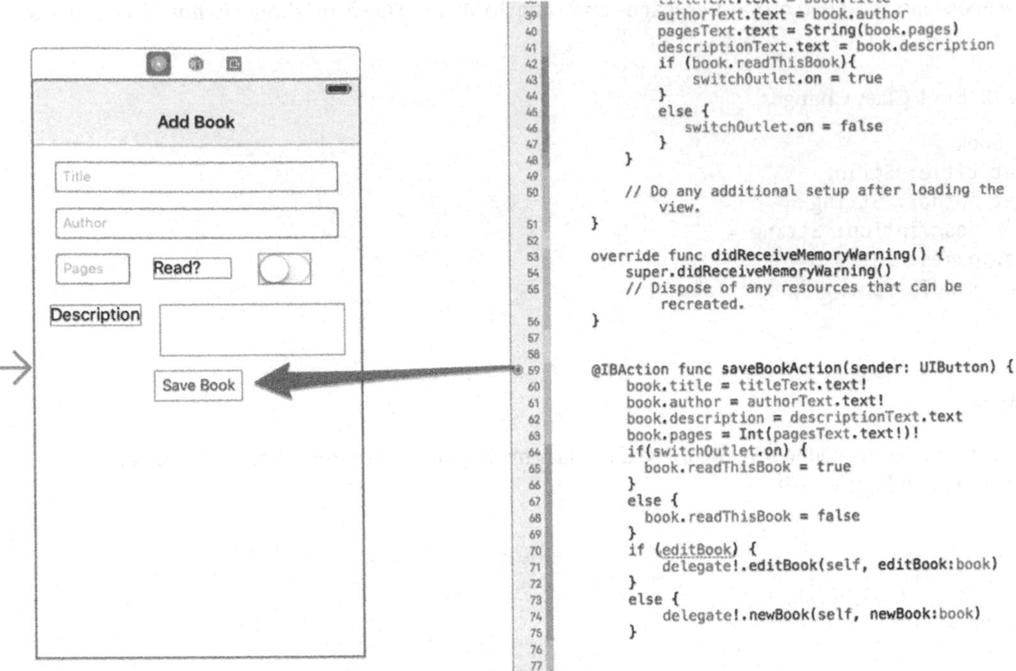

Figure 14-10. *Connecting the saveBookAction*

In the `DetailViewController` class, add the code shown in Listing 14-5.

Listing 14-5. New Properties

```
    @IBOutlet weak var pagesOutlet: UILabel!
    @IBOutlet weak var switchOutlet: UISwitch!

     var delegate: BookStoreDelegate? = nil


     var myBook = Book()
```

Alert Controllers

Add the controls for Pages, Read, and Edit for the `DetailViewController`. Connect the outlets by dragging the open circles to their controls, as shown in Figure 14-11.

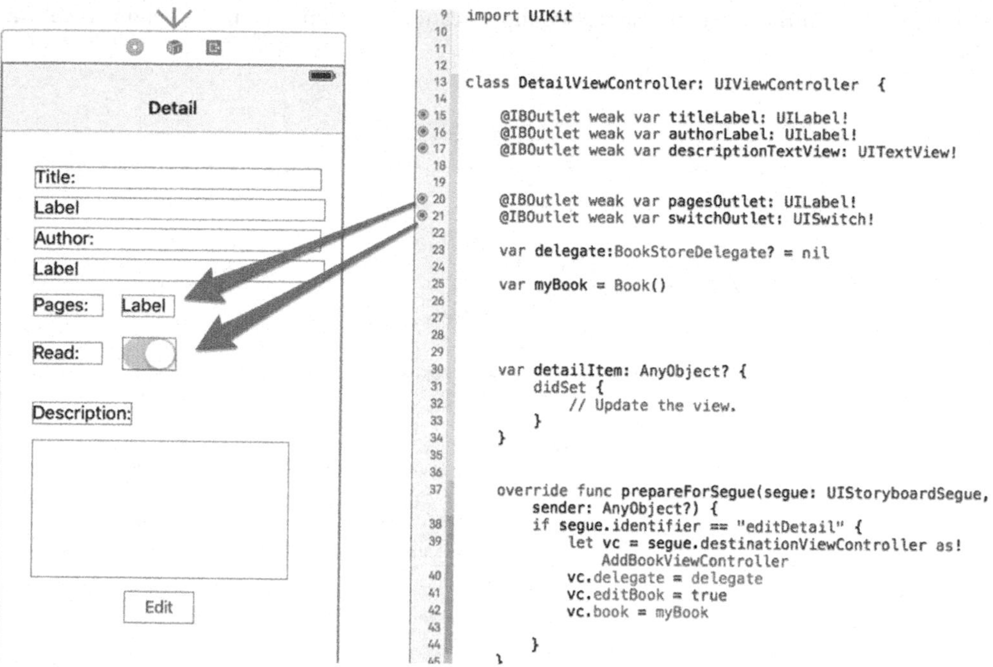
Detail
Title:
Label
Author:
Label
Pages:
Label
Read:
Description:
Edit
import UIKit
class DetailViewController: UIViewController {
@IBOutlet weak var titleLabel: UILabel!
@IBOutlet weak var authorLabel: UILabel!
@IBOutlet weak var descriptionTextView: UITextView!
@IBOutlet weak var pagesOutlet: UILabel!
@IBOutlet weak var switchOutlet: UISwitch!
var delegate:BookStoreDelegate? = nil
var myBook = Book()
var detailItem: AnyObject? {
didSet {
// Update the view.
}
}
override func prepareForSegue(segue: UIStoryboardSegue,
sender: AnyObject?) {
if segue.identifier == "editDetail" {
let vc = segue.destinationViewController as!
AddBookViewController
vc.delegate = delegate
vc.editBook = true
vc.book = myBook
}

Figure 14-11. *Adding the Pages and Read outlets*

The Read switch is disabled in this view by unchecking the `Enabled` property in the Attributes Inspector.

Add the code for displaying a `UIAlertController` when the Delete button is tapped on the DetailViewController, as shown in Listing 14-6.

Listing 14-6. Displaying a UIAlertController

```
    @IBAction func deleteBookAction(_ sender: UIBarButtonItem) {
        let alertController = UIAlertController(title: "Warning", message: "Delete this
        book?", preferredStyle: .alert)
        let noAction = UIAlertAction(title: "No", style: .cancel) { (action) in
            print("Cancel")
        }
        alertController.addAction(noAction)

        let yesAction = UIAlertAction(title: "Yes", style: .destructive) { (action) in
            self.delegate!.deleteBook(self)
        }
        alertController.addAction(yesAction)

        present(alertController, animated: false, completion: nil)
    }
```

Add the Delete Bar Button Item to the right navigation location and connect it to the action, as shown in Figure 14-12.

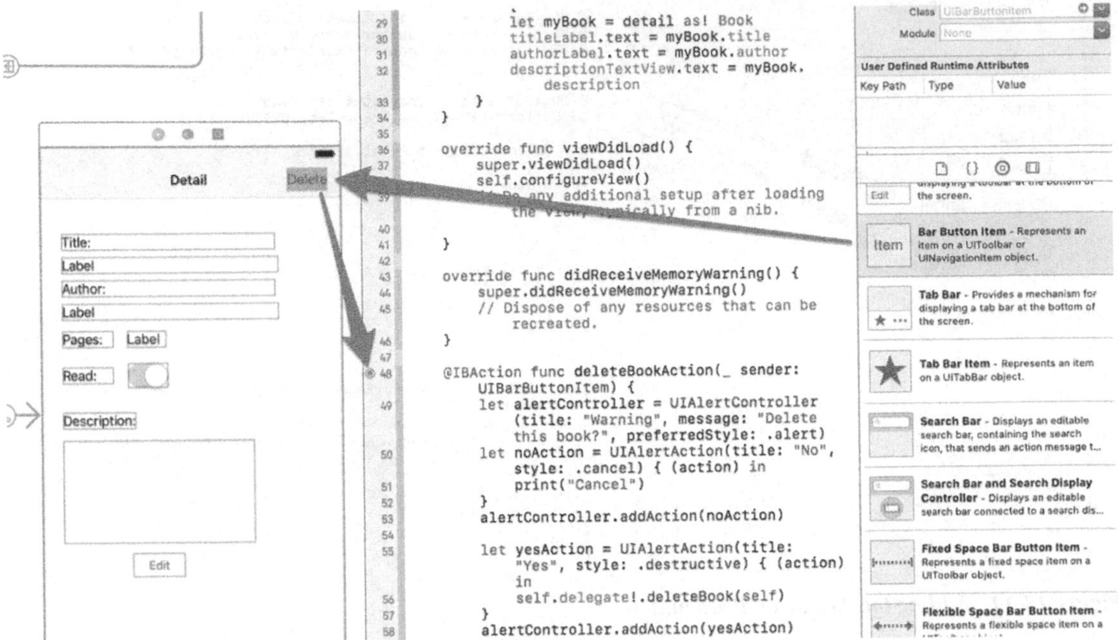

Figure 14-12. *Adding the Delete Right Bar Button Item and action*

The `UIAlertController` will warn the user that the book currently displayed in the `DetailViewController` is about to be deleted and will enable the user to decide whether to delete it. The `UIAlertController` has two buttons: Yes and No. When the user taps the right Bar Button Item (Delete), the `UIAlertController` will be as shown in Figure 14-13 when you are finished.

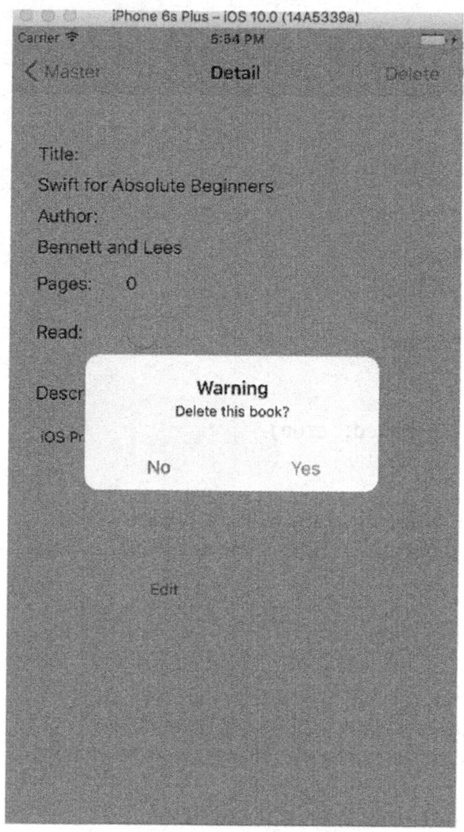

Figure 14-13. *UIAlertController being displayed*

When the user taps Yes to delete the book, you want to call the `deleteBook` delegate method as described in the `MasterViewController` class. Add the `BookStoreDelegate` as shown in Listing 14-7.

Listing 14-7. Adding the BookStoreDelegate

```
class MasterViewController: UITableViewController, BookStoreDelegate {
```

Let's now talk about the three delegate methods: `newBook`, `deleteBook`, and `editBook`, as defined in the `AddBookViewController` class in Listing 14-3 (lines 11 to 15). Add these three functions at the end of the `MasterViewController` class, as shown in Listing 14-8.

Listing 14-8. Conforming to the Protocol

```
// MARK: - Delegate Methods conforming to the protocol BookStoreDelegate as defined in
   the AddBookViewController
    func newBook(_ controller:AnyObject,newBook:Book) {
        myBookStore.theBookStore.append(newBook)
        tableView.reloadData()
        _ = navigationController?.popViewController(animated: true)
    }

```

```
106     func deleteBook(_ controller:AnyObject){
107         let indexPath = tableView.indexPathForSelectedRow
108         let row = (indexPath as NSIndexPath?)?.row
109         myBookStore.theBookStore.remove(at: row!)
110         tableView.reloadData()
111         _ = navigationController?.popViewController(animated:false)
112     }
113
114     func editBook(_ controller:AnyObject, editBook:Book){
115         let indexPath = tableView.indexPathForSelectedRow
116         let row = (indexPath as NSIndexPath?)?.row
117         myBookStore.theBookStore.insert(editBook, at: row!)
118         myBookStore.theBookStore.remove(at: row!+1)
119         tableView.reloadData()
120         _ = navigationController?.popViewController(animated: true)
121     }
```

The function newBook adds a new book to the bookstore; appending the array with the newBook does this, as shown in line 93. Line 94 then reloads the Table View by calling all the Table View delegate methods:

```
numberOfSectionsInTableView
numberOfRowsInSection
cellForRowAtIndexPath
```

Finally, you pop the `DetailViewController` from the navigation stack by calling `popToRootViewControllerAnimated(true)`. Popping the view from the navigation stack means the view is removed, similar to tapping the Back button.

The function `deleteBook` removes the book from the `bookStore` array. First, you determine which row was selected in the `tableView` and use that index to delete the book in the array by calling `removeAtIndex(row!)`, as shown on line 109.

The function `editBook` enables the user to edit an existing book in the `bookStore` array. To do this, the function inserts the edited book in the array at the row that was selected, as shown on line 111. Then the function deletes the original book that was pushed down one index when you inserted the book in the array, as shown on line 117.

Now add the Edit button to the bottom of the `DetailViewController` and add a Show Segue from the Edit button to the `AddBookViewController`, as shown in Figure 14-14.

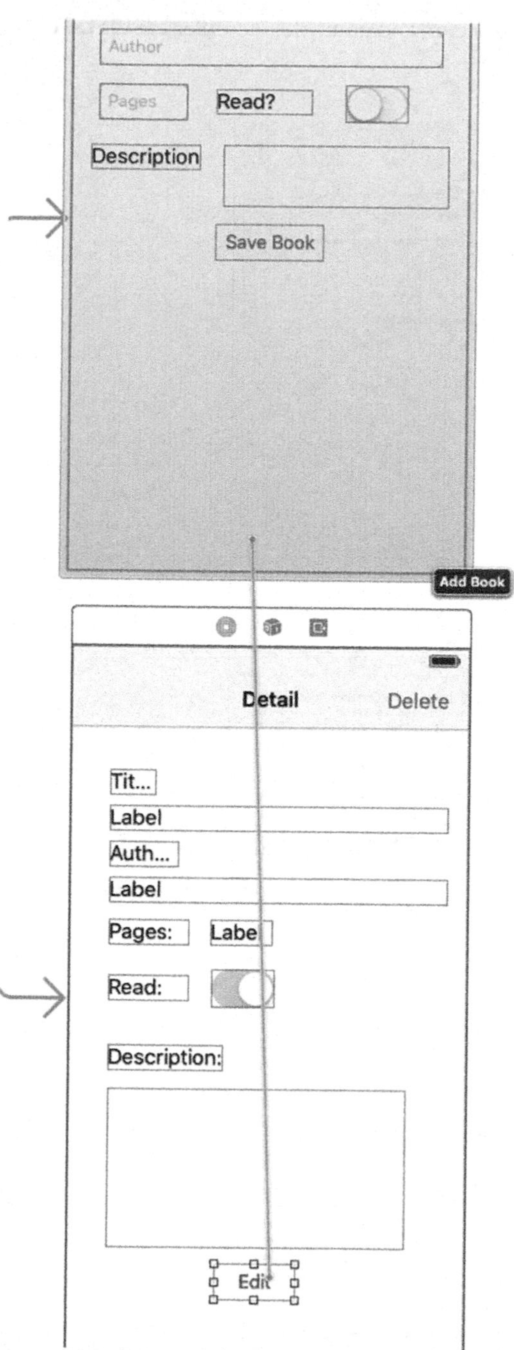

Figure 14-14. *Adding the Show Segue object*

Select the Segue you just created, select the Attributes Inspector, and name the identifier **editDetail**. See Figure 14-15.

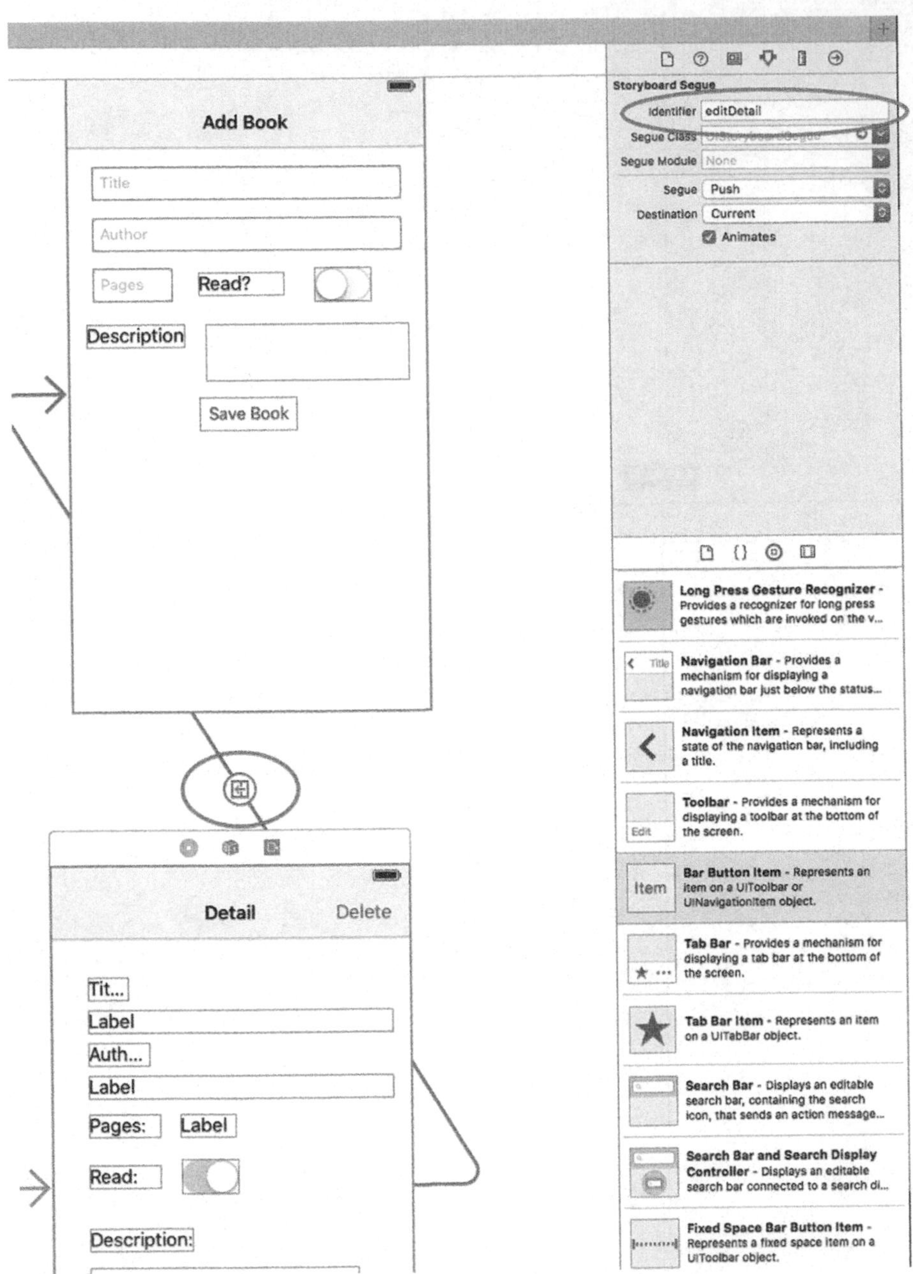

Figure 14-15. *Naming the Segue's identifier*

In the `DetailViewController`, add the `prepareForSegue` method before the `configureView` method, as shown in Listing 14-9.

Listing 14-9. Add the prepareForSegue Method

```
override func prepare(for segue: UIStoryboardSegue, sender: Any?) {
        if segue.identifier == "editDetail" {
            let vc = segue.destination as! AddBookViewController
            vc.delegate = delegate
            vc.editBook = true
            vc.book = myBook
        }
    }
```

Finally, modify the `configureView` function in the `DetailViewController` to properly populate the Pages and Read switch outlets, as shown in Listing 14-10.

Listing 14-10. Modify the configureView

```
func configureView() {
        if let detail = self.detailItem {
            myBook = detail
            titleLabel.text = myBook.title
            authorLabel.text = myBook.author
            descriptionTextView.text = myBook.description
            pagesOutlet.text = String(myBook.pages)
            if myBook.readThisBook {
                switchOutlet.isOn = true
            }
            else {
                switchOutlet.isOn = false
            }
        }
    }
```

App Summary

Compile and run the app. You should set breakpoints at the `delegate` functions to watch the program flow. It is a great app to see how delegates can be used to pass information from one view to another.

Additionally, you can add functionality to the app to make the information persistent by using Core Data or `NSUserDefaults`.

EXERCISES

- Add more books to the bookstore using the original program as a guide.
- Enhance the `Book` class so it can store another attribute—a price or ISBN, for example.
- Add persistence to the app by using Core Data or `NSUserDefaults`.

CHAPTER 15

Apple Watch and WatchKit

In September 2014, Apple announced the Apple Watch, which it considers to be the next chapter in Apple's history. This watch not only handles phone calls and text messages, but it also assesses the wearer's health by tracking heart rate and exercise. At the same time, Apple announced WatchKit, a framework designed for developing apps for the Apple Watch. WatchKit will be very familiar to developers already familiar with UIKit.

Initially, the Apple Watch had some serious limitations with development. The watch acted as an additional screen for an iPhone app. This required the watch to be close to the phone to function and also caused apps to run slowly. In June 2015, Apple announced watchOS 2.0. This new update included many new features, but the biggest one for developers was the ability to create apps that had code that ran on the Apple Watch instead of on the phone. Developers were able to create stand-alone apps that performed much better and were more responsive. Now, Apple has released watchOS 3.0 with even more developer improvements.

Considerations When Creating a watchOS App

One of the great things about developing for watchOS is that all of the development is done in Swift or Objective-C, just like with other iOS devices. The Apple Watch does have some different things that you need to consider before you jump into development.

- The Apple Watch screen is very small. You are limited to 38mm or 42mm, depending on the size of the watch. This means you will not have a lot of space for unnecessary UI elements. Your interface will need to be compact and well organized. Also, due to the two sizes being close in size, you have to create one interface and have it look good on either size.
- Sharing data between the phone and the watch requires some planning. With watchOS 3.0, Apple has made it even easier to share data. Primarily, Apple has enhanced the `WCSession` class. The use of this class is beyond the scope of this book.
- WatchKit for watchOS 3.0 provides many different ways to interact with users not only through apps, but also through glances, actionable notifications, and complications. Well-written apps can take advantage of multiple interactions where it makes sense. These interactions are beyond the scope of this book.

Creating an Apple Watch App

The first step is to create a new project in Xcode. AT the top, select Application under the watchOS header as the project type. Then select iOS App with WatchKit App, as shown in Figure 15-1.

G. Bennett and B. Lees, *Swift 3 for Absolute Beginners*, DOI 10.1007/978-1-4842-2331-4_15

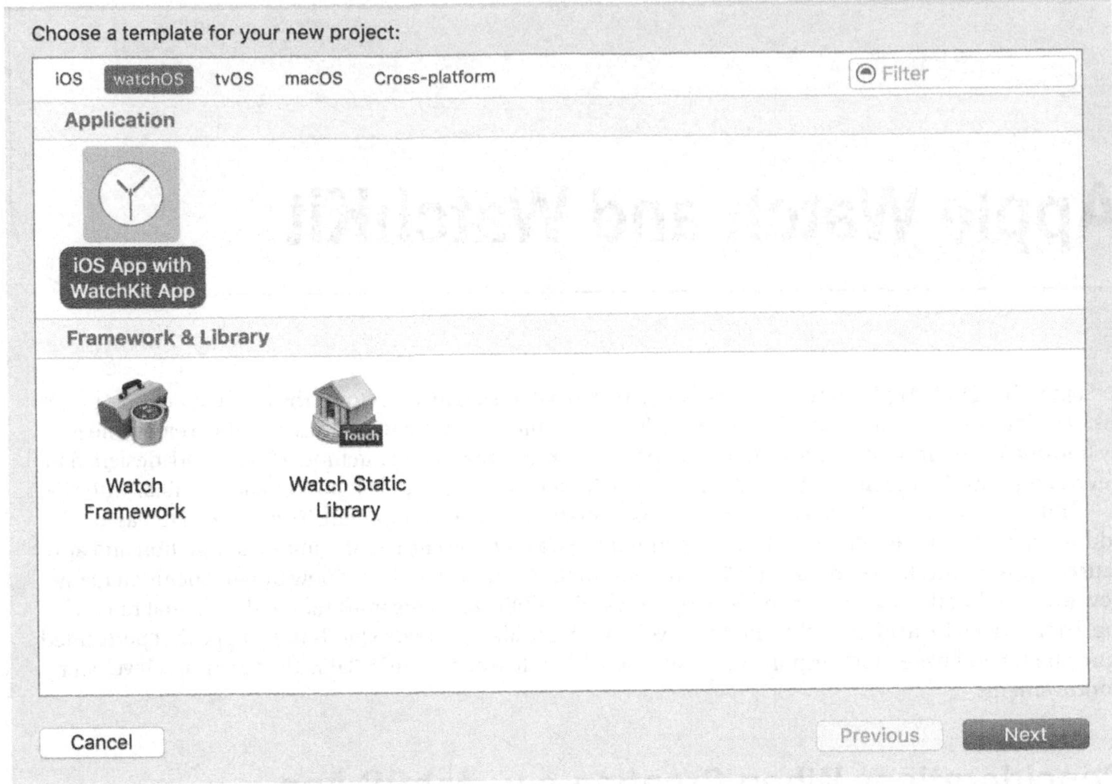

Figure 15-1. *Creating the watchOS app*

Next, you will be given the option of naming your project. We will call the one in this chapter `BookStore`. You will also notice that a watchOS app has different options from a standard iOS app. We will not be adding a notification or complication screne to this app, so make sure they are all unchecked, as shown in Figure 15-2.

■ **Note** WatchKit provides additional interaction types that not available in iOS apps. Glances are quick looks into your app. For example, a bookstore app might have a glance that shows the best sellers. Glances use a special interface on the watch. Complications allow your app to provide simple information on the watch face itself.

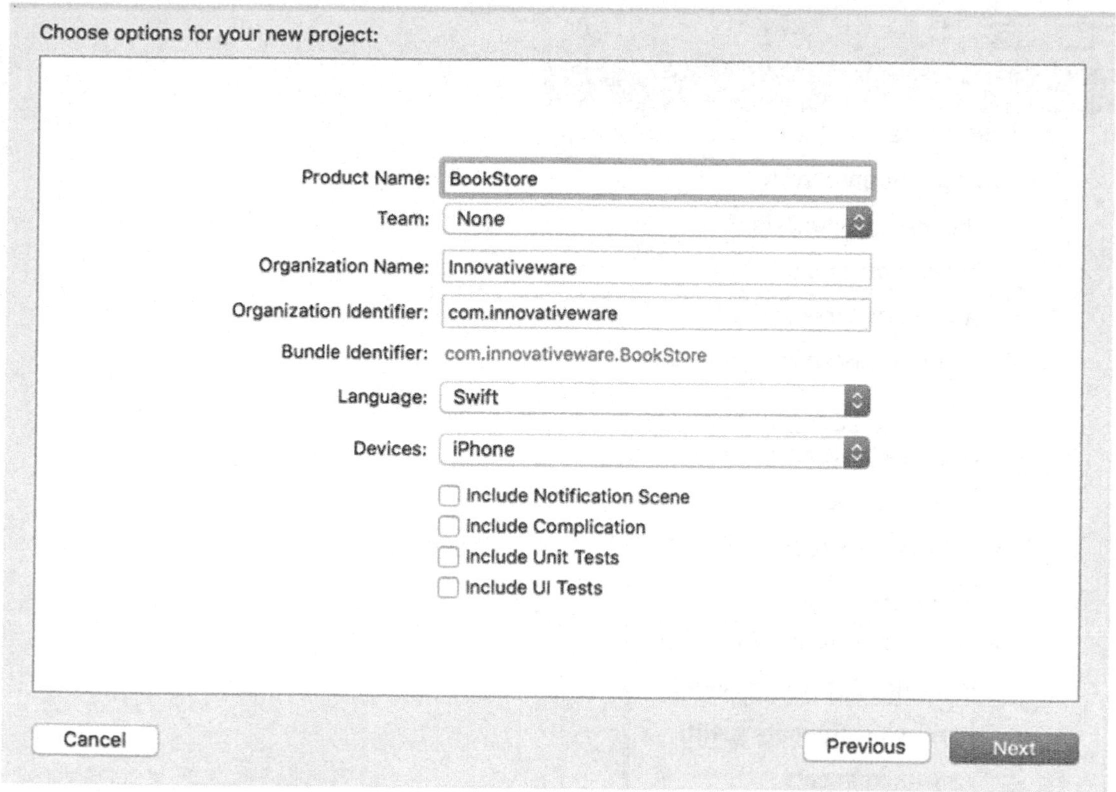

Figure 15-2. *watchOS App options*

Xcode will then prompt you to save your project. Once you've saved it, you will be presented with your new project. On the left side, you will notice two additional targets in your project. One is the BookStore WatchKit App, which contains the interface (storyboard and assets) for your app. The second new target is the BookStore WatchKit Extension. This will contain all of the code for your app to run on watchOS. See Figure 15-3.

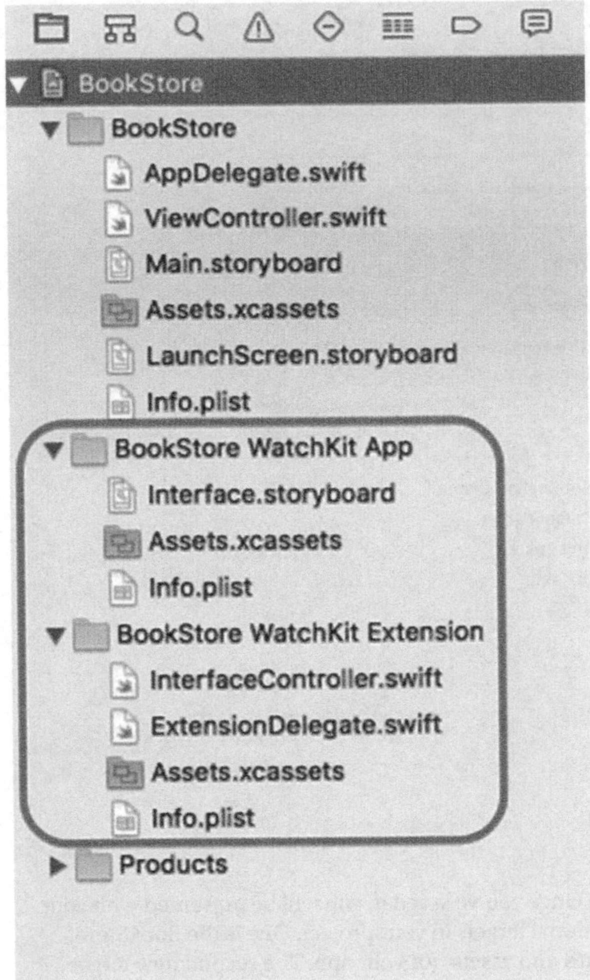

Figure 15-3. *New targets*

Click the `Interface.storyboard` in the BookStore WatchKit App target and you should see a screen similar to Figure 15-4. This is your empty watchOS app storyboard. You will notice the size is significantly smaller than a standard iOS storyboard.

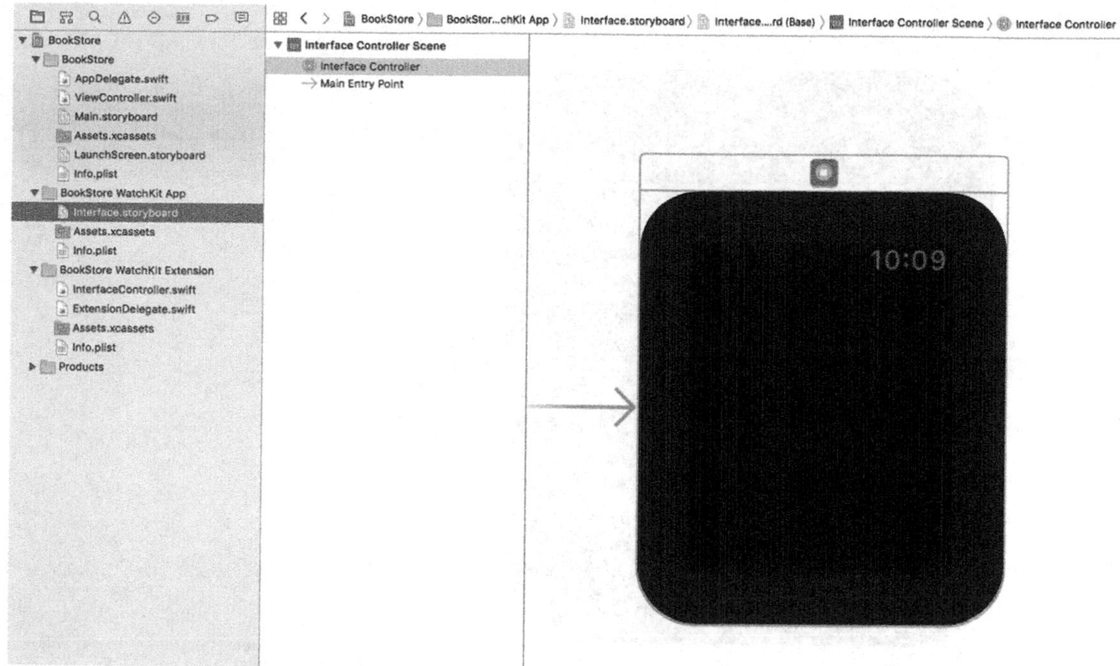

Figure 15-4. *Interface storyboard*

Since you are going to create a list of books for the watchOS app, you need to add a table to the storyboard. On the bottom right, search for table and drag the table into the Interface Controller Scene, as shown in Figure 15-5.

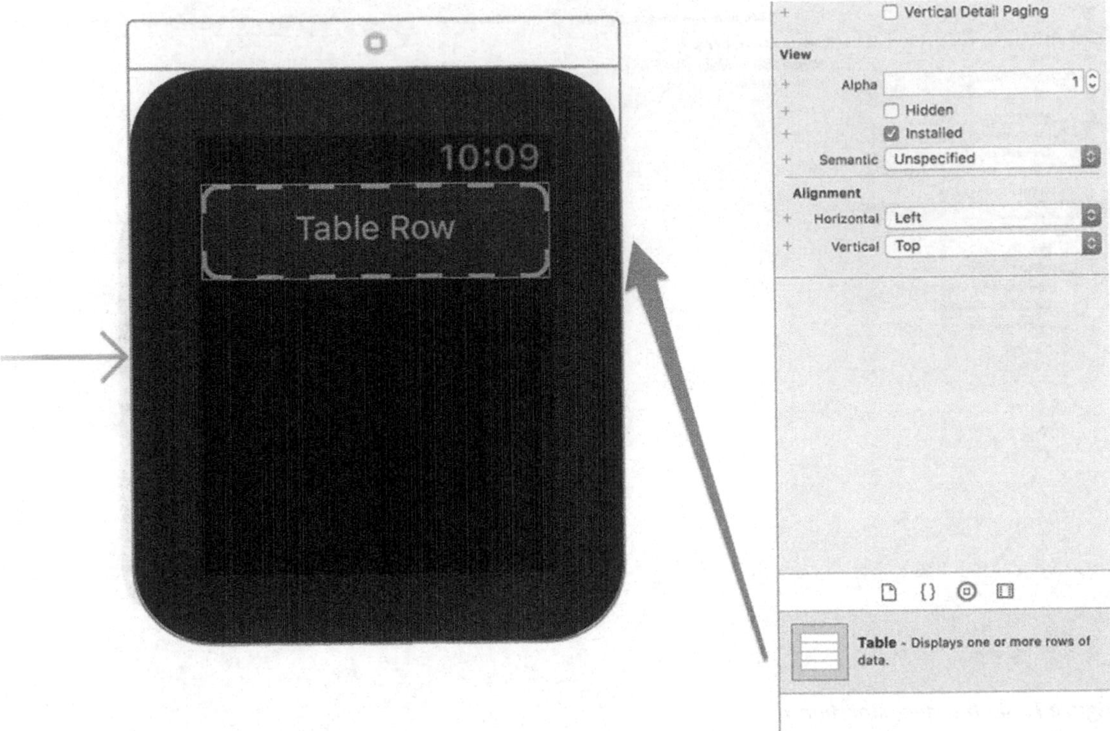

Figure 15-5. *Adding a table*

Xcode will now give you a Table Row as part of the table. This is similar to the prototype rows you used for creating table views in your iOS apps. You need to create a class to control it, but for now, you will add a label to it. Search for a label in the Object Library and drag one onto the row. See Figure 15-6.

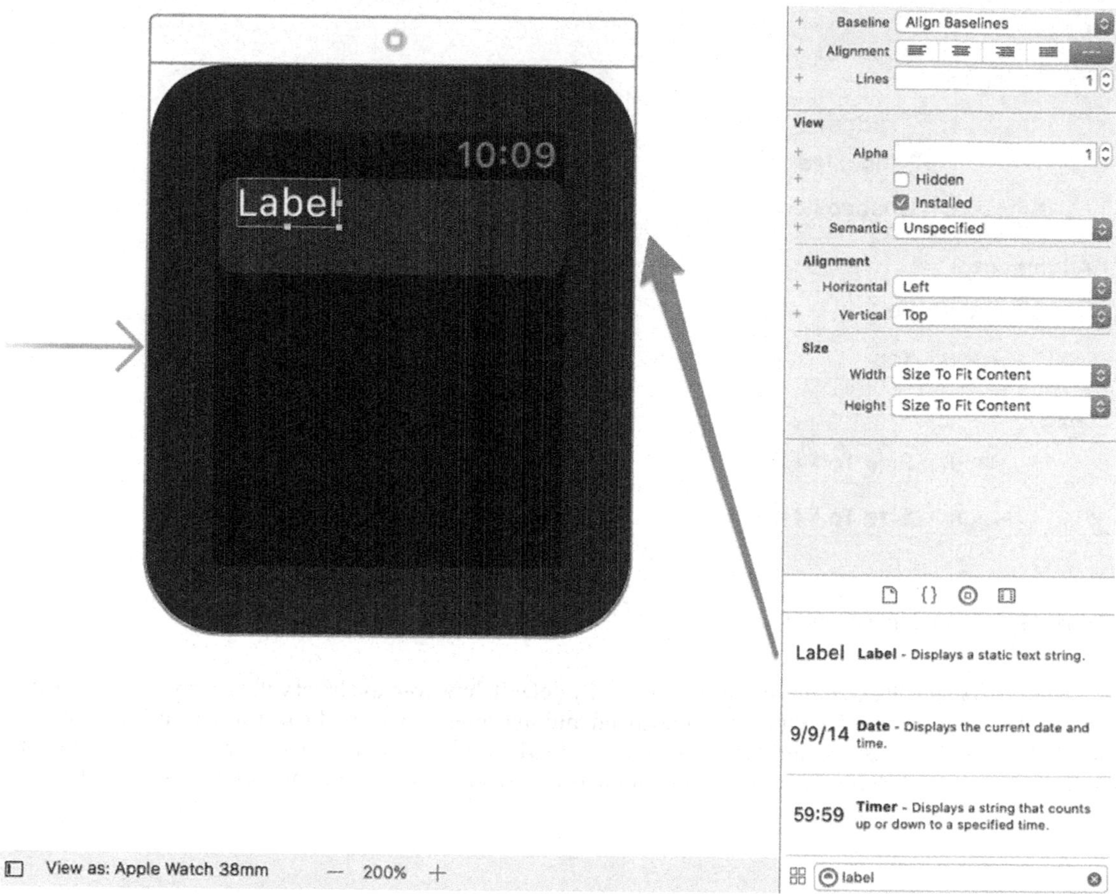

Figure 15-6. *Adding a label to the table row*

By default, the label will be located in the top-left corner of the Table Row. Check the Attribute Inspector to make sure the height and width can grow in size to fit the content. See Figure 15-7. This will help ensure that your app runs well on both sizes of Apple Watches.

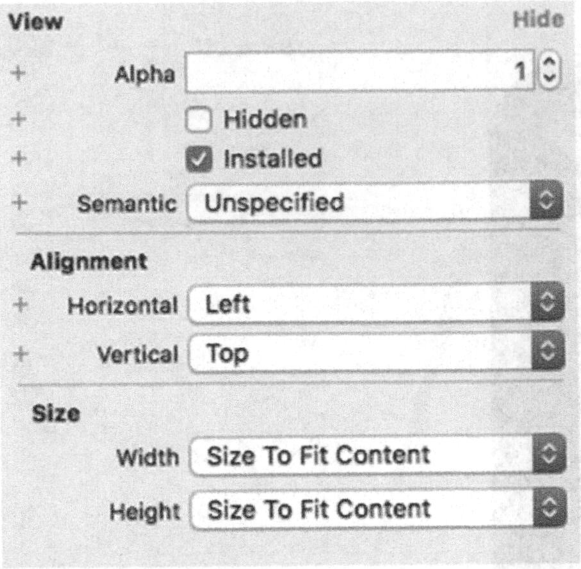

Figure 15-7. Allowing the label to grow

Now the label will expand to fit the entire row. By default, however, the label will only show one line of text. Since you are adding book titles, you may need multiple lines to fit all of the text you want to add. With the label selected, look in the Attributes Inspector on the right side. Find the `Lines` attribute and set it to 0, as shown in Figure 15-8. Setting the number of lines to 0 tells Xcode that it can use as many lines as needed.

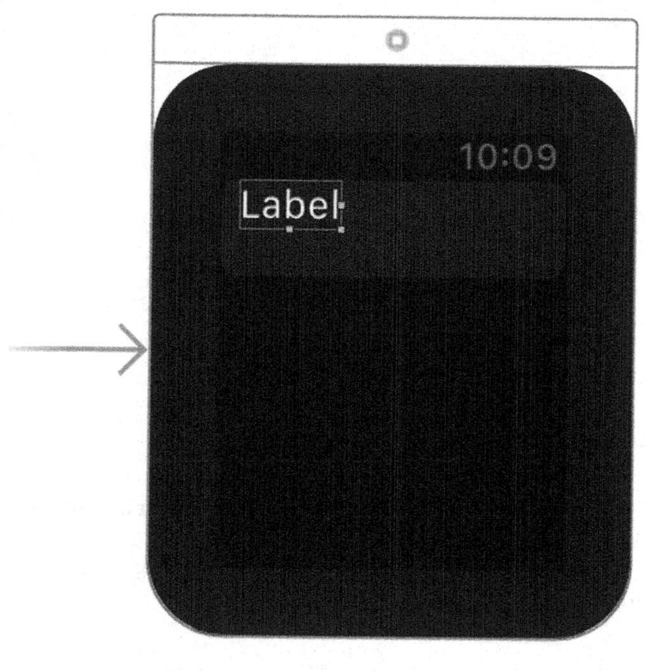

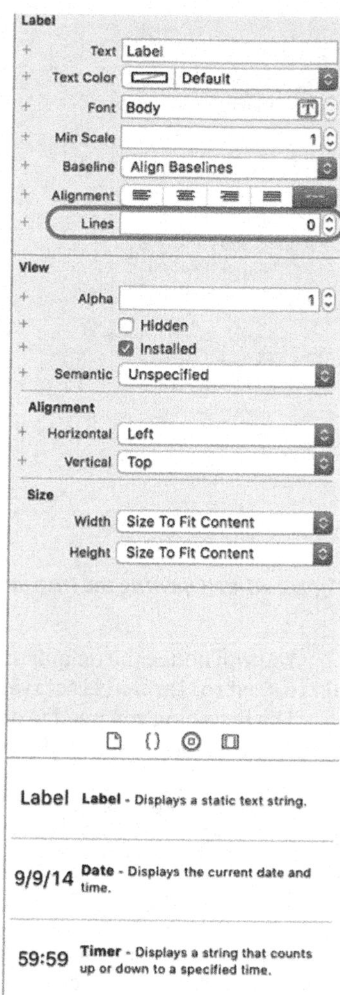

Figure 15-8. *Setting the Lines attribute*

Now you need to add some code to get the user interface working. On the left side, expand the BookStore WatchKit extension folder and select the `InterfaceController.swift` file, as shown in Figure 15-9. The `InterfaceController` is the default controller for the initial scene in a WatchKit storyboard.

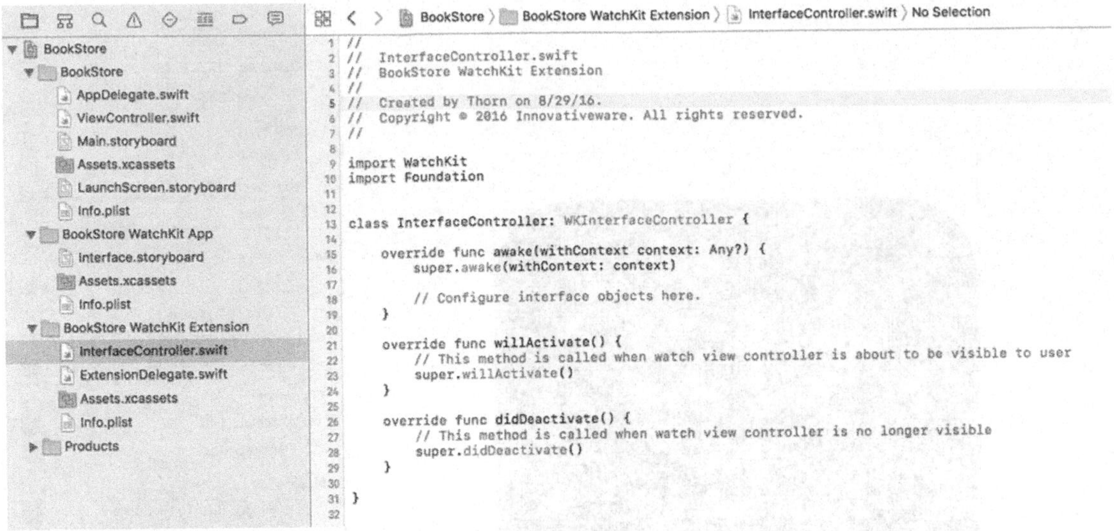

```
//
//  InterfaceController.swift
//  BookStore WatchKit Extension
//
//  Created by Thorn on 8/29/16.
//  Copyright © 2016 Innovativeware. All rights reserved.
//

import WatchKit
import Foundation


class InterfaceController: WKInterfaceController {

    override func awake(withContext context: Any?) {
        super.awake(withContext: context)

        // Configure interface objects here.
    }

    override func willActivate() {
        // This method is called when watch view controller is about to be visible to user
        super.willActivate()
    }

    override func didDeactivate() {
        // This method is called when watch view controller is no longer visible
        super.didDeactivate()
    }

}
```

Figure 15-9. *Opening the InterfaceController.swift file*

You will notice the default methods in the new controller file are different than they were for a standard `UIViewController`. `willActivate()` is equivalent to `viewWillAppear()`.

The first thing you need to do is add a class definition for a row. To do this, add the following code to the bottom of the file outside of the close brace (}) for the `InterFaceController` class.

```
1   class BookRow: NSObject {
2       @IBOutlet weak var bookLabel: WKInterfaceLabel!
3
4   }
```

Line 1 declares a new class called `BookRow`. It is a subclass of `NSObject`. Line 2 creates a property called `bookLabel`. `bookLabel`'s class is `WKInterfaceLabel`. This is similar to a `UILabel` that you have used before, but it works with WatchKit.

■ **Note** Swift allows for multiple classes to be declared in the same Swift file. This works well when you are only using that class with the other classes in the file. In this case, we are only going to use the row class with the `InterfaceController` class.

The `InterfaceController.swift` file will now look like Figure 15-10.

```swift
//
//  InterfaceController.swift
//  BookStore WatchKit Extension
//
//  Created by Thorn on 8/29/16.
//  Copyright © 2016 Innovativeware. All rights reserved.
//

import WatchKit
import Foundation


class InterfaceController: WKInterfaceController {

    override func awake(withContext context: Any?) {
        super.awake(withContext: context)

        // Configure interface objects here.
    }

    override func willActivate() {
        // This method is called when watch view controller is about to be visible to user
        super.willActivate()
    }

    override func didDeactivate() {
        // This method is called when watch view controller is no longer visible
        super.didDeactivate()
    }

}

class BookRow: NSObject {
    @IBOutlet weak var bookLabel: WKInterfaceLabel!

}
```

Figure 15-10. *Modified InterfaceController.swift file*

You can now connect the outlets to the interface. Select `Interface.storyboard`. Now select the Assistant Editor by selecting the icon with two circles in the top right of the Xcode window, as shown in Figure 15-11.

Figure 15-11. *Opening the Assistant Editor*

With the Assistant Editor, Xcode provides a quick way for developers to create objects and associate them with outlets in the interface. You will first need to create a table property representing the Table. Control-drag from the table in the Interface Controller Scene into the `InterfaceController` class on the right, as shown in Figure 15-12.

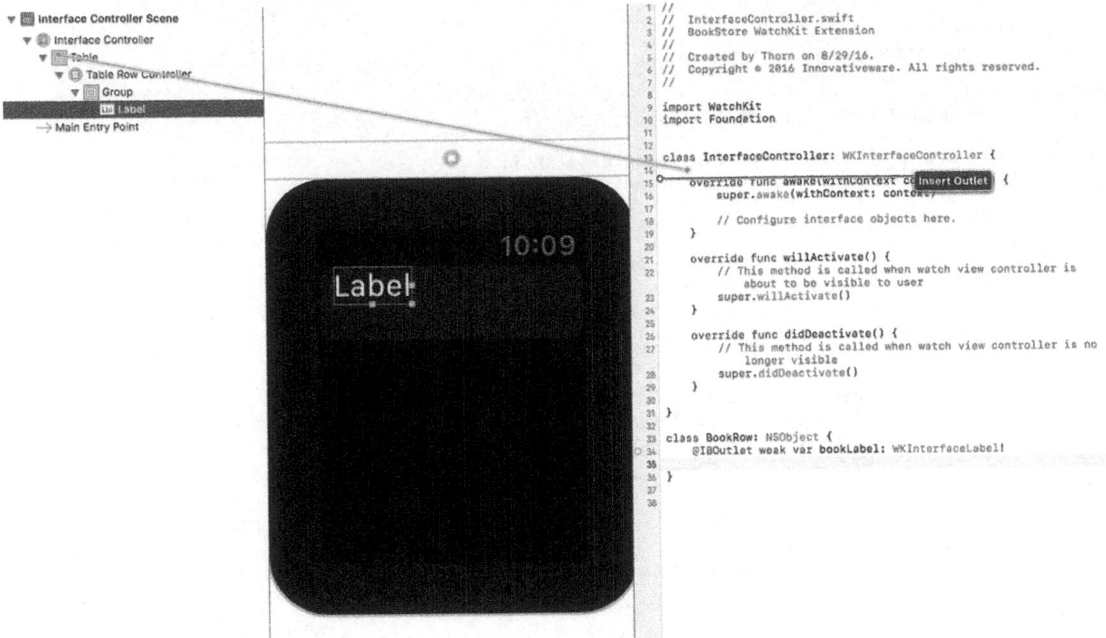

Figure 15-12. *Control-drag to create an outlet*

Once you release the `Table` object on the `InterfaceController` class, Xcode will prompt you to enter the type of outlet you are creating. Leave the defaults as is, except change the Name to `mainTable`, as shown in Figure 15-13.

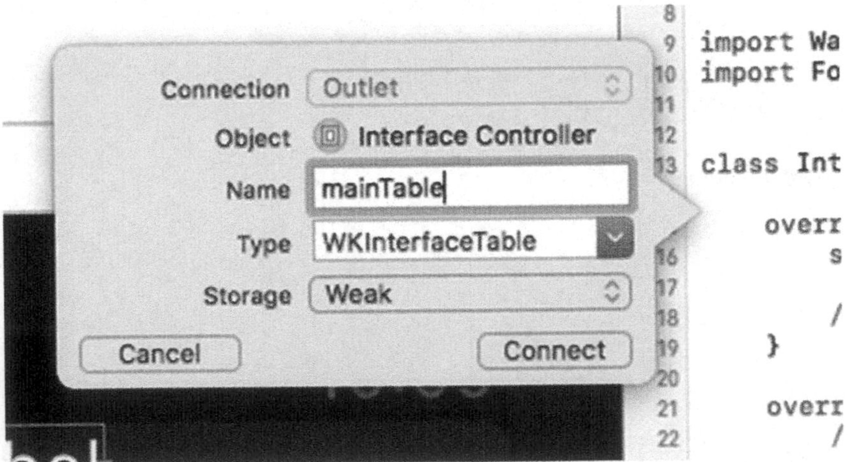

Figure 15-13. *Naming your outlet*

Select the "lines of text" icon in the top right of the Xcode window to return to the Standard Editor. Under the Interface Controller Scene, select the Table Row Controller, as shown in Figure 15-14.

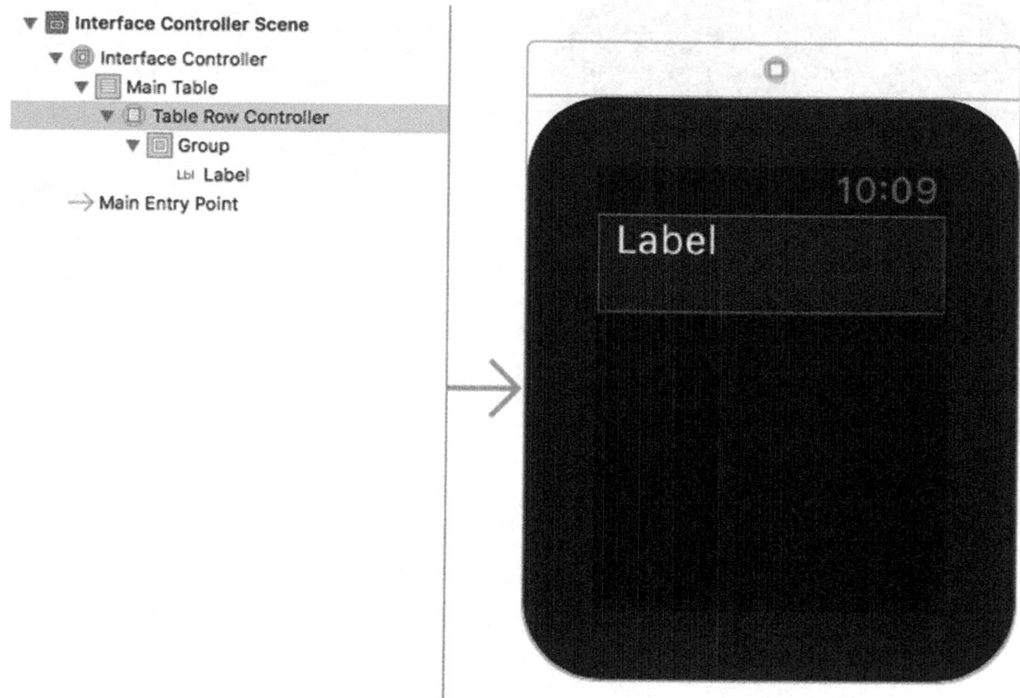

Figure 15-14. *Selecting the Table Row Controller*

Set the class of the Table Row Controller by selecting the Identity Inspector on the right side and selecting BookRow in the Class drop-down menu, as shown in Figure 15-15.

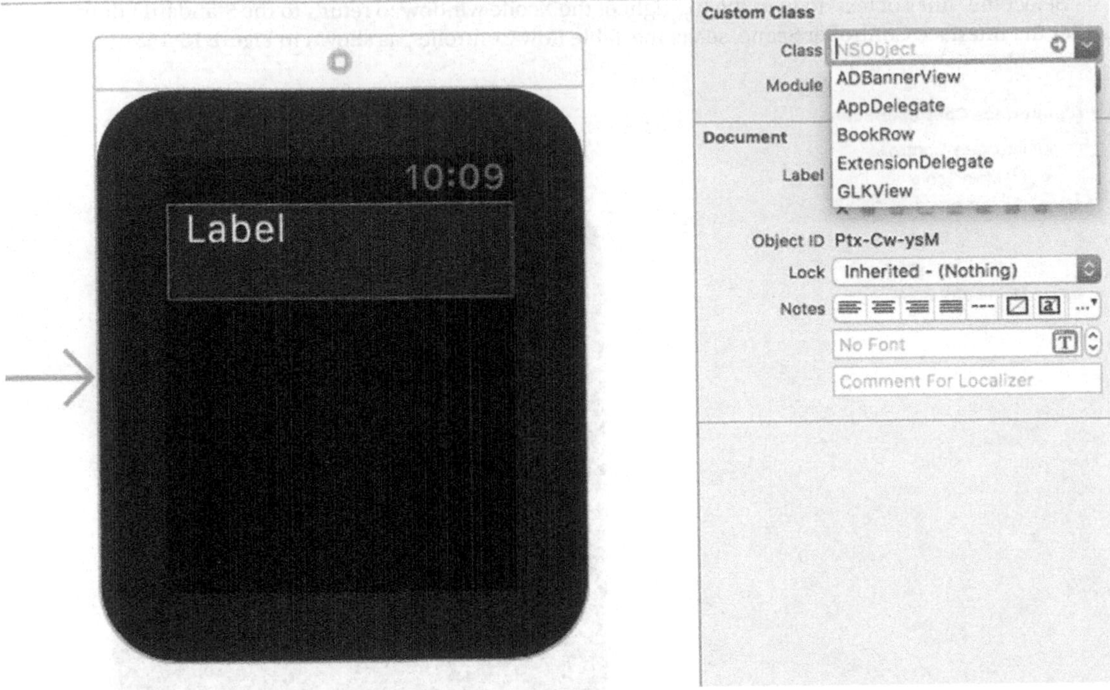

***Figure 15-15.** Changing the table row class to BookRow*

Now that your app knows the type of table row you are using in your code, you need to add an identifier for the row. This helps in the case you have multiple row types for a single table. Select the Attributes Inspector and enter `MyBookRow` as the identifier, as shown in Figure 15-16.

***Figure 15-16.** Changing the table row identifier*

You can now hook up the `WKInterfaceLabel` you created earlier. Under the Interface Controller Scene, control-drag from the book row to the label, as shown in Figure 15-17.

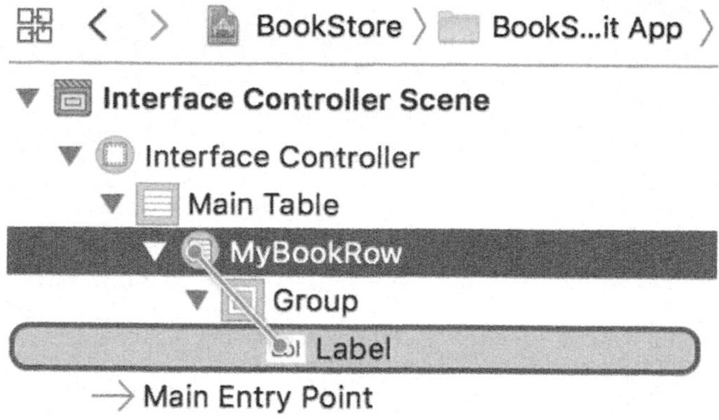

Figure 15-17. *Control-dragging from the row to the label*

You will be prompted to select an outlet from the available outlets, as shown in Figure 15-18. There is currently only one available outlet, so select `bookLabel`.

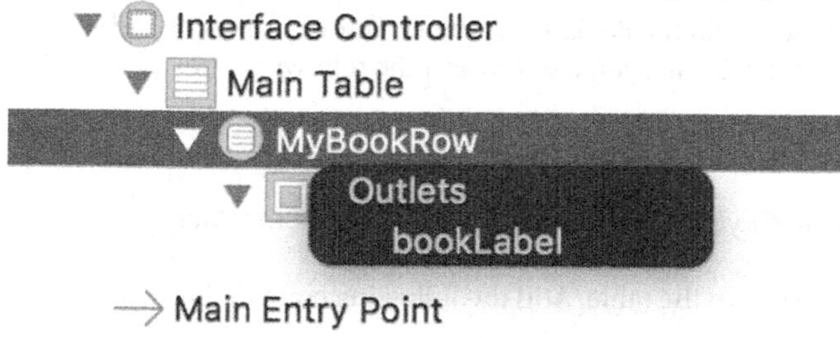

Figure 15-18. *Connecting the bookLabel outlet*

Your table and label are now all hooked up. Now you need some data to display. You are going to reuse some data you created in Chapter 8. Using the Finder on your Mac, drag the `Book.swift` and `BookStore.swift` files from the Chapter 8 folder into the BookStore WatchKit Extension folder in Xcode. Check the "Copy items if needed" check box to copy the files to the new project. Once you are done, you will have the `Book.swift and BookStore.swift` files in your target, as shown in Figure 15-19.

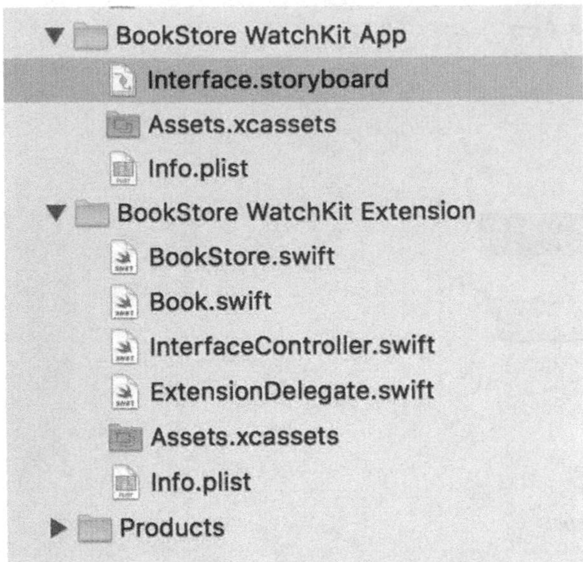

Figure 15-19. *Adding in the data files*

You have the data and interface complete. You now need to hook them up so the interface knows about the data. You need to declare a new property that will hold the `BookStore` object. Under your declaration of the `mainTable` object in the `InterfaceController.swift` file, you need to add the following line:

```
var myBookStore: BookStore = BookStore()
```

This creates a property of type `BookStore` called `myBookStore` and initializes it to an instance of `BookStore`.

We will use the `configureTable()` method to set up the table. Add the following code to the class, outside of any of the other methods:

```
1    func configureTable() {
2        mainTable.setNumberOfRows(myBookStore.theBookStore.count, withRowType:
         "MyBookRow")
3        for index in 0...(myBookStore.theBookStore.count - 1) {
4            if let myRow = mainTable.rowController(at: index) as? BookRow {
5                myRow.bookLabel.setText(myBookStore.theBookStore[index].title)
6            }
7        }
8    }
```

Line 1 declares the new method. Line 2 sets the number of rows in the table to the number of books in the bookstore. You'll use `myBookStore.theBookStore.count` to get that number. We also tell the table which row identifier to use with the table. Line 3 is a loop that assigns `index` to 0 and goes until it gets assigned to the number of books: 1. The reason you subtract 1 from the number of books is because Swift (and most modern programming languages) starts its arrays with 0. This means if you have an array with two items, the items will be in positions 0 and 1. If you try to look at position 2, you will receive an error.

Line 4 tries to create a new row for the table using the `index` variable you created in the previous line. Line 5 takes the row and assigns the `Book` title to `bookLabel`. Now we need to call `configureTable` when the view is being activated. Add the following line to the `willActivate` function:

```
configureTable()
```

After entering those lines, the `InterfaceController.swift` file will look like Figure 15-20.

```
//
//  InterfaceController.swift
//  BookStore WatchKit Extension
//
//  Created by Thorn on 8/29/16.
//  Copyright © 2016 Innovativeware. All rights reserved.
//

import WatchKit
import Foundation


class InterfaceController: WKInterfaceController {

    @IBOutlet var mainTable: WKInterfaceTable!
    var myBookStore: BookStore! = BookStore()

    override func awake(withContext context: Any?) {
        super.awake(withContext: context)

        // Configure interface objects here.
    }

    override func willActivate() {
        // This method is called when watch view controller is about to be visible to user
        super.willActivate()
        configureTable()
    }

    override func didDeactivate() {
        // This method is called when watch view controller is no longer visible
        super.didDeactivate()
    }

    func configureTable() {
        mainTable.setNumberOfRows(myBookStore.theBookStore.count, withRowType: "MyBookRow")
        for index in 0...(myBookStore.theBookStore.count - 1) {
            if let myRow = mainTable.rowController(at: index) as? BookRow {
                myRow.bookLabel.setText(myBookStore.theBookStore[index].title)
            }
        }
    }


}

class BookRow: NSObject {
    @IBOutlet weak var bookLabel: WKInterfaceLabel!

}
```

Figure 15-20. *InterfaceController.swift file*

You now have enough in place to run the app. From the target menu, select BookStore WatchKitApp and then select the size of the Apple Watch you would like the simulator to use, as shown in Figure 15-21. If this is your first time launching the Watch Simulator, it may take some time and ask for permissions on the Phone Simulator before the app will run successfully.

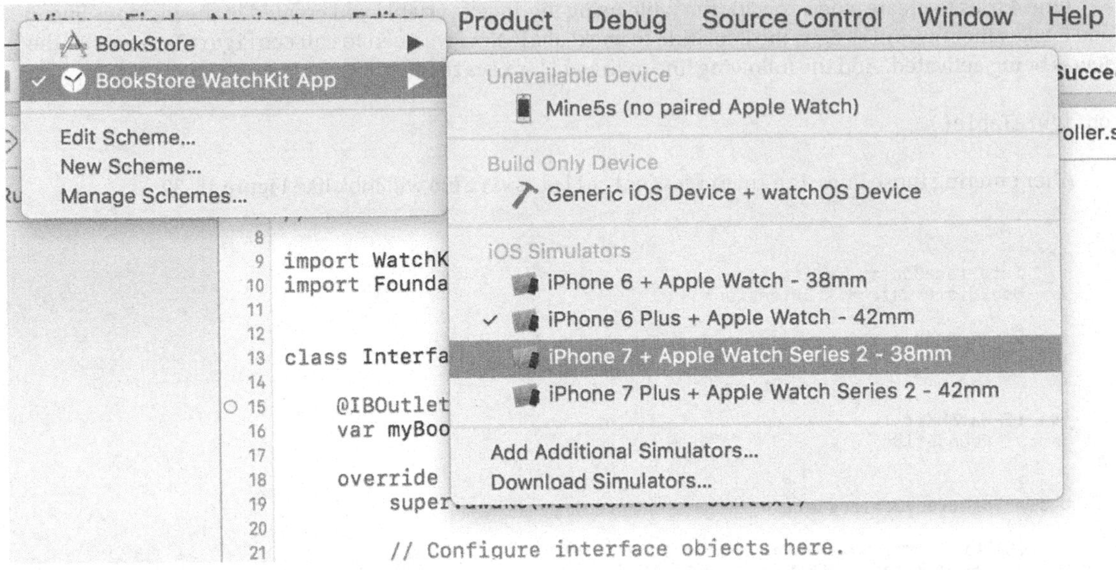

Figure 15-21. *Selecting the WatchKit target*

Once the app is launched, you will see a watch screen with the two books in the `myBookStore` object. You can go back to the `BookStore.swift` file and add more books if you want to play around with the scrolling. The app should look like Figure 15-22.

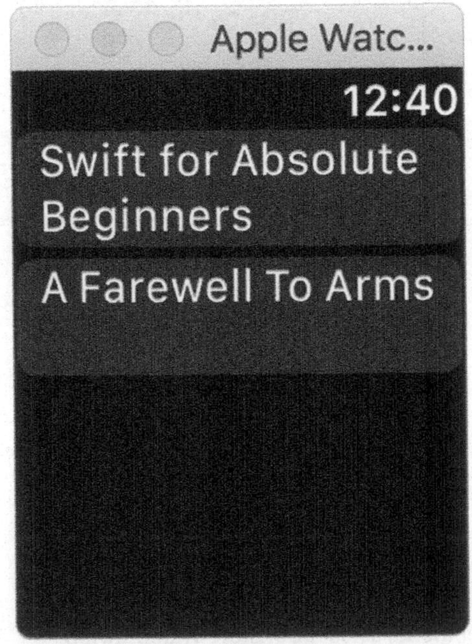

Figure 15-22. *First WatchKit app launch*

Adding More Functionality

In the last section, you created a WatchKit app, but it's very limited in functionality. In this section, you will add a new scene to the app to show book detail when a book is selected. Because you will be adding a scene, you will use an additional controller file. Right-click the BookStore WatchKit Extension folder and select New File, as shown in Figure 15-23.

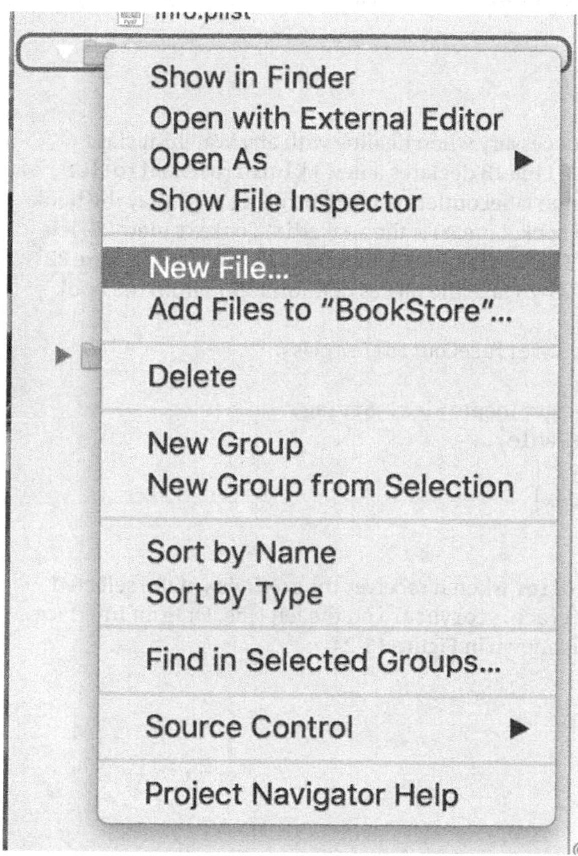

Figure 15-23. *Adding new controller file*

Make sure the new file is a Swift file and name it `DetailController.swift`. It should now appear in your file list. Add the following code after the `import Foundation` line:

```
import WatchKit


class DetailController: WKInterfaceController {
    @IBOutlet var labelTitle: WKInterfaceLabel!
    @IBOutlet var labelAuthor: WKInterfaceLabel!
    @IBOutlet var labelDescription: WKInterfaceLabel!

```

```
18          var book: Book!
19
20          override func awake(withContext context: Any?) {
21              super.awake(withContext: context)
22              if let book = context as? Book {
23                  labelTitle.setText(book.title)
24                  labelAuthor.setText(book.author)
25                  labelDescription.setText(book.description)
26              }
27          }
28      }
```

Line 10 imports the WatchKit framework. This is necessary when dealing with any WatchKit class such as `WKInterfaceController` or `WKInterfaceLabel`. Line 13 declares a new `WKInterfaceController` subclass called `DetailController`. Lines 14-16 create the label outlets you will be using to display the book information. Line 18 declares the `Book` property called book. Line 20 is the `awakeWithContext` method. It is passed an object called `context`, which is of type `Any`. This is where the `Book` object will be passed. Line 22 takes the context and assigns it to a book object. Lines 23-25 take the pieces of information from the book and assign them to the labels.

You now need to add the following method to the `InterfaceController` class:

```
override func contextForSegue(withIdentifier segueIdentifier: String,
                        in table: WKInterfaceTable,
                        rowIndex: Int) -> Any? {
        return myBookStore.theBookStore[rowIndex]
    }
```

This method passes the book to the `DetailController` when it receives the `rowIndex` of the selected row. Now you need to create the interface. Select `Interface.storyboard` on the left side. Drag an Interface Controller from the Object Library to the storyboard as shown in Figure 15-24.

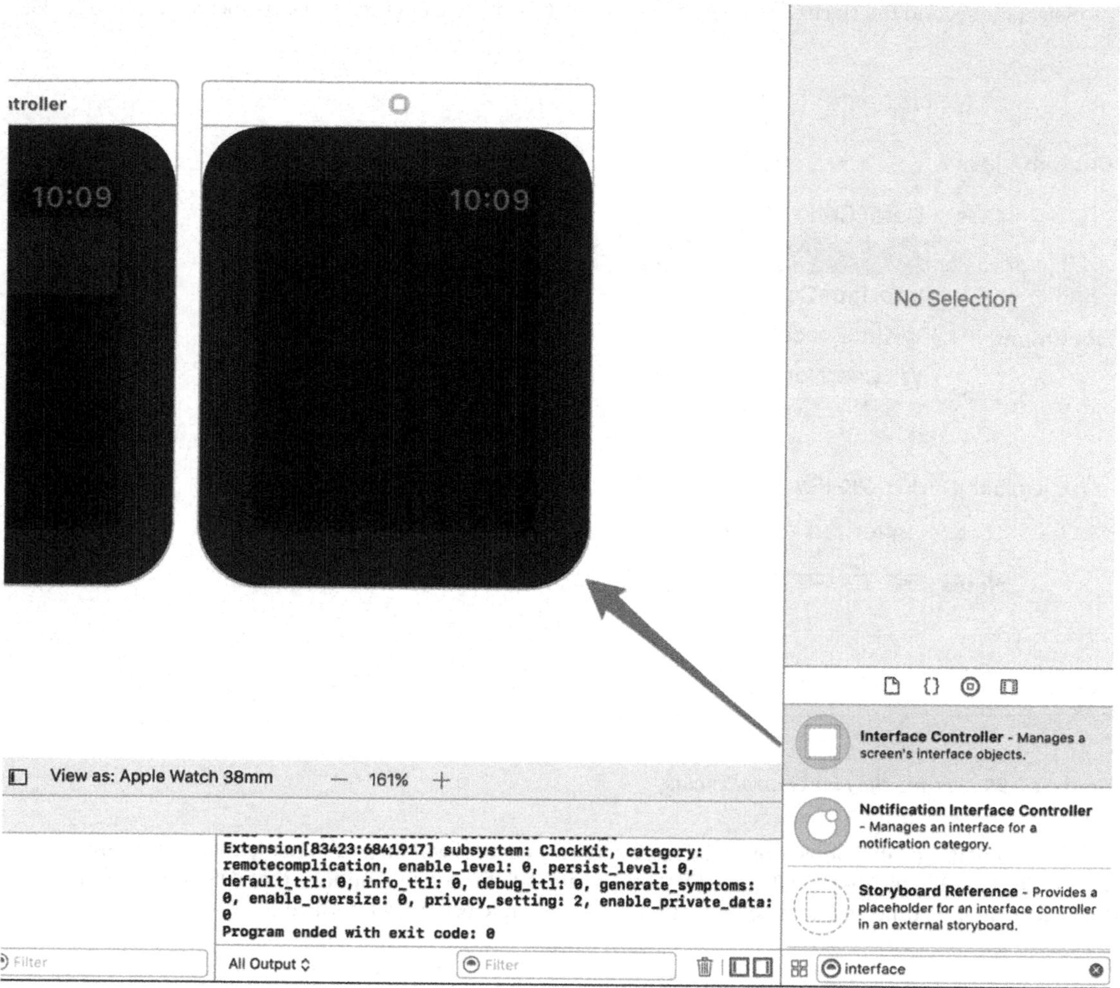

Figure 15-24. *Adding new controller file*

Select the second Interface Controller Scene and set the class to DetailController, as shown in Figure 15-25.

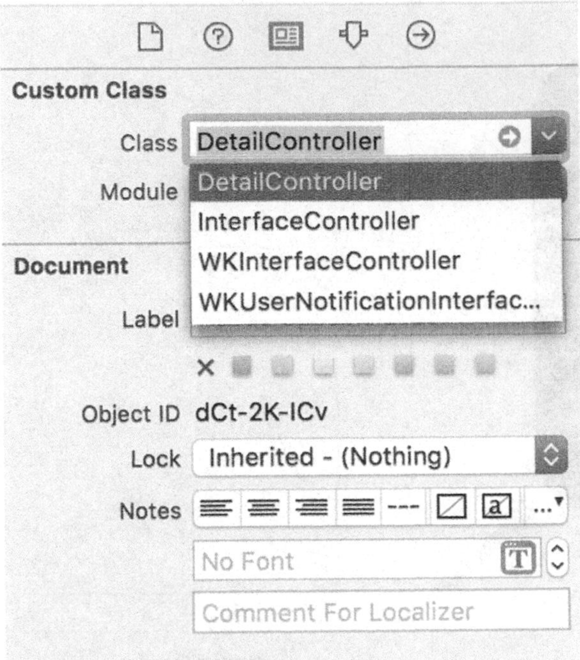

Figure 15-25. *Setting the new controller class*

Now drag three label objects onto the interface. These labels will be for the book title, author, and description. See Figure 15-26. watchOS does not provide all of the layout options that iOS, tvOS, or macOS do. As a developer, time will need to be spent designing simple watchOS interfaces.

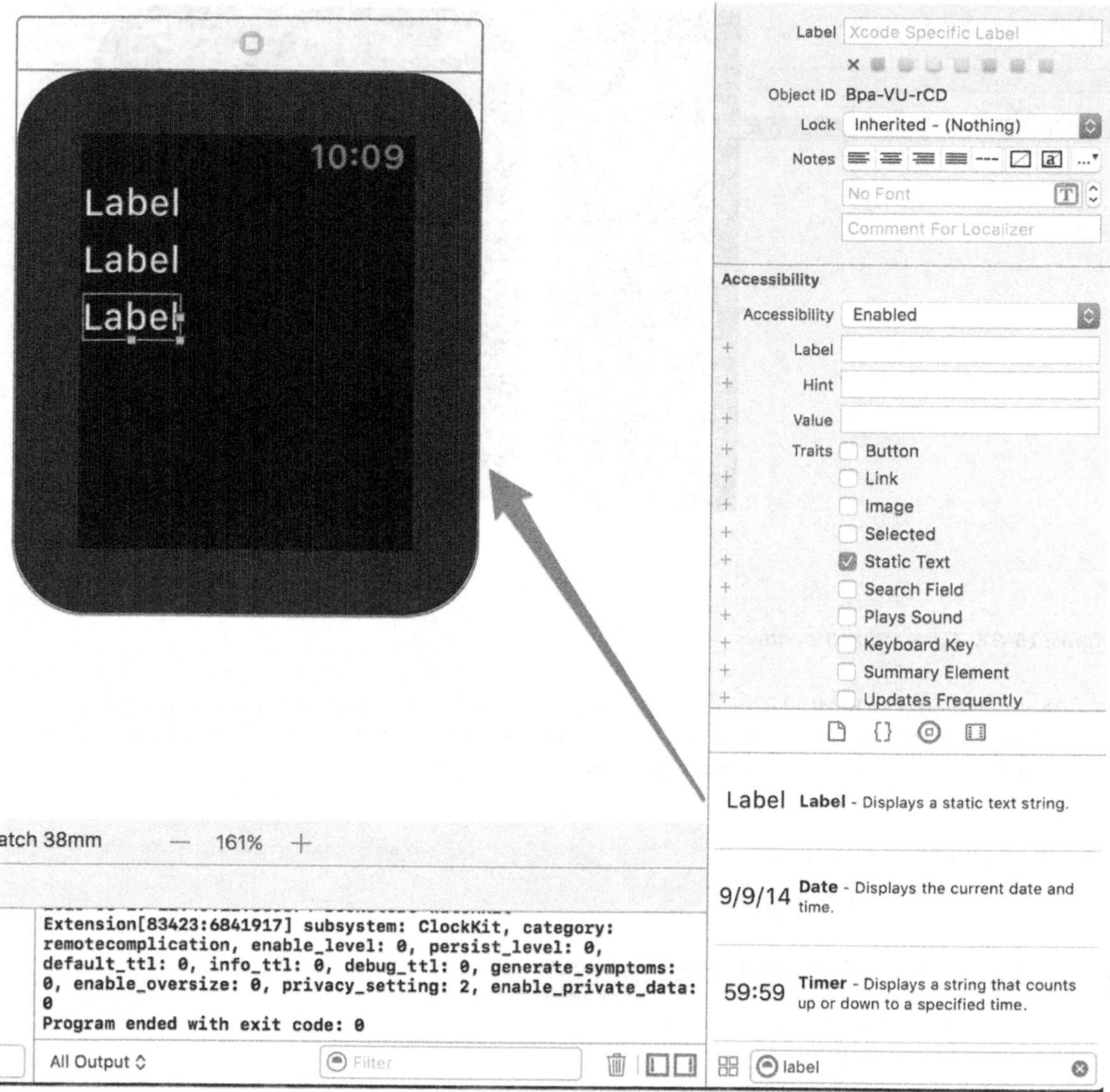

Figure 15-26. *New labels*

Now you need to connect the outlets of the new labels. Control-drag from the Detail Controller Scene to each of the labels and assign them to their respective property. See Figure 15-27.

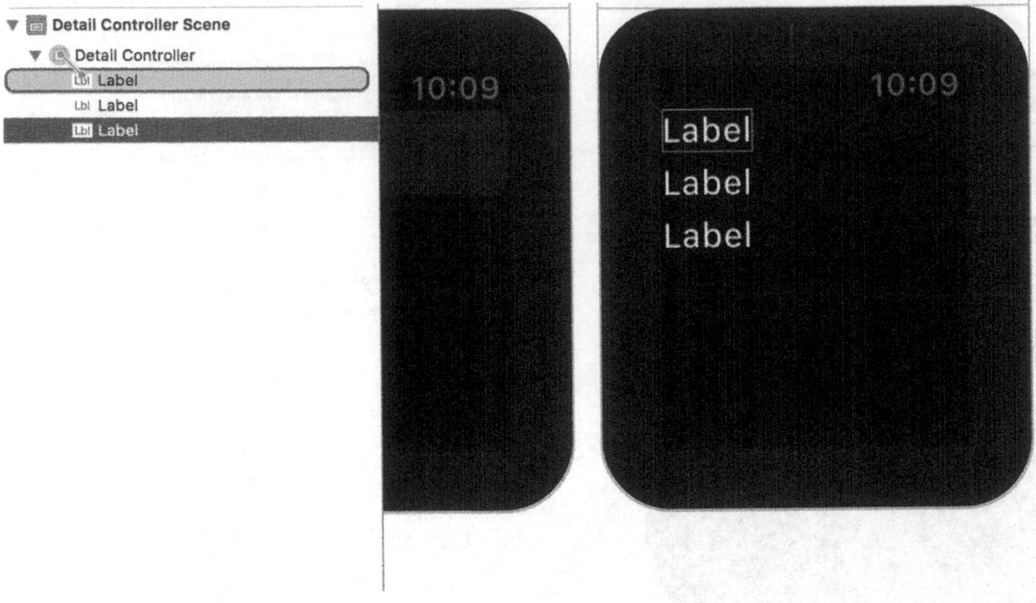

Figure 15-27. Connecting the outlets

The data should all be displaying now. You need to create the segue and test the app once again. Control-drag from the `MyBookRow` under the Interface Controller Scene to the Detail Controller. You will be prompted to select the type of segue. Select push. See Figure 15-28.

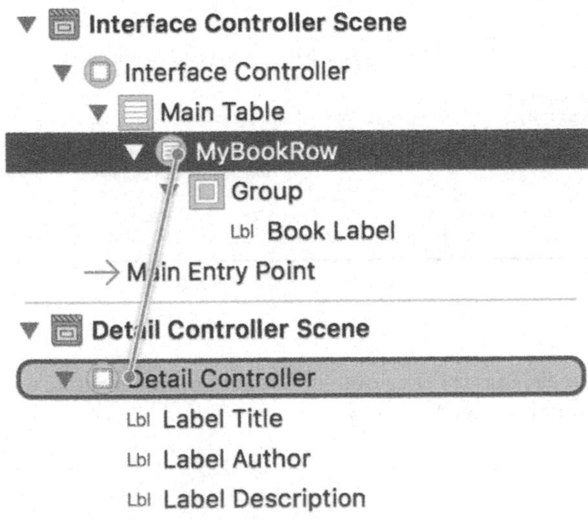

Figure 15-28. Creating the segue

Now run the app and select a row. You should see the detail controller you just created, as shown in Figure 15-29.

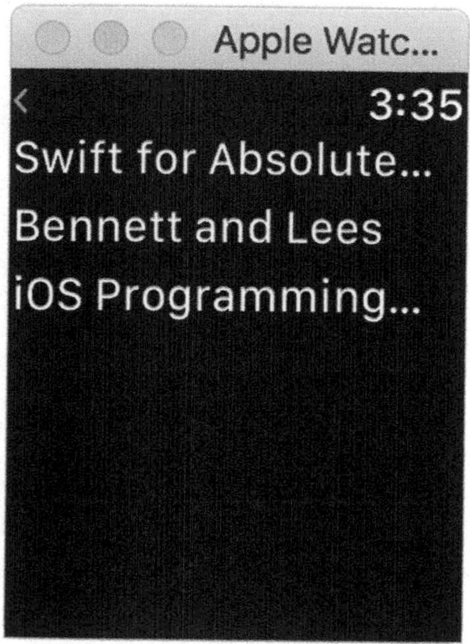

Figure 15-29. *Detail view scene*

Summary

This chapter covered an introduction to developing for the Apple Watch. Specifically, in this chapter, you learned the following:

- How to create a new WatchKit app
- How to use the WatchKit controls `WKInterfaceController`, `WKInterfaceTable`, and `WKInterfaceLabel`
- How to create multiple scenes and add segues between them
- How to handle passing data from one scene to the next

EXERCISES

- Set up the labels on the detail scene to display all of the data.
- Add more books to your `BookStore` so you can play with the scrolling in the app.

CHAPTER 16

A Swift HealthKit iPhone App

HealthKit enables iOS developers to integrate health and fitness devices with their app and integrate the data with Apple's easy-to-read dashboard. HealthKit enables health and fitness apps on an iOS device to work together and report device data in the Health app dashboard. See Figure 16-1.

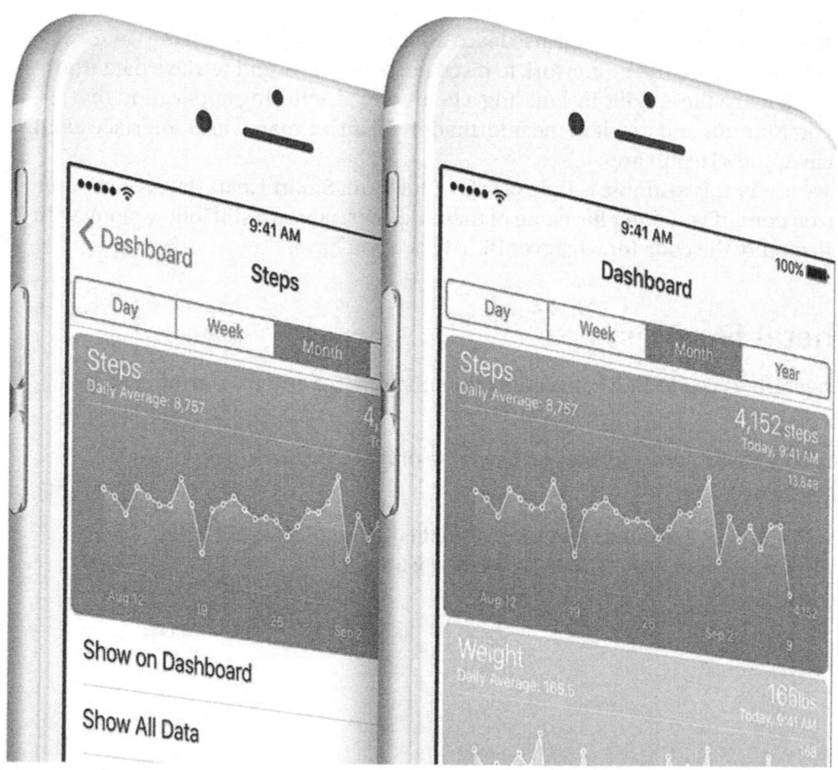

Figure 16-1. The Health app's dashboard

G. Bennett and B. Lees, *Swift 3 for Absolute Beginners*, DOI 10.1007/978-1-4842-2331-4_16

HealthKit is the accompanying developer SDK included in iOS 8 and newer. The SDK enables other applications to access health data with the user's permission. For example, a blood pressure application could share its information with the user's doctor.

A number of companies support HealthKit, including Polar, EPIC, Mayo Clinic, and RunKeeper.

■ **Note** To work through this example, you'll need an active developer account. You won't be able to enable the HealthKit Capability and access the HealthKit Store without one.

Introduction to Core Bluetooth

The Core Bluetooth framework lets your iOS apps communicate with Bluetooth's low-energy devices (Bluetooth LE or BLE, for short). BLE devices include heart rate monitors, digital scales, digital thermostats, and more.

The Core Bluetooth framework is an abstraction of the Bluetooth LE specification and defines a set of protocols for communicating with Bluetooth LE devices.

As you learn about HealthKit in this chapter, you'll also learn about the key concepts of the Core Bluetooth framework, including how to use the framework to discover, connect to, and retrieve data from BLE-compatible devices. You will learn these skills by building a heart rate monitoring application that communicates with a BLE heart monitor and displays the information on an animated user interface along with storing the information in Apple's Health app.

The heart rate monitor we use in this example is the Polar H7 Bluetooth Smart Heart Rate Sensor that can be purchased from Amazon.com. If you don't have one of these devices, you can still follow along with the tutorial, but you'll need to modify the code for whatever BLE device you have.

Central and Peripheral Devices

There are two major components involved in BLE communication: the ***central*** and the ***peripheral.*** (See Figure 16-2.)

- The *central* is the boss that wants information from one or more workers in order to accomplish a specific task.
- The *peripheral* is the worker that sends and receives data that is consumed by the central devices. The peripheral has the data the central wants.

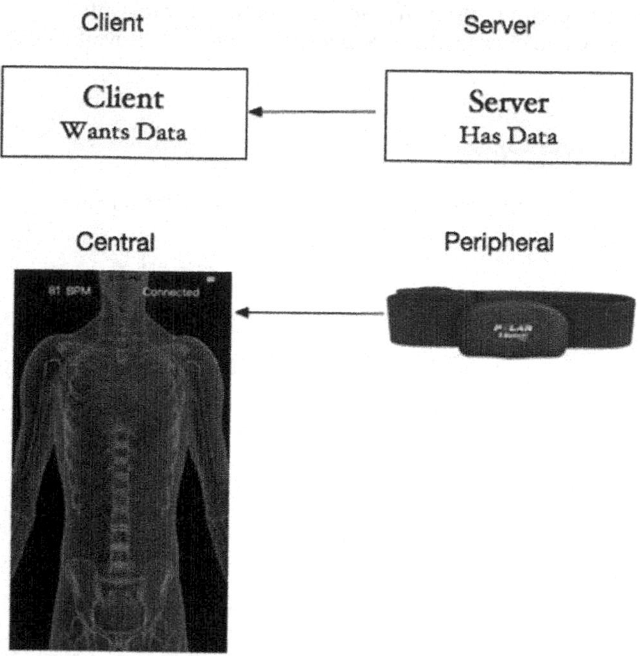

Figure 16-2. Understanding central and peripheral devices

Peripheral Advertising

Advertising is the primary way that peripherals make their presence known via BLE.

In addition to advertising their existence, advertising packets can also contain some data, such as the peripheral's name. The packets can even contain some extra data related to what the peripheral collects. For the heart rate monitor application, the packets also provide heartbeats per minute information.

The central scans for these advertising packets, identifies any peripherals it finds relevant, and connects to individual devices for more information.

Peripheral Data Structure

Advertising packets are very small and cannot contain large amounts of data, so to get more data, a central needs to connect to a peripheral to obtain all of the data available.

Once the central connects to a peripheral, it needs to choose the data it is interested in. With BLE, data is organized into ***services*** and ***characteristics***:

- A *service* is a collection of data and associated behaviors describing a specific function or feature of a device. A device can have more than one service. The heart rate monitor exposing heart rate data from the monitor's heart rate sensor is a great example of this.
- A *characteristic* provides additional details about a peripheral's service. A service can have more than one characteristic. The heart rate service, for example, may contain a characteristic that describes the intended body location of the device's heart rate sensor and an additional characteristic that transmits heart rate measurement data.

Once a central has established a connection to a peripheral, it is free to discover the full range of services and characteristics of the peripheral, and to read or write the characteristic values of the available services.

CBPeripheral, CBService, and CBCharacteristic

A peripheral is represented by the `CBPeripheral` object, while the services relating to a specific peripheral are represented by `CBService` objects. (See Figure 16-3.)

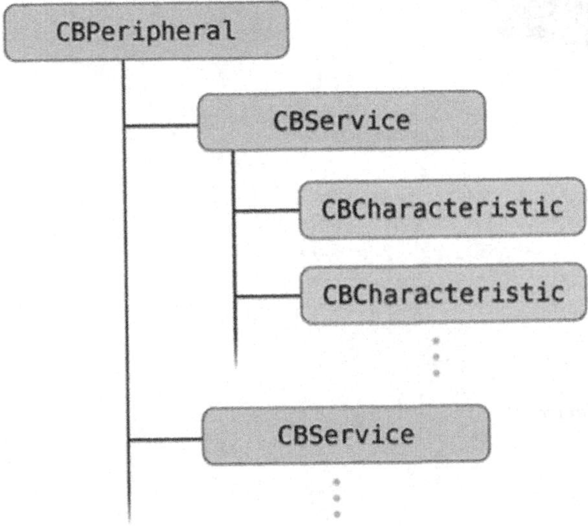

Figure 16-3. *Structure of a peripheral's services and characteristics object hierarchy*

The characteristics of a peripheral's service are represented by `CBCharacteristic` objects, which are defined as attribute types containing a single logical value.

Each service and characteristic you create must be identified by a universally unique identifier, or UUID. UUIDs can be 16- or 128-bit values, but if you are building your client-server (central-peripheral) application, you'll need to create your own 128-bit UUIDs. Also, make sure the UUIDs don't collide with other potential services in close proximity to your device.

Building the App

We are going to build a simple heart rate monitor app that works with a BLE heart rate monitor. In the process of building this app, you will learn a lot about HealthKit and BLE, such as the following:

- How to set up your heart rate monitor
- How to request permissions to access and store HealthKit data
- How to read BLE data and format it to show in the Health app
- How the Core Bluetooth Framework works
- How to display information from the heart rate BLE monitor (See Figure 16-4.)

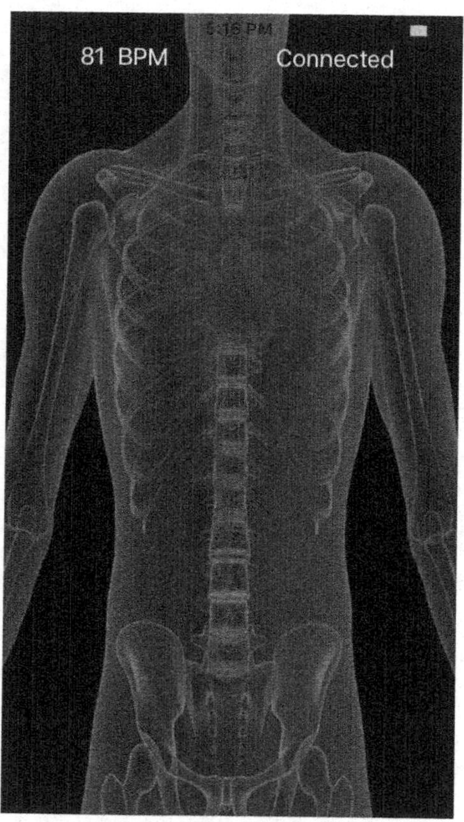

Figure 16-4. *The Heart Rate Monitor app*

1. Create a Single View Application, as shown in Figure 16-5.

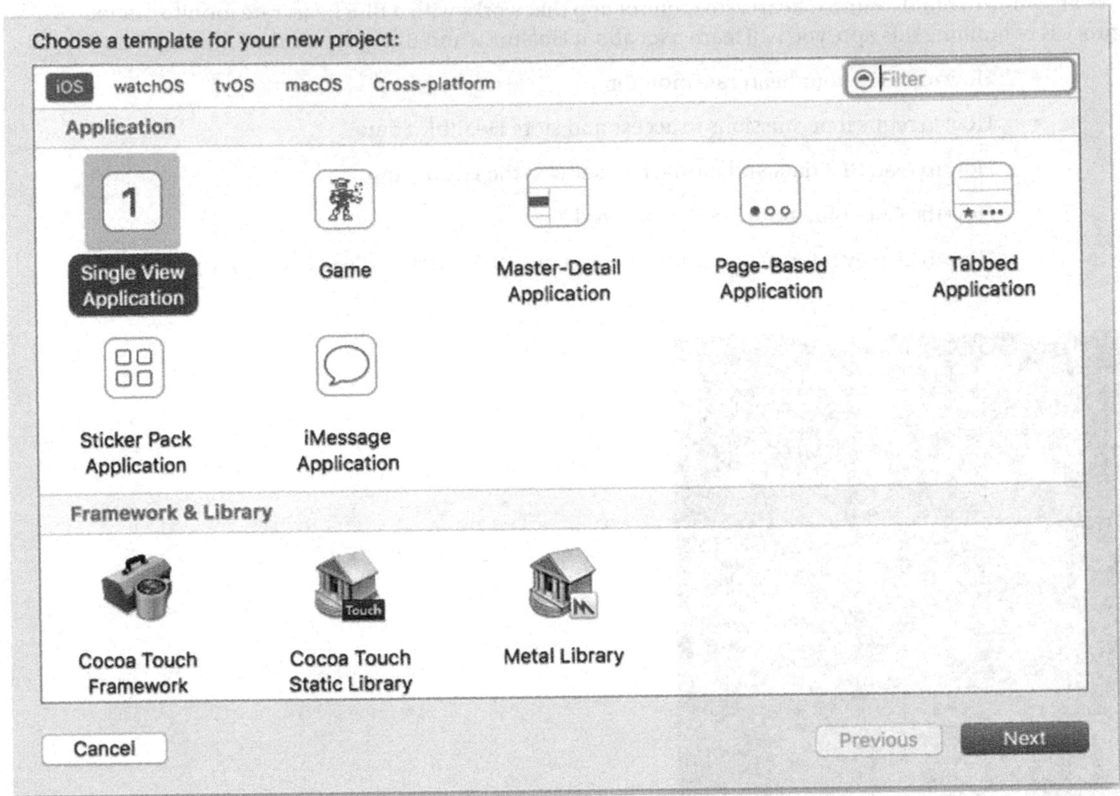

Figure 16-5. *Creating a single view application*

2. Name your app and save the project, as shown in Figure 16-6.

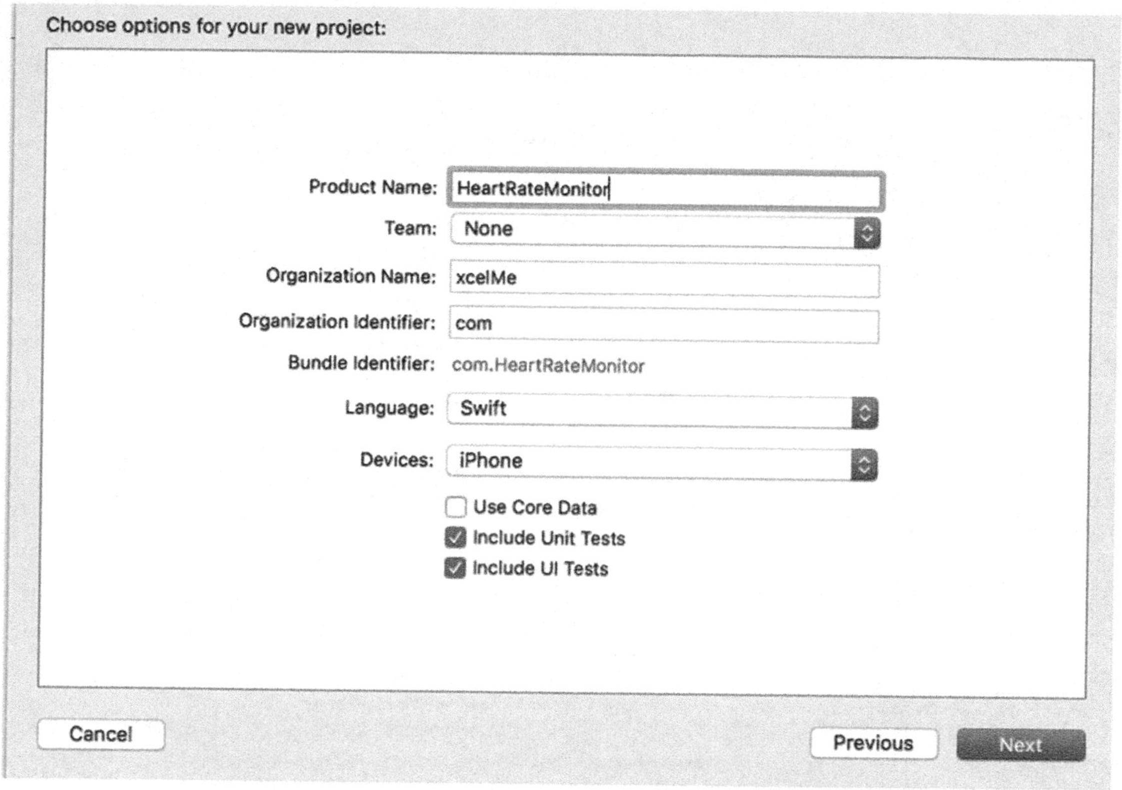

Figure 16-6. *Naming the project*

3. Change the bundle identifier to the identifier you are going to use to submit to the App Store and include the `HealthKit.framework`. Also, select your developer team, as shown in Figure 16-7.

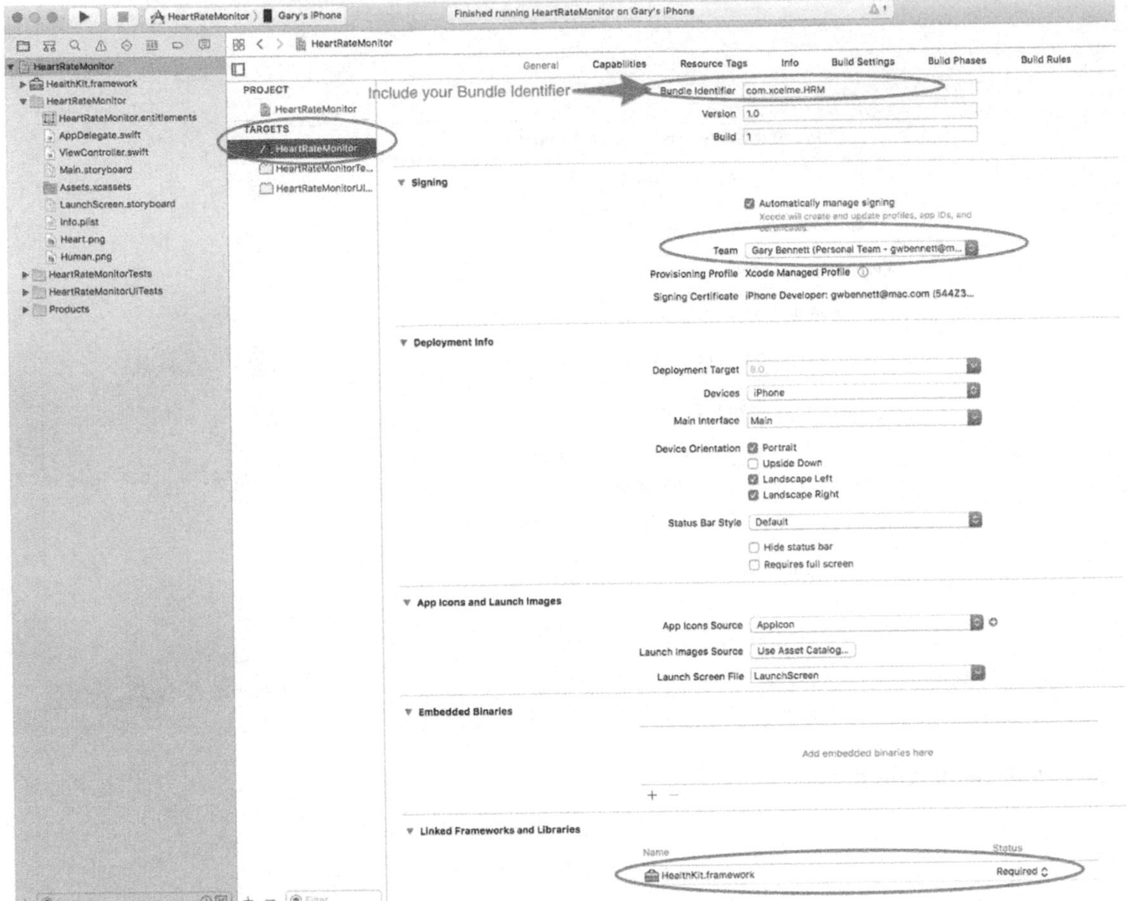

Figure 16-7. Adding your own bundle identifier, team, and HealthKit.framework

4. In order to use HealthKit, you need to add the HealthKit entitlement. Change the project's capabilities to add HealthKit, as shown in Figure 16-8.

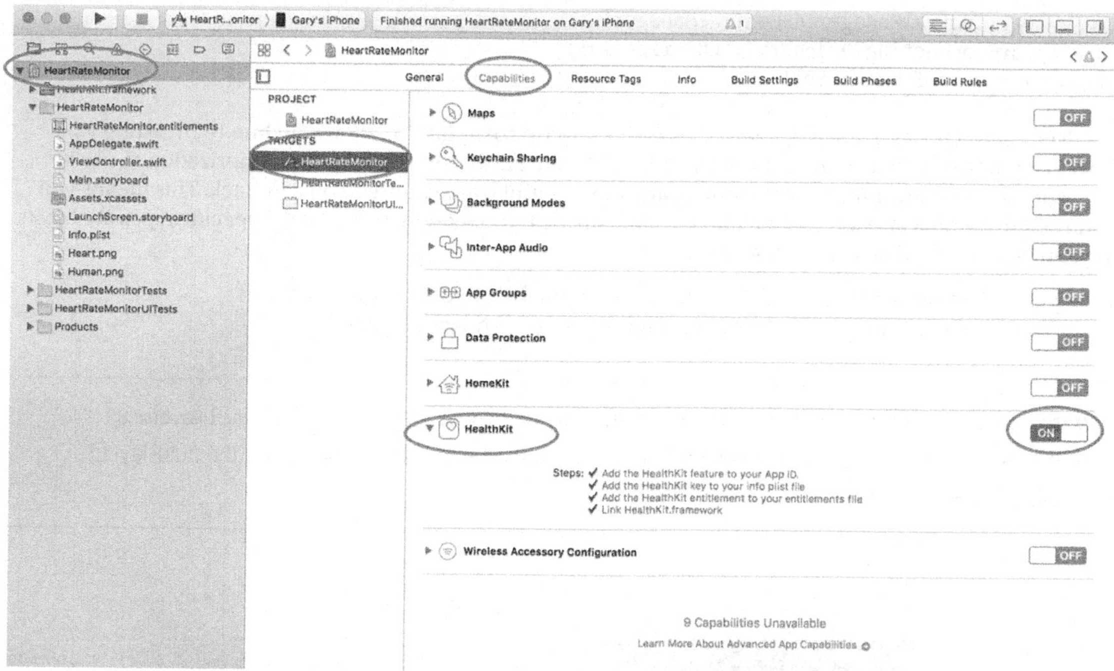

Figure 16-8. *Including the HealthKit capabilities in the project*

5. The app doesn't automatically get access to the HealthKit data, so it first needs to ask permission. Open the `ViewController.swift` file to add all of the related code this app needs.

6. Import the Core Bluetooth and HealthKit frameworks, add the Core Bluetooth delegate protocols, and declare the properties, as shown in Listing 16-1. The ViewController needs to implement the `CBCentralManagerDelegate` protocol to enable the delegate to monitor the discovery, connectivity, and retrieval of peripheral BLE devices. The ViewController also needs to implement the `CBPeripheralDelegate` protocol so it can monitor the discovery, exploration, and interaction of a remote peripheral's services and properties.

Listing 16-1. Adding Core Bluetooth, HealthKit, and Properties

```
import UIKit
import CoreBluetooth
import HealthKit


class ViewController: UIViewController, CBCentralManagerDelegate, CBPeripheralDelegate{

    let PULSESCALE: NSNumber = 1.2
    let PULSEDURATION: NSNumber = 0.2
    var heartRate: UInt16!
    let healthKitStore: HKHealthStore = HKHealthStore()
```

```
19      var centralManager:CBCentralManager!
20      var connectingPeripheral: CBPeripheral!
21      var pulseTime: Timer!
```

The core of the HealthKit Framework is the `HKHealthStore` class, as shown on line 18 in Listing 16-1. Now that you've created an instance of `HKHealthStore`, the next step is to request authorization to use it.

The users are the masters of their data, and they control which metrics you can track. This means you don't request global access to the HealthKit Store. Instead, you request access to the specific types of objects the app needs to read or write to the store.

7. Add the `Heart.png` and `Human.png` files from the Chapter 16 project to this project. Then create the outlets for the labels, as shown in Figure 16-9.

■ **Note** You can refer to the Chapter 16 project that can be downloaded from `forum.xcelme.com` as described in the introduction. It includes the PNG files used for the app and it shows you the auto-layout constraints if you need help.

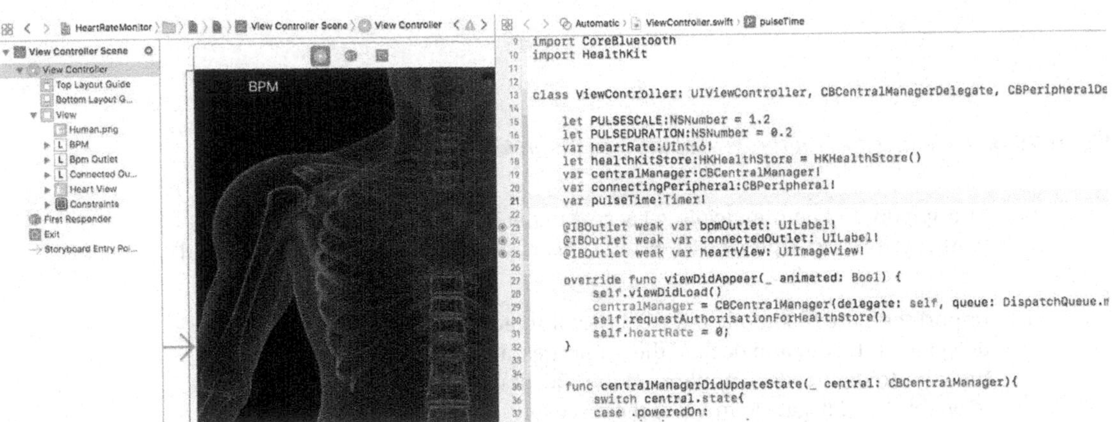

Figure 16-9. *Creating the HealthKit Store object and creating outlets*

8. Add the `viewDidAppear` method as shown in Listing 16-2. You need to instantiate the `centralManager` and request authorization to the HealthKit Store.

Listing 16-2. Add the init as Shown

```
override func viewDidAppear(_ animated: Bool) {
        super.viewDidAppear(animated)
        centralManager = CBCentralManager(delegate: self, queue: DispatchQueue.main)
        requestAuthorisationForHealthStore()
        heartRate = 0
```

9. 32 }Add the `centralManagerDidUpdateState` method as shown in Listing 16-3. This ensures that the device is BLE compliant and it can be used as the central device object of the `CBCentralManager`. If the state of the central manager is powered on, the app will receive a state of `CBCentralManagerStatePoweredOn`. If the state changes to `CBCentralManagerStatePoweredOff`, all peripheral objects that have been obtained from the central manager become invalid and must be rediscovered.

Listing 16-3. Add the centralManagerDidUpdateState Method

```
func centralManagerDidUpdateState(_ central: CBCentralManager){
        switch central.state {
        case .poweredOn:
            print("poweredOn")

            let serviceUUIDs: [CBUUID] = [CBUUID(string:"180D")]
            let lastPeripherals = centralManager.retrieveConnectedPeripherals(withServic
            es: serviceUUIDs)
            print(lastPeripherals.count)
            if lastPeripherals.count > 0 {
                connectingPeripheral = lastPeripherals.last as CBPeripheral?;
                connectingPeripheral.delegate = self
                centralManager.connect(connectingPeripheral, options: nil)
                connectedOutlet.text = "Connected"
            }
            else {
               centralManager.scanForPeripherals(withServices: serviceUUIDs, options: nil)
                connectedOutlet.text = "Disconnected"
            }

        default:
            print(central.state)
        }


    }
```

10. The next step is to determine if you have established a connection to the heart rate monitor. Add the `didDiscoverServices` and `didDiscoverServices` methods. When you establish a local connection to a peripheral, the central manager object calls the `didDiscoverPeripheral` method of its delegate object.

In the implementation, we first set the view controller to be the delegate of the peripheral object so that it can notify the view controller. If no error occurs, we next ask the peripheral to discover the services associated with the device. Then we determine the peripheral's current state to see if we have established a connection. (See Listing 16-4.)

Listing 16-4. Add the didDiscoverPeripheral and didDiscoverServices Methods

```
func centralManager(_ central: CBCentralManager, didDiscover peripheral: CBPeripheral,
  advertisementData: [String : Any], rssi RSSI: NSNumber) {

        connectingPeripheral = peripheral
        connectingPeripheral.delegate = self
        centralManager.connect(connectingPeripheral, options: nil)
        connectedOutlet.text = "Connected"
    }

    func centralManager(_ central: CBCentralManager, didConnect peripheral: CBPeripheral)
{


        peripheral.discoverServices(nil)
    }

    func peripheral(_ peripheral: CBPeripheral, didUpdateValueFor characteristic:
    CBCharacteristic, error: Error?) {
        if let actualError = error{
            print("\(actualError)")

        }else {
            switch characteristic.uuid.uuidString{
            case "2A37":
                update(characteristic.value!)
            default:
                print("")
            }
        }
    }

    func peripheral(_ peripheral: CBPeripheral, didDiscoverServices error: Error?) {

        if let actualError = error{
            print("\(actualError)")
        }
        else {
            for service in peripheral.services as [CBService]!{
                peripheral.discoverCharacteristics(nil, for: service)
            }
        }
    }
```

11. Now add the `didDiscoverCharacteristicsForService` method, as shown in Listing 16-5.

This method lets you determine the characteristics the service has. First, we check if the service is the heart rate service. Then we iterate through the characteristics array and determine if any of the characteristics are a heart rate monitor notification characteristic. If so, we subscribe to this characteristic, which tells the CBCentralManager to notify us when the characteristic changes.

If the characteristic is the body location characteristic, there is no need to subscribe. You just read the value. If the service is the device info service, look for the manufacturer name and read it.

Listing 16-5. Add the didDiscoverCharacteristicsForService Method

```
func peripheral(_ peripheral: CBPeripheral, didDiscoverCharacteristicsFor Service: CBService, error: Error?) {

        if let actualError = error{
            print("\(actualError)")
        }
        else {

            if service.uuid == CBUUID(string:"180D"){
                for characteristic in (service.characteristics as [CBCharacteristic]?)!{
                    switch characteristic.uuid.uuidString{

                    case "2A37":
                        // Set notification on heart rate measurement
                        print("Found a Heart Rate Measurement Characteristic")
                        peripheral.setNotifyValue(true, for: characteristic)

                    case "2A38":
                        // Read body sensor location
                        print("Found a Body Sensor Location Characteristic")
                        peripheral.readValue(for: characteristic)

                    case "2A39":
                        // Write heart rate control point
                        print("Found a Heart Rate Control Point Characteristic")

                        var rawArray: [UInt8] = [0x01];
                        let data =  NSData(bytes: &rawArray, length: rawArray.count)
                        peripheral.writeValue(data as Data, for: characteristic, type: CBCharacteristicWriteType.withoutResponse)

                    default:
                        print("")
                    }

                }
            }
        }
    }
```

To understand how to interpret the data from a BLE characteristic, you need to check the Bluetooth specification. For this example, visit `https://developer.bluetooth.org/gatt/characteristics/Pages/CharacteristicViewer.aspx?u=org.bluetooth.characteristic.heart_rate_measurement.xml`.

A heart rate measurement consists of a number of flags, followed by the heart rate measurement itself, energy information, and other data.

Add the `update` function shown in Listing 16-6. The `update` function is called each time the peripheral sends new data.

The `update` function converts the contents of the characteristic value to a data object. Next, you get the byte sequence of the data object. Then you calculate the `bpm` variable, which will store the heart rate information.

To calculate the BPM, we obtain the first byte at index 0 in the array as defined by `buffer[0]` and mask out all but the first bit. The result returned will either be 0, which means that the first bit is not set, or 1 if it is set. If the first bit is not set, retrieve the BPM value at the second byte location at index 1 in the array and convert it to a 16-bit value based on the host's native byte order.

12. Add the `pulse` method. Output the value of BPM to your `bpmOutlet UILabel`. Set up a timer object that calls pulse at 0.8-second intervals; this performs the basic animation that simulates the beating of a heart through the use of Core Animation, as shown in Listing 16-7.

Listing 16-6. Add the update Method

```
func update(_ heartRateData:Data){
        var buffer = [UInt8](repeating: 0x00, count: heartRateData.count)
        (heartRateData as NSData).getBytes(&buffer, length: buffer.count)

        var bpm:UInt16?
        if buffer.count >= 2 {
            if buffer[0] & 0x01 == 0 {
                bpm = UInt16(buffer[1])
            }else {
                bpm = UInt16(buffer[1]) << 8
                bpm =  bpm! | UInt16(buffer[2])
            }
        }

        if let actualBpm = bpm {
            print("actualBpm \(actualBpm)")
            bpmOutlet.text = String(actualBpm)

            let rate = 60.0 / Float(self.heartRate)
            print("\(rate)")
            saveHeartRateIntoHealthStore(Double(bpm!))

            let oldBpm = self.heartRate
            self.heartRate = bpm
            if oldBpm == 0 {
                pulse()
                self.pulseTime = Timer.scheduledTimer(timeInterval: 0.8, target: self,
                    selector: #selector(ViewController.pulse), userInfo: nil, repeats:
                    false)
            }

        } else {
            print("bpm \(bpm)")
            self.bpmOutlet.text = "\(bpm)"
        }
    }
```

Listing 16-7. The pulse function

```
    func pulse() {
        let pulseAnimation = CABasicAnimation(keyPath: "transform.scale")
        pulseAnimation.toValue = PULSESCALE
        pulseAnimation.toValue = NSNumber(value: 1.2)
        pulseAnimation.fromValue = NSNumber(value: 1.0)

        pulseAnimation.duration = PULSEDURATION
        pulseAnimation.duration = 0.2
        pulseAnimation.repeatCount = 1
        pulseAnimation.autoreverses = true
        pulseAnimation.timingFunction = CAMediaTimingFunction(name:
        kCAMediaTimingFunctionEaseIn)
        heartView.layer.add(pulseAnimation, forKey: "scale")
        let rate = 60.0 / Float(self.heartRate)
        self.pulseTime = Timer.scheduledTimer(timeInterval: TimeInterval(rate), target:
        self, selector: #selector(ViewController.pulse), userInfo: nil, repeats: false)
    }
```

13. Now add the `didUpdateValueForCharacteristic` method, as shown in Listing 16-8. The `didUpdateValueForCharacteristic` function will be called when `CBPeripheral` reads a value or updates a value periodically. We need to implement this method to check to see which characteristic's value has been updated, and then call one of the helper methods to read in the value.

Listing 16-8. Add the didUpdateValueForCharacteristic Method

```
func peripheral(_ peripheral: CBPeripheral, didUpdateValueFor characteristic:
CBCharacteristic, error: Error?) {
        if let actualError = error {
            print("\(actualError)")

        } else {
            switch characteristic.uuid.uuidString {
            case "2A37":
                update(characteristic.value!)
            default:
                print("")
            }
        }
    }
```

14. Add the `saveHeartRateIntoHealthStore` method, as shown in Listing 16-9.

In this method, you first create a sample object using `HKQuantitySample`. In order to create this sample, you need the following:

- A Quantity type object, like `HKQuantityType`, initialized using the proper sample type.
- A Quantity sample, like `HKQuantity`'s start and end date, which in this case is the current date and time in both cases.

Listing 16-9. Add the saveHeartRateIntoHealthStore Function

```
fileprivate func saveHeartRateIntoHealthStore(_ height:Double) -> Void
    {
        // Save the user's heart rate into HealthKit.
        let heartRateUnit: HKUnit = HKUnit.count().unitDivided(by: HKUnit.minute())
        let heartRateQuantity: HKQuantity = HKQuantity(unit: heartRateUnit, doubleValue:
        height)

        let heartRate : HKQuantityType = HKQuantityType.quantityType(forIdentifier:
        HKQuantityTypeIdentifier.heartRate)!
        let nowDate: Date = Date()

        let heartRateSample: HKQuantitySample = HKQuantitySample(type: heartRate
            , quantity: heartRateQuantity, start: nowDate, end: nowDate)
        self.healthKitStore.save(heartRateSample, withCompletion: { (success, error) ->
        Void in
            if( error != nil  ) {
                // Error saving the workout
                print("done")
            }
            else {
                // Workout saved
                print("done")

            }
        })
```

15. Add the requestAuthoriationForHealthStore function as shown in Listing 16-10. You're creating a Set with all the types you need to read from the HealthKit Store: characteristics (blood type, sex, and birthday), samples (body mass and height), and workouts.

Then you check if the HealthKit Store is available. For universal apps, this is crucial because HealthKit may not be available on every device. Finally, the app performs the actual authorization request; it invokes `requestAuthorisationToShareTypes` with the previously defined types for reads. Now that your code knows how to request authorization, you need to create a way for your app to invoke it.

Listing 16-10. Add the requestAuthorisationForHealthStore Function

```
fileprivate func requestAuthorisationForHealthStore() {

        let dataTypesToRead = Set(arrayLiteral:
            HKObjectType.characteristicType(forIdentifier:
            HKCharacteristicTypeIdentifier.dateOfBirth)!,
            HKObjectType.quantityType(forIdentifier: HKQuantityTypeIdentifier.
            bodyMass)!,
            HKObjectType.quantityType(forIdentifier: HKQuantityTypeIdentifier.height)!
        )

        //Requesting the authorization
        healthKitStore.requestAuthorization(toShare: nil, read: dataTypesToRead) {
        (success, error) -> Void in
```

```
                if( success )
                {
                    print("success")
                }
            }
        }
```

App Summary

You are done adding code, so run the app. When the app starts, it asks permission to access the HealthKit Store. If this is the first time the app has run, HealthKit Store asks the user for permission, as shown in Figure 16-10.

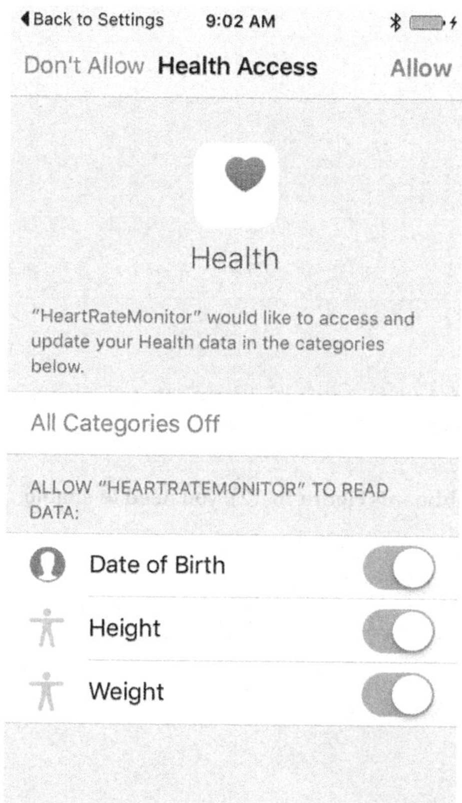

Figure 16-10. *HealthKit asking the user permission to access the app*

As the app runs and is displaying data, it is also storing data in the HealthKit Store. You can see that data by opening the Health app, as shown in Figure 16-11.

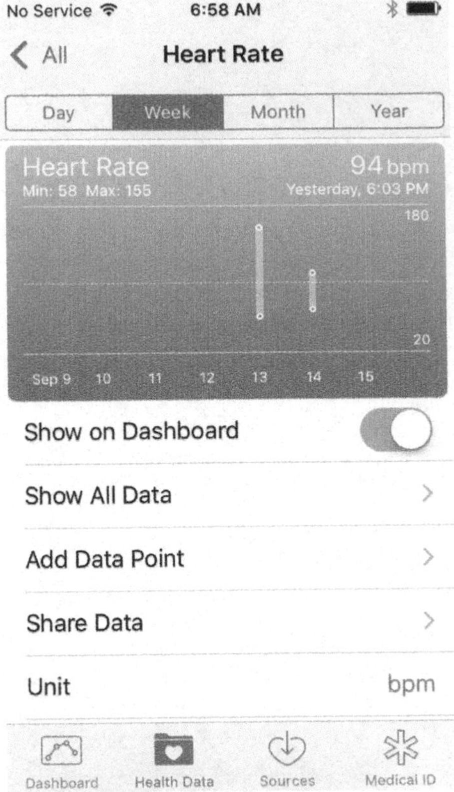

Figure 16-11. *The heart rate data being stored in the HealthKit Store*

If you want to view the heart rate data in the Health app's dashboard (Figure 16-12), you need to enable the Show on Dashboard switch, as shown in Figure 16-11.

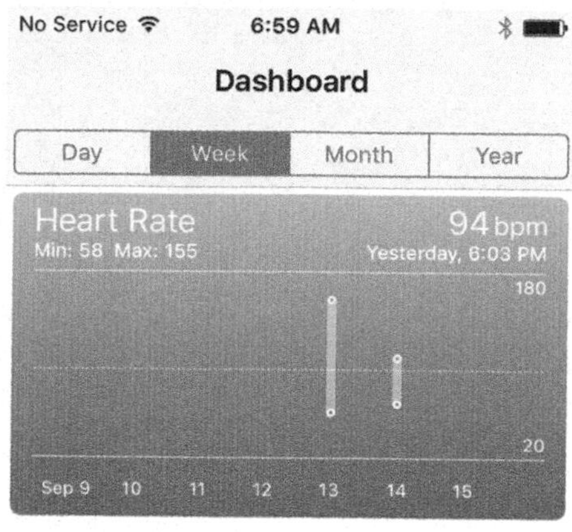

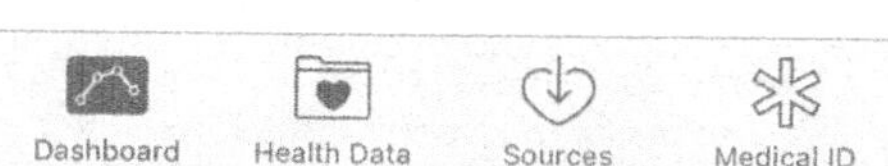

Figure 16-12. *The heart rate data being displayed in the dashboard*

What's Next?

You did it! You should have a great foundation to write outstanding apps. The best place to start is with your own idea for an app. Start writing it today. You are going to have lots of questions. That is how you are going to continue to learn. Keep moving forward and don't stop, no matter if you get discouraged sometimes.

If you do get discouraged, visit `www.xcelMe.com/forum`. There are great resources on this site for finding answers to your questions. There is a topic for this book and each chapter in the book. Feel free to post your own questions. The authors of this book help answer the posts. Also, there are free videos on `www.xcelMe.com`. In the live sessions, you can ask Gary Bennett questions. Just click the Free Videos tab at the top of the page, as shown in Figure 16-13.

Good luck and have fun!

EXERCISES

- Enable the app to read data from the HealthKit Store.
- Enable the app to connect and disconnect to the heart rate monitor.
- Enable the users to set visual and audible alarms when their heart rate gets too high.

Index

A

B

G. Bennett and B. Lees, *Swift 3 for Absolute Beginners*, DOI 10.1007/978-1-4842-2331-4

C

D, E

F, G

H

I, J, K

Q

R

S

T

U, V

W

X, Y, Z

CPSIA information can be obtained
at www.ICGtesting.com
Printed in the USA
LVOW05s1628280317
528763LV00005B/118/P